Gender Divide and the Computer Game Industry

Julie Prescott
University of Bolton, UK

Jan Bogg
University of Liverpool, UK

A volume in the Advances in Human and
Social Aspects of Technology (AHSAT)
Book Series

Information Science
REFERENCE

An Imprint of IGI Global

Managing Director:	Lindsay Johnston
Production Manager:	Jennifer Yoder
Development Editor:	Myla Merkel
Acquisitions Editor:	Kayla Wolfe
Typesetter:	Lisandro Gonzalez
Cover Design:	Jason Mull

Published in the United States of America by
Information Science Reference (an imprint of IGI Global)
701 E. Chocolate Avenue
Hershey PA 17033
Tel: 717-533-8845
Fax: 717-533-8661
E-mail: cust@igi-global.com
Web site: http://www.igi-global.com

Library of Congress Cataloging-in-Publication Data

Prescott, Julie, 1975-
  Gender divide and the computer game industry / by Julie Prescott and Jan Boggs.
    pages cm
Includes bibliographical references and index.
  Summary: "This book takes a look at the games industry from a gendered perspective and highlights the variety of ways in which women remain underrepresented in this industry"-- Provided by publisher.
  ISBN 978-1-4666-4534-9 (hardcover) -- ISBN 978-1-4666-4535-6 (ebook) -- ISBN 978-1-4666-4536-3 (print & perpetual access) 1. Video games industry--Social aspects. 2. Video games--Social aspects. 3. Women computer industry employees. 4. Sex discrimination in employment. I. Boggs, Jan, 1959- II. Title.
  HD9993.E452P74 2014
  331.4'87948--dc23
                              2013020690

This book is published in the IGI Global book series Advances in Human and Social Aspects of Technology (AHSAT) (ISSN: 2328-1316; eISSN: 2328-1324)

British Cataloguing in Publication Data
A Cataloguing in Publication record for this book is available from the British Library.

All work contributed to this book is new, previously-unpublished material. The views expressed in this book are those of the authors, but not necessarily of the publisher.

For electronic access to this publication, please contact: eresources@igi-global.com.

Advances in Human and Social Aspects of Technology (AHSAT) Book Series

Ashish Dwivedi
The University of Hull, UK

ISSN: 2328-1316
EISSN: 2328-1324

MISSION

In recent years, the societal impact of technology has been noted as we become increasingly more connected and are presented with more digital tools and devices. With the popularity of digital devices such as cell phones and tablets, it is crucial to consider the implications of our digital dependence and the presence of technology in our everyday lives.

The **Advances in Human and Social Aspects of Technology (AHSAT) Book Series** seeks to explore the ways in which society and human beings have been affected by technology and how the technological revolution has changed the way we conduct our lives as well as our behavior. The AHSAT book series aims to publish the most cutting-edge research on human behavior and interaction with technology and the ways in which the digital age is changing society.

COVERAGE

- Activism & ICTs
- Computer-Mediated Communication
- Cultural Influence of ICTs
- Cyber Behavior
- End-User Computing
- Gender & Technology
- Human-Computer Interaction
- Information Ethics
- Public Access to ICTs
- Technoself

IGI Global is currently accepting manuscripts for publication within this series. To submit a proposal for a volume in this series, please contact our Acquisition Editors at Acquisitions@igi-global.com or visit: http://www.igi-global.com/publish/.

Titles in this Series

For a list of additional titles in this series, please visit: www.igi-global.com

Emerging Research and Trends in Interactivity and the Human-Computer Interface
Katherine Blashki (Noroff University College, Norway) and Pedro Isaias (Portuguese Open University, Portugal)
Information Science Reference • copyright 2014 • 580pp • H/C (ISBN: 9781466646230) • US $175.00 (our price)

Creating Personal, Social, and Urban Awareness through Pervasive Computing
Bin Guo (Northwestern Polytechnical University, China) Daniele Riboni (University of Milano, Italy) and Peizhao Hu (NICTA, Australia)
Information Science Reference • copyright 2014 • 440pp • H/C (ISBN: 9781466646957) • US $175.00 (our price)

Gender Divide and the Computer Game Industry
Julie Prescott (University of Bolton, UK) and Jan Bogg (The University of Liverpool, UK)
Information Science Reference • copyright 2014 • 334pp • H/C (ISBN: 9781466645349) • US $175.00 (our price)

User Behavior in Ubiquitous Online Environments
Jean-Eric Pelet (KMCMS, IDRAC International School of Management, University of Nantes, France) and Panagiota Papadopoulou (University of Athens, Greece)
Information Science Reference • copyright 2014 • 325pp • H/C (ISBN: 9781466645660) • US $175.00 (our price)

Innovative Methods and Technologies for Electronic Discourse Analysis
Hwee Ling Lim (The Petroleum Institute-Abu Dhabi, UAE) and Fay Sudweeks (Murdoch University, Australia)
Information Science Reference • copyright 2014 • 546pp • H/C (ISBN: 9781466644267) • US $175.00 (our price)

Advanced Research and Trends in New Technologies, Software, Human-Computer Interaction, and Communicability
Francisco Vicente Cipolla-Ficarra (ALAIPO – AINCI, Spain and Italy)
Information Science Reference • copyright 2014 • 361pp • H/C (ISBN: 9781466644908) • US $175.00 (our price)

New Media Influence on Social and Political Change in Africa
Anthony A. Olorunnisola (Pennsylvania State University, USA) and Aziz Douai (University of Ontario Institute of Technology, Canada)
Information Science Reference • copyright 2013 • 373pp • H/C (ISBN: 9781466641976) • US $175.00 (our price)

Cases on Usability Engineering Design and Development of Digital Products
Miguel A. Garcia-Ruiz (Algoma University, Canada)
Information Science Reference • copyright 2013 • 470pp • H/C (ISBN: 9781466640467) • US $175.00 (our price)

Human Rights and Information Communication Technologies Trends and Consequences of Use
John Lannon (University of Limerick, Ireland) and Edward Halpin (Leeds Metropolitan University, UK)
Information Science Reference • copyright 2013 • 324pp • H/C (ISBN: 9781466619180) • US $175.00 (our price)

www.igi-global.com

701 E. Chocolate Ave., Hershey, PA 17033
Order online at www.igi-global.com or call 717-533-8845 x100
To place a standing order for titles released in this series, contact: cust@igi-global.com
Mon-Fri 8:00 am - 5:00 pm (est) or fax 24 hours a day 717-533-8661

Table of Contents

Chapter 6

Chapter 7

Chapter 8

Foreword

This book addresses the relationship between gender and computer gaming in three contexts. It considers the representation of gender within games themselves, the gender dynamics of gaming culture, and their production within the industry. The comprehensive examination of these issues provided in the included chapters is timely given that computer gaming continues to be perceived as both a male leisure activity and a male dominated industry. It also has wider relevance for understanding barriers to female employment in science and technology more generally, gender segregation in the labour market, and the gendering of leisure within society. Although it addresses these issues primarily from the perspective of social and organisational psychology, it also draws on relevant literature in related areas. This makes the book of relevance to a wide variety of academics, researchers and students, as well as those within the gaming and related industries.

The book sets out to examine both the myths and realities of the gendering of gaming in the specified contexts in order to identify the ways in this can be recognised, challenged and changed in both production and consumption. It effectively demonstrates the economic importance of gaming as an industry and leisure activity in contemporary society. This provides an important context for demonstrating the importance of the examination of women as producers and consumers of games. It also addresses the issue of gendered representation within games and associated interactions in online gaming spaces, and considers possibilities for resistance to traditional gender roles. The recognition that masculinity and femininity are not homogenous categories is important, and the book effectively argues for the need to give greater consideration to this issue when examining game preferences, the gender dynamics of the activity and the industry.

One of the most useful contributions is the presentation of the results of empirical research examining female experiences of working within the gaming industry itself. It also addresses emerging areas of gender and gaming, which have not currently received sustained empirical attention. These include family friendly games and parental mediation, as well as the implications of gendering for the educational use of games.

The final chapter of the book provides an excellent overview of the main issues covered in the earlier chapters. It effectively considers the three separate aspects of the gendering of gaming, but also provides an important consideration of their interrelationships. It identifies current gaps in the empirical and theoretical literature, and makes recommendations for industry and policy makers to address the current gender imbalance in the industry. It locates these identified gaps and recommendations within the wider social, economic and political contexts of the issue.

Overall the book provides an informative and detailed overview of the factors which influence the gendering of computer gaming. Its critical review of the existing literature and identification of future areas for both research and practical action provide an agenda for academics and practitioners alike to challenge both the myths and realities that characterise this issue.

Jo Bryce
University of Central Lancashire, UK

Jo Bryce *is Director of the Cyberspace Research Unit, University of Central Lancashire, United Kingdom. Her research focuses on the psychological, social, and forensic aspects of the Internet and related technologies, with a specific focus on their use by young people, associated risk exposure and e-safety. Other interests include the role of ICTs in the commission of criminal offences, online privacy and security, and online piracy and file-sharing.*

Preface

This preface describes both the need for, and purpose of this book – an interdisciplinary literature review of the multiple issues related to gender and computer games for women as both producers and consumers of computer games. The book's guiding message comes from the perspective that there is a need for women to be involved in the production of computer games and all forms of technology development at all levels. We will explore the issues women face working in this relatively new industry and present some of our UK based research. In general, the guiding message of our book is that computer games/games can be beneficial and women/girls should be involved in all aspects of the industry from consumer to developer. Throughout this book, computer games will refer to both computer games and game interchangeably.

INTRODUCTION

Women and men are segregated within the workforce, and although women are increasing in the workforce, they are segregated into certain jobs (horizontal segregation) and at lower levels (vertical segregation) within sectors and organisations. The underrepresentation of women in computing careers and the Information and Communication Technology (ICT) industries and the wider Science, Engineering, and Technology (SET) sectors generally forms the starting point and main impetus for this book. There are many internal and external factors as to why women are underrepresented in certain disciplines and occupations (see Prescott & Bogg, 2012, for an over view of the issues related to the issues of gendered occupational segregation in SET). Women have become increasingly more visible in games culture especially as gamers in recent years. However, the issue of gender and computer games is still very relevant (Kafai, et al., 2008). The relatively new industry (approximately four decades) of computer games development is interesting to explore, as it is a relatively new industry and part of the wider ICT and STEM/SET sectors, with recent figures suggesting that women represent just 4% of the UK's game industries workforce (Skillset, 2009). This is a decrease from 12% reported in 2006 (Skillset, 2006). Similar figures have also been reported in America (Gourdin, 2005) and Canada (Dyer-Whitheford & Sharman, 2005). The industry would benefit from attracting a more diverse workforce.

To illustrate the magnitude of the industry, in 2009, games were one of the biggest forms of entertainment in Britain, outselling films (including going to the cinema and DVD sales; Wallop, 2009). Highlighting the significance of the games industry to today's culture, Gillespie (2000) notes that: "This $9 billion market is art and is significant in today's culture in the same way that books, film, radio, television, and rock-and–roll were the significant media of the past" (Flanagan, 2003, p 361). The importance of the games industry towards the economic and culture landscape is highlighted and empathised in more detail in chapter one. Research shows women are active gamers, especially with more casual than hard-core games. However, the gendering of computer games may be changing. For instance, Braithwaite (2010) views the social network site Facebook, as a catalyst in which women are increasingly becoming more hard-core gamers. The image of the games industry, like the wider ICT and SET industries, is still very much "boys work." However, this image could change with a more diverse workforce and an increasing number of female gamers. The industry may begin to lose its "for boys only" masculine image. There is a general need for the industry to find ways to make computer games female friendly and remove male domination in game culture. This book will consider the position of females throughout the digital age and consider the digital divide from a gendered perspective, across other Web 2.0 applications, including, social media, the Internet, and computers more generally.

We will look at the computer games industry from a gendered perspective and provide a timely overview of gender and computer games. The book will provide a comprehensive overview on the issue of gender, computer games, and the ICT sector, taking into account the literature on interrelated issues associated with the gendering of computer games, from childhood through to adulthood (play and interests through to careers). The book considers whether this new industry could provide solutions for other male-dominated industries, due to the supposedly less bureaucratic working practices and potential new styles of working, or are the same old issues and stereotypes perpetuated, as previous research findings from the wider ICT/SET sectors suggest. We will discuss the issues using a range of relevant literature, from social psychology, organisational psychology, computer science, cultural studies, and sociology disciplines, and we use both qualitative and quantitative research to discuss the issues. Therefore, the book is of relevance to both academics and students in the social and behavioral science disciplines and groups interested in workforce issues in the ICT/SET industries. A number of the chapters will draw from our own relevant employment data, with both qualitative and quantitative research methods. This was extracted from our United Kingdom, Breaking Barriers project (Jan Bogg, Director, and Julie Prescott, senior researcher) and Julie Prescott's recent doctoral research, which focused specifically on women game developers (Jan Bogg was the PhD supervisor).

AIMS OF THIS BOOK

Computer games are gendered, and this book aims to give a comprehensive overview of the issues and discuss why women are underrepresented throughout the games industry and gaming culture generally. Computer games are important to today's society, significant both economically and culturally. Importantly, the computer game industry has a massive impact on culture, technology, and the media landscape today. The industry could widen its appeal through an increased awareness of the variety of roles and skills within the industry and through highlighting the benefits and rewards of working in such a creative, competitive, and growing industry. Findings from the research discussed at length within this book will highlight issues that could enable the games industry to review its policies and working practices in order to facilitate women and other minority groups in the working environment. Instead of women "fitting in or getting out," more can be done to eradicate career barriers and discriminatory work practices in all aspects of the games industry, as well as related game industry occupations such as game journalism.

The book is Western-international in scope, in that we utilize literature and examples from a variety of countries, most predominantly from the UK and USA. Statistics used to illustrate the underrepresentation of women in the computer games industry are, in the main, from the UK and the USA, with some acknowledgement, where possible, of the situation in Europe, Asia, and other parts of the world. The issues discussed are of relevance to Anglophone and Western European countries, although variations between these (and, of course, variations within countries) should be borne in mind.

ORGANISATION OF THE BOOK

In writing this book, we aim to cover a number of issues deemed important to the gendering of computer games, the computer games industry and digital technology more generally. In order to give the book structure, we present the text in two sections. The first section considers the literature and previous research on a number of issues related to gender and computer games to provide readers with a thorough understanding of the gender divide and computer games. The second section illustrates the career factors that influence the careers of women working in the games industry and highlights the issues women who currently work in the industry face.

Within each chapter, we have provided chapter aims to signpost what readers will gain from reading each chapter and included a useful key issues table. Throughout the chapters, we hope to highlight the range of ways in which women remain underrepresented with computer games, the wider gaming culture and the computer games industry.

Section 1

Chapter 1: Introduction – Why the Gender Divide in Computer
Games is an Important and Timely Issue

This introductory chapter provides an overview of some of the reasons and issues for why the authors feel the computer games industry is an important industry and considers the gender digital divide in computer games. In particular, the chapter focuses on the transferable skills and the technical ability computer games can potentially provide to gamers, as well as considers how games can be beneficial to wider society through a look at the research in the new area of pro-social games and gaming. Although this book has a gendered focus, the authors do recognize that computer games and the computer games industry has other minority and underrepresented groups. Within this chapter, they will also consider other underrepresented groups including those from non-white backgrounds, non-Western culture, and considerations for gamers who are older, gay, lesbian, bisexual, or transgender.

Chapter 2: The Computer Games Industry, Market, and Culture

This chapter considers the computer game industry's current climate, in particular the importance of the industry in terms of its economic and cultural impact. This is a relatively new industry, part of the wider SET and ICT sector, yet it is an important and increasingly influential industry. The aim of this chapter is to highlight and emphasize to the reader how the computer games industry impacts society, culture, and is a prominent force in the media landscape today. The chapter also discusses the issue of how games are mediated to provide readers with an indication of how attitudes and parenting style can influence what is played and by whom.

Chapter 3: Games and Society – Can Games Make a Better World?

This chapter explores the literature on serious games. In particular, this chapter reviews computer game use in the learning environment and games for learning with a look at the argument for and against their use. The chapter discusses how the younger generation (Net Generation), who have not known a world without technology, computers, and computer games, view technology as a learning tool. In keeping with the gendered digital divide, how the young generation views and uses technology from a gendered perspective is considered.

Chapter 4: Play, Preferences, and the Gendering of Gaming

This chapter explores the differences between the genders with regard to how games are played, what is played, and what motivates people to play. In discussing the issues, the authors focus on Massively Multiplayer Online Role-Playing Games (MMROPGs) as a specific game genre with an interesting gender divide. Also considered within the chapter is the gendering of space and the issue of access to and usage of computer games for girls/women.

Section 2

Chapter 5: Representation, Image, and Identity

This chapter emphasises that the underrepresentation of females is not restricted to the games themselves but extends to other aspects of the wider gaming culture. Females are under-represented within computer games, and when they feature in games, they are often hyper-sexualised, such as being scantily dressed, with small hips and large busts. The authors consider the impact that these images can have on both men and women. This chapter also considers avatars and their influence on identity especially for the identity of female gamers.

Chapter 6: Game Workers and the Gender Divide in the Production of Computer Games

This chapter will discuss the game workers who develop computer games and how and why the gender composition of the computer game workforce is an important consideration when discussing the gendering of computer games. In particular, the authors will focus on the issues of flexible working and work life balance.

Chapter 7: The Experience of Women Game Developers

Career motivation, person-environment fit, self-efficacy, self-esteem, work satisfaction, career factors, and life issues are all important constructs when looking at the career and career development of women. This chapter will discuss these constructs and the implications for women working in the games industry. This chapter includes findings from research with women games developers.

Chapter 8: Issues Career Women Face

This chapter focuses on the barriers women encounter in the workplace. There are a number of barriers, which prevent women entering certain occupations and progressing to senior roles. In particular, the chapter will address the issues of career progression, promotion and aspirations, career barriers, women in leadership/senior roles, and the characteristics of what makes a good leader.

Chapter 9: Reflections for the Future

Gendered occupational segregation has a detrimental effect on many aspects of women's careers, most specifically pay, promotion, and career opportunities. It is apparent that men and women experience the workplace differently. This chapter will consider the multifaceted issues in relation to careers of women.

Chapter 10: Final Thoughts and Concluding Comments

In the final chapter, the authors consider the findings, summarise key points, and guidepost further research. They provide useful international Internet resources for reading and networking opportunities. This chapter is a good starting point for research and resources in the area. Further research into the experiences of women working in the computer game industry and other male dominated sectors will enable those industries to alter working practices, which may not only attract but also retain a more diverse workforce.

A COMMON GROUND

In writing this book, we have focused on a psychosocial perspective and a multi-disciplinary viewpoint of gendered occupational segregation to explore the underrepresentation of women in all aspects of computer game culture. This book is our story of the gendering of computer games and the gendered digital divide; we hope it stimulates both reflection and action.

Julie Prescott
University of Bolton, UK

Jan Bogg
University of Liverpool, UK

REFERENCES

Brathwaite, B. (2010). *Women in games from famine to Facebook*. Retrieved from http://www. huffingtonpost.com/brenda-brathwaite/women-in-games-from-famin_b_510928.html

Dyer-Whitheford, N., & Sharman, Z. (2005). The political economy of Canada's video and computer game industry. *Canadian Journal of Communication*, *20*, 187–210.

Flanagan, M. (2003). Next level women's digital activism through gaming. In *Digital media revisited: Theoretical and conceptual innovation in digital domains* (pp. 359–388). Cambridge, MA: MIT.

Gourdin, A. (2005). *Game developers demographics: An exploration of workforce diversity*. International Game Developers Association.

Kafai, Y. B., Heeter, C., Denner, J., & Sun, J. Y. (2008). *Beyond Barbie and Mortal Kombat: New perspectives on gender and gaming*. Cambridge, MA: MIT Press.

Prescott, J., & Bogg, J. (2012). *Gendered occupational differences in science, engineering, and technology careers*. Hershey, PA: IGI Global. doi:10.4018/978-1-4666-2107-7

Skillset. (2006). *Skillset: Workforce survey 2006*. The Sector Skills Council for Creative Media.

Skillset. (2009). *2009 employment census: The results of the seventh census of the creative media industries december 2009*. The Sector Skills Council for Creative Media.

Wallop, H. (2009, December 26). Video games bigger than film. *The Daily Telegraph*.

Acknowledgment

We would like to thank the women in our research for providing their time and experiences of working in the computer games industry.

We thank the reviewers for taking the time to read and comment on the manuscript.

We would also like to thank the staff at IGI Global for their support during the entire process from original proposal to final publication.

Julie Prescott
University of Bolton, UK

Jan Bogg
University of Liverpool, UK

Section 1

Chapter 1
Introduction:
Why the Gender Divide in Computer Games is an Important and Timely Issue

ABSTRACT

We live in a technological world and any divide on gendered or other terms is detrimental. The aim of this chapter is to provide the reader with an introduction to the gendered digital divide and the gendered digital divide in relation to computer games specifically. In general, technology is viewed as masculine, and there are gender distinctions in relation to access to technologies and how technologies are used. In addition, there is a gender divide in terms of who is involved in the design and production of technology. This chapter also considers "otherness" aside from a gendered divide to include non-White representations, older gamers, and gay gamers. The chapter also considers the arguments as to whether games are good or bad, including a discussion on pro social games.

INTRODUCTION

This book explores gender within computer games, computer games culture and the computer games industry. We will present literature from a predominantly social and organizational psychology perspective as well as include research from other disciplines including game theory, media and cultural studies, and sociology to present a rich and varied picture of the complex interwoven issues surrounding gender within computer games. Our guiding message throughout is that computer games are gendered in a num-

DOI: 10.4018/978-1-4666-4534-9.ch001

ber of ways from consumption of the games through to the design of the games. We wish to reiterate that our book is written through the lens of an organisational/social/management psychology perspective. Our writing style is as psychologists and the content is reflective of this professional standpoint. This unique cognitive perspective invites the reader to consider the rich and varied internal and external factors, which encompass occupational gendered segregation.

Technology is often viewed as being masculine (i.e. Wajcman, 2007; Wilson, 2003) with gender distinctions applied to the access to technologies (Ulicsak, et al, 2009), and how technologies are used (Kelan, 2007). There is also gender divide in terms of who is involved in the design and production of technology; where there is a male dominance in who decide what technologies are made and for whom (Valenduc et al, 2004). The male dominance of the ICT workforce is a global issue and predominant in the UK and the USA. For instance in the USA in 2006 females represented just 16% of employed computer and information scientists educated to doctorate degree (National Science Foundation, 2011). Similarly in 2008 the number of employed female ICT professionals in the UK was 66,076, just 14.4% of employed ICT professionals (UKRC, 2008). In the USA the number of females that received bachelor's degree in the computer sciences decreased by 10% from 28% in 2000 to 18% in 2008 (National Science Foundation, 2011). Recent statistics in the UK shows that females

represented just 13% of all undergraduate degree acceptances in computer science in 2011 (UCAS, 2012).

Technology is increasing influencing our daily lives, making the ability to access and use technology increasingly more important. The development of Web 2.0 and associated technology has helped the increased usage of technology in the daily lives of many children and adults, of both genders, globally. Two recent reports in the UK by Ofcom, suggest that the frequency of Internet use has increased from 2004 to 2009, for both adults and children (Ofcom, 2011a, 2011b). According to the Ofcom report on children's digital literacy, 67% of 5-7 year olds, 82% of 8-11 year olds, and 90% of 12-15 year olds access the Internet at home. The number of hours children spend online varies by age, with 12-15 year olds spending the most hours at 15.6 hours per week. Research has found that males spend more time online and have higher Internet skills than females (Hargittai & Shafer, 2006; Ono & Zavodny, 2003).

Of particular relevance for this book, are the findings by Ofcom that the use of games consoles by 12-15 year olds to access the Internet has increased from 18% in 2009, to 23% in 2010 (Ofcom, 2011a). Suggesting the increasing usage of computer games and gaming devices have on children today. Furthermore, the social networking activity of children is continually increasing, notably an increase in the social networking activity of 5-7 year olds. The report also found that 34% of 8-12 year olds and 47% 0f 10-12 year olds, in the UK have a profile on sites such as Facebook, even though this requires users to register as being 13 or over (Ofcom, 2011a). Older generation usage has also increased, with 74% of people age 55-64 using the Internet in 2010. There has also been a growth in accessing the Internet via mobile phones (Ofcom, 2011b). Those aged 16-24 have the highest Internet use and those aged 55-74 the least (European Commission, 2008). Communication is the most popular type of activity for adult use; with weekly activity for individuals including; email (79%), social networking (45%), work/studies information (45%) and banking/paying bills (33%). Over half of adult Internet users say they have a social network profile (Ofcom, 2011b).

Due to the nature of this book it is apparent there is a gender divide within computer games in terms of gender representation within the games themselves, to gendered differences in how games are played, motivations for play, space and time to play as well as how games are produced by a predominantly male dominated industry producing games for men. However, it is not just female gamers that are seen as a minority by the games industry, as research on representations of race and culture within games, as well as older and gay gamers suggests. These issues are important and require debate, we will only briefly review these issues as the focus of our book is that of gender.

Ethnicity, Race and Culture in Computer Games

Media images still contain traces of long-standing cultural presumptions not only of essential racial difference but the hierarchy that idealizes Whiteness. (Entman & Rojecki, 2011, p57)

Few studies have looked at ethnicity and race within computer games. The studies that have looked at ethnicity and race have found that games have a strong tendency to have the main or primary character as white. Brand et al (2003) found from their analysis of 130 games that characters tended to be white or that it was difficult to determine the race of characters. Dill et al (2005) from their study found that 68% of game main characters were white, followed by Latino (15%) and Black (8%). In a more recent study White et al (2009) found that 81% of characters were white, followed by Black (11%), Asian (5%) and Hispanic (3%). With regards to gender and ethnicity, Jansz and Martis (2007) found that female characters in lead roles are almost exclusively white.

As with female characters it would seem non-white characters are either missing or stereotypically represented. Everett and Watkins (2008) found that nearly 70% of game protagonists are white male. Black representation is found in criminality, athleticism or terrorism. In 2001 a report by the American organisation 'Children Now' found black males typically appear in sports games and black females are 90% of the time represented as victims of violence (twice the percentage of white females). The Grand Theft Auto game series does have non-white playable characters however the black playable characters and black non-player characters are ghettoized and hyperviolent (Leonard, 2009). Leonard (2006) argues that the representation of black characters as violent reproduces fears of black masculinity. In general it appears that a number of racist stereotypes exist in games. For instance Asian characters are stereotyped as martial artists, speaking poor English found in a number of games (Dynasty Warriors, Crouching Tiger and Wrath of Heaven). Violent black athlete's (NBA live), the Arab terrorist (Desert Storm, Americas Army) and Latino criminals (GTA: Vice City). All these stereotypes contribute to our ideas about ethnicity and race.

Williams et al (2009) looked at the representation of race and gender in over 150 of the recent games of the time and found an over-representation of whiteness and masculinity which they argue is due to "a combination of developer demographics and perceived ideas about game players among marketers" (p. 831). Higgin (2009) reports that non-white bodies have been reduced in MMORG in recent years. Arguing that this reduction is not a result of colour blindness but adhering to white dominance. Leading Higgin's to suggest that race is a non-issue within cyberspace and gaming. Race is not even mentioned in the ESA's yearly essential facts about the industry. The racial composition of who plays and designs games is sparse. According to Skillset (2009), less than 4% of computer games employees in the UK are from an ethnic minority background; however accurate worldwide figures are sparse. Supporting Higgins view that race is not important within the industry. Brock (2011) suggests that games tend to draw from Western values of white masculinity. Brock looked at race within RE5 (Resident Evil 5) with a focus on the female black playable character; Sheva Alomar. The character of Sheva was found as being highly sexualised and exoticised with large breast, tiny waist and scant clothing despite going into battle, even wearing a bikini. Figure 1 illustrates Sheva in her costumes, which is not typical battle attire. The game was also found to be racist in that the African zombies are depicted as malevolent and savage, before becoming infected. Brock argues that "racism is a structural belief of Western culture" (p449).

In relation to culture, the Middle East is perhaps arguably the most stereotyped in the gaming world. In particular the Middle East is a favourite virtual battleground and in the current climate holds links with terrorism and Islamist extremism. Sisler (2008) looked at the representation of Arabs in games and found that games exploit cultural stereotypes much more so than other forms of media. Through content analysis of more than 90 European or American and 15 Arab games Sisler found that Western games relies on 'Orientalist' imagery which recreates Islamic society as a timeless and exotic entity which Sisler suggests excludes them from modernity. This is perhaps even more worrying since Sisler reports, games are currently and increasingly being used as a public relations tool for promoting the US Army and in army recruitment with games such as America's Army. Sisler also found that games produced by Arab developers is sparse but there are some games which have Arab and Muslim hero's and some which reflect accurate portrayals of significant conflicts (Sisler, 2008).

It is not just about increasing the representation of minority groups within games,

Figure 1. Sheva Alomar in Resident Evil 5™
(Source: weskerfreak105 at www.deviantart.com)

but having un-stereotypical representation of these groups within games, to reduce cultural stereotypes in this increasing media platform. Although not the focus of this book, we wish to briefly highlight that as with gender, other minority groups have similar issues.

The Older Gamer

The older gamer is overlooked by the gaming industry despite 26% of people over 50 in America playing games (ESA, 2011). Older adults are an increasing gamer market and although research on older gamers is sparse, research suggests older adults prefer sedentary rather than physically active games and games which can be played on varying levels of strategic complexity (Hoppes, Hally, & Sewel, 2000). According to Copier (2002), despite some older people playing games, in general games are not socially accepted amongst older generations(as cited in De Shuteer, 2010). However despite the paucity of research in the area of older gamers, it would appear that computer games are becoming an increasingly popular leisure activity amongst older generations (Pearce, 2008; De Schutter, 2010). Pearce (2008) suggests that the needs of older gamers is being ignored by both the mainstream computer games industry and the computer game press. Pearce's study of 'baby boom gamers', gamers who at the time of the study were aged over 40 (born between 1946 and 1964), found that women over 40 are one of the fastest growing gamer populations. The study of 300, mostly American participants, found a number of interesting things about the over 40 gamer. For instance, the majority are married with children, the over 40 gamer plays games in the home and the PC is the most popular platform. The most popular game genres for the over 40 gamer being those that tell a story with a sense of escape to another world and they spend between 10 to 40 hours per week playing games instead of watching TV or doing other leisure activities. There is a need for more research investigating older gamers, however the research that has been conducted on older gamers tends to focus on how to get older players to play rather than analysing the motives of those who already play (De Schutter, 2010). In a survey of 124 Flemish adults gamers aged between 45 and 85, De Schutter (2010) found, like Pearce's American study that the majority of older gamers played PC games, mostly casual games which are highly accessible and easy to learn. De Schutter also found that the majority of participants in the study were female and they enjoyed the challenge of puzzle games. Suggesting that older gamers are likely to be female and as such are not the games industries target audience. The industry is recognising the diversity of its audience with the 'games for all' concept first proposed by Nintendo with the development of the portable DS and Wii consoles. Taub (2006) reports how the Wii is making an appearance in nursing homes to increase older generations physical activity which also enables the Wii to reach a wider and more diverse audience.

Gay, Lesbian, Bisexual and Transgender (GLBT) Gamers

Another underrepresented group of gamers are often referred to as 'gaymers'. According to Kerr (2006) the industry workforce presumes the gamer population is homophobic, and hence why they do not include gay, lesbian, bisexual and transgender (GLBT) content in games. Although these gamers are an over-looked gaming audience, an early example of homosexuality in computer games was an Easter egg built into the game Sim Coter developed by Maxis in 1996. Easter eggs are "hidden messages, images and content found within games by those with the skill and motivation to look for them" (Shaw, 2009, p249). The Sim Coter game had predefined days of the year in which male characters would kiss. However the programmer of the Easter egg lost his job once the games publisher found out (Consalvo, 2007), perhaps indicating the industries aversion to homosexuality in games.

Despite this early objection by the developer Maxis, researchers suggest that sexualities other than heterosexual are starting to appear in games. Recently, Shaw (2009) looked at GLBT representation in games. Shaw acknowledges that research tends to focus on representations of gender and to a lesser extent race but representations of GLBT are rare, acknowledging that research by Consalvo, 2003a, 2003b are exceptions. Games that Shaw reports have a non-heterosexual content include; Bully developed by Rockstar in 2006, Fable developed by Microsoft Games Studios in 2004 and the Temple of Elemental Evil developed by Atari in 2003. Many games from Asian countries, predominantly Korea and Japan, contain and homoerotic content (Shaw, 2009). Research has found gamers can make their avatar in a number of games such as Fallout 1 and 2, The Sims, Fable and Bully have a relationship with either gender (Orchalla, 2006). According to Consalvo (2003) heterosexual romance plots within games reinforce the concept of compulsive heterosexuality. Schroder (2008) through analysis of gender and sexuality in the role playing game Gothic series, found that players often perform archetypical versions of masculinity, a hyper- identity., finding that whilst were sexual portrayals of women exist homosexuality is rare. Schroder, found male avatars reproduce the traditional concepts of masculinity, traditional gender roles are adhered to and compulsory heterosexuality is not challenged but affirmed in the Gothic series, supporting Consalvo's earlier research.

Eklund found some women try not to reveal they are female when playing online. Unwanted attention was found to occur when females disclosed their gender. Similarly homophobic references such as "fag" in online gaming spaces support the view point that gay gamers are viewed as other in games culture (Chonin, 2006; Leupold, 2006; Vargas, 2006). Interestingly, Palomares and Lee (2010) found that gender-matched avatars increase the likelihood of gender typical language use, whereas the converse was true for gender mismatched avatars which was found to promote counter typical language especially among women. Shaw's (2009) research found that gay gamers don't want to be marketed to specifically due to the ghettoization that occurred with

girl gamers discussed in chapter three. As is the case with female representation within games, there is a conflict between not being represented and being represented in a stereotypical way that is viewed as a difficulty with gay representation as highlighted by Sender, who asserts that "the history of gay visibility reveals the tensions between invisibility and limited visibility, between typification and stereotyping, and between needing to find telegraphic ways of representing gayness and doing so at the expense of gay people" (Sender, 2004, p13 in Shaw p 244). Indeed Shaw's study found that advertisement for gaymers appears in gay magazines not game magazines suggesting gaymers are not included in the wider games culture.

Again like with other underrepresented groups within games and games culture, the industry itself lacks a diverse workforce. Research suggests there is a lack of non-heterosexual game workers, especially in core content creation roles (Gourdin, 2005). This lack of representation with the workforce that creates the games has a significant impact on the lack of gay representation within the games themselves. Since industry professional's ability to express their sexual or gender identities impacts the representation of those identities in what they create (Sender, 2004).

The limited research on under-represented groups suggests that more research is needed, especially in terms of how race, ethnicity, culture, sexuality and gender intersect in games and can reproduce and perpetuate stereotypical attitudes amongst players. Shaw and Warf (2009) suggest the affective experience of games on the player is as an important area of research. Shaw's (2012) research provides a good starting point for considering the interplay of a number of categories. Research is starting to consider race and ethnicity in games more and it appears that there is a general need for more culturally inclusive game design, not based on stereotypical representations. Importantly, there is a need to create realistic female game characters and diverse characters. Greater diversity in gaming products would increase profits, through sales to diverse groups. This would benefit the industry and gaming culture. We will now turn our attention to the focus of this chapter gender in the digital age.

Gender and the Digital Age

Web 2.0 refers to a variety of Web enables applications built on open source and driven by user generated content. The most frequently used Web 2.0 applications include wikis (Wikipedia.org), podcasts (youtube.com) and social networking sites (Facebook.com, Twitter.com). Web 2.0 technologies are helping increase the appeal of technology and computer games to a female audience. This is particularly evident through female use of social networking sites such as Facebook. Indeed females are reported to now outnumber males on many social networking sites including Facebook and Twitter (Lam et al., 2011). Research has found that gender differences exist in the usage of social networking sites. In a recent study in Turkey female Facebook users were more likely to use Facebook for maintaining new relationships, and for academic purposes, whereas males were found to use Facebook for making new contacts (Mazman & Usluel, 2011). Whereas a recent American study found that female undergraduate students spent more time on Facebook and were more likely to experience negative effects from Facebook use such as loss of sleep, stress, addiction, and a negative self-body image (Thompson & Lougheed, 2012). Research on the information reference site Wikipedia has found gender bias to exist in a low representation of female editors as well and a gender bias on the topics of particular interest to female editors with the authors suggesting Wikipedia is 'growing in a way that is biased toward topics of interest to males'(Lam et al., 2011). In our opinion it is important that all voices are heard.

As this book will illustrate, females do play computer games close to parity with males, for certain genres and platforms i.e. online gaming so we need to ask "why is the activity still viewed male?"

Research suggests females tend to prefer social aspects of computing and computer games (i.e. Jansz et al, 2010). Computer games especially with the increase of multiplayer gaming may increase female participation in computer games as they become more and more social. Women are increasing becoming gamers, especially in MMORPG's games. Multiplayer online role-playing game (MMORPG) is a genre of computer role-playing games in which a large number of players interact with one another, within a virtual game world. Interestingly, MMORPGS are dominated by women (Consumer Electronics Association, 2007; Yee, 2006). Krotoski (2005) reported that women like

MMORPG games, such as *EverQuest, The Sims Online,* and *City of Heroes*, as they are able to choose a variety of selves, traditionally unavailable offline. It would appear that girls and women are increasingly engaging with technology from a consumer base, but less so from a productive base. There are a number of ways in which technology and specifically computer games are gendered. Indeed the relationship between gender and computer gaming is complex and operates on a number of different levels. The aim of this book is to look specifically at the gendering of computer games. This gendering takes place on a number of levels, from production through to consumption with gender situated beyond the game context.

Definition of Computer Games

Computer games are also referred to as video games, PC based or console games respectively but the terms are often used interchangeably. For the purpose of the current book the terms computer games and games will be used interchangeably to refer to all digital games. We will use Kirriemuir and McFarlane (2006) definition of games which states that a game:

... provides some visual digital information or substance to one or more players, takes some input from the players, processes the input according to a set of programmed game rules and alters the digital information provided to the players. (p6)

There are single player, multiplayer and massively multiplayer games. Computer games are played (operate) on a device (plat-form) specially made for game play called a game console, or a personal computer (PC) or a mobile phone. Examples of game consoles include Microsoft Xbox, Sony Play Station, Nintendo Wii and the handheld Nintendo DS.

Gaming is a worldwide leisure activity. There are reportedly 4 million active gamers in the Middle East, 10 million in Russia, 10 million in Vietnam, 10 million in Mexico, 13 million in Central and South America, 15 million in Australia, 17 million in South Korea, 100 million in Europe, 105 million in India, 183 million in America and a staggering 200 million in China. Figure 2 shows a visual representation of these figures which clearly illustrates the differences between countries.

Collectively, the planet is spending more than 3 billion hours a week gaming (McGonigal, 2011). According to the ELSPA (Entertainment and Leisure Software Publishers Association), in 2004 there were a staggering 20.8 million consoles and handheld game consoles in UK homes (Krotoski, 2004). In 2009 it was reported that a staggering 68% of US households play games and 42% of US homes have at least one gaming console (Entertainment Software Association, 2009), this has since risen to 49% in 2012 (ESA, 2012). Since 1998 more than 335 million computer games and leisure software have been sold in the UK alone (ELSA, 2008). 273.5 million games were sold in the USA in 2009 (ESA, 2011b), and in 2009, computer games outsold films (including trips to the cinema and DVD sales) (Wallop, 2009). 12 years is the overall average number of years American gamers have been playing; with adult males averaging 16 years, adult females 12 years and all adults

Figure 2. Illustrates the number of gamers worldwide in millions

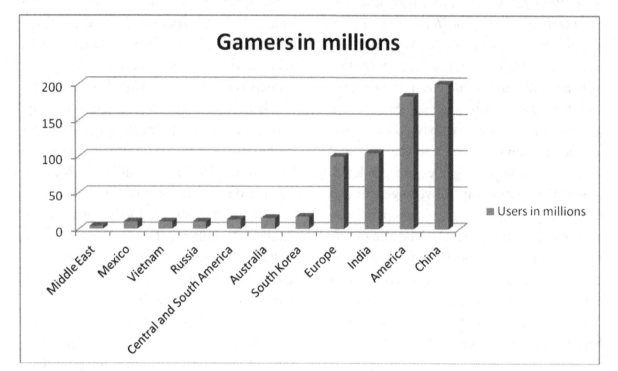

averaging at 14 years. According to the ESA (2011a) most American gamers expect to continue playing games for the rest of their lives. Despite the popularity of games there are many gender differences which we aim to illustrate throughout this book. For example boys of all ages have been found to be more likely to own a games console than girls (Ulicsak et al., 2009). It is reported that men spend more money on hardware and software for digital play than females (Bertozzi & Lee, 2010).

Computer Games Good or Bad?

Previous research looking at the psychological aspects of games tended to focus on aggression and the violent content of games. Research on computer games has moved on from this focus, particularly in recent years. However this is still an important area and we feel it is important to consider the potential bad as well as good of computer games. One of the major negative aspects of games is the violent and aggressive content, promoting violence and aggressive behaviour (i.e. Anderson et al 2008). The General Aggression Model suggests violent games increase aggression in the player (Anderson and Bushman, 2001). In particular Anderson et al, (2003) found violence in games to be significantly related to violence in the real world. Research also suggests there are gender differences with the effects of violent games with men becoming more hostile and aggressive after play than women (Bartholow & Anderson, 2002). Wang et al's (2011) recent research found violent video game play has a long-term effect on the brain functioning of men, but they did not compare the effects on women.

The majority of studies which report violent game effects have been criticised for being based on correlational associations between playing games and aggression in children and adults which does not necessarily confirm a causal link between the two variables (i.e. Ferguson & Kimburn, 2009; Ferguson et al, 2008a, 2008b). According to the ESA (2011B) violent crime amongst the young in America has decreased since the early 1990's whilst computer game popularity and use has increased, the opposite effect if there was a causal link. Indeed, the US Supreme Court argues that:

... psychological studies purporting to show a connection between exposure to violent video games and harmful effects on children do not prove that such exposure causes minors to act aggressively. (ESA, 2011b, p1)

Violence and aggression are associated with masculinity and therefore the studies of violence and aggression in computer games; although worthwhile in their own right also highlight the gendered nature of games. Due to the association of violence and games with masculinity it could be argued that the masculine dominance of computer games and the computer games culture is perpetuated and reinforced through these games, games considered 'mainstream' by the industry and hard core gamers. Indeed, after controlling for gender and previous gaming experience, Peng et al (2008) found people with more

physical-aggressive personalities engage in a more aggressive style of playing. With the same game, more aggressive people played the game more violently. Leading to the question of whether games induce violence or people play violent games due to their personalities and personal preferences?

Although gaming has been associated with increases in aggression and aggressive behaviour there is the argument that games actually enables the release of pent up aggression known as the Catharsis Theory and therefore has a positive effect on the player (Emes, 1997). Research has also suggested that playing violent games can lead to positive outcomes, such as the increase in memory, attention and spatial cognition. In particular, violent games have been associated with significant increases in visuo-spatial ability (Castel et al, 2005; Green & Bavelier 2003, 2006; Rosser et al, 2007). For instance, Ferguson, Cruz and Rueda (2008b) found playing violent video games was associated with higher visual memory recall. They suggest there are positive aspects of violent game use and that research should turn its focus on the positive aspects rather than focusing solely on the negative aspects of such games. Indeed a violent first person shooter game (Re-Mission) has been developed for cancer education and proved beneficial to young cancer patients (Kato and Beale, 2006). Feng, Spence and Pratt (2007) suggest that women in particular benefit from playing games due an increase in spatial attention and mental rotation in both genders. Feng, Spence and Pratt (2007) argue that games can therefore help reduce the gender gap in spatial cognition. Cultural differences must also not be ignored as Ferguson (2010) found that exposure to violence in games was not related to acts of aggression in Hispanic youths in USA. It should also be noted that much of this earlier research on computer games and violence did not take into account the issue of gender (with the few exceptions as mentioned), this focus on male aggression may be a reflection that computer games are viewed as a male activity. Research that does not take account of demographic differences such as gender could arguably be perpetuating the view that gaming is a male activity, rendering and reinforcing the viewpoint of the female gamers as 'other'.

However it is not just violence and aggression that research has found can have a negative impact on players. For instance Gentile et al's (2011) longitudinal study of children in Singapore found pathological gaming can lead to depression, anxiety, social phobias and lower school performance. The study found children who perform poorly at school are more likely to play more games as they gain as sense of mastery which eludes them at school. Other negative aspects of computer games include addiction, social isolation, and the negative imagery of women which is gender specific and will be discussed in chapter five. Gentile (2011) posits that there are five dimensions on which video games can affect players simultaneously: amount of play, content of play, game context, structure of the game, and the mechanics of game play. By considering all these dimensions Gentile suggests games can have both perceived positive and negative effects on players; games are therefore neither good nor bad. We agree that a variety of factors affect players and argue that genres such as action/adventure and sport are questionable from a gendered perspective.

Although there are some popular discourses that portray computer games as negative, especially violent games as discussed, the converse can also be noted, that playing computer games can be associated with some positive outcomes. For instance, research has found that in general game players are more likely to be academically successful, go to University and have better employment prospects (Harris, 2001). Playing games has been associated with a number of positive outcomes in children's abilities. For instance, games have also been found to help children learn about technologies, play with others (Brand, 2007), improve children's performance on instructional tasks (Pillay, 2002), develop their strategic thinking (Kirriemuir & McFarlane, 2004), improve their mental rotation (De Lisi & Wolford, 2002) improve their basic math abilities (Brand, 2007; Jones, 2009) and mathematical thinking skills (Devlin, 2011). Recently, Vitassari et al's (2010) preliminary findings suggest computer games enhance the learning of multiplication tables in maths for primary school children in Malaysia. Although computer games are frequently associated with improved visual spacial and mathematical abilities they have also been linked to other educational benefits in children. For instance Skoric et al (2009) found Singaporean children who spent more time playing games scored significantly better on their English test scores. Research has also found game play associated in the development of communication skills, negotiating skills, group decision making and data handling (Kirriemuir & McFarlane, 2004).

It is evident from our view point and through an examination of past research that games can be beneficial in a number of aspects despite the studies on violence and aggression. In order to consider the good versus the bad of games, we need to view the full gambit of games available as not all computer games contain violent and aggressive content. One of the most widely discussed games regarding aggression and violence is the Grand Theft Auto series produced by Rockstar Games. Grand Theft Auto (GTA) enables players to be aggressive and violent and the game even allows players to engage in sexual practices with female prostitutes and kill them to retrieve the fee paid. To illustrate this point, we have included three images from the GTA series (Figures 3-5). The selected images capture the violent theme of these type of games and the representation of females within the games. This is a relvant gender issue and will be discussed in chapter five.

Despite these graphic violent and sexually explicit images some researchers suggest

Figure 3. GTA™ gangster imagery
(Source: Downloaded from http://free-wallpaper-site.blogspot.co.uk/2011/11/grand-theft-auto-san-andreas-wallpaper.html)

Figure 4. GTA™ violence
(Source: Downloaded from http://free-wallpaper-site.blogspot.co.uk/2011/11/grand-theft-auto-san-andreas-wallpaper.html)

Figure 5. GTA™ female representation
(Source: Downloaded from http://free-wallpaper-site.blogspot.co.uk/2011/11/grand-theft-auto-san-andreas-wallpaper.html)

this game could be beneficial in terms of a resource to stimulate morality debates within the classroom (Gillespie, 2000). It appears there has been a shift in recent years to not focus on the negative or potentially negative aspects of games as illustrated by Gillespie with regards to the GTA series, instead researchers now looking into how games can actually improve the individual and maybe even society. These games have become known as pro social games and form an important area of studying computer games as discussed later in this chapter. So far we have tended to focus on the more negative or potentially negative aspect of computer games. We as authors want to encourage women and girls to be more interested and play more computer games in order to develop their technological competence and skills. Computer games have the potential to provide transferrable skills and we would like to discuss those in more detail and how they impact women especially in terms of the gendered digital divide.

Technical Ability and Transferable Skills

With regard to gender, a major benefit to narrowing the gendered skills gap is increasing female usage, interest and engagement with technology, and games are viewed as one potentially vital way in doing just that. Playing with technology increases comfort level with technology as well as having the potential to develop an interest in technology, which could go beyond playing. Smith et al (2005) found students with high computer technology domain identification, were more likely to consider a career in a computer technology field compared to students with low computer technology domain identification.

A lack of efficacy and interests by women has been put forward as a reason why so few women seek a career within Information and Communication Technology (ICT). Self-efficacy is one's belief in one's ability on a specific task such as computers/technology and an important psychological construct of the self. In an American study of the IT industry, Michie and Nelson (2006) found that men had greater self-efficacy for IT occupations and more passion for computing than females. The study also found that men had a less positive attitude towards women's capabilities for IT, resulting in gender biases with computers, in particular computer work, viewed as a male domain. Similarly, Singh and Allen (2007) found that women rate their abilities lower and report lower confidence than men do in computer related tasks. This is despite equal or superior task performance. Men in the study also displayed a more relaxed approach and playful attitude towards computers.

Digital play may enable women to gain an interest in computers as well as allow for the freedom of play for experimentation and personal growth. Female gaming should be encouraged as it could provide important technological knowledge as well as having the potential to make women more comfortable with technology. Previous research found that through playing games as children can form a significant role in developing children's attitudes towards technology (Bennett & Bruner, 2000). According to Bertozzi and Lee (2010) "playing with computer technology appears to be related to feeling comfortable with and competent in terms of computer technology because play affects attitudes" (p. 200). Suggesting girls should be exposed to and encouraged to play complex games as early as possible to increase their technological self-efficacy. Bertozzi and Lee (2010) found that encouraging digital gameplay in females' increases self-efficacy with technology which could help address the underrepresentation of females in technology related fields, a view which we support. From a three year longitudinal study of an after school gaming club for boys and girls in several Canadian schools, Jenson and de Castell (2011) found a number of gender differences in terms of education, gender and gaming. For instance from their study they found that although all children lived in a home with at least one games console, girls had little or no consistent access to console games. Another interesting finding was that the girls reported that they never turned the consoles on or set them up at home but once shown how to do so in the after school clubs they started setting them up. On the other hand, none of the boys admitted to not knowing how to set the consoles up; they either knew or learned by doing. Jenson and de Castell's (2011) study supports affirmative action of girls' only groups in order to encourage engagement in gaming and computer use more generally. Interestingly, Jenson and de Castell (2011) found that for the boys in their study gameplay was connected to their identity; they were good or bad, a winner or a loser. Dovey and Kennedy (2006) use the term 'technicity' (p64) to refer to the interconnectedness of identity and technical competence.

According to Dovey and Kennedy computer game play is a vital site for displaying technicity. Therefore playing computer games can provide the gamer with valuable skills which can be transferred to other social and work related uses of technology. Playing games may also spark an interest in computers and ultimately an interest in computer related careers which is particularly important for women/girls due to the underrepresentation of females in ICT as discussed in chapter six. Having looked at some of the potential skills computer games may provide players in terms of their wider technological competence and knowledge, we would now like to consider a more recent and emerging area of study into the benefits of gaming; what has become known as pro social gaming.

Pro Social Games/Gaming

Games don't distract us from our real lives. They fill our real lives: with positive emotions, positive activity, positive experiences, and positive strengths. (McGonigal, 2011, p354)

Game designer Jane McGonigal argues that games can change the world and that game developers have a responsibility to steer games in the direction of improving real world problems. Jane McGonigal's inspirational book 'reality is broken' (2011) advocates the benefits of games and more importantly the potential benefits pro social games and gamers can have on society. Some areas for the application of games for change include; human rights, poverty, environmental issues, global conflict, news, business, public policy, politics, public health and economics. According to McGonigal, games are not separate from our real lives. Gamers aren't escaping their real lives but through games are making their lives more rewarding. Social learning theory posits that children imitate what they observe (Bandura, 1977). Computer games go one step further as they allow players to not only observe but also enact in virtual behaviours. Research is increasingly considering games for ethical and moral reasoning development. For example some recent games that could enhance pro social behaviour in games include Nintendogs where players have to look after and nurture a puppy, whereas both Fable and Fallout are two games that offer players morality points for making good choices.

Previous research on the effects of computer games tends to concentrate on the negative effects of games as we have just briefly discussed. More recently research has started to look at the potential benefits or positive effects of playing computer games, this is especially so with the increase of pro social games. Research on the pro social aspects of games have found they have the potential capacity to deepen moral reasoning, give players a new perspective, enable players to practice cooperation as well as shape and reinforce positive behaviours. Greitemeyer and colleagues have conducted a number of experiments investigating the effects of playing pro social games on pro social behaviour. Greitemeyer and Osswald (2009) in two experiments found that playing pro social compared to neutral computer games decreased aggression responses. Greitemeyer and Osswald (2010) through four experiments

found playing pro social as opposed to neutral computer games increased helping behaviour. However the helping behaviour that was tested in the experiments were; picking up spilled pencils, more willingness to assist in future experiments and help an harassed experimenter. However some might question whether this is really pro social behaviour. Greitemeyer, Osswald and Brauer (2010) found pro social games increased interpersonal empathy and decreased pleasure of other's misfortune.

Other researchers support the body of work of Greitemeyer et al. For instance, Narvaez and Mattan (2006) found that participants who played a game with a helping scenario were more likely to be pro social after the game. Gentile et al (2009) found playing pro social computer games was related to pro social behaviour, such as cooperation, sharing and empathy. Whitaker and Bushman (2011) conducted two experiments which found that playing violent games made participants more aggressive whereas relaxing games decrease aggression and can make people happier and more kind, thus increasing pro social behaviour. In general the research suggests that pro social games increase pro social outcomes and degrease antisocial outcomes.

Buckley and Anderson (2006) expanded the GAM (general aggression model) into a GLM (general learning model) which suggests, as GAM does, that media exposure affects a person's state and behavioural reactions. Greitemeyer (2011) found exposure to media with pro social content increased the accessibility of pro social thoughts, empathy and helping behaviour, whilst decreasing aggression. What is particularly interesting and striking from the research on pro social games and gaming, is that there is no mention of any gender differences. According to gender role theory, women have traits such as nurturing and caring, whereas men are meant to have more aggressive and competitive traits (i.e. Schein, 1973). Therefore, one would presume that gender would be a pertinent issue in pro social gaming research. However, in the studies mentioned there has been no reference to any consideration in relation to gender. More research is needed on this area of gaming more generally, but specifically with regards to considering any possible gender differences and even investigating to see if there is any difference in pro social behaviour as a result of playing a pro social game between the genders. However it could be argued that games which could be considered as having a pro social element such as Nintendogs appeal to a larger female audience than a male audience which is perhaps due to the nurturing element of the game. The issue of gendering of genres will be discussed in detail in chapters four and five which will highlight the difference preferences the genders as a generality have, with females preferring more social, and causal games than males.

CONCLUSION

We live in a technological world and any divide is detrimental. The aim of this chapter was to provide the reader with an introduction to the gendered digital divide and the gendered digital divide in relation to computer games specifically. As we have mentioned, this is a recent area of research and much more research is required to gain a better understanding of the impact of games on prosocial behaviour. Technology is viewed as masculine and there are gender distinctions in relation to access to technologies, and how technologies are used. In addition, there is a gender divide in terms of who is involved in the design and production of technology. Men have greater self-efficacy and women have lower confidence than men do in computer related tasks. In addition, males are reported to spend more time online and have higher Internet skills than females, yet females now outnumber males on many social networking sites, including Facebook and Twitter.

There are a number of studies that have considered the impact of computer games on the gamer. Researchers tend to be split between the view point that games can have either a negative or positive impact or effect. Table 1 shows the main negative and positive aspects of computer games and the impact

Table 1, The main negative and positive aspects of computer games

Negative Impact on Player/ Gamer	Positive Impact on Player/ Gamer
Increases aggressive behaviour	Learn about technology and computers
Addiction	Promote empathy and helping behaviour
Depression	Enables role play
Social isolation	Social interaction
Distraction from other activities	Collaboration/team work
	Maths skills
Negative Aspects of the Game	Communication skills
Violent content	Increase memory
Sexual content	Increase attention
Negative portrayals of women	Increase special cognition
Negative portrayals of race, ethnicity and non-western culture	

Table 2. The gendered digital divide: The Key Issues

Gender Differences and Reasons for the Gender Divide in Computer Games	Core Issues Involved	How May the Issue be Addressed
Gender divide in technology	• Technology is viewed as masculine. • There are gender distinctions with regard to the access of technologies, and how technologies are used. • Males are reported to spend more time online and have higher Internet skills than females. • Web 2.0 technologies are helping increase the appeal of technology and computer games to a female audience. • Females are reported to now outnumber males on many social networking sites including Facebook and Twitter • Research on the information reference site Wikipedia has found gender bias to exist in low representation of female editors as well and a gender bias on the topics. • There is a gender divide in terms of who is involved in the design and production of technology. With a lack of female representation in technology related education and careers. • Men have greater self-efficacy for IT occupations and more passion for computing than females • Women have lower confidence than men do in computer related tasks.	• The image of technology needs to change to incorporate a female view. • The increasing use of technology is making technology more inclusive. However, major gender differences exist to the detriment of females. More is required to reduce this gendered gap especially with regard to confidence and self-efficacy. • For instance, increasing female interest and participation with computers and particularly with computer games could attract more women into technology and computing careers.
Computer games	• There are gender differences with the effects of violent games with men becoming more hostile and aggressive after play than women. • Research suggests playing violent games has been associated with significant increases in visuo-spatial ability. • Females have less access to console games in the home.	• Due to the association of violence and games with masculinity, the masculine dominance of computer games and the computer games culture is perpetuated and reinforced through games considered 'mainstream' by the industry and hard core gamers. • The benefits of playing games could help reduce the gender gap in spatial cognition. • Future research on computer games needs to take into account gender differences.

these aspects may have on gamers in order to give the reader a quick overview.

Due to the immersion and interactive nature of games, they are viewed by many as potentially valuable learning tools that can engage the NetGeneration. This generation has not known a world without technologies, such as the Internet and computer games. The literature and research, tends to focus on the negative aspects of games, yet games can be use-

ful. For instance, games in the area of learning, and behaviour change, which we will discuss in detail in chapter three. Technology is evolving to become more inclusive, it is crucial for the image of technology to change to incorporate a female view, as major gender differences exist to the detriment of females. More is required to reduce this gendered gap, especially in relation to confidence and self-efficacy. Increasing female interest and participation with computers and particularly with computer games could attract more women into technology and computing careers. This would assist in changing perceptions of the computer industry as being 'for the boys'. Women need to be involved in the games industry, in greater numbers and this is the focus of the next chapter.

REFERENCES

Anderson, C. A., Beerkowitz, L., Donnerstein, E., Huesmann, R. L., Johnson, J., & Linz, D. et al. (2003). The influence of media violence on youth. *Psychological Science in the Public Interest*, *4*, 81–110.

Anderson, C. A., & Bushman, B. (2001). Effects of violent video games on aggressive behaviour, aggressive cognition, aggressive affect, psychological arousal, & prosocial behaviour: A meta-analytic reviews of the scientific literature. *Psychological Science*, *12*, 353–359. doi:10.1111/1467-9280.00366 PMID:11554666

Anderson, C. A., & Dill, K. E. (2000). Video games & aggressive thoughts, feelings, and behavior in the laboratory & in life. *Journal of Personality and Social Psychology*, *78*(4), 772–790. doi:10.1037/0022-3514.78.4.772 PMID:10794380

Anderson, N., Lankshear, C., Timms, C., & Courtney, L. (2008). Because it's boring, irrelevant & I don't like computers: Why high school girls avoid professionally-oriented ICT subjects. *Computers & Education*, *50*, 1304–1318. doi:10.1016/j.compedu.2006.12.003

Bandura, A. (1977). *Social learning theory*. New York: General Learning Press.

Bartholow, B. D., & Anderson, C. A. (2002). Effects of violent video games on aggressive behavior: Potential sex differences. *Journal of Experimental Social Psychology*, *38*(3), 283–290. doi:10.1006/jesp.2001.1502

Bennett, D., & Bruner, C. (2000). The role of gender in the design of electronic learning environments for children. *Tech Learning's Well-connected Educator Journal, 21*.

Bertozzi, E., & Lee, S. (2010). Not just fun & games: Digital play, gender and attitudes towards technology. *Women's. Studies in Communications*, *30*(2), 179–204.

Brand, J. E. (2007). *Interactive Australia 2007: Facts about the Australian computer and video game industry*. Queensland, Australia: Bond University.

Brand, J. E., Knight, S., & Majewski, J. (2003). *The diverse worlds of computer games: A content analysis of spaces, population, styles and narratives*. Academic Press.

Buckley, K. E., & Anderson, C. A. (2006). A theoretical model of the effects & consequences of playing video games. In *Playing video games: Motives, responses, and consequences*. Mahwah, NJ: Lawrence Erlbaum Associates.

Cassell, J., & Jenkins, H. (1998). *From Barbie to Mortal Kombat: Gender & computer games*. Cambridge, MA: MIT Press.

Castel, A., Pratt, J., & Drummond, E. (2005). The effects of action video game experience on the time course of inhibition of return & the efficiency of visual search. *Acta Psychologica, 119*, 217–230. doi:10.1016/j.actpsy.2005.02.004 PMID:15877981

Chonin, N. (2006, February 5). MMORPG! WOW! TOS! GLBT! Sexual harassment! *San Francisco Chronicle.*

Clegg, S., & Trayhurn, D. (2000). Gender & computing: Not the same old problem. *British Educational Research Journal, 26*(1), 75–89. doi:10.1080/014119200109525

Consalvo, M. (2003a). Hot dates & fairy-tale romances: Studying equality in video games. In *The video game theory reader* (pp. 171–194). London: Routledge.

Consalvo, M. (2003b). *It's a queer world after all: Studying the Sims & sexuality.* New York: GLAAD Centre for the Study of Media & Society.

Consalvo, M. (2007). *Cheating: Gaining advantage in videogames.* Cambridge, MA: MIT Press.

Consumer Electronics Association. (2007). *Five tech trends to watch.* Retrieved from http://www.ce.org/PDF/2007–2008_5_Tech_Trends_to_Watch.pdf

De Lisi, R., & Wolford, J. (2002). Improving children's mental rotation accuracy with computer game playing. *The Journal of Genetic Psychology, 163*, 272–282. doi:10.1080/00221320209598683 PMID:12230149

De Schutter, B. (2010). Never too old to play: The appeal of digital games to an older audience. *Games & Culture: A Journal of Interactive Media.* doi:10.1177/1555412010364978

Devlin, K. (2011). *Mathematical education for a new era: Video games as a medium for learning.* London: AK Peters. doi:10.1201/b10816

Dill, K. E., Brown, B. P., & Collins, M. A. (2008). Effects of exposure to sex-stereotyped video game characters on tolerance of sexual harassment. *Journal of Experimental Social Psychology, 44*, 1402–1408. doi:10.1016/j.jesp.2008.06.002

Dill, K. E., Gentile, D. A., Richter, W. A., & Dill, J. C. (2005). Violence, sex, & age in popular video games: A content analysis. In *Featuring females: Feminist analyses of media* (pp. 115–130). Washington, DC: American Psychological Association. doi:10.1037/11213-008

Dill, K. E., & Thill, K. P. (2007). Video game characters & the socialization of gender roles: Young people's perceptions mirror sexist media depictions. *Sex Roles, 57*, 851–864. doi:10.1007/s11199-007-9278-1

Dovey, J., & Kennedy, H. W. (2006). *Game culture: Computer games as new media.* Berkshire, UK: Open University Press.

Emes, C. E. (1997). Is Mr Pac Man eating our children? A review of the effects of video games on children. *Canadian Journal of Psychiatry, 42*, 409–414.

Entman, R. M., & Rojecki, A. (2011). *The Black image in the White mind: Media & race in America*. Chicago, IL: University of Chicago Press.

ESA. (2011a). *Video games & the economy*. Retrieved from http://www.theesa.com/gamesindailylife/economy.pdf

ESA. (2011b). *Essential facts about the computer & video game industry*. Retrieved from www.theesa.com

ESA. (2011c). *Essential facts about games & violence*. Retrieved from http://www.theesa.com/facts/pdfs/ESA_EF_About_Games_&_Violence.pdf

European Commission. (2008). *Women in ICT: Status & the way ahead*. Brussels: European Commission.

Everett, A., & Watkins, S. G. (2008). The power of play: the portrayal & performance of race in video games. In K. Salen (Ed.), *The ecology of games: Connecting youth, games, & learning* (pp. 141–166). Cambridge, MA: The MIT Press.

Feng, J., Spence, I., & Pratt, J. (2007). Playing an action video game reduces gender differences in spatial cognition. *Psychological Science*, *18*(10), 850–855. doi:10.1111/j.1467-9280.2007.01990.x PMID:17894600

Ferguson, C. J. (2007). Evidence for publication bias in video game violence effects literature: A meta-analytic review. *Aggression and Violent Behavior*, *12*, 470–482. doi:10.1016/j.avb.2007.01.001

Ferguson, C. J. (2010). Introduction to the special issue on video games. *Review of General Psychology*, *14*(2), 66–67. doi:10.1037/a0018940

Ferguson, C. J., Cruz, A. M., & Rueda, S. M. (2008b). Gender, video game playing habits and visual memory tasks. *Sex Roles*, *58*, 279–286. doi:10.1007/s11199-007-9332-z

Ferguson, C. J., & Kimburn, J. (2009). The public health risks of media violence: A meta-analytic review. *The Journal of Pediatrics*, *154*, 759–763. doi:10.1016/j.jpeds.2008.11.033 PMID:19230901

Ferguson, C. J., Rueda, S. M., Cruz, A. M., Ferguson, D. E., Fritz, S., & Smith, S. M. (2008a). Violent video games and aggression: Causal relationship or by product of family violence & intrinsic violence motivation? *Criminal Justice and Behavior*, *35*, 311. doi:10.1177/0093854807311719

Gentile, D. A., Choo, H., Liau, A., Sim, T., Li, D., Fung, D., & Khoo, A. (2011). Pathological video game use among youths: A two-year longitudinal study. *Paediatrics*, *127*(2), e318–e329. doi:10.1542/peds.2010-1353

Gentile, D. A., Yerson, C. A., Yukawa, S., Ihori, N., Saleem, M., & Ming, K. L. et al. (2009). The effects of prosocial video games on prosocial behaviors: International evidence for correlational, longitudinal & experimental studies. *Personality and Social Psychology Bulletin*, *35*, 752–763. doi:10.1177/0146167209333045 PMID:19321812

Gillespie, R. (2000). When no means no: Disbelief, disregard and deviance as discourses of voluntary childlessness. *Women's Studies International Forum*, *23*(2), 223–234. doi:10.1016/S0277-5395(00)00076-5

Green, S., & Bavelier, D. (2003). Action video game modifies visual selective attention. *Nature*, *423*, 534–537. doi:10.1038/nature01647 PMID:12774121

Green, S., & Bavelier, D. (2006). Enumeration versus multiple object tracking: The case of action video game players. *Cognition*, *101*, 217–245. doi:10.1016/j.cognition.2005.10.004 PMID:16359652

Greitemeyer, T. (2011). Effects of prosocial media on social behavior: When & why does media exposure affect helping & aggression? *Current Directions in Psychological Science*, *20*(4), 251–255. doi:10.1177/0963721411415229

Greitemeyer, T., & Osswald, S. (2009). Prosocial video games reduce aggressive cognitions. *Journal of Experimental Social Psychology*, *45*, 896–900. doi:10.1016/j.jesp.2009.04.005

Greitemeyer, T., & Osswald, S. (2010). Effects of prosocial video games on prosocial behavior. *Journal of Personality and Social Psychology*, *98*(2), 211–221. doi:10.1037/a0016997 PMID:20085396

Greitemeyer, T., Osswald, S., & Brauer, M. (2010). Playing prosocial video games increases empathy & decreases schadenfreude. *Emotion (Washington, D.C.)*, *10*(6), 796–802. doi:10.1037/a0020194 PMID:21171755

Grusec, J. E., & Lytton, H. (1988). *Social development: History, theory, & research.* New York: Springer-Verlag.

Hargittai, E., & Shafer, S. (2006). Differences in actual and perceived online skills: The role of gender. *Social Science Quarterly*, *87*(2), 432–448. doi:10.1111/j.1540-6237.2006.00389.x

Harris, J. (2001). *The effect of computer games on young children -A review of the research.* London: Home Office Research, Development & Statistics Directorate. doi:10.1037/e668282007-001

Hoppes, S., Hally, C., & Sewell, L. (2000). An interest inventory of games for older adults. *Physical & Occupational Therapy in Geriatrics*, *18*(2), 71–83. doi:10.1080/J148v18n02_05

Jansz, J., Avis, C., & Vosmeer, M. (2010). Playing the Sims2: An exploration of gender differences in players' motivations & patterns of play. *New Media & Society*, *12*(2), 235–251. doi:10.1177/1461444809342267

Jansz, J., & Martis, R. G. (2007). The Laura phenomenon: Powerful female characters in video games. *Sex Roles*, *56*, 141–148. doi:10.1007/s11199-006-9158-0

Jenson, J., & deCastell, S. (2011). Girls@ play. *Feminist Media Studies*. doi:10.1080/14680777.2010.521625

Jones, J. (2009). Video games help music & math education. *Convergence*. Retried from http://www.convergemag.com/edtech/Video-Games-Music-Math-Education.html

Kato, P. M., & Beale, I. L. (2006). Factors affecting acceptability to young cancer patients of a psychoeducational video game about cancer. *Journal of Paediatric Oncology, 23*(5), 269–275. doi:10.1177/1043454206289780 PMID:16902082

Kelan, E. K. (2007). Tools & toys: Communicating gendered positions towards technology. *Information Communication and Society, 10*(3), 358–383. doi:10.1080/13691180701409960

Kerr, A. (2006). *The business & culture of digital games: Gamework/gameplay.* London: Sage.

Kirriernuir, J., & McFarlane, A. (2006). *Literature review in games & learning.* Retrieved from www.futurelab.org.uk

Krotoski, A. (2004). *Chicks & joysticks: An exploration of women & gaming* (White paper). Entertainment & Leisure Software Publishers Association (ELSPA).

Krotoski, A. (2005). Socialising, subversion & the self: Why women flock to massively multiplayer online role playing games. In N. Garrelts (Ed.), *Digital gameplay: Essays on the nexus of game & gamer.* Jefferson, NC: McFarland Press.

Lam, S. K., Uduwage, A., Dong, Z., Sen, S., Musicant, D. R., Terveen, L., & Ridel, J. (2011). *WP:Clubhouse? An exploration of Wikipedia's gender imbalance.* Paper presented at WikiSym 2011, Mountain View, CA.

Leonard, D. J. (2006). Not a hater, just keepin' it real: The importance of race-& gender-based games studies. *Games and Culture, 1*(1), 83–88. doi:10.1177/1555412005281910

Leonard, D. J. (2009). Young, black (& brown) & don't give a fuck: Virtual gangstas in the era of state violence. *Cultural Studies. Critical Methodologies, 9*, 248–272. doi:10.1177/1532708608325938

Leupold, T. (2006). Is there room for 'gaymers' in the gaming industry? *Oakland Tribune.* Retrieved from http://findarticles.com/p/aticles/mi_qn4176/is_20060407/ai_n16142589/

Mazman, S. G., & Usluel, Y. K. (2011). Gender differences in using social networks. *The Turkish Online Journal of Educational Technology, 10*(2), 133–139.

McGonigal, J. (2011). *Reality is broken: Why games make us better & how they can change the world.* New York: Penguin Press.

Michie, S., & Nelson, D. L. (2006). Barriers women face in information technology careers: Self-efficacy, passion & gender biases. *Women in Management Review, 21*(1), 10–27. doi:10.1108/09649420610643385

Narvaez, D., & Mattan, B. (2006). Practicing goodness: Playing a prosocial video game. *Centre for Ethical Education.* Retrieved from http://cee.nd.edu/news/documents/PracticingGoodnessReportFINAL.pdf

Natale, M. J. (2002). The effect of a male-orientated computer gaming culture on careers in the computer industry. *Computers & Society,* 24–31. doi:10.1145/566522.566526

National Science Foundation. (2011). *Women, minorities & persons with disabilities in science & engineering: 2011 special report NSF.* Arlington, VA: NSF.

Ochalla, B. (2006). *Boy on boy action: Is gay content on the rise?* Retrieved from http://www.gamasutra.com/features/20061208/ochalla_01.shtml

Ofcom. (2011a). *UK children's' media literacy.* Retrieved from http://stakeholders.ofcom.org.uk/market-data-research/media-literacy/archive/medlitpub/medlitpubrss/ukchildrensml/

Ofcom. (2011b). *UK adults' media literacy.* Retrieved from http://stakeholders.ofcom.org.uk/binaries/research/media-literacy/media-lit11/Adults.pdf

Ono, H., & Zavodny, M. (2003). Gender & the internet. *Social Science Quarterly, 84*(1), 111–121. doi:10.1111/1540-6237.t01-1-8401007

Palomares, N. A., & Lee, E.-J. (2010). Virtual gender identity: the linguistic assimilation to gendered avatars in computer-mediated communication. *Journal of Language and Social Psychology, 29*(1), 5–23. doi:10.1177/0261927X09351675

Pearce, C. (2008). The truth about baby boomer gamers: A study of over-forty computer game players. *Games and Culture, 3*(2), 142–174. doi:10.1177/1555412008314132

Peng, W., Liu, M., & Mou, Y. (2008). Do aggressive people play violent computer games in a more aggressive way? Individual differences & idiosyncratic game-playing experience. *Cyberpsychology & Behavior, 11*(2), 157–161. doi:10.1089/cpb.2007.0026 PMID:18422407

Pillay, H. (2002). An investigation of cognitive processes engaged in by recreational computer game players: Implications for skills for the future. *Journal of Research on Technology in Education, 34*(3), 336–350.

Rosser, J., Lynch, P., Cuddihy, L., Gentile, D., Klonsky, J., & Merrell, R. (2007). The impact of video games on training surgeons in the 21st century. *Archives of Surgery, 142,* 181–186. doi:10.1001/archsurg.142.2.181 PMID:17309970

Schein, V. (1973). The relationship between sex role stereotypes & requisite management characteristics. *The Journal of Applied Psychology, 57*(1), 95–100. doi:10.1037/h0037128 PMID:4784761

Schroder, A. (2008). We don't want it changed, do we? Gender & sexuality in role-playing games. *Eludamos Journal of Computer Game Culture, 2*(2), 241–256.

Shaw, A. (2009). Putting the gay in games: Cultural production & GLBT content in video games. *Games and Culture, 4*(3), 228–253. doi:10.1177/1555412009339729

Shaw, A. (2012). Do you identify as a gamer? Gender, race, sexuality, & gamer identity. *New Media & Society, 14*(1), 28–44. doi:10.1177/1461444811410394

Shaw, I. G. R., & Warf, B. (2009). *Worlds of affect: Virtual geographies of video games.* Environment & Planning. doi:10.1068/a41284

Singh, K., & Allen, K. R. (2007). Women in computer-related majors: A critical synthesis of research & theory from 1994 to 2005. *Review of Educational Research, 77*(4), 500–533. doi:10.3102/0034654307309919

Sisler, V. (2008). Digital Arabs: Representation in video games. *European Journal of Cultural Studies, 11*(2), 203–219.

Skoric, M. M., Ching Teo, L. L., & Neo, R. L. (2009). Children & video games: Addiction, engagement & scholastic achievement. *Cyberpsychology & Behavior, 12*(5), 567–572. doi:10.1089/cpb.2009.0079 PMID:19624263

Smith, J. L., Morgan, C. L., & White, P. H. (2005). Investigating a measure of computer technology domain identification: A tool for understanding gender differences & stereotypes. *Educational and Psychological Measurement, 65*(2), 336–355. doi:10.1177/0013164404272486

Taub, E. (2006). Nintendo at AAP event to count the grayer gamer. *New York Times.*

Taylor, T. L. (2003). Multiple pleasures: Women & online gaming. *Convergence, 9*(1), 21–46. doi:10.1177/135485650300900103

Thompson, S. H., & Lougheed, E. (2012). *Frazzled by Facebook? An exploratory study of gender differences in social network communication among undergraduate men & women.* Retrieved from http://www.freepatentsonline.com/article/College-Student-Journal/285532023.html

UCAS. (2012). *Data search.* Retrieved from http://search1.ucas.co.uk/f&f00/index.html

UKRC. (2008). *Women's underrepresentation in SET in the UK: Key facts.* UK Resource Centre for Women in Science, Engineering & Technology. Retrieved from http://www.theukrc.org/resources/key-facts-&-figures/underrepresentation

Ulicsak, M., Wright, M., & Cranmer, S. (2009). *Gaming in families: A literature review: Futurelab.* Retrieved from archive.futurelab.org.uk/resources/...reviews/Gaming_Families.pdf

Valenduc, G., et al. (2004). *Widening women's work in information & communication technology.* European Commission. Retrieved from http://www.ftu-namur.org/fichiers/D12-print.pdf

Vargas, J. A. (2006, March 11). For gay gamers, a virtual reality checks. *The Washington Post.*

Vitasari, P., Muhammad, P. V., Wahab, P. N. V., Othman, A., & Awang, A. G. (2010). A research for identifying study anxiety sources among university students. *International Education Studies, 3*(2), 189–196.

Wajcman, J. (2000). Reflections on gender & technology studies: In what state is the art? *Social Studies of Science, 30*(3), 447–464. doi:10.1177/030631200030003005

Wajcman, J. (2007). From women & technology to gendered techno science. *Information Communication and Society, 10*(3), 287–298. doi:10.1080/13691180701409770

Wallop, H. (2009, December 26). Video games bigger than film. *The Daily Telegraph.*

Wang, P., Lawler, J. J., & Shi, K. (2011). Implementing family-friendly employment practices in banking industry: Evidences from some African & Asian countries. *Journal of Occupational and Organizational Psychology.* doi:10.1348/096317910X525363

Whitaker, J. L., & Bushman, B. J. (2011). *Remain calm, be kind: Effects of relaxing video games on aggressive & prosocial behavior.* Social Psychological & Personality Science. doi:10.1177/1948550611409760

Williams, D., Martins, N., Consalvo, M., & Ivory, J. D. (2009). The virtual census: Representations of gender, race & age in video games. *New Media & Society, 11,* 815–834. doi:10.1177/1461444809105354

Williams, M. J., Levy Paluck, E., & Spence-Rodgers, J. (2010). The masculinity of money: Automatic stereotypes predict gender differences in estimated salaries. *Psychology of Women Quarterly, 34,* 7–20. doi:10.1111/j.1471-6402.2009.01537.x

Wilson, F. (2003). Can compute, won't compute: Women's participation in the culture of computing. *New Technology, Work and Employment, 18*(2), 127–142. doi:10.1111/1468-005X.00115

Yee, N. (2006). The demographics, motivations & derived experiences of users of massively-multiuser online graphical environments. *Presence (Cambridge, Mass.), 15,* 309–329. doi:10.1162/pres.15.3.309

Yee, N. (2007). Motivations of play in online games. *Journal of CyberPsychology & Behavior, 9,* 772–775. doi:10.1089/cpb.2006.9.772 PMID:17201605

KEY TERMS AND DEFINITIONS

Aggression: Behavior, or a disposition, that is forceful, hostile, or attacking.

Ethnicity: A person's ethnic origin.

Gender Divide: A divide between the genders based on being either male or female.

Older Gamers: Gamers viewed outside the age demographic of the general gamer population.

Pro Social Games: Games that enhance or encourage pro social behaviour such as empathy or helping others.

Violence: The intentional use of physical force or power, threatened or actual, against oneself, another person, or against a group or community, which either results in or has a high likelihood of resulting in injury, death, or psychological harm.

Chapter 2
The Computer Game Industry, Market, and Culture

ABSTRACT

Games have become an important leisure activity for children and adults, and they are becoming an increasingly important part of our culture as a whole. This chapter gives readers an insight into the impact of computer games both culturally and economically. The chapter also considers the technical impact of computer games and how this might impact the gendered digital divide. For instance, it is often noted that playing computer games can be a gateway to computing careers due to increasing confidence and skills in computing as well as developing an interest in computers due to familiarity. Indeed, computer games and gaming might be an initial intro-duction for children to digital technologies generally. In turn, developing their confidence and skills in their usage of technology, leading to an increased utilisation and interest in a career in computer science and information technology. All issues are important when considering the gender divide in computer games.

INTRODUCTION

The computer games industry is the most established of all the sectors of the emergent new media landscape. (Dovey & Kennedy's, 2006, p2)

Although the computer games industry forms part of the wider ICT (Information and Com-munication Technology) and SET (Science, Engineering and Technology) sector, and despite being a relatively new industry of approximately four decades, it is becom-

DOI: 10.4018/978-1-4666-4534-9.ch002

ing an important and established industry within itself. As the opening quote by Dovey and Kennedy illustrates, it is an established industry in the new media landscape and its impact has only increased in recent years and continues to do so. The new media landscape includes digital technologies such as Web 2.0 applications, online dating, and mobile phone technologies. The computer games industry has become one of the biggest of the digital technology industries in both economic and cultural terms. The games industry is a multibillion-dollar business and its products have become a major part of the media landscape. Worldwide, it's a $41.9 billion USD industry (Vancouver Film School, VFS, 2010). Games are a mainstream form of entertainment and there has been an explosive growth in the impact of games over the last decade. Indeed computer games have become one of the most popular leisure activities for children and adults in Western and Asian societies (Hartmann & Kilmmt, 2006). According to the Entertainment and Software Association (ESA) in 2012 72% of American households play computer games. To illustrate the increasing impact of computer games over recent years, the ESA (2011) reports that in 1996 the American entertainment and software industry sold about $2.6 billion in sales revenue, in 2009 sales were £20 billion. According to Dove and Kennedy (2006):

Economic, technical and cultural impacts all need to be taken into consideration when trying to understand the forces which determine the production of mainstream console games. (Dovey & Kennedy, 2006, p43).

The purpose of this chapter is to highlight the pervasive impact of computer games in today's society in order to enable the reader to comprehend the significance of the gender divide within both the production and consumption of games. In order to do this, this chapter is divided into a number of subsections looking at the cultural, economic and technical impact of computer games.

In order to understand the gender divide it is important to consider the history of the industry and how it has developed. Games are a growing part of Western and Asian cultures with a number of related activities including computer games magazines and Internet communities having emerged. Games are sneaking into all aspects of our lives including the workplace, with research suggesting that 61% of CEO's and other senior executives say they take daily game breaks at work (Reinecke, 2009) again emphasising the popularity of games and their significance today. The popularity of computer games has also been increasing with advances in technology in particular the increasing use of mobile phones, especially smart phones. According to the ESA mobile phone games are viewed as an important contribution to game sales and there were 4.6 billion mobile phone subscribers worldwide in 2009, compared with one billion in 2002 (ESA, 2011b). From a psychological and social science perspective computer games have been linked to addiction, skill development, health promotion and learning as will be discussed in subsequent chapters of this book. Many have questioned whether this increasingly popular leisure activity is harmful or beneficial. In particular, do children (and adults) learn from spending hours playing computer games and if so, what do they learn? Chapter three will discuss the research around computer games and learning in more depth. However it is not just children that play computer games. Indeed the average age of an American game player in 2011 was 37 and the average age of a game buyer was 41 (ESA, 2011a). In 2012 the average age of an American game player was 30 and 35 was the average age of a game buyer so quite a big age reduction between the year which may be an indication that more younger gamers are emerging or that gamers stop gaming as they get older. It is suggested that games have a number of benefits. For instance family friendly games can bring families together and the increase in pro social games have highlighted a number of benefits to individuals and society. This chapter will look at family friendly and prosocial games as well as illustrate the significance of computer games through a look at their impact economically and culturally. But first a definition of computer games in the context of this book is required.

THE COMPUTER GAMES INDUSTRIES CURRENT CLIMATE: THE CULTURE OF GAMES AND THEIR ECONOMIC IMPACT

The games industry is significant in that is has never been the product of one particular culture. (Consalvo, 2006, p123)

The games industry itself is an interesting industry and has developed in accordance with the popular demand of games themselves. The game industry has grown over approximately four decades from a small sector, niche market into a thriving multi-billion dollar industry and a mainstream entertainment choice for millions globally. Advances in both technology and the changing gamer demographic of the last decade have been instrumental in the evolution of the industry which seems set to grow. The relatively new computer games industry has accelerated from small firms and individuals programming in their bedrooms to an industry dominated by multinational hardware producers. Despite the games industry being a global industry with game development companies in the UK, USA, Australia, Iceland, Brazil, and South Korea to name but a few; Gaudioso (2003) argues that the current games industry is controlled by a handful of multinational publishers, mainly Electronic Arts (EA), Sony, Nintendo, and Activism. It is clear that the industry has three distinct geographical areas; North America, Europe and Japan; producing cultural products distinct to their geographical area. The greatest difference in the nature of games occurs between Japan in the East and the American and European markets of the West. The Japanese games industry is based on comic books, such as Manga, with the games sold in Japan being produced by Japanese producers whereas the other two markets (the American and European) interrelate more (Johns, 2006). According to Mia Consalvo, the game industry is:

... a hybrid encompassing a mixture of Japanese and American businesses and (more im-

portantly) cultures to a degree unseen in other media industries. (Consalvo, 2006, p117)

This hybrid of cultures is interesting and in a case study of Japanese game publisher Square Enix, Consalvo found distinctions between what the company produces for its home market and what they successfully sell abroad. For instance Consalvo found countries give characters a more 'native' look and more 'native' items such as Asian objects in the Sims game.

Through a brief look at the history of computer games it seems the American and Japanese markets have always had a close, yet competitive relationship. The first electronic game, tennis for two, was developed in 1958 by William Higginbotham at the US Department of Nuclear Energy's Brookhaven National Laboratory (Kline et al, 2003). In 1977 Atari released the 2600 home computer console in America, whilst Nintendo released its first console in Japan. In 2004 it was reported that North America accounts for approximately 40% of the global games market, Europe nearly the same with the remainder divided between Japan and the rest of Asia (DFC, 2004). The top game producing countries are; the USA, Japan, Britain, Germany and France, followed by Canada (DTI, 2002 in Dyer-Witheford and Sharman (2005). Currently the games industry in America directly and indirectly employs more than 120,000 people in 34 states (ESA, 2011c). According to Dyer-Witheford and Sharman (2005) the creation of games is divided into three stages: development, publishing and software. Canada's games industry earned approximately $2 billion USD in 2008, which according to the VFS (2010) is more than many parts of the entertainment sector. The games industry is made up of a number of specialism's including development, production, design, level design, audio design, art and testing. The UK industry supports an estimated 28,000 jobs, directly, and indirectly (Oxford Economics, 2008). Within Europe, Britain has the highest number of games development studios across Europe (ISFE, 2004, see Krotoski, 2004). With more recent figures suggesting that the UK games industry has 9900 employees (Oxford Economics, 2008). Just over two thirds of these people work in games development, with the remainder focused on publishing, marketing and other core business functions.

It has been suggested that 10% of games make 90% of the money (Dyer-Witheford & Sharman, 2005). This is because major game publishers prefer clones of proven hits rather than experimentation, as indicated by the 'franchises' that dominate the best seller list (Dyer-Witheford & Sharman, 2005). This can have a significant impact as game developers develop games for their target audience and therefore successful games continue to be produced. This leads to what Shaw (2009) viewed as a 'narrow vision': "as economically successful genres are reproduced, this results in a narrower vision of what 'gamers' play" (Shaw, 2009, p232). What gamers play can also be impacted by the design teams as it has been found that masculine fantasies dominate game design (Gansmo, Nordli, & Sorenson, 2003). This male dominance has a specific gender impact perpetuating the masculine culture of computer games. Publishers also avert risk by basing games on blockbuster films (i.e. Enter the Matrix), popular books (i.e. Harry Potter) and television programmes (i.e. The Simpsons Road Rage). This could potentially be beneficial to a female game consumer since a variety of games will be produced based on other popular media. On the other hand basing games on other popular cultural forms could perpetuate gender if leisure is viewed as a predominantly male pursuit. In our view women need to be part of the gaming culture in order to put across a female perspective that is not based on male fantasises or interpretations of what females want.

The games industry is one of the fastest growing sectors of the 21st century (Krotoski, 2004). It has even been reported that more digital games are sold in the US and UK than books (Bryce & Rutter, 2001). In 2004, the industries worldwide worth stood at 20bln Euros for software and hardware (ISFE, 2004, see Krotoski, 2004). The estimated turnover of the UK computer games industry in 2008 was £625 million, having a direct contribution to UK GDP (Gross Domestic Product) of approximately £400 million (Oxford Economics, 2008). According to research and analysis of the US economy by IBISWorld, in 2008 the games industry (including development, production and retailing) was a $40 billion USD business. More recently the Vancouver Film School (2010) suggests that in 2009 the worldwide games industries worth stood at 41.9 billion USD. It should also be bore in mind that the games industry also influences sales in other industries such a as increasing the demand for HDTV's (ESA, 2011c), so games are big business.

There appears to be mixed views on the industry during the current economic climate with the situation viewed more positively in the USA and Canada than in the UK. According to PricewaterhouseCoopers the computer games sector will remain "one of the above-average growth segments of the global entertainment industries through 2011" (ESA, 2011b). It appears that despite the economic down turn faced by a number of countries including America games sales, both hardware and software increased in 2008 despite the country's economic downturn (Snider, 2009). According to the IBISWorld report, the industry was not expected to be hit by the current recession but instead it was expected to grow by 9.5% in 2009. The report also projects a yearly forecast thereafter of 10%, which is estimated to reach $63.2 billion by 2013 (IBISIWorld, 2008). A report by the Vancouver film school (VFS) in 2009, suggested the games industry was strong enough to survive the recession due to the growth in the industries software sales globally. The report suggests that in 2008 across the globe the games industry revenue figures in billions US dollar were; USA 21.3, Canada 20, Europe 17.9, Korea 1.7, China 7.9, Japan 6.3, Latin America 1.0 and India 0.2. However findings in the UK may not be so optimistic. According to the Oxford Economics report (2008) despite the industries 10% per annum growth since 2004, the industries decline in the UK is a possibility. One of the major reasons the report suggests for this possible decline is due to the expansion of the industry in other regions such as Canada, China and Korea. Many newer gaming countries provide support for the industry. For example from a study of the Korean online games industry, Jin and Chee (2008) found that the Korean government has been instrumental in supporting the industry by providing financial subsidies and incentives to developers. The Oxford Economic report goes on to suggest that the UK 's games development industry could be £350 million lower by the year 2013, with a loss of 10,000 jobs supported both directly and indirectly by the games industry. At the time of writing, it appears the industry is doing much better than most, the ESA (2012) reported a total of $24.75 billion spend by American customers. After all the same report stated that 42% of game players viewed games as the most value for money leisure activity compared to DVD, music or the cinema.

ECONOMIC IMPACT OF PLAYING GAMES

The economic impact of computer games is not restricted to a countries GDP and employment by the industry and related sectors. Indeed, there are now a number of potential economic benefits from actually playing games. One of the major economic benefits of playing games is that the popularity of games has led to the creation of professional gamers. The Cyberathlete Professional League (CPL) allows gamers to pursue full time careers in playing games. The CPL is the world's most recognised brand in professional games tournaments (Burgess, Stermer, & Burgess, 2007). The CPL has a series of tournaments transforming game competitions into a pro-

fessional sport (Burgess et al, 2007). In Asia (especially South Korea) professional gamers are treated with high esteem and even treated as sports celebrities (Chee, 2006). Through an investigation of pro gamers Taylor (2008) found a gender segregation of pro gamers and an increase in more single sex teams and single sex competitions. Taylor found that women were at a disadvantage within professional gaming since the higher prize winnings went to male teams the research revealed there to be a secondary status for female competitions and prize winnings.

However you do not have to be a professional gamer to benefit economically from playing computer games and many people are making this popular leisure activity into a self-employment opportunity. For instance Lee and Lin (2011) found that income can be earned by trading virtual objects and currencies used in MMORPG (Massively Multiplayer Online Role-Playing Games); a form of economic activity known as real money trade (RMT). Lee and Lin's 2011 study focused on RMT workers as an example of new cyber workers who lack traditional identity sources such as workplaces, company names or associations with existing occupations. According to Lee and Lin (2011), RMT workers "play in the virtual worlds of MMOs, collect virtual currency and objects and sell them to other players for real money" (Lee and Lin, 2005, p452). RMT workers are an interesting category of new workers as they combine not only home with work but also home and work with leisure. Lee and Lin found that RMT workers use various strategies to separate home from work and leisure related play from work related play. Heeks (2008) estimated that there were at least 60,000 RMT related enterprises in operation worldwide in 2008.

Recent years has seen brand placement and advertising in games (Shaw and Warf, 2009) and games such as Second Life enable players to generate real money from virtual businesses. Taiwanese entrepreneur Anshe Chung became a multimillionaire virtually. Players even pay other players to get them to higher, more challenging levels of games (Barboza, 2005). Books have been published on the subject of making money in the virtual world. For example Daniel Terdiman has published a book in 2007 entitled: 'The Entrepreneur's Guide o Second Life: Making Money in the Metaverse' about how to build profitable business in the virtual world of Second Life. Economic activity and playing games as employment (outside of game development) is a new area and one which needs much more research. Currently it is unclear of the gender of RMT workers and if there is a gender divide within this form of work. However due to the general male dominance of games and the gaming culture more generally we can speculate that a large proportion of RMT workers will be male, however this is just our speculation. What is particularly interesting about RMT work and gender is the interlink between not just work and the home but also between work, the home and leisure making traditional gender roles interesting and an important area of future study.

New media industries have been associated with a new style of working, a style that may not be advantageous to women. Gill (2002) put forward that the image of new media work as cool, non-hierarchical and equalitarian is entrenched in gender inequalities relating to education, access to work and pay. She also found a number of new forms of gender inequality emerging connected to the features of work that are valued such as informality, autonomy and flexibility. In a study of 125 freelance media workers in six European countries, Gill (2002) found that as freelance workers, workers were not connected to any particular workplace or organization; as virtual workers they could not be located in any specific place. Participants in the study characterized their work as multimedia content creation, digital art, computer game design, animation, video art, Web broadcasting, Internet and Website design. As we will discuss in chapter six, these are similar characteristics as game developers, in that, the media workers were young, aged 25-35 and the majority had a University degree; with half having a postgraduate education. They were mostly art graduates rather than computer science graduates and most defined themselves as artist, especially the women, rather than programmers. Gill found that women and men have different experiences of work in new media, challenging the egalitarian view of the industry. For example, women earned less money and they were more likely to work from home, which was seen as a disadvantage in the industry due to the lack of networking available. Networking was deemed necessary within new media work for attracting new contracts or projects. Indeed finding new projects was found to be through whom you know not what you know. This was perceived by some women as a form of gender exclusion, similar to the 'old boys' network' of more established industries such as the wider ICT and SET sector. Therefore, this style of working is not meritocratic or egalitarian when based on connections rather than open competition. The study found that women emerged as clear losers in terms of the number of contracts and the money earned within the industry. Gill (2002) concludes that:

... patterns of discrimination are naturalized and inequality and injustice wear an egalitarian mask. (p86).

This is encapsulated by one participant's view of the industry in Gill's (2002) study:

... give me a formal hierarchy any day over the fake democracy and pseudo-equality of this work. (p83).

We will look at the position of, as well as the experiences of female game workers from past literature and our own research in chapters six, seven and eight. Now we will turn our attention to the technical impact of games.

THE UPGRADE CULTURE: THE TECHNICAL IMPACT OF COMPUTER GAMES

A major feature of the SET and ICT sector is the upgrade culture and this is particularly evident in the games industry. Technology is never stable, but is always in what Kline et al (2003) calls a state of 'perpetual innovation' (Dovey & Kennedy, 2006, p73). The continual release of new technologies such as new consoles, games, editing software etc. is

an issue across a range of sectors including the games industry. In a study of first year games students in the North West of England and London and interviews with five professional designers, Ashton (2011) examined the contexts and practical means associated with upgrading the self (keeping up) with regards to issues such as anxiety and identity for those working in an upgrade culture. Skills are continually reinvented across both the production and consumption of games; therefore it is not just the game developers who have to keep up to date with their skills but also the gamers. In her study of Web design skills Kotamraju (2002) suggests that:

... skill is at the core of identity. In many instances, skill is what we perceive as giving us worth not only within the marketplace, but within our lives as well. Anxiety provoked by out dated or inadequate skills often reflects uncertainty about our place in the world. (p2)

Therefore the upgrade culture can have a significant impact on game workers and is an important consideration when looking at the inclusiveness of the workforce. There is however a paucity of research in this area and much more research is needed especially in terms of the gender divide and the upgrade culture. For instance how do women who have taken time out of their careers for maternity leave and childcare get back into the culture and what barriers in particular do they face when they need to keep updated on their skills so frequently?

As games become increasingly more popular and the games industry grows, games courses are also growing throughout Universities; however they tend not to be appealing to women; only 5% of games students in the UK, in 2004 where women (Haines, 2004). Haines suggests that women are unaware of the potential opportunities within the games industry. Our research which will be discussed at length in chapters seven and eight, suggests girls/women are unaware of the variety of skills and roles within the industry. The academic route is viewed as beneficial to women in order for them to break into the male domain of the games industry (Fullerton et. al., 2008). According to Fullerton et. al. (2008) women could benefit from a University background in games as it may enable them to develop skills, confidence and explore their own creative interests and insights in game design in an academic environment before breaking into the games industry. They also acknowledge that women do not have to be hard core gamers in order to break into the industry via an academic route (Fullerton et. al., 2008). However one of the concerns of teaching gaming within higher education is that the games industry moves very fast in terms of technological development. David Braben, boss of UK developer, Frontier has criticised University games courses and highlights the difficulties of teaching for such a fast paced upgrade culture. Braben suggests that the courses are "failing students and the industry because they are teaching skills that are between five and ten years out of date." This quote highlights how the upgrade culture associated with this industry can be an issue throughout. Next we would like to look at the cultural impact of one of the world's major entertainment and leisure pursuits.

GAMES AND THEIR CULTURAL IMPACT

Culture is not something ready-made which we "consume," culture is what we make in the practices of consumption. (Storey, 2000, p59, as cited in Dovey & Kennedy, 2005, p63)

The popularity of games has increased dramatically over the past few decades making games one of the most popular media outlets today and a powerful aspect of our cultural landscape. Games are an increasingly pervasive leisure activity for a diverse audience of gamers playing a wide genre of games on various platforms. It is reported that in 2010 67% of American households owned some form of computer games console and 41% of Americans purchased a game in that year (ESA, 2010). The extent of the impact computer games impact is not restricted to America. Indeed, according to Juul (2010), more than 50% of the population in the Western world play computer games and games are also hugely popular throughout Asian countries. Some of the games that are produced themselves become cultural phenomena. For instance, Nintendo's Pokemon, in a similar vein as Pac-Man and The Mario Brothers games before it, are examples of games that have moved from games to cultural phenomena. Pokemon has become a television show, film, toys and other merchandise have all been produced from the game.

The games industry has a pervasive impact upon popular culture which is influenced by, and influences other media and popular culture including, games being turned into books (i.e. Assassins Creed) and into films (i.e. Tomb Raider). It is one of the fastest growing sectors in the British economy and the bestselling games turn over sums comparable to hit films and music titles (Haines, 2004). In particular the games industry is influencing the current film industry. The Prince of Persia: The Sands of Time is currently the highest grossing movie based on a computer game. Excluding DVD sales, the movie has made $312,583,548 USD worldwide (Mai, 2010). The games industry is also having an impact on the music industry. Games such as Rock Band and Guitar Hero are not only popular gaming activities that are highly social, but they also enable musicians to reach a wider audience and music labels to generate revenue (ESA, 2011b). According to the ESA (2011b), 40 million paid songs have been sold via download through the Rock Band franchise since its launch in 2007 and the first video game compilation album released worldwide 'Video games live: volume one' album was released in 2008 reaching number 10 in the American Billboard charts. Interestingly it would seem that playing computer games can also inspire other leisure pursuits. In a 2008 study of more than 7000 Rock Band and Guitar Hero players, 67% of the non-musicians in the study were inspired to play a real instrument whereas the musicians in the study had increased the amount of time they played (Brightman, 2008). This inspiration for other leisure pursuits from playing computer games extends beyond music. For instance Crawford (2005) found no evidence to support the view that playing computer games results in reduced levels of sports participation. Crawford suggests that for some adult gamers playing sports games

can actually increase interest and knowledge of sports. However Crawford did find that there were gender differences in the findings resulting from the gender differences in game genres played with sports games being a particularly male dominated genre of game.

According to the Entertainment and Software Association (ESA, 2011d) computer games are considered works of art in themselves as well as influencing other art forms. The games industry recognises games for their entertainment value and the art community, according to the ESA is starting to recognise them for their cultural value (ESA, 2011d). Highlighting the current impact and significance of games, in 2010 the Museum of Video Games opened in Paris in order to celebrate the artistic and technical history of video games (ESA, 2011d). Due to this pervasive impact the computer games industry is starting to receive increasing attention from social scientists. This growing industry is viewed an important industry of study due to the connections computer games have with other cultural sectors (Johns, 2006). Recently Terlecki et al (2011) suggested that "as computer technology continues to pervade every facet of life, the study of video game playing becomes more relevant" (p 22). We would tend to agree with this view point and encourage the study of all aspects of computer games and the industry especially from a gendered perspective. This is especially so since the industry is relatively new and increasingly significant today.

The quote by Storey at the start of this subsection helps to illustrate why it is important for women and a more diverse workforce to be a part of the production and development of computer games in order for a more diverse workforce to be a part of the making and meaning of today's cultural landscape. Women (and other underrepresented groups) are becoming more and more a part of the computer games consumer market but they are still notably missing from the production and development of games culture. It appears that a masculine culture exists in computer games as this book will discuss throughout and according to Jenkins, "video games are characterized by masculine play styles, and marked specifically by 'boy culture'" (Jenkins, 2000, p270). The ICT industry in particular computers has had problems with image. With an image often perceived as 'geeky', the work is often viewed as unsociable, solo technical work (Miller et al., 2004). Focus group research by Edwards and Stephenson (2002) found that in the UK young people viewed the ICT sector as boring, geeky and dominated by male workers (as cited in Miller et al., 2004). Australian senior high school girls perceive computing subjects as boring (Anderson et al., 2008). Symonds (2000) found similar results in a study of New Zealand female high school students who described IT work as boring, anti-social with little communication, despite the female students acknowledging the career benefits of high salaries and good job opportunities associated with work in the sector (in Harries and Wilkinson, 2004). Understanding gender and technology may provide further insight into gender in society. Technology has a gender specific association which helps perpetuate the gender gap in ICT. This gender specific association of technology and the ICT industry is perhaps even more pronounced with computer games and computer game culture. In his book 'Die tryin': video games, masculinity, culture'; Burrill (2008) put forward that computer games are play grounds for the construction and performance of masculinity. According to Burril, the games industry presumes the player is male. This presumption of a gamer as male could lead to female gamers being viewed as 'other' within the wider gaming culture., yet despite this label of 'other' women have had an impact. Chapter six will describe in more detail the impact of women on the gaming market and their influence as gamers, as well as discuss the underrepresentation of women and other groups in the development and production of computer games. We would now like to consider family friendly games as these are viewed as a way of including females as gamers.

FAMILY FRIENDLY GAMES AND GAMES FOR ALL

It has been suggested that games are less intergenerational than television (Orleans & Laney, 2000). In recent years the games industry has seen a steady increase in the number of what have become known as family friendly games – games that can be played by the whole family. Family friendly games are viewed as beneficial as they can bring families together through play. According to the ESA, half of American parents play games at least once a week with their children (ESA, 2011b). In America findings suggest that

64% of parents with children under 18 view games positively. The main reasons research has found as to why parents play computer games with their children is because parents view them as fun for the entire family, their children ask them too and they feel it is a good opportunity to socialise with their children as well as monitor the game content (ESA, 2011b). Indeed research has found a number of benefits in playing games with other family members. Adolescents who play games have been found to have more family closeness, increased school engagement, more involvement in other leisure activities, a positive mental health, a positive self-concept and increased friendship networks (Durkin & Barber, 2002). Reasons for playing games as a family have been found to be similar across Europe, the UK and the USA including it is fun, enabling parents to spend time together with children, monitor the games played as well as the time spent playing. There is also the benefit of social interaction with extended family and friends i.e. through Facebook since the social networking site Facebook has many family friendly games such as FarmVille which are becoming increasingly popular with Farm-Ville reaching 90 million active players in 2010 (McGonigal, 2011).

The Wii console by Nintendo is at the forefront of family friendly games helping to close the generational gap in computer games. When the Nintendo Will system was released in 2006 it introduced a different kind of gaming system; a more community-centric gaming system with Wii being a play on 'we'. According to Nintendo the 'ii' was meant to visually represent the image of two people standing together and playing (Carless, 2006). Even the controller for the Wii is far removed from the traditional joysticks and controllers and reflects more realistic actions whilst playing. The systems Mii's (the playable characters and non-playable characters) also define the system as sociable since gamers develop Mii's of family and friends and even when those other players are not playing their Miis are on screen as members of the crowd as non-playable characters. Due to its sociable game play the Wii is being utilised in ever increasingly diverse environments such as medical schools and school physical education classes for educational purposes (Boyle et al, 2011), and in nursing homes (Taub, 2006) in an attempt to reach a wider audience and a more diverse demographic of gamer. Fron et. al. view the Wii console as important in appealing to a wider and more diverse audience as they suggest "the Wii may be as significant as the Model T Ford in creating videogames for the people" (Fron et. al., 2007; p316).

The family friendliness and games for all view point is not viewed popular with the hard core gamer market. For instance in April 2008 video game industry analyst Michael Pachter was quoted saying:

Wii Fit is just not aimed at hard core gamers...It's defiantly aimed at the Oprah crowd. I bet they sell a million units a week for every pound that Oprah says she lost on it. (Balance Blackboard Blog, 2008).

Whether the consoles and games are viewed as hard core or not and accepted into 'mainstream game culture or not, Nintendo with their handheld DS and Wii consoles are currently leading the console market (Ulicsak et al, 2009). Both the Nintendo consoles are marketed as a family console which has led to other consoles developing family-friendly games such as the cross-platform guitar hero and rock band games. In 2009 the top selling Wii games, which out sold those for the Xbox and Sony consoles, were family friendly games (Mathews, 2009). Indeed in 2011, 39.3% of games sold in America were rated for everyone (ESA, 2012).

In a literature review of gaming and families produced by Futurelab, Ulicsak et al (2009) defines family gaming as including "any kinship grouping where the players come from different generations" (p 2). The Futurelab report found no gender difference in the time spent playing computer games but there was a gender difference in what games they were playing. Young children of both genders were found as preferring puzzle and action adventure games but as they aged boys preferred first person shooter, racing and action games whilst girls tended to stay with puzzle and simulations. Gender is a potential issue for playing games as a family due to this difference in their preference towards preferred game genre, as well as the priority the different genders give to gaming. Research suggests that males are more likely to make time to play games whereas females tend to fit play around other interests and activities (Dawson et al, 2007). Boys are also more likely to own a console than girls (Ulicsak et al, 2009), this ownership may perhaps give boys more decision making power and control within the family of what is played and when.

In light of the issue of family friendly games it is important to consider the gender divide in terms of parental mediation, that is, how parents view games for their children and how this is dependent on gender in terms of the parents views and the mediation of the child(ren).

PARENTAL MEDIATION OF COMPUTER GAMES

According to the Entertainment Software Association (ESA, 2008) 91% of parents are present at the time a game is purchased or rented and that 86% of children gain their parents' permission before purchasing or renting a game. In America the Entertainment Software Rating Board (ESRB), an industry self-regulatory body assigns aged-based rating to games to guide retailer and consumers (ESRB.org). However, the ESRB has no official enforcement power and games are often sold to younger consumers (Kutner et al, 2008). The Pan European Game Information (PEGI) is the equivalent classification system which runs in Europe.

There are three main types of parental mediation; active mediation which consist of talking about the games content whilst the child is playing the game, restrictive mediation which involves setting rules that restrict the use of the medium, including restrictions on time spent, location of use or content, and co-playing which involves actively participating with the game (Millwood, Hargrave

& Livingstone, 2007). Studies investigating parental mediation of games suggest that parents tend to mediate games as they mediate television (Nikken & Jansz, 2006, 2007). However games are interactive and require an active player to feed input into the game (Newman, 2002). Gaming is much more immersive than watching television and games require investment of playing time in order to be able to operate the interface and understand the games structure (Vorderer, 2000). Indeed, Sherry Turkle encapsulates the difference between television and games in that:

Television is something you watch, video games are something you do, a world you can enter, and, to a certain extent, they are something you "become". (Turkle, 1984p 66-67)

Gender and the age of a child have both been found as being important factors and significantly affect parental mediation. For instance Nikken and Jansz (2007) found that younger children and girls were more often subjected to mediation than males and older children. In their Dutch study, Nikken and Jansz (2006) used an online questionnaire to investigate parental mediation of computer games. They found a child's age and parent's game behaviour were the most important factors that influenced parental mediation. Findings revealed that parents applied more restrictive and active mediation when they viewed games as having negative behavioural effects with more co-playing mediation behaviour when the parent expected more positive benefits from game play. Parents who played games were more optimistic about the positive

effects and less worried about the negative effects of computer games (Nikken & Jansz, 2006). The study also found that parents are more likely to be involved in co-playing when they expected positive social-emotional effects of game playing on their children (Nikken & Jansz, 2006). Therefore parental attitude is important and can have a huge impact on a child's game playing. In an American study, Shin and Huh (2011) conducted a survey of teenagers and parents to look at what specific perceptual and demographic factors influence parents to monitor their teenage children's gaming and to explore how different forms of parental mediation are associated with game playing behaviours. The study found parents who viewed negative effects of games where more likely to engage in restrictive mediation, whereas parents who viewed games as having a positive influenced were more involved in permissive forms of mediation such as co-playing. Only game rating checking was a significant and positive predictor of teenagers' game playing behaviours. Teenagers who receive a higher level of game rating checking mediation were found to play more games and were more likely to engage in deceptive gaming activities.

Research on the parental mediation of television has previously found that mothers are more likely to exert more mediation than fathers' (Valkenburg et al, 1999; van der Voort et al, 1992). This has also been found to be the case for the parental mediation of computer games (Nikken & Jansz, 2006). However, both genders were found to equally mediate through co-play. Previous research suggests that parents are concerned about a number of negative effects of games, in particular the violent content of games desensitising children towards real life violence and the amount of time spent gaming, which parents feel could be spent doing more worthwhile pursuits such as exercising, studying or socialising, issues discussed in chapter one (Oosting et al, 2010). A recent qualitative study conducted in the Netherlands, found parents tend to choose restrictive mediation most often through limiting play time and/or prohibiting game content (Oosting et al, 2010). The study also found parents expressed a need for more comprehensive information regarding game content.

The ability to access and use technology is becoming increasingly more important as technology is used in our daily lives. Parental mediation is an important area of consideration when looking at computer games and their impact on the cultural landscape. In July 2012 the UK made the PEGI game ratings legally enforceable so that retailers that sell games to under aged children can be subject to prosecution (BBC News, 2012). Mediation is important for all technologies and across platforms when it comes to game play since it has been reported that 34% of 8-12 year olds and 47% of 10-12 year olds in the UK have a Facebook profile despite the minimum age being 13 (Ofcom, 2011). In terms of this book the gender divide in who is mediated and who does the mediating is interesting. Again these gender divides place females in a different position than males. Interestingly girls are mediated more than males which could be interpreted as gaming not viewed as suitable or as acceptable for girls as it is for

boys. Again reinforcing the view that computer games are a male pursuit and leisure activity not a female one. The research finding that mothers mediate more than fathers, especially when more mediation has been linked with a more negative attitude towards gaming, again suggesting gaming is a male domain. This finding can also be linked to game playing attitudes since less women play all game genres as will be discussed in chapter four, they therefore do not understand the benefits or at least the potential benefits of game play. More research is needed to

CONCLUSION

Games have become an important leisure activity for children and adults and they are becoming an increasingly important part of our culture as a whole. Emphasizes the importance of games in society today is a quote by game designer Jesse Schell who suggests computer games are a medium for everyday life; "beyond Facebook, beyond consoles and even computer screens games are becoming the medium for everyday life" (DICE Summit February, 2010). It is apparent from this introductory chapter that this is an important industry in the global media and entertainment industries. It is often noted that playing computer games can be a gateway to computing careers due to increasing confidence and skills in computing as well as developing an interest in computers due to familiarity (i.e. Cassell & Jenkins, 1998; Gorriz & Medina, 2000). Indeed computer games and gaming might be an initial introduction for children to digital technologies generally. In turn, developing their confidence and skills in their usage of technology; leading to an increased utilisation and interest in a career in computer science and information technology. It is important to remember the games industry is big business and constantly growing:

Key Facts About the Games Industry

- Gaming is a worldwide leisure activity but viewed mainly as a male leisure pursuit.
- Computer games industry has accelerated from small firms and individuals programming in their bedrooms to an industry dominated by multinational hardware producers.
- Worldwide, it's a $41.9 billion USD industry.
- There are reportedly 4 million active gamers in the Middle East, 10 million in Russia, 10 million in Vietnam, 10 million in Mexico, 13 million in Central and South America, 15 million in Australia, 17 million in South Korea, 100 million in Europe, 105 million in India, 183 million in America and a staggering 200 million in China.
- Collectively, the planet is spending more than 3 billion hours a week gaming.
- In 2012 72% of American households play computer games.
- In 2012 the average age of an American game player was 30 and 35 was the average age of a game buyer.
- In 2009, computer games outsold films sales.

- It has been suggested that 10% of games make 90% of the money.
- In 2008 across the globe the games industry revenue figures in billions US dollar were; USA 21.3, Canada 20, Europe 17.9, Korea 1.7, China 7.9, Japan 6.3, Latin America 1.0 and India 0.2.
- The UK industry supports an estimated 28,000 jobs, directly, and indirectly.
- The estimated turnover of the UK computer games industry in 2008 was £625 million, having a direct contribution to UK GDP (Gross Domestic Product) of approximately £400 million (Oxford Economics, 2008).
- In the UK in 2009 women represent just 4% of the computer games industries workforce.
- 2012 figures suggest women represent 47% of American gamers.
- Women represent 51% of Wii users and 53% of DS users.
- The casual game association in 2007 was worth $2.25 billion USD.
- Men makeup 48% of casual game players and women 52%.

It is evident that the games industry is big business and there is an increasing blurring between the virtual and real world. This blurring is discussed in chapter five where we will take into account computer games, identity in the virtual worlds. We must not ignore the cultural significance of computer games as well as how culture helps shape gendered gaming preferences. The identity of the gamer has changed in recent years and a more diverse audience is being attracted to games as a leisure activity. This attraction to games by more females and a more diverse demographic is in part due to the increase in family friendly games, pro social games and games that can be played via social networking sites such as Facebook and through more mobile platforms such as mobile phones.

More and more girls and women are playing games, it is important to look at the games industry and gaming culture in terms of the gender divide to understand how women fit in the industry as both producers and consumers.

We hope this chapter has given readers a good overview of the industry in terms of its economic, cultural and technical impact. In particular, the intention of this chapter was to provide an introduction to some of the gendered issues that are involved in computer games as well as highlight the inherent gender

Table 1. The computer games industry and its significance today: The key issues

Gender Differences and Reasons for the Gender Divide in Computer Games	Core Issues Involved	How May the Issue be Addressed
Economic issues	• Men spend more money on hardware and software for digital play than females. • The games industry also influences sales in other industries such a as increasing the demand for HDTV's. • Women are disadvantaged within professional gaming with a secondary status for female competitions and prize winnings.	• Equal status needs to be given to female professional gamers and gaming competitions. • Women play games and if this was more widely acknowledged then this would help reduce the male image of computer games.
Technological issues	• Game play has increased with the advancement of mobile phone technologies such as smart phones. This is particularly so for female game play. • Women working in the industry are disadvantaged because of the upgrade culture within the industry and the constant need to update skills due to maternity leave and childcare issues.	• This fast moving industry needs to take into account the skill needs of it employers. This is especially important in retaining a female workforce. • Female game workers should be encouraged to retain after maternity leave and given the support to update or regain their skills needed for their role.
Cultural issues	• Computer games are one of the most popular leisure activities for children and adults in Western and Asian societies • Some computer games are based on other forms of media, such as popular TV shows and books. This game design basis could potentially be beneficial to a female game consumer since a variety of games will be produced based on other popular media. • The computer games industry influences other media industries such as film and music.	• There needs to be a more diverse workforce to be a part of the making and meaning of today's cultural.
General issues	• Younger children and girls are more subjected to parental mediation of their game play than males and older children. • Parents who played games were more optimistic about the positive effects and less worried about the negative effects of computer games. • Fathers have been found to be more likely to play computer games with their children, than mothers. • Mothers are more likely to impose restrictive mediation on game playing, than fathers.	• If the image of computer games became more gender neutral, perhaps females would receive as equal parental mediation as their male counterparts. • Family friendly games are increasing the demographic diversity of gamers. • Parental attitude is important and can have a huge impact on a child's game playing. • More guidance is needed to enable parents to make informed choices regarding their children's game play.

divide which exists and persists throughout. Amongst other issues this chapter has considered family friendly games and issues around parental mediation. The next chapter will consider games for learning and how the gender divide is an issue when considering games in a learning context.

REFERENCES

Anderson, N., Lankshear, C., Timms, C., & Courtney, L. (2008). Because it's boring, irrelevant & I don't like computers: Why high school girls avoid professionally-oriented ICT subjects. *Computers & Education, 50*, 1304–1318. doi:10.1016/j.compedu.2006.12.003

Ashton, D. (2011). Upgrading the self: Technology & the self in the digital games perpetual innovation economy. *Convergence, 17*(3), 307–321.

Balance Blackboard Blog. (2008). *Wii fit advertising killing*. Retrieved from http://www.balanceboardblog.com/2008/04/analyst-wii-fit-advertising-killing.html

Bogg, J. (2007). Dr Jekyll & Ms Hide: Where are the women in science? & what would attract them from other sectors? *Nature, 447*.

Boyle, E., Connolly, T. M., & Hainey, T. (2011). *The role of psychology in understanding the impact of computer games*. Entertainment Computing. doi:10.1016/j.entcom.2010.12.002

Brightman, J. (2008, November 25). Guitar Hero, Rock Band players showing increased interest in real instruments. *Game Daily*. Retrieved from http://www.gamedaily.com/games/rock-b&-2/playstation-3/games-news/guitar-hero-rock-b&-players-showing-increased-interest-in-real-instruments/

Bryce, J., & Rutter, J. (2001) *In the game – In the flow: Presence in public computer gaming*. Paper presented at Computer Games & Digital Textualities. Copenhagen, Denmark. Retrieved from http://www.digiplay.org.uk

Bryce, J., & Rutter, J. (2003). The gendering of computer gaming: experience & space. In *Leisure cultures: Investigations in sport, media & technology* (pp. 3–22). Leisure Studies Association.

Burgess, M. C., Stermer, S. P., & Burgess, S. R. (2007). Sex, lies, & video games: The portrayal of male & female characters on video game covers. *Sex Roles, 57*, 419–433. doi:10.1007/s11199-007-9250-0

Burrill, D. A. (2008). *Die tryin': Videogames, masculinity, culture*. New York: Peter Lang Publishing Inc.

Carless, S. (2006). IGA's Townsend on BF2142 in-game ads. *Gamasutra*. Retrieved from http://www.gamasutra.com/php-bin/news_index.php?story=11300

Cassell, J., & Jenkins, H. (1998). *From Barbie to Mortal Kombat: Gender & computer games*. Cambridge, MA: MIT Press.

Consalvo, M. (2006). Console video games & global corporations: Creating a hybrid culture. *New Media & Society, 8*(1), 117–137. doi:10.1177/1461444806059921

Crawford, G. (2005). Digital gaming, sport & gender. *Leisure Studies, 24*(3), 259–270. doi:10.1080/0261436042000290317

Dawson, C. R., Cragg, A., Taylor, C., & Toombs, B. (2007). *Video games*. Retrieved from www.bbfc.co.uk/downloads/pub/Policy%20&%20Research/BBFC%20Video%20Games%20Report.pdf

DFC. (2004). *DFC intelligence releases new market forecasts for video game industry*. Retrieved from http://www.dfcint.com/news/prsep222004.html

Dovey, J., & Kennedy, H. W. (2006). *Game culture: Computer games as new media*. Berkshire, UK: Open University Press.

Durkin, K., & Barber, B. (2002). Not so doomed: Computer game play & positive adolescent development. *Applied Developmental Psychology, 23*, 272–392. doi:10.1016/S0193-3973(02)00124-7

Dyer-Whitheford, N., & Sharman, Z. (2005). The political economy of Canada's video & computer game industry. *Canadian Journal of Communication, 20*, 187–210.

ESA. (2001). *State of the industry report 2000-2001*. Entertainment Software Association. Retrieved from http://www.theesa.com/facts/econdata.asp

ESA. (2008). *Essential facts about the computer & videogame industry 2008: Sales, demographics & usage data*. Retrieved from http://www.thesa.com/facts/pdfs/ESA_EF_2008.pdf

ESA. (2010). *Sales, demographics & usage: Essential facts about the computer & video games industry*. Retrieved from http://www.theesa.com/facts/pdfs/ESA_Essential_Facts_2010.PDF

ESA. (2011a). *Essential facts about the computer & video game industry*. Retrieved from http://www.theesa.com/facts/pdfs/ESA_EF_About_Games_&_Violence.pdf

ESA. (2011b). *The evolution of mobile games*. Retrieved from http://www.theesa.com/gamesindailylife/mobile_games.pdf

ESA. (2011c). *Video games & the economy*. Retrieved from http://www.theesa.com/gamesindailylife/economy.pdf

ESA. (2011d). *Video game design influencing art*. Retrieved from http://www.theesa.com/gamedesigninfluencingart.pdf

ESA. (2012). *Essential facts about the computer & video game industry 2012 sales, demographic & usage data*. Entertainment Software Association.

Fron, J., Fullerton, T., Morie, J. F., & Pearce, C. (2007). *The hegemony of play*. Paper presented at the Situated Play. New York, NY.

Fullerton, T., Fron, J., Pearce, C., & Morie, J. (2008). Getting girls into the game: Towards a virtuous cycle. In *Beyond Barbie & Mortal Kombat: New perspectives on gender & gaming* (pp. 161–176). Cambridge, MA: The MIT Press.

Gansmo, H. J., Nordli, H., & Sorensen, K. H. (2003). The gender game: A study of Nigerian computer game designers. In *Strategies of inclusion: Gender & the information society: Experiences from private & voluntary sector initiatives* (pp. 139–159). Trondheim, Norway: NTNU.

Gaudioso, J. (2003). Magazine names top games suppliers. *Video Store Magazine, 25*(45), 10.

Gill, R. (2002). Cool, creative & egalitarian? Exploring gender in project-based new media work in Europe. *Information Communication and Society, 5*(1), 70–89. doi:10.1080/13691180110117668

Gorriz, C. M., & Medina, C. (2000). Engaging girls with computers through software games. *Communications of the ACM, 43*, 42–49. doi:10.1145/323830.323843

Green, L., Miles, I., & Rutter, J. (2007). *Hidden innovations in the creative sectors.* Manchester, UK: Manchester Institute for Innovation Research.

Haines, L. (2004). *Why are there so few women in games?* Retrieved from http://archives.igda.org/women/MTNW_Women-in-Games_Sep04.pdf

Harries, R., & Wilkinson, M. A. (2004). Situating gender: students' perceptions of information work. *Information Technology & People, 17*(1), 71–86. doi:10.1108/09593840410522189

Hartmann, T., & Klimmt, C. (2006). Gender & computer games: Exploring females' dislikes. *Journal of Computer-Mediated Communication, 11*, 910–931. doi:10.1111/j.1083-6101.2006.00301.x

Heeks, R. (2008). *Current analysis & future research agenda on 'gold framing'.* Retrieved from http://www.sed.manchester.ac.uk/idpm/research/publications/wp/di/di_wp32.htm: University of Manchester.

IBIS Word. (2008). Retrieved from http://www.ibisworld.com/pressrelease/pressrelease.aspx?prid=133

Jenkins, H. (2000, September). *Art form for the digital age.* Retrieved from http://www.geocities.com/lgartclass/h&outs/ArtfortheDigitalAge/ArtFormfortheDigitalAge.html

Jin, D. Y., & Chee, F. (2008). Age of new media empires: A critical interpretation of the Korean online game industry. *Games and Culture, 3*(1), 38–58. doi:10.1177/1555412007309528

Johns, J. (2006). Video games production networks: Value capture, power relations & embeddedness. *Journal of Economic Geography, 6*, 151–180. doi:10.1093/jeg/lbi001

Juul, J. (2010). *A casual revolution: Reinventing video games & their players.* London: MIT Press.

Kline, S., Dyer-Witheford, N., & de Peuter, G. (2003). *Digital play: The interaction of technology, culture & marketing*. Montreal, Canada: McGill-Queen's University Press.

Kotamraju, N. (2002). Keeping up: Web design skill & the reinvented worker. *Information Communication and Society, 5*(1), 1–26. doi:10.1080/13691180110117631

Krotoski, A. (2004). *Chicks & joysticks: An exploration of women & gaming. Entertainment & Leisure Software Publishers Association*. ELSPA.

Kutnet, L. A., Olson, C. K., Warner, D. E., & Hertozog, S. M. (2008). Parents' & sons' perspectives on video game play: A qualitative study. *Journal of Adolescent Research, 23*(1), 76–96. doi:10.1177/0743558407310721

Lee, Y.-H., & Lin, H. (2011). Gaming is my work: Identity work in Internet-hobbyist game workers. *Work, Employment and Society, 25*(3), 451–467. doi:10.1177/0950017011407975

Mai, P. (2010). *The highest & lowest grossing video game-based movies*. Retrieved from http://blogs.ocweekly.com/heardmentality/2010/07/hollywoods_lowest_grossing_vid.php

Matthews, M. (2009). *Exclusive: U.S. year-to-date console top 5s reveal 2009's victors so far*. Retrieved from www.gamasutra.com/phpbin/news_index.php?story=24481

Miller, L., Neathey, F., Pollard, E., & Hill, D. (2004). *Occupational segregation, gender gaps & skill gaps*. Equal Opportunities Commission.

Millwood Hargrave, A., & Livingstone, S. (2007). *Ofcom's submission to the Byron review*. Retrieved from http://stakeholders.ofcom.org.uk/binaries/research/telecoms-research/annex6.pdf

Newman, J. (2002). In search of the video gamplayer: The lives of Mario. *New Media & Society, 4*(3), 404–422.

News, B. B. C. (2012). *UK enforces Pegi video game ratings system*. Retrieved from http://www.bbc.co.uk/news/technology-19042908

Nikken, P., & Jansz, J. (2006). Parental mediation of children's videogame playing: A comparison of reports by parents & children. *Learning, Media and Technology, 31*(2), 181–202. doi:10.1080/17439880600756803

Nikken, P., & Jansz, J. (2007). Parents' interest in videogame ratings & content descriptors in relation to game mediation. *European Journal of Communication, 22*(3), 315–336. doi:10.1177/0267323107079684

Ofcom. (2008). *Annex 3 media literacy audit: Report on UK children by platform*. Retrieved from www.ofcom.org.uk/advice/media_literacy/medlitpub/medlitpubrss/ml_childrens08/cannex.pdf

Ofcom. (2011). *UK children's media literacy*. Retreived from http://stakeholders.ofcom.org.uk/binaries/research/media-literacy/medialit11/childrens.pdf

Orleans, M., & Laney, M. (2000). Children's computer use in the home. *Social Science Computer Review, 18*, 56–72. doi:10.1177/089443930001800104

Osting, W., Ijsselsteijn, W. A., & de Kort, Y. A. W. (2010). *Parental perceptions & mediation of children's digital, game play at home: A qualitative study.* Retrieved from http://www.carmster.com/families/workshop/uploads/Main/Oosting2.pdf

Oxford Economics. (2008). *The economic contribution of the UK games industry: Final report.* Retrieved from http://www.oef.com/FREE/PDFS/GAMESIMPACT.PDF

Reinecke, L. (2009). Games at work: The recreational use of computer games during work hours. *Cyberpsychology. Behavior & Social Networking, 12*(4), 461–465.

Shaw, A. (2009). Putting the gay in games: Cultural production & GLBT content in video games. *Games and Culture, 4*(3), 228–253. doi:10.1177/1555412009339729

Shaw, I. G. R., & Warf, B. (2009). Worlds of affect: Virtual geographies of video games. *Environment & Planning, 41*(6), 1332–1343. doi:10.1068/a41284

Shin, W., & Huh, J. (2011). Parental mediation of teenagers' video game playing: antecedents & consequences. *New Media & Society, 13*(6), 945–962. doi:10.1177/1461444810388025

Snider, M. (2009). *Video game sales hit record despite economic downturn.* Retrieved from http://www.gamesindustry.biz/content_page.php?aid=30008

Symonds, R. (2000). Why IT doesn't appeal to young women. In *Women, work & computerization: Charting a course to the future.* Vancouver, Canada: Kluwer Academic Publishers.

Taub, E. (2006). Nintendo at AAP event to count the grayer gamer. *New York Times.*

Taylor, T. L. (2008). Becoming a player: Networks, structures, & imagined futures. In *Beyond Barbie® & Mortal Kombat: New perspectives on gender & gaming.* Cambridge, MA: MIT Press.

Terlecki, M., Brown, J., Harner-Steeiw, L., Irvin-Hannum, J., Marchetto-Ryan, N., Ruhl, L., & Wiggins, J. (2011). Sex differences & similarities in video game experience, preferences, & self-efficacy: Implications for the gaming industry. *Current Psychology (New Brunswick, N.J.), 30*, 22–33. doi:10.1007/s12144-010-9095-5

Ulicsak, M., Wright, M., & Cranmer, S. (2009). *Gaming in families: A literature review.* Retrieved from http://www.archive.futurelab.org.uk/resources/...reviews/Gaming_Families.pdf

Valkenburg, P. M., Kremar, M., Peeters, A. L., & Marseille, N. M. (1999). Developing a scale to assess three styles of television mediation: Instructive mediation, restrictive mediation, & social co-viewing. *Journal of Broadcasting & Electronic Media, 43*(1), 523–553. doi:10.1080/08838159909364474

Van der Voort, T., Nikken, P., & van Lil, J. (1992). Determinants of parental guidance of children's television viewing: A Dutch replication study. *Journal of Broadcasting & Electronic Media, 36*(1), 52–66. doi:10.1080/08838159209364154

Vancouver Film School (VFS). (2009). *The game industry: Now & in the future*. Vancouver, Canada: Vancouver Film School.

Vancouver Film School (VFS). (2010). *The game industry now & in the future 2010: Industry facts, trends & outlook*. Vancouver, Canada: Vancouver Film School.

Vorderer, P. (2000). Interactive entertainment & beyond. In D. Zillamann, & P. Vorderer (Eds.), *Media entertainments*. Mahwah, NJ: Erlbaum.

KEY TERMS AND DEFINITIONS

Computer Games Industry: A term that refers to the industry and the people who work within that industry that is responsible for the development of the computer games themselves.

Culture: The ideas, customs, and social behaviour of a particular people or society.

Economic Impact: Financial impact of the product.

Gender Divide: A divide between the genders based on being either male or female.

Media Landscape: A term that refers to various communication media and how it is used.

Upgrade Culture: A term that refers to the situation within the technology industries that are forever changing and advancing technologies.

Chapter 3
Games and Society:
Can Games Make a Better World?

ABSTRACT

In this chapter, the authors consider how computer games can be beneficial for learning and education purposes. How computer games can start the learning progress, capture the imagination, enable creativity and storytelling, and provide an understanding of the power of computing is discussed. Also considered is how games might introduce girls (and boys) to a wide range of 21st century skills, which may lead to greater engagement in science, technology, and engineering subjects. However, due to the masculinity of computer games and the computer game culture more generally, the gender divide is a major disadvantage in the uptake of games for learning.

INTRODUCTION

Why might we want or need to consciously design and use computer and video games for learning? (Prensky, 2005, p97)

The chapters opening quote by Prensky poses an interesting question. This is an interesting question especially in terms of discussing the gender divide in computer games. As the

introductory chapter highlighted, computer games are increasingly invading all aspects of our lives and it seems will continue to do so. The increase in the development of games and virtual environments for fun, learning, health and litigation is rapidly increasing. The potential opportunity for women to enter the labour market as developers, or be retained should be grasped by the sector. Illustrating both the prominence of computer games,

DOI: 10.4018/978-1-4666-4534-9.ch003

especially for the younger generation that has grown up with computers and the gender divide is some recent study findings. A study investigating how students' use technology in an academic context found the majority of the 470 Australian 1st year students played games (77%), with 34% playing daily or weekly, and a significantly higher percentage of males played games compared to females (90% and 70% respectively) (Corrin, Lockyer, & Bennett, 2010). The study does however highlight that despite the gender differences, females do play computer games just maybe not to the intensity of both frequency and duration a males. Games are increasingly being used for educational purposes; especially stimulation games however there is a paucity of research on how these games are used for learning. Games are repetitive and interactive two elements that potentially make them influential (Anderson & Bushman, 2001). Games are also supposed to be fun which is important for engagement, motivation and immersion (Agarwal & Krarhanna, 2002).

In chapter one, a definition of computer games was provided. We now need to consider what makes a game a game. According to Reiber (1996) play usually has the following attribute; that it is voluntary, intrinsically motivating, involves some form of active engagement and has a make-believe quality. More recently McGonigal (2011) suggests that a game has four core elements; a goal, the rules, the feedback system, and voluntary participation. According to McGonigal everything else within a computer game is an effort to reinforce and enhance these four core elements. Therefore, competition and winning are not defining traits of games. Computer games in particular can enhance a number of emotional and psychological aspects including happiness, fear, power, and competition. Computer games also include a number of elements which make them appealing for the learning environment such as collaboration with other players, intrinsic motivation, interaction and engagement.

Games can aide learning because they are interactive, engaging, they can build in feedback and assessment and they promote 21st century skills. This chapter will discuss games and society, firstly a definition of what we mean by the term 'serious games' 'is needed.

... the label [serious games] refers to a broad swathe of video games produced, marketed, or used for purposes other than pure entertainment; these include, but are not limited to, educational computer games, edutainment and advertainment[...] and also health games and political games. [...] in theory, any video game can be perceived as a serious game depending on its actual use and the player's perception of the game experience. (Egenfeldt-Nielsen et al. 2008, p.205)

Serious Games are defined as digital games and equipment with an agenda of educational design and beyond entertainment. (Sorensen & Meyer, 2007, p.559)

[Serious games aim] to use new gaming technologies for educational or training purposes .it investigates the educational, therapeutic

and social impact of digital games built with or without learning outcomes in mind. (Felicia, 2009, p6)

The purpose of this chapter is to provide an overview of the literature on games and learning, taking into account the gendering of games and the impact this can have on learners. This chapter will consider both the benefits and drawbacks of using computer games for learning and education, and discuss technology use, learning styles and the net generation.

LEARNING, TECHNOLOGY AND THE NET GENERATION

The current generation of students has never experienced the world without information, and communication technology (ICT). They have grown up with computers, the Internet and computer games. The Net generation learn through interaction (Oblinger & Oblinger, 2005; Prensky, 2001; Tapscott, 1998). However, there is evidence to suggest it is not the instructional technique but how students perceive the technique, that encourages learning (Konings, et al, 2005). A definition of games for learning is provided by de Freitas (2006) "applications using the characteristics of video and computer games to create engaging and immersive learning experiences for delivering specified learning goals, outcomes and experiences" (p9). Technologies are playing an increasing role in higher education. Teaching and learning in higher education is said to be undergoing a transformation due to technologies of learning (Kellner, 2003). It has been suggested that there is a shift in students' aptitude and behaviour of students born in or after 1980 as a result of their level of exposure to technology over the course of their lives (Oblinger & Oblinger, 2005; Barnes et al, 2007). This shift has prompted the suggestion that teaching needs to adapt to the learning styles and needs of this generation as well as close the gap on the digital divide between students of the Net Generation (Tapscott, 1998) and their digital immigrant teachers (Prensky, 2001; Oblinger & Oblinger, 2005). Studies show that today's students learning preferences are strongly shaped by new media technologies such as computer games, virtual reality environments, the Internet and social networking tools. The technology acceptance model (TAM, Davis, 1989) identifies two user beliefs; perceived usefulness and perceived ease of use. The TAM suggests that when users are presented with a new technology, a number of factors influence their decision about how and when they will use it (Figure 1), notably:

- **Perceived Usefulness (PU):** This was defined by Davis as "the degree to which a person believes that using a particular system would enhance his or her job performance."
- **Perceived Ease-of-Use (PEOU):** Davis defined this as "the degree to which a person believes that using a particular system would be free from effort" (Davis, 1989).

With regard to computer games, experience with computer games will influence both

Figure 1. The Technology Acceptance Model as defined by Davis (1989)

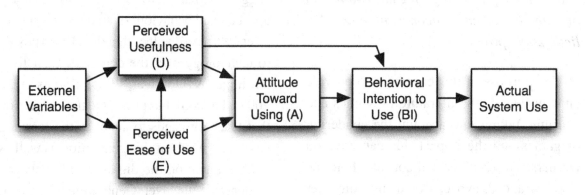

students' acceptance of working with games in the classroom and their learning processes. Indeed, game based learning is viewed as 'a new literacy' (Gee, 2003, 2005, 2007). However, Gee does not take into account this 'new literacy' that computer games offer in terms of a gendered digital divide.

In a recent English study, Hosein, Ramanau and Jones (2010) found generational differences in that younger students tend to use technology for social and leisure, whereas older students were more likely to use technology for study. The authors found that the frequency of using ICT was related to students' perception of competence. However, Hosein, Ramanau and Jones (2010) question whether "the frequent use of living technologies by Net Generation aged students' provide an advantage to them over the older students when it comes to using learning technologies at university?" (p405). Hosein, Ramanau and Jones (2010) concluded that students use learning technologies (slightly) more often than living technologies on an average day, regardless of age. They go on to suggest that technology needs to be seamlessly integrated and perhaps viewed by students as a hybrid of a

recreational and study tool to be used successfully as a learning technology. Interestingly, the study also found that older students were able to close the digital divide with the Net Generation students as younger students are not able to transfer their skills automatically to study and learning (Hosein, Ramanau, & Jones, 2010; Corrin, Lockyer, & Bennett, 2010; Kirkwood & Price, 2005).

GENDER DIFFERENCES IN TECHNOLOGY USE

As well as there being a difference between generations in terms of technology use, confidence and efficacy, there are also a number of differences in technology use and competence between students of the Net Generation. The most prominent digital divide is with regards to gender. Indeed the digital divide has been found to go beyond access and includes how women and men use, contribute to and are represented within technology (Van Dijk, 2005; Royal, 2010). For instance Royal (2010) analysed the content of a number of Websites targeted at a female demographic and found a gender digital divide consistent with the gender divide of women=private domain and men=public domain. A number of differences between the genders has been found in relation to access, usage and competence in regards to a number of technologies including computer games (e.g. Krotoski, 2004), Internet use (e.g. Kennedy, Wellman, & Clement, 2003), and general computer use (e.g. Michie & Nelson, 2006). In terms of looking at technology for educational and learning use, the Internet is of particular importance and a number of gendered differences have been found. For instance women have been found to use the Internet more for social reasons (Kennedy, Wellman, & Clement, 2003), have less Internet efficiency (Cheong, 2007) and less identification with the Internet (Joiner et al, 2007). Joiner et al (2005), found that male undergraduate students in England were more likely to have their own Web page and use the Internet more, particularly to use game Websites and downloaded material from the Internet, more than their female counterparts.

The Internet is becoming increasing used for educational purposes and can provide learners with distant, interactive, individualised and inquiry-based learning activities (e.g. Tsai, 2001; Chou & Tsai, 2002). Therefore, differences in Internet use, efficiency and attitudes towards the Internet are important issues of research. For instance, Eachus and Cassidy (2006) found self-efficacy influential for computer and Internet use among college students within the context of e-learning. According to Peng, Tsai, and Wu (2006) students with positive attitudes and high self-efficacy view the Internet as a functional tool. From

their research Peng, Tsai and Wu (2006) found males had a more positive attitude towards the Internet than females. Joiner et al (2007) found that students in the UK and Australian who were more anxious about using the Internet used it less.

According to Konijn and Nije Bijank (2009), games have the potential to support the development of adolescent identity construction. They suggest the appeal and impact of games are; wishful identification, immersion and presence, mastery and challenge and perceived realism. Suggesting adolescents can use role play to learn and develop. An underdeveloped area of research of the impact of games is the developmental process involved in the game play of adolescents and children at the developmental stages of their lives. One of the major drawbacks to using games for learning is the gendering of games. This gendering of computer games and technology generally perhaps comes to light more when discussing serious games. Girls do play games, yet as we have seen in chapter 2, girls and women often have different play styles and attitudes associated with games, including game preferences. Gender differences could be due to a number of interrelated factors. This includes the masculine image of games and technology, access to and the gendering of space and time limitations. In addition, the lack of female representation in computer games, especially in some game genres, the hyper-sexualised and eroticised representation of females within games and the gendering of leisure is important. Gendered socialisation in that computer games are for boys, and gender role expectations, all may lead to a lack of confidence and a general attitude that computer games and technology generally are for boys.

The number of female gamers is increasing but they still play fewer games and spend less time doing so than their male counterparts (Kafai et al., 2008). Although females are an increasing gamer population, there is still a gender divide in computer games; boys and men tend to play more games and dominate the gaming culture generally. This early and sustained exposure of boys with computer games potentially places them at an advantage in terms of computer competence and computer confidence in school and beyond. With the increased focus of serious games and games being brought into the classroom in recent years, it has been acknowledged that the computer disadvantage for girls will be intensified in the uptake of game-based learning in education (Goode et al, 2006; Klawe, 2005). Games used for learning could alienate inexperienced and female students and students of all genders not interested in playing computer games (Carr and Pelletier, 2008). Indeed, Jenson and de Castell (2011) suggest that it is important for serious game designers to better understand girls' perspectives on gaming and how to best engage and involve them in games for educational purposes and games generally. As we have previously acknowledged, boys tend to have more access to computers and game consoles and computers are viewed as a more masculine domain as highlighted throughout the literature and research reported in this book. So does this mean females are at a disadvantage in the learning environment when learning is

through computer games and other computer related methods? We must not be drawn into the duality of female non-players and male players as differences exist within as well as between genders. We are also aware of the 'essentialisation' of girls and boys, in that all same sex children and adults have the same likes and dislikes. Boyle and Connolly (2008) suggest that designers must consider gender differences in game styles when designing games for learning.

SERIOUS GAMES: GAMES FOR LEARNING

... the perception of the use of games in particular has presented a belief in the potential for widening participation to new learner groups who have previously been excluded due to language and writing difficulties. (de Freitas, 2006, p352).

Gaming can enable players to develop a number of general transferable skills including technological competencies, critical thinking skills, and team working skills. This brings into question the difference between informal and formal learning as skills may be being learnt which the game is not intending to teach According to Bennerstedt et al (2011) games foster transferrable skills beyond the game itself; skills which Bennerstedt et al argue can prepare children for life. Indeed Kambouri et al (2006) found games attract and improve the literacy's and ICT skills in young adults who play game's for leisure and who have not been able to learn in formal education. According to Whitton (2011), learner engagement is important for effective learning to occur. Whitton, from her study, found participants were not prepared to learn from a game purely because it was a game. The game needed to be an effective learning tool and this finding was irrelevant as to whether the participant played games from leisure. According to flow theory certain factors add to the enjoyment of an experience; these factors are:

1. A challenge that requires skill to achieve with an attainable goal and known rules.
2. Complete absorption in the activity.
3. Clear goals.
4. Immediate feedback.
5. Concentration on the task in hand.
6. A sense of control, lacking the sense of worry about losing control.
7. Loss of self-consciousness.
8. Transformation of time. (p598)

Whitton suggests a five-factor model of learning engagement (see Figure 2) and the greater the five-factors are present, the greater the engagement. The five factors are similar in level of importance:

- **Challenge:** Motivation to undertake the activity, clarity as to what is involved and a perception that the task is achievable.
- **Control:** Fairness of the activity, the level of choice over types of action available in the environment and the speed and transparency of feedback.
- **Immersion:** Extent to which the individual is absorbed in the activity.

Figure 2. Depiction of Whitton's five model factor of learning engagement

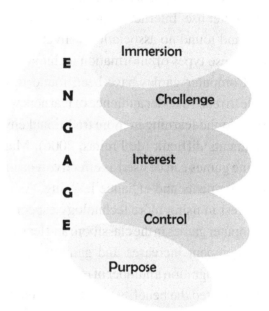

- **Interest:** Intrinsic interest of the individual in the activity or its subject matter.
- **Purpose**: Perceived value of the activity for learning, its benefit.

In the wider occupational context, games have uses for example in training for athletes and the US Army, with games are being developed to prepare police and fire fighters for terrorist attacks. IBM use games to teach business management and CISCO to teach networking concepts (see Kron et al, 2010). Games have been linked to improving skills useful to the performance of mathematics, engineering and science (Subrahmanyam, Smahel, & Greenfield, 2006). Interestingly in a recent study Jackson et al (2011) found more game playing in 12 year olds to be associated with greater creativity, regardless of gender or race. The authors also looked at creativity and computer use, Internet use and mobile phone use and found no association with creativity and these types of information technologies.

Computer games have been found to be able to reach a wider audience of learners who have found learning in more traditional environments difficult (de Freitas, 2006). Many argue games can be used as effective learning environments and enhance learning. As the interest in using more technology especially computer games in the classroom and learning environment increases and gains more and more recognition a number of researchers have investigated the benefits or potential benefits to this new learning approach. Games have been found to increase engagement (Prensky, 2001, 2006) retention (Grithiths, 2002), motivation (Yee, 2007) and collaboration (McGonigal, 2011) Computer games can enhance students experiences through active participation (Grimley et al, 2011), increase creative thinking (Eow et al, 2009), as well as provide powerful and meaningful contexts for learning (Shaffer, 2006). Through games players are no longer limited to, and restricted by the real world. This is especially important when considering role-playing games, which may enable players to understand a different perspective and view situations from another perspective.

Studies have started to look at how students feel about computer games in the classroom. Recently Grimley et al (2011) explored the student experience of learning with computer games. The study found many benefits of using games for learning compared to lectures in-

cluding, increased alertness, increased feeling of involvement and increased perception of challenge. The study also reports evidence of improved attainment concluding that "interactive approaches such as computer games, student learning experiences and attainment may be improved" (p 45). Interactivity in particular is an important element of computer games. Interactivity encourages the maintenance of players' attention which has ramifications for their enjoyment, immersion in the game and their ability to learn from the experience (Sellers, 2006) According to Lieberman (2006) interactive games provide the player feedback. Indeed it has been suggested that computer games make failure fun through the feedback given (McGonigal, 2011).

Motivation is an important factor in all learning (Wang & Liu, 2000). Learning should be integrated into the design of computer game not added in afterwards (Hoffman, 2009). According to Van Eck (2006) there are three ways to integrate games into learning; "have students build games from scratch; have educators and/or developers build educational games from scratch to teach students; and integrate commercial off-the-shelf (COTS) games into the classroom" (p57). A major way students have been found to learn through computer games is through designing the computer games themselves. Gamers develop game literacy through playing games, but they can also gain skills through the process of designing and developing games (Pelletier, 2008). For example Kovacevic et al (2012) wanted to see if designing rather than playing games increases learning and learning motivation and how. Results indicate that designing computer programs raises curiosity and a useful learning tool for students. Females often differ in their play styles. Indeed, Subrahanyam and Greenfield (2009) found that girls prefer nonaggressive, less fantasy based games as opposed to boys who prefer the contrast; aggressive and highly fantasy based games.

Whitlock, McLaughlin, and Allaire (2012) found computer games improve the attention and spatial orientation of older adults (aged 60-77). There is a growing interest in the use of computer games for training cognitive abilities. Games can be complex and use multiple cognitive abilities, can offer motivational rewards and played socially. Games have been shown to improve younger adults cognitive abilities in areas such as visual attention and mental rotation ability (i.e. Feng, Spence, & Pratt, 2007). Virtual worlds can help autistic children develop their social skills (Alcorn et al, (2011).

Physical therapy games improve gait and balance in people with Parkinson's disease (Dowling et al, 2011) and research suggests motivational games as well as regular physical therapy improve Parkinson's patients (Assad et al, 2011). Dance and exercise games are becoming increasingly popular with the motivational properties of these games potentially changing behaviour of young people to keep fit. Papastergiou (2009) found benefits of computer games including increasing physical fitness and motivation for physical exercise. Games also have the potential to increase player knowledge about health problems and illnesses, support patient rehabilitation, increase physical activity and support health promotion (Skiba, 2008).

COMPUTER GAMES IN THE CLINICAL EDUCATION ENVIRONMENT, GAME PLAY TO CHANGE HEALTH BEHAVIOUR, HEALTH PROMOTION AND ATTITUDES

As well as learning practical skills, gaming is potentially a good method for learning clinical decision making and patient interaction. Games are increasingly used in the clinical educational setting and recent research looking at the attitudes of games in nursing education (Lynch-Sauer et al, 2011) found gaming and new technologies was viewed positively. In particular, the study found that student nurses in the study were interested in using multiplayer online health care situations that would realistically replicate the experience of being a professional in practice. Boyle et al (2011b) used the Nintendo Wii to improve the surgical performance of medical students with no prior game experience. Boyle et al found games can provide cheap, convenient and effective attention to current training. Rosser et al (2007) found surgeons who played games for more than 3 hours a week made fewer errors, were faster and scored better on laparoscopic training courses than surgeons who never played. Interestingly Harper et al (2007) found game experience correlated inversely with ability to learn robotic suturing. Does this mean non-gamers will be at a disadvantage if games are incorporated in the classroom?

Kron et al (2010) investigated the attitudes of medical students' attitudes toward games and new media in medical education and found that the majority of medical students in the study were favourable of these technologies being incorporated into education and that education should make better use of such technologies. However, the Persky et al (2007) survey of attitudes towards games in education of pharmacy students in America and found students found games enjoyable but questioned how much they learned. Supplement to traditional methods but not a replacement. What students learn through games appears to be an important factor and important for validating the use of games in the classroom.

In terms of designing games and applications for health women are an untapped talent in terms of designers of apps for health and could contribute to making such apps female friendly. Many health care systems are now creating novel ways to incorporate Internet technologies into clinical practice. Many applications continue to be developed to assist in healthcare. Any software application that may be used on a mobile phone, is a mobile application. Development ranges from applications that provide health coaching to those that collect clinical health data, deliver health care information and provide real-time monitoring of patient data. Mobile technology is becoming ubiquitous to all socioeconomic groups. In healthcare, using technology as a tool is a useful adjunct to clinical therapy. For example, in the care of diabetes there are apps that run on mobile phones and online patient portals can provide patients with detailed information about their glucose levels. Downloading data from equipment onto their computers or mobiles, such as downloading the data from glucose meters, allows patients to organize data and distinguish patterns in their blood glucose levels. Skype can be used to conduct counselling sessions the integration of technology can present unique challenges such as patient ability to use the technology.

Mobile applications and text messaging aid in delivering the help, support and information that a specific patient requires. Support via technology can be linked to behaviour change and can be used in heath promotion by providing the patient with information, action plans for change and feedback on progress. Tailoring a treatment plan, then supporting it with text messages for support or reminders to check blood glucose, can supply the patient with ongoing 'real-time' support to assist in diabetes self-management. Patients could also choose to participate in online distance learning program, as opposed to attending diabetes information sessions. This provides the opportunity for diabetes education to be provided in a format that the patient wants. For example, written information provided on the Internet, allowing with a click for the information to be read aloud, translated into another language, read frequently asked questions, refer to other reliable resources and ask questions about their diabetes care. Technology facilitates this. Furthermore, quick response (QR) codes, expand the amount of information that a person can receive. The patient can scan the QR code embedded into a leaflet or on a poster, with their phone camera and be taken to a Website or link with more information. Research has demonstrated promising results in the use of technology to assist in patient care. For example, Harris (2011), found that using Skype, to communicate via Webcam with adolescents with diabetes, to supplement clinic visits improved their diabetes self-management. The Apple iTunes store has numerous applications or 'apps' available, such as Lose It! or the Atkins Carb Counter, which log caloric intake and physical activity, to help individuals monitor their diet and exercise. However, who has access to such apps and the digital divide generally is an issue. Examples of research in the area include (for more examples, see http://www. projecthealthdesign.org/projects):

- A computer-based personal health application for diabetes self-management that provides customized recommendations.
- Serendipity apps encourage individuals to overcome fear of uncertainty, useful with anxious patients. Apps like Getlostbot, encourages users to break old routines and try different routes and places. The app silently monitors where individuals go and when it notes a predictable routine, Getlostbot sends directions to somewhere different, in the location i.e. a new café not visited before.
- A chronic disease medication management system that uses a cellphone application for people with diabetes to record their blood glucose levels, blood pressure, diet and exercise, and quickly upload these readings, via a cellphone to their health care provider.
- A mobile app for youths with obesity and depression. The app tracks food, exercise, mood and socializing. It will analyse then communicate with a

health coach, in real-time, then share summary reports with their physicians and nurses.

Technology providing computer- or mobile phone based support, such as blood sugar reading or education may be helpful. Tapping into the psychosocial aspects of why a patient should change their behaviour are important. Development of applications for health, may assist in improving adherence to change, such as in diet, medication, exercise or blood glucose testing. However, for any behaviour to change, the patient must still be motivated and willing to change behaviour.

Games are also being designed to look at how humans communicate, for example the Embodied Communication Game (ECG; Scott-Phillips et al., 2009). In the game two players interact with one another, only via a pair a networked computers. A key feature of the ECG is that participants have to find a way to indicate that some of their actions are communicative, whilst others are not. The Embodied Communication Game (ECG) is an interactive, two-player game in which the participants collaborate to score as many points as possible. Each player controls a stick person, who moves around his or her own four-quadrant box. The box is coloured red, blue, green or yellow, at random. To score points players must use certain movements, or combinations of movements, to refer to their intended destination. The instructions state that participants should attempt to 'coordinate' their behaviour with the other player. The challenge is to make it apparent to one's partner, which movements are communication and which are simply used to travel around the box. In this way communication systems develop. This type of research demonstrates the ways novel communication systems emerge and develop in pairs or groups of interacting individuals (Scott-Phillips et al., 2009).

Tapping into virtual reality games, computer-generated exhibits (CGE) are newly emerging in the courtroom. This may be seen as a progression of technology into the courtroom and legal representatives now have access to increasingly realistic animations and virtual-reality (VR) techniques (Schofield & Mason, 2010). CGEs may be beneficial in contributing to the understanding of events in a trial. However, there is substantial variability on the acceptance of CGEs in the courtroom and few formal guidelines as to the content and style the exhibits should adhere. For example, the US National Transportation Safety Board created a 45 minute animated sequence of events of a plane crash, using data from the flight recorder and the audio of conversations between the pilots and air traffic control. The prosecutors were able to show in 'real-time' how the aircraft was involved in a severe weather pattern. Pilot error was determined as the key contributing factor to the crash. Additional training and aircraft warning systems were introduced following the findings.

DRAWBACKS TO GAMES FOR LEARNING AND THE GENDERING OF COMPUTER GAMES

As we have highlighted there have been a number of criticisms of computer games

generally which obviously become even more important issues when considering games for learning. Provenzo (1991) suggests that there are four concerns about games for learning;

- Can lead to violent aggressive behaviour.
- Employ destructive gender stereotyping.
- Promote unhealthy attitudes.
- Stifle creative play.

However, games have developed in recent years and as we have seen there are a number of benefits that have been put forward that games can bring to the learner experience. However, despite the numerous potential benefits there are a number of criticisms for using games in the classroom. For instance a lack of resources, a lack of interest from teachers, they may be difficult to learn especially by non-gamers and there is an issue of ensuring alignment between the game and learning outcomes. One major influential factor is teachers' personal interest in using games as using games in the classroom requires a change in the attitude towards games and investment in game development relevant to the curriculum. Koh et al (2012) investigated teacher perceptions of using games in Singapore schools and found that the majority of the 479 teachers in the study had a positive attitude and felt that games can lead to better learning outcomes for students in terms of cognition, motor skills and affective learning. Barriers included; time, lack of resources, high costs, the relevance of games, parents attitude and lack of school support. It is not just teachers, but parents who are influential. In a recent study investigating parents' attitudes of the use of computer games in the classroom

Bourgonjon et al (2011) found that parents are influenced by the media's negative portrayal of games in games used for learning tools. Parents could benefit from more information on the benefits of game related learning. In an earlier study Bourgonjon et al (2010) looked into students attitudes of using games for learning. The study found that student experience with playing games had a direct impact on students' preference for games, ease of use, learning opportunities and usefulness. The study found that students who are more immersed in video game technology do prefer a different kind of education, suggesting that this method of learning is more suitable to some students and perhaps a disadvantage to many students. For instance, Bonanno and Kommers's (2005) study found, many students, a significant proportion of which were female, do not have much experience with game technology. Students are not a homogeneous group of gamers, as the research on differences in technology use suggests, educators should not presume all students have the same interests and level ability in technology use especially computer games.

Aside from the differences within students' abilities and attitudes, and teachers' abilities, willingness and attitude towards computer games for learning there is the difficulty in finding the balance between entertainment and educational value in computer games (Moreno-Ger, Burgos & Martinez-Ortiz, 2008). Research on games or learning is still relatively new and much more research is needed to evaluate the effects of computer game based learning and consider if different types of game based learning and different learning and engagement. A major challenge for game designers is to be able to create games that are appealing and accessible to all, making games appeal to educators and providing educators with the knowledge that students have equal access to learning through game play. Women are an under used employment resource and an underdeveloped gamer market. In 2004, 27.2% of all active gamers in the UK were women with an average age of 30-35 years playing on average 7.2 hours per week (Krotoski, 2004). Game design teams that have more women in key design and production roles have produced products women enjoy. For example, Maxis, makers of The Sims, the game is estimated to have approximately 50% female players, has a workforce of 50% female designers and 40% female producers. The Sims development team has more women than average than other team at Electronic Arts (Fullerton, Fron, Pearce, & Morie, 2007). Recruiting and retaining women game designers will contribute to the development of rich and varied serious games.

CONCLUSION

Games start the learning progress, capturing the imagination, enabling creativity, storytelling and providing an understanding of the power of computing. Introducing girls (and boys) to a wide range of 21st century skills, may lead to greater engagement in science, technology and engineering subjects. Perhaps this will lead to them choosing a related career. More work is required to understand the benefits of learning through making games. It may be the case that there are no gender differences in game play, merely that boys play more games. For example, Durkin and Barber (2002) found a number of benefits, with no negative outcomes in playing computer games in adolescence, leading the authors to conclude that computer games can be a positive feature of a healthy adolescence. Positive outcomes included, family closeness activity involvement, positive school engagement, good mental health, self-concept, and friendship networks. In the United States, the Federation of American Scientists (2006) issued a white paper calling for more research into the use of games for science, technology, engineering and mathematics (STEM) related learning. Hayes (2011) and others, in relation to how to engage girls in IT-related learning, using games such as The Sims computer game and the virtual world of Teen Second Life, suggests games can enhance computational understanding and skills (Gee & Hayes, 2009). Games can develop skills, for example learning 'cheating' enables an understanding of programming language and coding. User-centred design and sociotechnical analysis, can enable players to see how technology is embedded in social systems and critically analyse the design of technological artefacts' (Mumford, 1987, see Hayes).

Many health care systems are now creating novel ways to incorporate Internet technologies into clinical practice. Many applications continue to be developed to assist in healthcare. Mobile applications and text messaging aid in delivering the help, support and information that a specific patient requires. Support via technology can be linked to behaviour change and can be used in heath promotion by providing the patient with information, action plans for change and feedback on progress. Research has demonstrated promising results in the use of technology to assist in patient care. Development of applications for health, may assist in improving adherence to change, such as in diet, medication, exercise or blood glucose testing. However, for any behaviour to change, the patient must still be motivated and willing to change behaviour. There are a number of benefits that games can bring to the learner experience and equally a number of criticisms, which are particularly important when considering games for learning. However, we must remember, learning through games is dependent on the game itself in conjunction with the social interactions that take place around the game. Girls tend to play a narrower range of game genres than boys and a number of game design software has been designed to appeal to girls (i.e. Storytelling Alice and Rapunzel). Research has looked specifically at designing games as a primary source of learning for girls (Kelleher, 2008; Denner et al, 2009). Serious games can be fun, as well as being educational, engaging, impactful, meaningful and purposeful. Serious games can still potentially fulfil entertainment desires. Becoming increasingly viable platforms for learning, skill development and behaviour change. Students today are comfortable with technology and may welcome the possibility of using interactive media in an educational setting. We want to highlight gender bias in that, most game genres are considered masculine, this may limit attraction to and retention of female students. In terms of designing games and applications for health, women are an untapped talent in terms of designers of apps for health and could contribute to making such apps female friendly. Women are an under used employment resource and an underdeveloped gamer market. Recruiting and retaining women game designers will contribute to the development of rich and varied serious games. Overcoming gender bias will benefit women, computer games development, the games industry and society.

Table1. Gender and serious games: The key issues

Gender Differences and Reasons for the Gender Divide in Computer Games	Core Issues Involved	How May the Issue be Addressed
Technology use	• The digital divide has been found to go beyond access and includes how women and men use, contribute to and are represented within technology. • The Internet is becoming increasing used for educational purposes and can provide learners with distant, interactive, individualised and inquiry-based learning activities Women have been found to use the Internet more for social reasons, have less Internet efficiency and less identification with the Internet than men. • Male undergraduate students in England have been found to be more likely to have their own Web page, use the Internet more, particularly to use game Websites and downloaded material from the Internet more than their female counterparts. • Males have a more positive attitude towards the Internet than females.	• There is a need to reduce the gender digital divide through education initiatives that focus on getting girls to the same confidence level with ICT as boys. • Research suggests girls only initiatives help improve girls' interest in, and usage of technologies such as computer games. • Initiatives need to be more widely available and include a number of digital technologies used in everyday lives in order to help reduce this gap. • Girls/women should be equally encouraged to engage with technology.
Games and gender	• Girls do play games, but females have different play styles and attitudes associated with games, including game preferences. • Gender differences could be due to a number of interrelated factors, including the masculine image of games and technology, access to and the gendering of space and time limitations. • Gendered socialisation in that computer games are for boys, influenced by the lack of female representation in computer games, especially in some game genres, the hyper sexualised and eroticised representation of females within games and the gendering of leisure. • Gender role expectations can lead to a lack of confidence. • Although females play games they play fewer games and spend less time doing so than males.	• The gendering of computer games and technology is highlighted, when discussing serious games. • Using games in the classroom may reduce the gendered digital divide. • In order for the gendered divide to close, those who use, and advocate the use of computer games in the learning environment must be aware of gendered issues, associated with computer games and other forms of technology.
Games and learning	• Games can aide learning because they are interactive, engaging, they can build in feedback and assessment and they promote 21st century skills. • Early and sustained exposure of boys with computer games potentially places them at an advantage in terms of computer competence and computer confidence in school and beyond. • The computer disadvantage for girls could be intensified in the uptake of game-based learning in education. • Games used for learning could potentially alienate inexperienced students and students of all genders not interested in playing computer games.	• Emphasise that games provide players the opportunity to use role play to learn and develop. • Computer games for learning, should focus on any students unfamiliar with game technologies. • Be aware that some students may be less confident in playing computer games. • Extra support provided to students as necessary. • Ensure no student is disadvantaged, through using technology in learning.

REFERENCES

Agarwal, R., & Krarhanna, E. (2002). Time flies when you are having fun: cognitive absorption & beliefs about information technology usage. *Management Information Systems Quarterly*, *24*(4), 665–694. doi:10.2307/3250951

Assad, O., Hermann, R., Lilla, D., Mellies, B., Meyer, R., & Shevach, L. et al. (2011). Motion-based games for Parkinson's disease patients. *Lecture Notes in Computer Science*, *6972*, 47–58. doi:10.1007/978-3-642-24500-8_6

Bennerstedt, U., Ivarsson, J., & Linderoth, J. (2011). *How gamers manage aggression: Situating skills in collaborative computer games*. Computer-Supported Collaborative Learning. doi:10.1007/s11412-011-9136-6

Bonanno, P., & Kommers, P. A. M. (2008). Exploring the influence of gender & gaming competence on attitudes towards using instructional games. *British Journal of Educational Technology*, *39*(1), 97–109.

Bourgonjon, J., Valcke, M., Soetaert, R., de Wever, B., & Schellens, T. (2011). Parental acceptance of digital game-based learning. *Computers & Education*, *57*, 1434–1444. doi:10.1016/j.compedu.2010.12.012

Bourgonjon, J., Valcke, M., Soetaert, R., & Schellens, T. (2010). Students' perceptions about the use of video games in the classroom. *Computers & Education*, *54*, 1145–1156. doi:10.1016/j.compedu.2009.10.022

Boyle, E., Connolly, T. M., & Hainey, T. (2011a). *The role of psychology in understanding the impact of computer games*. Entertainment Computing. doi:10.1016/j.entcom.2010.12.002

Boyle, E., Kennedy, A.-M., Traynor, O., & Hill, A. D. K. (2011b). Training surgical skills using nonsurgical tasks- can Nintendo Wii improve surgical performance? *Journal of Surgical Education*. doi:10.1016/j.jsurg.2010.11.005 PMID:21338974

Carr, D., & Pelletier, C. (2008). Games, gender & representation. In E. R. Ferdig (Ed.), *Handbook for research on effective electronic gaming in education* (Vol. 2, pp. 911–921). Hershey, PA: IGI Global. doi:10.4018/978-1-59904-808-6.ch052

Cheong, P. H. (2007). Gender & perceived Internet efficacy: Examining secondary digital divide issues in Singapore. *Women's. Studies in Communications*, *30*(2), 205–228.

Chou, C., & Tsai, C.-C. (2002). Developing web-based curricula: Issues & challenges. *Journal of Curriculum Studies*, *34*, 623–636. doi:10.1080/00220270210141909

Corrin, L., Lockyer, L., & Bennett, S. (2010). Technological diversity: an investigation of students' technology use in everyday life & academic study. *Learning, Media and Technology*, *35*(4), 387–401. doi:10.1080/17439884.2010.531024

Davis, F. D. (1989). Perceived usefulness, perceived ease of use, & user acceptance of information technology. *Management Information Systems Quarterly, 13*(3), 319–340. doi:10.2307/249008

de Freitas, S. I. (2006). Using games & simulations for supporting learning. *Learning, Media and Technology, 31*(4), 343–358. doi:10.1080/17439880601021967

Denner, J., Bean, S., & Martinez, J. (2009). Girl game company: Engaging Latina girls in information technology. *Afterschool Matters, 8*, 26–35.

Dowley, G. (2011). *Computer games help people with Parkinson's disease, pilot study shows.* Retrieved from http://www.sciencedaily.com/releases/2011/10/111019180024.htm

Durkin, K., & Barber, B. (2002). Not so doomed: Computer game play & positive adolescent development. *Applied Developmental Psychology, 23*, 373–392. doi:10.1016/S0193-3973(02)00124-7

Eachus, P., & Cassidy, S. (2006). Development of the web users self-efficacy scale (WUSE). *Journal of Issues in Informing Science & Information Technology, 3*, 199–211.

Egenfeldt-Nielsen, S., Smith, J. H., & Tosca, S. P. (2008). *Understanding video games: The essential introduction.* London: Routledge.

Eow, Y. L., Ali, W. Z. B., Mahmud, R. B., & Baki, R. (2009). Form one student's engagement with computer games & its effect on their academic achievement in a Malaysian secondary school. *Computers & Education, 53*(4), 1082–1091. doi:10.1016/j.compedu.2009.05.013

Federation of American Scientists. (2006). *Harnessing the power of video games for learning.* Retrieved from http://www.fas.org/gamesummit/Resources/Summit%20on%20Educational%20Games.pdf

Felicia, P. (2009). *Digital games in schools: A handbook for teachers.* Retrieved from http://games.eun.org/upload/GIS_HANDBOOK_EN.PDF

Feng, J., Spence, I., & Pratt, J. (2007). Playing an action video game reduces gender differences in spatial cognition. *Psychological Science, 18*(10), 850–855. doi:10.1111/j.1467-9280.2007.01990.x PMID:17894600

Fullerton, T., Fron, J., Pearce, C., & Morie, J. (2007). Getting girls into the games: Towards a 'virtous cycle. In *Beyond Barbie & Mortal Kombat: New perspectives on gender & computer games.* Cambridge, MA: MIT.

Gee, J. P. (2003). *What video games have to teach us about learning & literacy.* New York: Palgrave Macmillan. doi:10.1145/950566.950595

Gee, J. P. (2005). Learning by design: Good video games as learning machines. *E-Learning & Digital Media*, 2(1), 5–16. doi:10.2304/elea.2005.2.1.5

Gee, J. P. (2007). *Good video games + good learning: Collected essays on video games, learning, & literacy*. New York: Peter Lang.

Gee, J. P., & Hayes, E. (2009). No quitting without saving after bad events: Gaming paradigms & learning in the Sims. *International Journal of Learning and Media*, 1(3), 1–17. doi:10.1162/ijlm_a_00024

Goode, J., Estrella, R., & Margolis, J. (2006). Lost in translation: Gender & high school computer science. In J. M. Cohoon, & W. Aspray (Eds.), *Women in IT: Reasons on the underrepresentation* (pp. 89–114). Cambridge, MA: The MIT Press. doi:10.7551/mitpress/9780262033459.003.0003

Griffiths, M. (2002). The educational benefits of video games. *Education for Health*, 20(3), 47–51.

Grimley, M., Green, R., Nilsen, T., Thompson, D., & Tomes, R. (2011). Using computer games for instruction: The student experience. *Active Learning in Higher Education*, 12(1), 45–56. doi:10.1177/1469787410387733

Harper, E. P., Baldwin, R. G., Gansneder, B. G., & Chronister, J. L. (2001). Full-time women faculty off the tenure track: Profile & practice. *Review of Higher Education*, 24, 237–257. doi:10.1353/rhe.2001.0003

Hayes, E. (2011). The Sims as a catalyst for girls' IT learning. *International Journal of Gender. Science & Technology*, 3(1), 121–147.

Hoffmann, L. (2009). Learning through games. *Communications of the ACM*, 52, 21–22. doi:10.1145/1536616.1536624

Hosein, A., Ramanau, R., & Jones, C. (2010). Learning & living technologies: A longitudinal study of first-year students' frequency & competence in the use of ICT. *Learning, Media and Technology*, 35(4), 403–418. doi:10.1080/17439884.2010.529913

Jackson, L. A., Witt, E. A., Games, A. I., Fitzgerald, H. E., von Eye, A., & Zhao, Y. (2011). Information technology use & creativity: Findings from the children & technology project. *Computers in Human Behavior*. doi:doi:10.1016/j.chb.2011.10.006

Jenson, J., & deCastell, S. (2011). Girls@ play. *Feminist Media Studies*. doi:10.1080/14680777.2010.521625

Joiner, R., Brosnan, M., Duffield, J., Gavin, J., & Maras, P. (2007). The relationship between internet identification, internet anxiety & Internet use. *Computers in Human Behavior*, 23, 1408–1420. doi:10.1016/j.chb.2005.03.002

Joiner, R., Gavin, J., Duffield, J., Brosnan, M., Crook, C., & Durndell, A. et al. (2005). Gender, internet identification & internet anxiety: Correlates of internet use. *Cyberpsychology & Behavior*, 8(4), 371–378. doi:10.1089/cpb.2005.8.371 PMID:16092894

Kafai, Y. B. (2009). Serious games for girls? Considering gender in learning with digital games. In U. Ritterfield, M. Cody, & P. Vorderer (Eds.), *Serious games mechanisms & effects* (pp. 221–235). London: Routledge.

Kambouri, M., Thomas, S., & Mellar, H. (2006). Playing the literacy game: A case study in adult education. *Learning, Media and Technology*, *31*(4), 395–410. doi:10.1080/17439880601022015

Kelleher, C. (2008). Using storytelling to introduce girls to computer programming. In *Beyond Barbie & Mortal Kombat: New perspectives in gender, games & computing*. Boston: MIT Press.

Kellner, D. (2003). *Technological transformation, multiple literacies, & the re-visioning of education*. Retrieved from http://www.gseis.ucla.edu/faculty/kellner/essays.html

Kennedy, T., Wellman, B., & Clement, K. (2003). Gendering the digital divide. *IT & Society*, *1*(5), 72–96.

Kirkwood, A., & Price, L. (2005). Learners & learning in the twenty-first century: What do we know about students' attitudes towards & experiences of information & communication technologies that will help us design courses? *Studies in Higher Education*, *30*(3), 257–274. doi:10.1080/03075070500095689

Kirkwood, A., & Price, L. (2005). Learners & learning in the 21st century: What do we know about students' attitudes & experiences of ICT that will help us design courses? *Studies in Higher Education*, *30*(3), 257–274. doi:10.1080/03075070500095689

Klawe, M. M. (2005). *Increasing the number of women majoring in CS: What works?* Paper presented at ACM SIGCSE 2005 Symposium. St. Louis, MO. Retrieved from www.princeton.edu/seasWeb/dean/Klawe/SIGCSE 2005.pdf

Koh, E., Kin, Y. G., Wadhwa, B., & Lim, J. (2012). Teacher perceptions of games in Singapore schools. *Simulation & Gaming*, *43*(1), 51–66. doi:10.1177/1046878111401839

Konijn, E. A., & Nije Bijvank, M. (2009). Doors to another me: Identity construction through digital game play. In U. Ritterfield, M. Cody, & P. Vorderer (Eds.), *Serious games mechanisms & effects* (pp. 167–179). London: Routledge.

Konings, K. D., Br-Gruwel, S., & van Merrienboer, J. J. G. (2005). Towards more powerful learning environments through combining the perspectives of designers, teachers, & students. *The British Journal of Educational Psychology*, *75*(4), 645–660. doi:10.1348/000709905X43616 PMID:16318683

Kovacevic, I., Minovic, M., de Pablos, P. O., & Starcevic, D. (2012). Motivational aspects of different learning contexts: my mom won't let me play this game..... *Computers in Human Behavior*. doi:doi:10.1016/j.chb.2012.01.023 PMID:22393270

Kron, F. W., Gjerde, G.L., & Sen, A., & Fetters. (2010). Medical students attitudes toward video games & related new media technologies in medical education. *BMC Medical Education*, *10*(50), 1–11. PMID:20074350

Krotoski, A. (2004). *Chicks & joysticks: An exploration of women & gaming. Entertainment & Leisure Software Publishers Association.* ELSPA.

Lieberman, D. (2006). What can we learn from playing interactive games? In P. Vorderer, & J. Bryant (Eds.), *Playing video games: Motives, responses, & consequences* (pp. 379–397). Mahwah, NJ: Elbaum.

Lynch-Sauer, J., VenBosch, T.M., Kron, F., Livingston Gjerde, G., Arato, N., Sen, A., & Fetters, M.D. (2011). Nursing students' attitudes toward video games & related new media technologies. *The Journal of Nursing Education, 50*, 1–11. doi:10.3928/01484834-20110531-04 PMID:21627050

McGonigal, J. (2011). *Reality is broken: Why games make us better & how they can change the world.* New York: Penguin Press.

Michie, S., & Nelson, D. L. (2006). Barriers women face in information technology careers: Self-efficacy, passion & gender biases. *Women in Management Review, 21*(1), 10–27. doi:10.1108/09649420610643385

Moreno-Ger, P., Burgos, D., & Martines-Ortiz, I. (2008). Educational game design for online education. *Computers in Human Behavior, 24*, 2530–2540. doi:10.1016/j.chb.2008.03.012

Oblinger, D., & Oblinger, J. (2005). Is it age or IT: First steps toward understanding the net generation. In *Educating the net generation.* Boulder, CO: EDUCAUSE.

Papastergiou, M. (2009). Exploring the potential of computer & video games for health & physical education: A literature review. *Computers & Education, 53*, 603–622. doi:10.1016/j.compedu.2009.04.001

Pelletier, C. (2008). Gaming in context: how young people construct their gendered identities in playing & making games. In *Beyond Barbie & Mortal Kombat: New perspectives on gender & gaming* (pp. 145–160). Cambridge, MA: The MIT Press.

Peng, H., Tsai, C.-C., & Wu, Y.-T. (2006). University students' self-efficacy & their attitudes toward the Internet: The role of students' perceptions of Internet. *Educational Studies, 32*(1), 73–86. doi:10.1080/03055690500416025

Persky, A. M., Stegall-Zanation, J., & Dupuis, R. E. (2007). Students perceptions of the incorporation of games into classroom instruction for basic & clinical pharmacokinetics. *American Journal of Pharmaceutical Education, 71*(2), 1–9. doi:10.5688/aj710221 PMID:17429501

Prensky, M. (2001). Digital natives, digital immigrants. *Horizon, 9*(5), 1–6. doi:10.1108/10748120110424816

Prensky, M. (2005). Computer games & learning: Digital game-based learning. In J. Raessens, & J. Goldstein (Eds.), *Handbook of computer games studies.* Cambridge, MA: The MIT Press.

Prensky, M. (2006). *Don't bother me, Mom, I'm learning! How computer & video games are preparing your kids for 21st century success & how you can help*. St. Paul, MN: Paragon House.

Provenzo, E. F. (1991). *Video kids: Making sense of Nintendo*. Cambridge, MA: Harvard University Press.

Reiber, L. (1996). Seriously considering play: Designing interactive learning environments based on the blending of microworlds, simulations, & games. *Educational Technology Research and Development*, *44*, 43–58. doi:10.1007/BF02300540

Rosser, J., Lynch, P., Cuddihy, L., Gentile, D., Klonsky, J., & Merrell, R. (2007). The impact of video games on training surgeons in the 21st century. *Archives of Surgery*, *142*, 181–186. doi:10.1001/archsurg.142.2.181 PMID:17309970

Royal, C. (200). *Gendered spaces & digital discourse: Framing women's relationship with the internet*. VDM Publishing.

Sellers, M. (2006). Designing the experience of interactive play. In P. Vorderer, & J. Bryant (Eds.), *Playing video games: Motives, responses, & consequences* (pp. 379–397). Mahwah, NJ: Elbaum.

Shaffer, D. W. (2006). Epistemic frames for epistemic games. *Computers & Education*, *46*(3), 223–234. doi:10.1016/j.compedu.2005.11.003

Sherry, J. L., Lucas, K., Greenberg, B. S., & Lachlan, K. (2004). *Video game uses & gratifications as predictors of use & game preference*. Retrieved from http://icagames.comm.msu.edu/vgu%26g.pdf

Skiba, D. J. (2008). Games for health. *Nursing Education Perspectives*, *29*(4), 230–232. PMID:18770953

Sorensen, B. H., & Meyer, B. (2007). Serious games in language learning & teaching-a theoretical perspective. In *Proceedings of the 2007 Digital Games Research Association Conference* (pp. 559-560). GRAC.

Struyven, K., Dochy, F., Gielen, S., & Janssens, S. (2008). Students' experiences with contrasting learning environments: The added value of students' perceptions. *Learning Environments Research*, *11*, 83–109. doi:10.1007/s10984-008-9041-8

Subrahmanyam, K., & Greenfield, P. (2009). Designing serious games for children & adolescents: What developmental psychology can teach us. In U. Ritterfield, M. Cody, & P. Vorderer (Eds.), *Serious games mechanisms & effects* (pp. 167–179). London: Routledge.

Subrahmanyam, K., Smahel, D., & Greenfield, P. M. (2006). Connecting developmental processes to the Internet: Identity presentation & sexual exploration in online teen chatrooms. *Developmental Psychology*, *42*, 1–12. doi:10.1037/0012-1649.42.3.395 PMID:16420114

Tapscott, D. (1998). *Growing up digital: The rise of the net generation*. New York: McGraw-Hill.

Tsai, C.-C. (2001). The interpretation construction design model for teaching science & its applications to Internet-based instruction in Taiwan. *International Journal of Educational Development*, *21*, 401–415. doi:10.1016/S0738-0593(00)00038-9

Van Dijk, J. G. M. (2005). *The deepening divide: Inequality in the information society*. Thousand Oaks, CA: Sage Publications.

Van Eck, R. (2006). Digital game-based learning: It's not just the digital natives who are restless. *EDUCAUSE Review*, *41*(2), 55–63.

Wang, Z., & Liu, P. (2000). The influence of motivational factors, learning strategy, & the level of intelligence on the academic achievement of students. *Chinese Journal of Psychology*, *32*, 65–69.

Weaver, A. J., & Lewis, N. (2012). Mirrored morality: an exploration of moral choice in video games. *Cyberpsychology, Behavior, &. Social Networking*, *15*(11), 1–5.

Whitlock, L. A., Collins McLaughlin, A., & Allaire, J. C. (2012). Individual differences in response to cognitive training: Using a multi-modal, attentionally demanding game-based intervention for older adults. *Computers in Human Behavior*. doi:10.1016/j.chb.2012.01.012 PMID:22393270

Whitton, N. (2011). Game engagement theory & adult learning. *Simulation & Gaming*, *42*(5), 596–609. doi:10.1177/1046878110378587

KEY TERMS AND DEFINITIONS

Education: The process of receiving or giving systematic instruction, especially at a school or university.

Learning: The acquisition of knowledge or skills through study, experience, or being taught.

Net Generation: A term to refer to the current generation who have never experienced the world without information and communication technology (ICT). They have grown up with computers, the Internet, and computer games.

Serious Game: A game designed for a primary purpose other than pure entertainment. The "serious" adjective is generally prepended to refer to products used by industries like defense, education, scientific exploration, health care, emergency management, city planning, engineering, religion, and politics.

Chapter 4
Play Preferences and the Gendering of Gaming

ABSTRACT

The aim of this chapter is to highlight the gender divide in regards to play styles and game preferences. The chapter considers how gender differences in relation to play and preferences reinforce and perpetuate the view that computer games are a male domain and a predominantly male leisure pursuit. Additionally, the authors discuss what makes women, and girls play differently and in what ways the genders differ and why this might be. The chapter also discusses the view of masculinity as the dominant ideology of play within the game industry, with feminine play viewed as "other," trivialised and marginalised by the mainstream industry.

INTRODUCTION

Computer gameplay as a specific activity takes place within and forms part of a culture that is not gender neutral. (Dovey & Kenedy, 2006, p. 36)

After discussing the impact of computer games in society and culture it is not surprising to hear that a large proportion of American teenagers play games (Jones, 2003; Pew Internet and American Life Project, 2008). However the gamer population is by no means restricted to teenagers. According to recent findings by the Entertainment and Software Association the average age of a gamer regardless of gender was 30 in 2012 a reduction from age 37 in 2011 (ESA, 2011a, 2012). In this chapter we want to consider the gender divide with regards to play and preferences, including play styles and game genre preference's that have been found to differ between the genders. Chapter

DOI: 10.4018/978-1-4666-4534-9.ch004

one highlighted the importance of computer games in the current climate; specifically in terms of their current economic, cultural and media impact. This chapter will discuss the specifics of play and consider how play styles and preferences can differ; between the genders. In 2008 the Pew Internet and American Life Project found that game play was nearly universal across teens in America and it could even be suggested that for children in many countries including America, the UK, Australia, many parts of Europe and amongst many Asian countries to not play computer games is viewed unusual.

According to sociologist John Huizinga (1955) play is vital and an essential part of human life. Play in childhood is viewed as a means for children to understand the social world (Mead, 1934) and role-playing games in particular enable children to understand different roles, gain a sense of empathy and the viewpoints of others (Kato, 2010). The growing popularity and importance of games in our culture makes a discussion of the gender divide within games a pertinent and timely issue. As this chapter will discuss, play including digital play is deeply affected by the cultural construction of gender. Play and leisure, like work, are embedded in our cultures and therefore discussions of play with regards to the gendered digital divide is an important area of research and may enable a deeper understanding of gender and culture.

Computer game consumers are becoming more diverse especially in the advent of game consoles such as the Nintendo Wii, Nintendo DS and Microsoft X Box Kinect which play more social and interactive games. Women in particular are increasingly making up the gamer population and market especially in terms of the afore mentioned Nintendo consoles with recent figures saying that women represent 51% of Wii users and 53% of DS users (ESA, 2011b). However, as we will discuss throughout this chapter, and ultimately throughout this book, there are a number of gender differences that exist within games culture. In general, games are viewed as a male pursuit and females are less immersed in the culture of games. Highlighting the importance of games in culture today Jenson and de Castell (2011) argue that "over a remarkably short span of time, digital games have come to command an increasingly important role in social communications" (p. 1), and therefore they suggest, to which we agree, that it is important for us to find out "how and under what conditions girls and women play the way they do, without attributing to that way of playing in and of itself any enduring or fixed significance" (Jenson & de Castell, 2011, p. 10). The beginning quote again by Jenson and de Castell also acknowledges that computer games have moved on significantly from the lone socially isolated player image and are now part of how people communicate; they are social and allow players to interact with each other. This aspect will be explored later in the chapter through a specific look at MMORPG's.

Gender differences have been found in relation to a number of aspects of game play. For instance, Lucas and Sherry (2004) surveyed 534 young adults and found females played less frequently, they had less motivation to play in social situations and females where less in favour of competitive games and games with 3-D rotation than males. However despite these findings which suggest women are generally less favourable towards games, women are the fastest growing group of computer game consumers, making up an estimated 38% of USA players (IBISWorld, 2008). Women over 18 make up more of the game-playing population than males under 17 (ESA Industry Facts, 2012). According to an Entertainment Leisure Software Publishers Association (ELSPA) white paper (Krotoski, 2004), in 2004, 27.2% of all active gamers in the UK were women. These female gamers have an average age of 30-35 years old, playing on average 7.2 hours per week. Internationally, women in the UK represent a slightly lower proportion of gamers (27.2%) compared to women gamers in America (38%), Japan (36.8%) and Korea (65.9%). More recent figures from the ESA (2012) suggest women represent 47% of American gamers.

It must be bore in mind when discussing the gender divide and computer games that neither women nor men are homogenous groups. Research has often conflated age groups to make broad assumptions about 'females'. Taylor (2003) points this out in her study of Everquest players critiquing early research on gender and computer games, suggesting that

While some work in the 1990s was notable for its nuanced approach in understanding the relationship between gender and games, much of it presented stereotypical formulations of girls' relationships to technology. In addition, little was done to disentangle the

experience of play across age and life cycle. Research on girls thus often was extrapolated to apply to women. (p. 99)

Hence, the insistence that throughout this book we shall consider gender differences with regards to both gender and age (women/men, girls/boys). There is also consideration within categories. For instance within the category of 'women' Royse et al (2007) recognised there are different attitudes towards gaming. Royse et. al. (2007) identified three levels of game consumption by female adults. The power gamer, where gender and technology are highly integrated and women enjoy multiple pleasures from gaming; moderate gamers, who play games to cope with their real lives and enjoy controlling the gaming environment or use gaming as a distraction from life; and finally, the non-gamers who view games as a waste of time. In order to look at the gender divide with regard to play and preferences, this chapter will consider the technical ability and transferable skills games can provide, discuss motivation for game play, gender differences in computer use and game play, gender differences in terms of game genre and preferences, games for girls and the gendering of game space.

MOTIVATION FOR GAME PLAY

When the medium is designed so that female players are able to meet their primary gratification of control, they will be more inclined to play. (Lucas and Sherry, 2004, p. 518)

People spend a lot of money, time and energy on computer games so it is important to understand what motivates them to participate in this leisure activity. In order to understand play it is important to consider what motivates people to play games. Early research by Malone (1981) found three main motivations for playing computer games: fantasy, challenge and curiosity. More recently one of the most frequently cited motivations for game play, for both genders, is fun. According to a survey by the ESA (2001) fun was the most popular motivation for play, followed by; challenging, the need for an interactive social experience and because they provide good value for money with regards to entertainment. Games can even make failing fun (McGonigal, 2011). However because games vary enormously Poole (2000) suggests there are complex reasons why people play. According to Poole "videogames are powerful but they are nothing without humans to play them. So the inner life of videogames—how they work—is bound up with the inner life of the player" (p 9, as cited in Kirriemuir & McFarlane, 2004).

Synthesizing the research on motivation for game play, it would appear that there are five influencing factors as to why people play games. These factors are fun, challenge, social interaction, immersion and time to play (see Figure 1), whilst motivation may vary between the genders, the factors are co-influencing, for example a woman might find games not fun, as not the type of game they would want to play and not have the time to play.

In the earlier history of computer games, games were viewed as a distraction from more

Figure 1. Signpost to the five main factors that influence motivation to play games

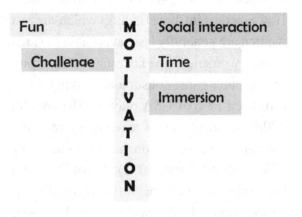

worthy activities such as homework or play involving physical exercise (Kirriemuir & McFarlane, 2004).

Research has found that people play games for a variety of reasons; including relaxation, competence and escape from daily concerns (Ryan, Rigby, & Przybyiski, 2006). Players have been found to focus and feel a sense of control, loss of a sense of time and place and find play intrinsically rewarding. This focus has been termed 'flow' by Csikszentmihalyi (1990). It has been suggested that games are unique and are unlike other forms of media in that they are not fixed but rather dynamic simulations (Aarseth, 2001). Since games are developed in the strive for realism, this allows players immersion and engagement with games (Pold, 2005). Indeed, Sherry et al (2004) put forward the uses and gratification theory in order to look at the motivations for gamers to play games. They suggest that game use is more purposeful and active than television use due to the costs involved in game play; investment in a console, games, pc etc. They found the most prominent motivation for game use was social interaction, contradicting the viewpoint that game play is a solitary activity.

Sherry et al. (2006) developed the most consistently used scale to understand people's motivations for play -The Analysis of Video Game Uses and Gratifications instrument (AVGUG). Bryce and Rutter (2002) suggest there is a lack of research looking into gender specific motivations and experiences of game play. They suggest gender and games need to be researched within a wider social context. Looking at the motivations to play online games, Yee (2007) suggests there are three main motivational components; achievement, social aspects and immersion. According to Yee (2007) different people choose to play games for very different reasons, and thus, the same video game may have very different meanings or consequences for different players. Yee found demographic factors such as gender, age and game usage patterns important to game play motivation. Supporting Yee's assertions of demographic differences Erfani et al. (2010) suggest that age, gender and prior gaming experience impact performance on games and performance is a key component to motivation.

Research on the motivations of children's game play has also found significant gender differences (McFarlane et al., 2002). In a study of British school children McFarlane found girls were more likely to play games because they were bored whereas boys more likely to play games as a first choice activity. This finding perhaps confirms the male dominance of computer games and the assertion that boys are more fully immersed in gaming culture

than females. Females in particular have been found to more likely to site communication as a fun element and motivation to play games (Bertozzi & Lee, 2010). Females have also been found to be more likely than males to enjoy the social nature of gaming. The social nature of massively multiplayer online role playing games has been suggested as to why the genre is becoming increasingly more popular with women despite the games being time intensive as they require long blocks of time to complete a task (Cassell & Jenkins, 1998).

One potentially important motivational factor is having the time to play. In particular gender differences have been found to exist in the amount of time available to play games. Difference in the amount of leisure time the two genders have; according to the National Statistics (2004) in the UK men have an hour and half more free time per day then women with similar gendered differences found across Europe and USA with men gaining between 30 minutes and up to 2 hours more free time then women (Eurostat, 2005). For women, due to their domestic responsibilities (which is also highly gendered) this tends to take precedence over their leisure time; resulting in women playing games less (Schott & Horrell, 2000). This view is also supported by Krotoski (2004), who puts forward that women's game choices reflect their time limitations. In that, women tend to prefer games which are easy to master and do not require a great amount of negotiation with a controller. Lack of time has been suggested as an important factor and could be the main reason as to why women tend to play more casual games (Angelo, 2004). Research by

Winn and Heeter (2009) suggests that women play fewer games due to less leisure time and their free time is in smaller chunks resulting in them playing games in shorter periods of time than men. However research in America has found the gender time gap spent on game play is narrowing with men averaging 7.6 hours of play per week and women 7.4 hours according to the entertainment software association (ESA, 2010). Research also suggests that women complain significantly more about the amount of time their male partner plays games (Ogletree & Drake, 2007). As illustrated throughout chapter one, women do play games and so now we need to consider how women pay and how play itself may be gendered in the computer gaming context.

GENDER DIFFERENCES IN COMPUTER USE AND GAME PLAY

Women play despite the game. (Taylor, 2003, p.36)

Judith Butler (1990) describes gender as performance, Butler suggests that our actions (performances) are what constitute our gender. Despite more women and girls becoming gamers, both hard core and casual games, computer games and games culture is still viewed as a male, rather than a female pursuit or leisure activity. There are a number of differences that previous research has found with regards to play and play preferences. For instance research suggests that older generations prefer playing online whilst younger generations prefer consoles (Lenhart et al, 2008), that males

prefer all-male characters whereas females prefer more variation (Williams et al, 2009), and males are more likely to play alone than females (Yee, 2006b). In particular a number of studies have looked at what women play and how they differ from male gamers (Carr, 2005; Cassell & Jenkins, 1998; Schott & Horrell, 2000). Without considering other demographical differences such as gender, age and race we are left with a narrow and stereotyped image of how people play. This section of the chapter will look specifically at the gendering of computer game play.

Despite the potential benefits of playing games, as previously discussed, a substantial gender difference in computer game involvement has been observed in many countries including America, the UK and throughout Europe. For example, studies have found gender differences in interests in computer games, confidence in computer games and the amount of time spent playing computer games (Bonanno & Kommers, 2008; Angelo, 2004; Krotoski, 2004; Natale, 2002; Schott & Horrell, 2000). Research by Yee (2006a) found that women are more likely to play with a partner (this was a male partner in the research looking at heterosexual couples) and will have more than likely been introduced to games by their partner then men. Similarly, Ogletree and Drake (2007) found many college aged female players had been drawn to gaming by their male partners. Suggesting a gender divide in that gaming is viewed as a male pursuit with males often introducing females to the leisure activity.

The image of computers and computer games have also been found to be gender specific, with research finding that children of both genders perceive computer users as male (Mercier, Barron, & O'Connor, 2006). Men are also considered more computer literate and computer confident than women, due to playing computer games (Natale, 2002). In contrast however research by Clegg and Trayhurn (2000) found no evidence of a gender difference in the confidence and skills of using computers. However, they did find differences between the women and men in their study in respect to home computer use, with women not using computers as much in the home, compared to men who used them more frequently and from childhood in the form of computer games. Terlecki et al (2011) in a study of over 2,000 undergraduate student's game experience, preferences and self-efficacy found males had more experience and were more confident in game play. Bonanno and Kommers (2008) developed a measurement of attitudes towards computer games which had four components; affective, behavioural, perceived control and perceived usefulness. The authors found a number of gender differences with regard to each of the four components and general attitude towards gaming. They found males to be less apprehensive, more confident with game controls and navigating through games and much more in control of the computer or console than females. Males in the study felt games relaxed them, whereas females did not tend to share this belief. The males also tended to have a more positive attitude towards gaming than females. Through playing games the authors concluded that males are more likely to regard computers as toys whereas females are more

likely to view computers as a tool for work (Bonanno & Kommers, 2008). Similarly, Kelan (2007) found that viewing technology as a toy, was associated with masculinity, whilst technology is viewed as a tool with femininity. These findings again reinforce the view that computers generally and computer games specifically are masculine. In contrast to Bonanno and Kommers findings, Oosterwegel et al. (2004) found no sex differences in attitudes towards computers for 12/13 year olds. However, they did find, like Bonanno and Kommer, that both boys and girls in the study thought that boys used and enjoyed computer games more than girls and that girls used and enjoyed word processing (using computers as a tool rather than a toy) more than boys. Similarly, Chan et. al. (2000) found that despite Canadian female students spending as much time using computers as their male counterparts; females used computers for e-mail and work assignments and spent less time playing games, programming or surfing the Internet than male students. From these studies it appears there is a gender difference in the usage of computers for different tasks and goals and this usage may have a significant impact on attitudes towards computers, and gaming technology.

GENDER, GAME GENRE AND PREFERENCES

One major distinction between the genders is regards to game genres preference. In general it is claimed that females prefer causal compared to more hard core games, which has made a gendered dichotomy between hard and casual games making hard core and more mainstream 'real games' male. For instance, in a British study of players aged between seven and 40 years, found girls/women played more puzzle and life-simulation games than first person shooter, violent and sports games (Dawson et al, 2007). First person shooter, violent and sports games are amongst the 'hard core' game genres. Casual games include puzzle games, card games, board games and simple action or light management games (De Schutter, 2011). Casual games are increasingly growing segment of the games market especially due to Facebook games such as Farmville and Bejeweled Blitz (Casual Games Association, 2010). Therefore there is a gendered dichotomy of the female casual gamer, Facebook gamer and the male hard core 'real' gamer (Juul, 2010).

There is not a single woman and therefore not a single game genre for women. Players change their preferences and habits over time. However, some game genres are becoming increasingly more played by female gamers. For instance, women and girls are more likely to play digital replicas of analog games such as solitaire (Fallow, 2005; Bertozzi and Lee, 2010) which fall into the casual games genre. Research suggests that more males play complex games than females (Bertozzi & Lee, 2010) and according to Bertozzi and Lee, "complex games combine physical and mental challenges in digital environments" (p. 200). Angelo (2004) found that women play more 'casual games' such as Tetris and Solitaire or simulation games such as the Sims. The term "casual games" is used to describe games that are easy to learn, utilize simple controls and aspire to forgiving game play. Men are

viewed as more hard core gamers, which is a widely used term applied to describe a type of gamer who prefers to take significant time and practice on games, with many hard core gamers priding themselves on mastering the rules or use of a game. However, casual gamers can be as equally committed to their preferred games as hardcore gamers are. Many researchers also suggest that men play more offline games than women whilst online gaming via Internet-linked PCs or modem-equipped consoles are increasingly popular mode of game play especially by female gamers (i.e. Dawson et al, 2007; Hartmann & Kilmmt, 2006); de Castell & Jenson, 2006; Ogletree & Drake, 2007). Peng et al.'s (2008) study adds weight to the perspective that individual playing experience of a single game varies enormously and environmental factors such as on a phone verses a 40 inch screen and playing against another person or the computer may influence how a game is played. Table 1 highlights the main differences between the casual and hard core gamer dichotomy.

Despite the gendered dichotomy of games the most popular game genre in the UK, for all gamers, is puzzle and quiz games, followed by action/adventure (Oxford Economics, 2008). The casual game association in 2007 reported that the casual games industry is worth $2.25bn, with men making up 48% of casual game players and women 52%; suggesting a more equal gender balance than Angelo and other researchers suggest. Research in Malaysia also found gender differences in game genres with women preferring puzzle games and men preferring racing games (Yong & Tiong, 2008). Other research dis-

Table 1. Main differences between the hard core and casual gamer

Hard Core Gamer	Casual Gamer
Play complex games.	Games are easy to learn.
Games take time and practice to master rules.	Games have simple controls.
Games take time and practice to master controls.	Games have forgiving gameplay.
Genres include: first person shooter, action/adventure and racing games.	Genres include: puzzle, analog games and Facebook games.
Play on Microsoft Xbox 360 and Sony Play Station 3 consoles.	Play on Nintendo Wii and DS consoles.
Viewed as male games.	Viewed as female games.
Violent content.	Non-violent content .

agrees with this gendering of game genres. Through participant observation of gamers aged 20-35, Yates and Littleton (2001) found women had a wide range of gaming interests that were not always tied to gendered expectations. However, the difference in findings could be due to cultural factors.

There have been a number of reasons suggested as to why there is a gender difference with regards to interest in playing different game genres with one reason for the difference being due to the way games look. Bogost (2006) suggests that female gamers prefer 2 Dimensional (2D) games and male gamers 3 Dimensional (3D) games, a finding Lucas and Sherry in 2004 also found. Bogost found that in order to appeal to a female market, games need to be fun, easy to understand and have dreamlike graphics. In order to appeal to male gamers, games need to be fun, challenging and have realistic graphics. However,

Bogost's study was conducted on a small sample (n=34) of 13-14 year olds so may not be representative of the general population. Due to the complexity and diversity of game play difference should be considered both in terms of play between as well as within game genres. The is illustrated by Jansz, Avis, and Vosmeer (2010) recent research that found that not all women and girls that played the Sims2 can be subsumed under one category of 'female gamers', since many females gamers had much in common with their male counterparts. However the study did reveal some gendered differences in that males and females that played the game did so for fun but the males in the study were more motivated by the challenge and social interaction elements of the game.

Denner and Campe (2008) developed the Girls Creating Games (GCG) programme in order to help increase interest, confidence and skills in IT for 126 girls aged 11-14 in America. The girls had to work in pairs to create a computer game with an interactive story structure, which limited the games they could make. The authors found that girls made games with three main themes; competition and conflict, real-world applications and challenges to gender stereotypes. The girls tended to like to solve real world problems in real world settings. Their games also tended to have bright vivid colours and they won through achievement rather than competition. Most of the games allowed the player to choose the gender of the character and they found girls seek to explore different identities and experiment with different notions of femininity. This potential need to explore identity is explored in more detail in the next chapter.

Similar findings have also been found by Heeter et al. (2009) in a study of 5th and 8th graders in America. Heeter et al., found that the designer's gender did influence the design outcome of games. Through mixed methods research, the results suggest that girls expected that they would find the girl-designed games significantly more fun than the boy-designed games and vice versa for the boys in the study. A significant finding from the study is that girls tended to design games with both girls and boys in mind, whereas boys designed for just boys. Their findings support the first half of the 'virtuous cycle' as proposed by Fullerton et. al. (2008), in that, games designed by women are more likely to attract women than games designed by men. Fullerton et. al. (2008) argue that more women would be interested in games if more games existed that girls and women liked to play and if work environments could be found that were more supportive of their values and work styles. The authors refer to this as the 'virtuous cycle'; 'making games that appeal to women and girls attracts more women to work on games, resulting in the creation of more games that appeal to women and girls' (p. 141). Researchers and the games industry still need to explore whether more women playing games will result in an increase in women being attracted to the industry as a career. These issues will be discussed in more detail in chapter six.

MASSIVELY MULTIPLAYER ONLINE ROLE-PLAYING GAMES (MMORPG's)

These games are not only the future of gaming, they are huge social experiments that will affect and shape the future of human communication. (Aareseth, 2004, p. 54)

MMORPG's have attracted players from both genders through games such as second life and EverQuest as they offer a variety of play styles and avenues for self-expression. This genre of game is important and compelling enough when discussing the gender divide and the play styles of women that we felt is deserved its own separate section within the discussion of game genre and preferences. This genre is popular with both men and women but with specific gender related differences. These games encompass several types of play style, and the variety of mechanics and the functionality of the games make them more personal and a more tailored gaming experience to individual players.

More than 16 million people around the world log into virtual worlds every day (MMOGchart, 2008).

It was therefore felt that MMORPGs needed a separate section within this chapter due to the impact virtual worlds have not only on play and preferences but also in terms of understanding gaming and its impact which is captured in the above opening quote by Aareseth (2004) empathising the impact of MMORPG's on human communication. Boellstorff (2008) goes further and suggests that virtual worlds are cultures to be analyzed in their own right. It is important to look at how people play games we can gain an understanding of how they make sense of their world through games. According to Corliss (2011) "the futures of telecommunications, information technologies, user interface, and interactivity are all closely connected with the development of and participation of MMO games" (p. 6). Massively multiplayer online role-playing game (MMORPG) is a genre of computer role-playing games in which a large number of players interact with one another within a virtual game world. Every day, millions of people interact with each other in the online environments of MMORPGs (Yee, 2006b). Game companies provide the game servers in return for a subscription fee. What is interesting and perhaps surprising about this genre is that they have a significant impact on gaming culture and they tend to be increasingly popular with women (Consumer Electronics Association, 2007; Yee, 2006b).

What may attract female gamers is that MMORPG's are often viewed as social gaming. Taylor (2003) suggests women enjoy these games within social communities as they allow the opportunity to play out different aspects of self-identity in a safe environment, allow for exploration with others as a team and they support the pleasure associated with success. Taylor (2003) explored the pleasures women derive from MMORPG's and found the relationship between gender and computer games as complex. Taylor studied women who play EverQuest, one of the most popular MMORPG's with a subscriber base of around 430,000; of which approximately 20-30% were at the

time of the study female. She found women enjoyed many of the aspects to games previously viewed as undesirable to women, such as violence and competition (Hayes, 2007). Taylor found women enjoyed not just the community and socialisation aspect of the game, but also many other aspects such as identity play, mastery and status, exploration, as well as team sport and combat. Women also gained enjoyment from identity play and the role-play involved in developing their avatars, which may or may not reflect aspects of themselves. Women enjoyed mastery and status through achieving personal goals, of gaining skills and attaining levels through competition, with themselves or with other players. Exploration was found enjoyable through navigating in a space were women are no more threatened than their male counterparts and team sport and combat was deemed enjoyable through using violence to express their mastery of the game. Similarly, Cunningham (2000) argues that women like to play violent and aggressive games since it enables them to do so in a safe context. It could also be that games allow women to be violent and aggressive in contrast to societal gendered expectations of the role of women. Similarly, Krotoski's (2005) study investigating why women like MMORPG, such as EverQuest, The Sims Online, and City of Heroes, found women can choose a variety of selves, traditionally unavailable offline. The issue of identity and games will be discussed in more detail in chapter five. However, it appears from both Taylors and Krotoski's research that what MMORPG's offer in the way of identity is appealing to female gamers.

World of Warcraft (WoW) has 12 million subscribers (Blizzard, 2010) making it currently the biggest and most successful MMORPG in the world. Indeed, the games world of Azeroth has "as many players as Sweden or Bolivia has inhabitants" (Corneliussen & Rettburg, 2008). The amount of time the world has spent playing WoW, since it was launched in 2004 is 5.93 million years or 50 billion collective hours. WoW players spend on average between 17 and 22 hours per week, which is more than any other game, with 11.5 million subscribers in 2010 earning its creators Blizzard $5 million a day in subscription fees (McGonigal, 2011). WoW is set in a Tolkien-inspired fantasy world (Azeroth) where players get together or play solo moving around the world in quest of monsters to kill, treasure to find and honour to gain. Players subscribe to a monthly fee and chat with other players in real time. The game is considered both a hard core and a casual game, as it has a multitude of play styles to appeal to different players. To emphasise the impact of WoW on general culture, WoWWiki created by WoW fans, is the single largest Wiki after Wikipedia.

MMORPG's have a UK female majority of up to 60%, most of whom are over 30 (Krotoski, 2004). However, according to Yee (2006b) women are in the minority (15%) of players of WoW, the world's biggest and most successful MMORPG. Yee suggests this female minority status is due to the context of the game which Yee suggests deters women from playing rather than the game itself. WoW is becoming a part of, as well as embedded into, the wider culture and it has featured in TV shows such as *South Park* and

The Simpsons. In WoW, players complete quests in a virtual world and receive rewards. This allows their character to gain levels and move forward to more complex challenges. Many of the challenges in WoW require collaboration and social interaction with other human players. WoW is a game that requires multi-tasking and switching between multiple cognitive abilities. More research is needed to understand the gendered dynamics of playing WoW. This genre of game is time intensive, as it requires long blocks of time to complete a task. However, despite the time issue, which we have previously acknowledged is a reason for the lack of female gamers, this genre of game is viewed as attractive to women due to the social nature of the genre (Cassell & Jenkins, 1998). Yet for now male players outnumber females, in the most successful MMORPG game.

GAMES FOR GIRLS' VS. GAMES FOR ALL: PINK GAMES

Creating a subgenre of games that appeals to stereotypes of gendered play habits resulted in the "ghettoization" of girl games and few- thought this may be changing-attempts to incorporate women into mainstream video gaming culture. (Shaw, 2009, p. 233)

In recent years games companies have made games in an attempt to attract a female audience this has created gendered ghettos (Jenkins, 1999). These ghettos determine the ways girls/women should play games. According to Taylor (2003) females are given signals from the broader gaming culture and the games industry that games are not meant for them. Therefore according to Taylor women and girls are unable to make informed choices with regard to what games to play, as they don't know what is out there or what they may enjoy. Girl/women games means a female audience is specifically targeted during the development and marketing of a game. Not a genre definition in itself, as girls games can constitute a number of different genres, including but not limited to, adventure and role playing. Several factors or characteristics distinguish girl's/women's games such as having a; dating feature, the controls are simple as is the overall game play. According to Gansmo et al. (2003), designers build games for a traditional feminine stereotype around social relations, romance, emotions and role playing.

As we have already noted, women are a larger audience of casual gamers which some have critiqued for focusing on self-help (which is gendered), rather than fun and are gendered as they focus on the family. Many (so called) computer games, such as for self-help or to improve skills, are still played on a gaming platform. The Sims is a poplar game amongst females a game that centres around consumerism and the family, with no precise goals players move forward in fictional lives. Second life developed by Linden Lab in 2003 attracts many women (Hayes, 2008). Wow and second life are both MMORP games but very different. WoW is about quests whereas second life is primarily a virtual world for socialising which maybe the increasing appeal of the game

to female gamers; this may be a reason why one game attracts substantially more female gamers than the other game.

There is some dispute as to whether this is actually a game, but the first girls game to appear in the US was Barbie Fashion Designer, published by Mattel in 1996 which was essentially an electronic version for dressing up Barbie (Cassell & Jenkins, 1998). The success of this game sparked discussion and concern over the stereotypical gender representations that initiated the Purple Moon Software's Rockett Movado games, which had a less gender stereotypical focus (Cassell & Jenkins, 1998). However the situation in the Japanese games industry seems completely different from the experience for girl games in the Western market. The first game developed for a female audience in Japan was Angelique for the Super Nintendo Entertainment System in 1994 published by Koei and developed by Ruby Party an all-female team within Koei (Marfica, 1999, as cited in Kim, 2009). Games made for girls share familiar codes of Shoujo manga (girls comics), "they share some common aspects with Purple Moon and Mattel, yet are positioned differently in the Japanese gaming industry and interact in a unique way with the fans" (p. 183). Despite utilising established codes of femininity and heterosexual fantasy, girl games developed by the Japanese designers for Japanese girls claim to develop a niche market enabling the relationship between publisher and audience to be closer and potentially more empowering (Kim, 2009).

According to Kim (2009) "Japanese women's games are significant for their history, influence and function as a site for female gamers to play out various female identities" (p. 165). Kim puts forward that Japanese women's games, in existence since 1994, can offer a wider definition of games for girls and she suggest even a counter argument against the critique of gender-specific games. Kim suggests that Japanese games "offer their audience avatars and genre structures that enable a certain type of feminine identification and narrative unavailable on games for a general audience or a predominantly male audience" (Kim, 2009, p. 169).

However, from our perspective computer games need to get rid of the gendered stereotypes within games and within the games industry more generally in order to meet the needs for inclusion and engagement of female gamers. As highlighted throughout this chapter women play a wide variety of game genres and we believe more women making games will increase the different types of games made, with different play styles, attracting a much wider and diverse audience and making games of all genres that appeal to a more inclusive gamer audience. We believe in the premise put forward by Newman (2004) that game developers should be making good games for everybody over limiting girl games. Before closing this chapter on play and preferences, we feel it is also important to consider space and how space with reference to game play is gendered and how this in turn influences play and game preference.

GENDERED SPACE

Gaming space has been viewed as a gender issue. Gaming occurs in both public and private spaces, as well as across networks, the biggest being the Internet. Dovey and Kennedy's (2006) book 'Games culture: computer games as new media' suggests that space occupied by computer games is often experienced differently dependent on age, gender, ethnicity, class and geography. Differences occur due to the location of consoles or computers in the home as it may prohibit access to particular members of that household. Research suggests there is a male dominance of technology, in particular a male dominance of computer games in the home and that boys are more likely to own a console (Ofcom, 2008). Indeed game space is viewed as being "gendered through its creation and embedded in the structure of games" (Flanagan, 2000). Jenson and de Castell's (2011) recent study mentioned earlier in this chapter highlights the gender divide with regards to girl's access to game consoles within the home. Since gaming is ultimately viewed as a male leisure activity boys are given priority when it comes to gaming and game consoles within the home environment. This issue was raised in chapter 1 with regard to family friendly gaming and the difficulty parents may experience in attracting both boys and girls in this leisure pursuit. Bryce and Rutter (2003, 2005) have studied how the physical space of gaming, such as in arcades, living rooms, bedrooms are materially and discursively positioned as male spaces.

Bryce and Rutter (2002) suggest computer games are a site for challenging dominant gender stereotypes, yet through game content, activities and game spaces the authors argue that gaming is reproducing gendered stereotypes and roles. Game spaces are gendered and exclude women. According to Bryce and Rutter women are granted limited access and assume particular roles within gaming and leisure more generally. This is especially so for public gaming spaces including gaming competitions. Reinforced by the stereotypical and offensive behaviour of males towards females such as belittlement 'only girls', and patronising as well as objectification. The anonymity of virtual games spaces allows female gamers the space to compete free from their gender, reducing stereotypical behaviour.

The apparent gendering of game playing space is not restricted to the home. Indeed, Bryce and Rutter (2003) looked at the social organisation of computer gaming and the way in which gaming is a gendered leisure activity. They suggest that all gaming spaces are still very much male domains, but more specifically, public gaming spaces. This, they argue, is due to the stereotypical view of gamers being male; acting as a psychological barrier to women's participation in public gaming. A study with Taiwanese students supports Bryce and Rutter's findings, suggesting that girls access to public leisure space is restricted (Lin, 2005). For some women, computer games can be an important social activity. Women are the main player of mobile phone games (Krotoski, 2004). Mobile phones may offer women a less restricted and a more accessible leisure

activity than other platforms and spaces, which are viewed both culturally and by the gaming industry as belonging to. More recently social networking sites such as Facebook have been viewed as paving the way for the next generation of hard core gamers, especially amongst women, allowing games to be played with friends across the site (Brathwaite, 2010). Therefore, social networking sites are another viable platform that allows women 'space' to play games. However, there is the issue of the hard core versus casual games dichotomy, this leaves women/girls outside of the mainstream gamer market and reinforces the view that games are for boys.

CONCLUSION

Computer supported play and pleasure might allow for them [females], as it has so successfully done for men and boys, a new form of play and pleasure, new avenues for learning and creativity, and new and highly profitable careers. (Jenson & de Castell, 2010, p. 64).

The above quote by Jenson and de Castell (2010) encapsulates the overall premise and main purpose of this book. The importance of this chapter has been to highlight the power struggle and tensions between the male and female gamer. This chapter has discussed the literature around play, highlighting how play is an important leisure activity, how computer games are becoming an increasing part of peoples leisure time and how computer game play is gendered, to the determent of girls and women, in a number of ways. According

Table 2. Play and preferences: The key issues

Gender Differences and Reasons for the Gender Divide in Computer Games	Core Issues Involved	How May the Issue be Addressed
Motivations for game play	• Females have less leisure time. • Females prefer easy to master games. • Girls play games due to boredom; whereas boys play as a first choice activity. • Communication and fun main motivations for female gamers • Challenge and fun main motivations for male gamers. • The social nature of games is more appealing to female gamers than male gamers.	• More understanding is needed of the difference in game play and what attracts both male and female gamers to play computer games. • More understanding of what makes games fun and is fun for different demographics. • The sexual division of labour within the home in terms of domestic and childcare responsibilities leads to women having less leisure time then males. This is a pertinent issue and one that extends beyond computer game play. • The increase in family friendly games is making games more social and increasing female participation in the leisure pursuit. However more games need to be made which are gender neutral in all genres.
Gender differences in computer use and computer game play	• Males prefer all-male characters whereas females prefer more variation. • Males are more likely to play alone than females. • Males have more interest in computer games. • Males have more confidence in computer games. • Males spend a greater amount of time playing computer games • The image of computers and computer games is male. • Males view computers as a toy, girls view computers as a tool.	• Encourage females to play games and increase their confidence in both computer games and computers more generally. • Eradicate the image of computers and specifically computer games as 'for boys only' image. • Less stereotypically gendered advertisement of computer games may help increase its image as not just a male leisure pursuit.
Game genre and preferences	• There is a dichotomy within game play that is gendered. Males are viewed as the hard-core gamers whereas female are viewed as the casual gamer. • Males play complex games, females play simple games • Girl/women games means a female audience is specifically targeted during the development and marketing of a game. • So called 'pink games' ghettoize female gamers, as a subgenre of gamer which makes them 'other' to the male mainstream of computer games. • Girl games have a traditional feminine stereotype around social relations, romance, emotions and role playing. • There is a parity between the genders with regards to playing MMORPG's. • MMORPG's are often viewed as social gaming given as a reason for large female interest in the genre. • Male players currently outnumber females in the most successful MMORPG game; World of Warcraft (WoW).	• It should be recognized that there is not a single woman and therefore not a single game genre for women despite women preferring casual games. • To reduce the gender dichotomy it should be recognised that 'casual gamers' can be as equally committed to their preferred games as so called 'hardcore gamers' are. • Women play a wide variety of game genres and we believe more women making games will increase the different types of games made, with different play styles, attracting a much wider and diverse audience. • Games of all genres need to appeal to a more inclusive gamer audience. • Game developers should be making good games for all.

continued on following page

Table 2. Continued

Gender Differences and Reasons for the Gender Divide in Computer Games	Core Issues Involved	How May the Issue be Addressed
Gendered space	• There is a male dominance of technology. • Males dominate computer games in the home. • Males are more likely to own a console. • Since gaming is ultimately viewed as a male leisure activity boys are given priority when it comes to gaming within the home environment in terms of access and usage. • Females have less access to computer gaming technology within the home. • Females are even more restricted with regard to gaming in public spaces including gaming competitions. • Women are the main player of mobile phone games. • Mobile phones may offer women a less restricted and a more accessible leisure activity than other platforms and spaces. • Social networking sites such as Facebook allow a viable platform which allows women 'space' to play games.	• Gaming is a gendered leisure activity. There is a need for gaming to be a more accepted leisure activity for females. • Parents need encouragement to enable girls within the home to have equal access to computer gaming technology. • Encourage females to play games on alternative platforms and spaces, such as mobile phones and social networking sites, to increase female participation. • Virtual games spaces allow female gamers the space to compete free from their gender, reducing stereotypical behaviour in game play. This should be encouraged and acknowledged as a benefit to game play.

to Dovey and Kennedy (2006), gender is a prominent force within the computer games culture, suggesting that

... computer games have emerged from within a set of contexts which figure as highly masculine (science, mathematics, technology, the military) and have therefore inherited this particular cultural coding. (p. 36)

It is this cultural coding, we want to highlight and discuss ways that may help reduce its impact. Although games and the computer games culture is generally viewed as 'masculine', women are an increasing gamer population. The literature suggests women are a huge gaming market in a number of gaming genres with the potential of becoming an even larger one. The games industry is recognising that there is a massive untapped market in the female population. For example, Japanese game giant Nintendo revealed its

strategy of attracting the 'non-gamer' market such as women and older gamers through the introduction of consoles such as the portable DS, with games such as Brain Age and the Wii console with its 'games for all' focus. The focus and increase on more family friendly games in particularly as discussed previously also has the potential to attract a more gender inclusive audience.

Computers games have been highly criticised for their violent content, especially in terms of increasing aggression and desensitising aggression in game players. However, as chapter one has shown research is starting to consider the benefits of games and game-play. Games are now being designed to improve, and enhance skills, knowledge and overall behaviour. In particular, games increase confidence in computing generally and overall technical ability, which are transferable skills, highly important, in this ever-increasing digital age. Despite the gendered differences observed in the motivation and reasons for playing games, female gamers both young and old have been found to view games as valuable spaces for socializing such as playing with friends and family as well as meeting new people via games (i.e. Royse et al, 2007; Yee, 2006b). Games are becoming more social and more accessible in the advent of mobile phone and social networking sites such as Facebook, providing less gendered space and time restrictions. Despite the differences between the genders in terms of play it is apparent that all gamers despite age and gender want fun, with fun being considered the most motivating factor of computer game play.

The gendered difference in terms of what games the genders p[refer to play has led to the development of a binary between hardcore and casual gamers and this binary is based on gendered lines. It could be argued, that this binary not only positions female gamers as 'other' but also supports cultural expectations about who is expected to play. It could be posited that women do not feel they have the right to leisure time and when they do, leisure time for women usually involves things that can be done in short time periods that are easily interruptible. Therefore, through understanding play we can understand larger issues of gender and culture. Throughout this chapter the issue of identity, especially in terms of online identities of players playing

The next chapter will focus more specifically on identity and computer games, enabling the reader to gain an insight into identity as portrayed within the games themselves as well as taking into account issues of identity from a gamer perspective. The chapter will also look at one of the major criticisms of computer games, that of hyper sexualised representation and also the general under-representation of females, within games and the wider gaming culture.

REFERENCES

Aarseth, E. (2001). Computer game studies, year one. *Game Studies*, *1*(1), 1–10.

Aarseth, E. (2004). Genre trouble: Narrativism & the art of simulation. In *First person: New media as story, performance, & game* (pp. 45–55). Cambridge, MA: The MIT Press.

Angelo, J. (2004). *New study reveals that women over 40 who play online games spend more time playing than male or teenage gamers*. Business Wire.

Boellstorff, T. (2008). *Coming of age in Second Life: An anthropologist explores the virtually human*. Princeton, NJ: Princeton University Press.

Bogost, I. (2008). *Girls prefer 2D games to 3D games*. Retrieved from http://kotaku.com/gaming/research/girls-prefer-2d-games-to-3d-games-335041.php

Bonanno, P., & Kommers, P. A. M. (2008). Exploring the influence of gender & gaming competence on attitudes towards using instructional games. *British Journal of Educational Technology*, *39*(1), 97–109.

Brathwaite, B. (2010). *Women in games: From famine to Facebook.* Retrieved from http://www.huffingtonpost.com/brenda-brathwaite/women-in-games-from-famin_b_510928.html

Bryce, J., & Rutter, J. (2002). The gendering of computer gaming: Experience & space. In *Leisure cultures: Investigations in sport, media & technology* (pp. 3–22). Leisure Studies Association.

Bryce, J., & Rutter, J. (2003). Gender dynamics & the social & spatial organization of computer gaming. *Leisure Studies, 22,* 1–15. doi:10.1080/02614360306571

Bryce, J., Rutter, J., & Sullivan, C. (2005). Gender & digital games. In J. Rutter, & J. Bryce (Eds.), *Understanding digital games.* London: Sage.

Bushman, B. J., & Anderson, C. A. (2002). Violent video games & hostile expectations: A test of the general aggression model. *Personality and Social Psychology Bulletin, 28,* 1679. doi:10.1177/014616702237649

Butler, J. (1990). *Gender trouble: Feminism & the subversion of identity.* London: Routledge.

Butler, J. (1993). *Bodies that matter: On the discursive limits of sex.* London: Routledge.

Carr, D. (2005). Contexts, gaming pleasures, & gendered preferences. *Simulation & Gaming, 36*(4), 464–482. doi:10.1177/1046878105282160

Cassell, J., & Jenkins, H. (1998). *From Barbie to Mortal Kombat: Gender & computer games.* Cambridge, MA: MIT Press.

Casual Games Association. (2007). *Casual games market report 2007: Business & art of games for everyone.* Retrieved from http://www.regonline.com/register/Checkin.aspx?EventId=164417

Chan, V., Stafford, K., Klawe, M., & Chen, G. (2000). Gender differences in Vancouver secondary students: Interests related to information technology careers. In *Women, work & computerization: Charting a course to the future* (pp. 58–69). Boston: Kluwer Academic Publishers.

Clegg, S., & Trayhurn, D. (2000). Gender & computing: Not the same old problem. *British Educational Research Journal, 26*(1), 75–89. doi:10.1080/014119200109525

Consumer Electronics Association. (2007). *Five tech trends to watch.* Retrieved from http://www.ce.org/PDF/2007–2008_5_Tech_Trends_to_Watch.pdf

Corliss, J. (2011). Introduction: The social science study of video games. *Games and Culture, 6*(1), 3–16. doi:10.1177/1555412010377323

Corneliussen, H., & Walker Rettberg, J. (Eds.). (2008). *Digital culture, play, & identity a world of warcraft® reader.* Cambridge, MA: MIT Press.

Csikszentmihalyi, M. (1990). *Flow, the psychology of optimal experience.* New York: Harper & Row.

Cunningham, S. (2000). Re-inventing the introductory computer graphics course: Providing tools for a wider audience. *Computers & Graphics, 24*(2), 293–296. doi:10.1016/S0097-8493(99)00164-8

Dawson, C., Cragg, A., Taylor, C., & Toombs, B. (2007). Video games: Research to improve understanding of what players enjoy about video games, & to explain their preferences for particular games. *British Board of Film Classification*. Retrieved from http://www. bbfc.co.uk/downloads/pub/Policy%20&%20 Research/BBFC%20Video%20Games%20 Report.pdf

De Castell, S., & Jenson, J. (2006). *You're going to die: Gender, performance & digital gameplay*. Paper presented at the Ninth International Association of Science & Technology for Development Conference on Computers & Advanced Technology in Education. Lima, Peru.

De Schutter, B. (2011). Never too old to play: The appeal of digital games to an older audience. *Games and Culture*, 6(2), 155–170. doi:10.1177/1555412010364978

Denner, J., & Campe, S. (2008). What games made by girls can tell us. In *Beyond Barbie & Mortal Kombat: New perspectives on gender & gaming* (pp. 129–144). Cambridge, MA: The MIT Press.

Dovey, J., & Kennedy, H. W. (2006). *Game culture: Computer games as new media*. Berkshire, UK: Open University Press.

Erfani, M., El-Nasr, M. S., Milam, D., Aghabeigi, B., Lameman, B. A., & Riecke, B. E. et al. (2010). The effect of age, gender, & previous gaming experience on game play performance. *Human-Computer Interaction IFIP Advances in Information & Communication Technology*, 332, 293–296. doi:10.1007/978-3-642-15231-3_33

ESA. (2010). *Sales, demographics & usage: Essential facts about the computer & video games industry*. Retrieved from http:// www.theesa.com/facts/pdfs/ESA_Essential_Facts_2010.PDF

ESA. (2011a). *Essential facts about the computer & video game industry*. Retrieved from www.theESA.com

ESA. (2011b). *Essential facts about games & violence*. Retrieved from http://www.theesa. com/facts/pdfs/ESA_EF_About_Games_&_ Violence.pdf

ESA. (2011c). *Video games & the economy*. Retrieved from http://www.theesa.com/ gamesindailylife/economy.pdf

ESA. (2012). *Essential facts about the computer & video game industry 2012 sales, demographic & usage data*. Entertainment Software Association.

Eurostats. (2005). *Comparable time use statistics: National tables from 10 European countries*. European Commission.

Fallows, D. (2005). *How women & men use the internet*. Retrieved from http://www.pewInternet.org/pdfs/PIP_Women_&_Men_online. pdf

Flanagan, M. (2000). Navigable narratives: Gender +narrative spatiality in virtual worlds. *Art Journal*, 59(3), 74–85. doi:10.2307/778029

Fron, J., Fullerton, T., Morie, J. F., & Pearce, C. (2007). *The hegemony of play*. Paper presented at the Situated Play. New York, NY.

Fullerton, T., Fron, J., Pearce, C., & Morie, J. (2008). Getting girls into the game: Towards a virtuous cycle. In *Beyond Barbie & Mortal Kombat: New perspectives on gender & gaming* (pp. 161–176). Cambridge, MA: The MIT Press.

Gansmo, H. J., Nordli, H., & Sorensen, K. H. (2003). The gender game: A study of Neregian computer game designers. In *Strategies of inclusion: Gender & the information society: Experiences from private & voluntary sector initiatives* (pp. 139–159). Trondheim, Norway: NTNU.

Hartmann, T., & Klimmt, C. (2006). Gender & computer games: Exploring females' dislikes. *Journal of Computer-Mediated Communication*, *11*(4), 910–931. doi:10.1111/j.1083-6101.2006.00301.x

Hayes, E. (2007). Gendered identities at play: Case studies of two women playing Morrowind. *Games and Culture*, *2*(1), 23–48. doi:10.1177/1555412006294768

Heeter, C., Egidio, R., Mishra, P., Winn, B., & Winn, J. (2009). Alien games: Do girls prefer games designed by girls? *Games and Culture*, *4*(1), 74–100. doi:10.1177/1555412008325481

Huizinga, J. (1955). *Homo ludens: A study of the play-element in culture*. Boston: BeaconPress.

Jansz, J., Avis, C., & Vosmeer, M. (2010). Playing the Sims2: An exploration of gender differences in players' motivations & patterns of play. *New Media & Society*, *12*(2), 235–251. doi:10.1177/1461444809342267

Jenkins, H. (1999). Voices from the combat zone: Game grrlz talk back. In *From Barbie to Mortal Kombat: Gender & computer games*. Cambridge, MA: MIT Press.

Jenkins, H. (2006). *Reality bites: Eight myths about video games debunked*. Retrieved from http://www.pbs.org/kcts/videogamerevolution/impact/myths.html

Jenson, J., & deCastell, S. (2010). Gender, simulation, & gaming: Research review & redirections. *Simulation & Gaming*, *41*(1), 51–71. doi:10.1177/1046878109353473

Jenson, J., & deCastell, S. (2011). Girls@play. *Feminist Media Studies*. doi:10.1080/14680777.2010.521625

Jones, S. (2003). *Let the games begin: Gaming technology & entertainment amongst college students*. Retrieved from http://www.pewInternet.org/PPF/r/93/report_display.asp

Juul, J. (2010). *A casual revolution: Reinventing video games & their players*. London: MIT Press.

Kato, P. M. (2010). Video games in health care: Closing the gap. *Review of General Psychology*, *14*(2), 113–121. doi:10.1037/a0019441

Kelan, E. K. (2007). Tools & toys: Communicating gendered positions towards technology. *Information Communication and Society*, *10*(3), 358–383. doi:10.1080/13691180701409960

Kim, H. (2009). Women's games in Japan: Gendered identity & narrative construction. *Theory, Culture & Society*, *26*(2-3), 165–188. doi:10.1177/0263276409103132

Kirriernuir, J., & McFarlane, A. (2006). *Literature review in games & learning.* Retrieved from www.futurelab.org.uk

Krotoski, A. (2004). *Chicks & joysticks: An exploration of women & gaming. Entertainment & Leisure Software Publishers Association.* ELSPA.

Krotoski, A. (2005). Socialising, subversion & the self: Why women flock to massively multiplayer online role playing games. In N. Garrelts (Ed.), *Digital gameplay: Essays on the nexus of game & gamer.* Jefferson, NC: McFarland Press.

Lenhart, A., Kahne, J., Middaugh, E., Macgill, A. R., Evans, C., & Vitak, J. (2008). *Teens, video games, & civics.* Pew Internet & American Life Project. Retrieved from http://www.pewInternet.org/Reports/2008/Teens-Video-Games-&-Civics.aspx

Lin, H. (2005). *Gendered gaming experience in social space: From home to Internet cafe.* Paper presented at the Changing Views - Worlds in Play. New York, NY.

Lucas, K., & Sherry, J. L. (2004). Sex differences in video game play: A communication-based explanation. *Communication Research, 31,* 499–523. doi:10.1177/0093650204267930

Malone, T. (1981). Toward a theory of intrinsically motivating instruction. *Cognitive Science, 4,* 333–369. doi:10.1207/s15516709cog0504_2

McFarlane, A., Sparrowhawk, A., & Heald, Y. (2002). *Report on the educational use of games.* Retrieved from http://www.teem.org.uk/publications/teem_gamesined_full.pdf

McGonigal, J. (2011). *Reality is broken: Why games make us better & how they can change the world.* New York: Penguin Press.

Mead, G. H. (1934). *Mind, self & society.* Chicago: University of Chicago Press.

Mercier, E. M., Barron, B., & O'Connor, K. M. (2006). Images of self & others as computer users: The role of gender & experience. *Journal of Computer Assisted Learning, 22,* 335–348. doi:10.1111/j.1365-2729.2006.00182.x

MMOGchart. (2008). *Total MMOG active subscription.* Retrieved from http://massively.joystiq.com/2008/02/14/mmog-charts-updated-wow-keeps-its-huge-lead/

Natale, M. J. (2002). The effect of a male-orientated computer gaming culture on careers in the computer industry. *Computers & Society, 20,* 24–31. doi:10.1145/566522.566526

National Statistics. (2004). *Focus on gender.* Retrieved from http://www.unece.org/fileadmin/DAM/stats/gender/publications/UK/Focus_on_Gender.pdf

Newman, J. (2004). *Video games.* London: Routledge.

Ogletree, S. M., & Drake, R. (2007). College students' video game participation & perceptions: Gender differences & implications. *Sex Roles, 56,* 537–542. doi:10.1007/s11199-007-9193-5

Oosterwegel, A., Littleton, K., & Light, P. (2004). Understanding computer-related attitudes through an idiographic analysis of gender & self-representations. *Learning and Instruction, 14,* 215–233. doi:10.1016/S0959-4752(03)00093-8

Oxford Economics. (2008). *The economic contribution of the UK games industry: Final report*. Retrieved from http://www.oef.com/FREE/PDFS/GAMESIMPACT.PDF

Pelletier, C. (2008). Gaming in context: How young people construct their gendered identities in playing & making games. In *Beyond barbie & mortal kombat: new perspectives on gender & gaming* (pp. 145–160). Cambridge, MA: The MIT Press.

Peng, W., Liu, M., & Mou, Y. (2008). Do aggressive people play violent computer games in a more aggressive way? Individual differences & idiosyncratic game-playing experience. *Cyberpsychology & Behavior, 11*(2), 157–161. doi:10.1089/cpb.2007.0026 PMID:18422407

Pew Internet & American Life Project. (2008). *Major new study shatters stereotypes about teens & video games*. Retrieved from http://www.pewInternet.org/press-releases/2008/major-new-study-shatters-stereotypes-about-teens-&-video-games.aspx

Pold, S. (2005). *Interface realisms: The interface as aesthetic form in postmodern culture*. Baltimore, MD: The John Hopkins University Press.

Poole, S. (2000). *Trigger happy: Videogames & the entertainment revolution*. Arcade Publishing.

Royse, P., Lee, J., Undrahbuyan, B., Hopson, M., & Consalvo, M. (2007). Woman & games: Technologies of the gendered self. *New Media & Society, 9*, 555–576. doi:10.1177/1461444807080322

Ryan, R. M., Rigby, C. S., & Przybyiski, A. (2006). The motivational pull of video games: A self-determination theory approach. *Motivation and Emotion, 30*(4), 344–360. doi:10.1007/s11031-006-9051-8

Schott, G., & Horrell, K. (2000). Girl gamers & their relationship with the gaming culture. *Convergence: The International Journal of Research into New Media Technologies, 6*(4), 36–53. doi:10.1177/135485650000600404

Shaw, A. (2009). Putting the gay in games: Cultural production & GLBT content in video games. *Games and Culture, 4*(3), 228–253. doi:10.1177/1555412009339729

Sherry, J. L., Lucas, K., Greenberg, B. S., & Lachlan, K. (2004). *Video game uses & gratifications as predictors of use & game preference*. Retrieved from http://icagames.comm.msu.edu/vgu%26g.pdf

Sherry, J. L., Lucas, K., Greenberg, B. S., & Lachlan, K. (2006). Video game uses & gratifications as predicators of use & game preferences. In *Playing video games: Motives, responses & consequences* (2nd ed., pp. 525–548). Mahwah, NJ: Lawrence Erlbaum Association.

Taub, E. (2006). Nintendo at AAP event to count the grayer gamer. *New York Times*.

Taylor, T. L. (2003). Multiple pleasures: Women & online gaming. *Convergence*, *9*(1), 21–46. doi: doi:10.1177/135485650300900103

Terlecki, M., Brown, J., Harner-Steeiw, L., Irvin-Hannum, J., Marchetto-Ryan, N., Ruhl, L., & Wiggins, J. (2011). Sex differences & similarities in video game experience, preferences, & self-efficacy: Implications for the gaming industry. *Current Psychology (New Brunswick, N.J.)*, *30*, 22–33. doi:10.1007/s12144-010-9095-5

Ulicsak, M., Wright, M., & Cranmer, S. (2009). *Gaming in families: A literature review*. Retrieved from http://archive.futurelab.org.uk/resources/documents/lit_reviews/Gaming_Families.pdf

Williams, D., Martins, N., Consalvo, M., & Ivory, J. D. (2009). The virtual census: Representations of gender, race & age in video games. *New Media & Society*, *11*, 815–834. doi:10.1177/1461444809105354

Winn, J., & Heeter, C. (2009). Gaming, gender, & time: Who makes time to play? *Sex Roles*, *61*, 1–13. doi:10.1007/s11199-009-9595-7

Yates, S., & Littleton, K. (2001). Understanding computer games culture: A situated approach. In *Virtual gender: Technology, consumption & identity* (pp. 103–123). London: Routledge.

Yee, N. (2006a). The demographics, motivations & derived experiences of users of massively-multiuser online graphical environments. *Presence (Cambridge, Mass.)*, *15*, 309–329. doi:10.1162/pres.15.3.309

Yee, N. (2006b). Motivations for play in online games. *Cyberpsychology & Behavior*, *9*(6), 772–775. doi:10.1089/cpb.2006.9.772 PMID:17201605

Yong, S.-T., & Tiong, K.-M. (2008). Video/computer games: Differences in the gender preferences, participation & perception. *Games Journal*. Retrieved from www.game-journal.org

KEY TERMS AND DEFINITIONS

Game Genre: Used to categorize games based on their gameplay interaction rather than visual or narrative differences. A video game genre is defined by a set of gameplay challenges. They are classified independent of their setting or game-world content, unlike other works of fiction such as films or books. For example, an action game is still an action game, regardless of whether it takes place in a fantasy world or outer space.

Gendered Space: A space that is divided on gender, viewed as either a male or a female space.

Girl Games: Computer games that have been developed specifically for a female audience.

MMORPRG's: Acronym for Massively Multi-user Online Role-Playing Games.

Motivation: The process that initiates, guides, and maintains goal-oriented behaviors. Motivation is what causes us to act.

Play: To engage in activity for enjoyment and recreation rather than a serious or practical purpose.

Section 2

Chapter 5
Representation, Image, and Identity

ABSTRACT

Throughout this book, the authors have disproved the dominant White, heterosexual, teen gamer image through highlighting current gamer facts and figures, as well as the research and literature in the area. However, despite these facts, figures, and previous research findings, it is apparent that the industry designs games for a White, heterosexual, male audience. Females tend to be underrepresented in games. This chapter looks at how female characters are often missing from games, especially as main characters, and when females are represented in games, they are often secondary characters and stereotypically represented most often in a hyper-sexualised way. This chapter identifies how computer games are designed for a male audience leaving female gamers as "other" within computer games and the wider gaming culture. It Discusses how females are underrepresented in games and the wider gaming culture reinforcing the "otherness" of the female gamer. It Reviews how the industry sexualises and eroticises women, and it considers how this might impact both male and female gamers as well as perpetuate the image that computer games are for boys.

INTRODUCTION

In this chapter, we would like to discuss issues around female representation and sexuality within computer games. Gender has been found to moderate outcomes including; skill (Brown et al, 1997), aggression (Sherry, 2001), game content (Kafi, 1999) and game preference (Sheldon, 2004) as discussed in previous chapters. Despite gender being a predominant issue in games culture the issue of female representation within com-

DOI: 10.4018/978-1-4666-4534-9.ch005

puter games as sexualized and second class characters is a dominant theory put forward as a reason why many women/girls are not attracted to games as players and ultimately as game developers. The guiding message of this book is that the games industry and games culture should attract more females in all aspects; from consumers to developers as they may potentially influence each other. It was therefore deemed essential to look, in some depth, into the image and representation of women and girls within computer games and computer games culture. This chapter will discuss the literature and previous research in the area of image and representation as well as discuss the implications of these dominant images and representations in terms of the gender divide and the gendering of games.

Computer games have tended to be targeted towards a male audience (Cassel & Jenkins, 1998; Provenzo, 1991). Indeed, it has been suggested that male is the default gender of computer games (Carr, 2005). A dichotomy in relation to gender in computer game characters has been found in numerous research studies. Previous research into female representation within computer games has found that women are in general underrepresented; as both active and playable characters (Ivory, 2006; Dietz, 1998), and these nonessential, passive characters of women also tend to be represented in an overly sexualised way (Dietz, 1998; Taylor, 2003, Graner Ray, 2004). Much of the research on gender and computer games has criticised the representation of women within the computer games, with their hyper sexualised representation of women. This hyper sexualisation takes the form of large breasts,

tiny waits and little/scant clothing. Ogletree and Drake (2007) found female characters within games are viewed as more helpless and sexually provocative than male characters and they are less likely to be strong and aggressive. Whereas Hartmann and Klimmt (2006) found that a lack of social interaction, followed by violent content and sex role stereotyping of game characters were the main reasons why German women disliked computer games. It is not just the representation of women and girls within games that sexualise women as Sheri Graner Ray noted. According to Graner Ray (2004) 'booth babes' and sexually orientated themes at the numerous professional games gatherings and conferences suggest the industry is for "boys only" (p. 150) (booth babes are scantily clad/sexily dressed females hired to hand out flyers and entice people to individual game stands at games conferences). One reason why women may not be adequately represented within games it is suggested is due to the prevalence of the I-methodology, which posits that designers designing for themselves in game designs (Faulkner & Lie, 2007). According to Faulkner and Lie (2007), designers who are usually young or middle aged men, make what they view as interesting and when designing for girls/women they tend to build on stereotypical females or females they view aesthetically pleasing.

It is generally accepted that females are sexually objectified within games and games culture (e.g., Beasley & Standley, 2002; Dietz, 1998; Heintz-Knowles & Henderson, 2002, as cited in Ivory, 2006). Haninger and Thompson (2004) go as far as suggesting that female representation in computer games also involves female characters indulging in sexually suggestive behaviour. One of the most controversial computer games, especially when discussing violence as mentioned in chapter one, or when discussing the representation of women in games is the Grand Theft Auto (GTA) series, which is among the top selling games worldwide. The major controversy of the game lies in its violent content and that in one of the games; GTA: Vice City the male character can hire and even kill female prostitutes. This game in particular does not represent women in a good light.

Despite the poor female portrayal in the GTA series female characters have started to increase within computer games with Lara Croft being hailed as the first serious action/adventure game to feature a female character as the primary character often viewed as being aimed at female gamers and to increase female gamer participation in this genre of games. Lara is a strong character, however the character is again hyper sexualised due to her large breasts, tight fitting top and very short shorts. This hyper sexualised representation has led some to the question as to whether this game was really designed for female gamers (Kennedy, 2002). The issues of female representation within games are not just limited to the games themselves. Through content analysis of game reviews from Internet sites, Ivory (2006) found that female characters where underrepresented in games and those that were included within games where more often sexualised in comparison to their male counterparts. This led Ivory to pose an interesting question; the question that if women within games are portrayed in a sexualised

way then should their numbers be increased within games? This is an interesting question and through this chapter we hope to argue for more games females want and more choice in how female characters are portrayed. After all chapter one illustrated this industry is an important industry in a number of ways, especially in shaping the cultural landscape. As this brief introduction highlights, the issue of image and representation with regard to games is highly gendered. In this chapter we will discuss the image and representation of females within computer games. We will look at the literature as to why there is a lack of female characters in computer games, consider how females are represented in the wider games culture and the effects of under representation and hyper sexualised representation, on both male and female gamers and potentially non-gamers. The chapter will then move onto discuss identity in games, through a look at the hyper sexualisation of female characters and the identity of game avatars.

FEMALE UNDER-REPRESENTATION IN COMPUTER GAMES: WHY THE LACK OF WOMEN WITHIN GAMES?

Video game images and stories are a dynamic part of our social worlds, providing information about what we should or could do, think and feel. (Dill et al., 2008, p. 1407)

The above quote by Dill et al (2008) as well as the information on the impact of the computer games industry in today's culture and society as discussed in chapter two, highlights why both the underrepresentation of females and their image within games is an important issue for discussion. According to Shaw and Warf (2009), "The most notable portrayal of women is actually their invisibility" (p. 6) indicating that women are 'other' to computer games, and that when females do exist they are there as something tokenistic and pleasing for male gamers voyeuristic gaze. This invisibility as noted by Shaw and Warf could include not just female characters but also female gamers, since female gamers needs are second, if at all, within games. Dietz (1998) is considered the first to study to examine gender roles and violence in games that were aimed at children. In 1998, Dietz found a distinct lack of females in computer games with 41% of the 33 popular games of the time having no female human characters in them and 30% had no female characters human or otherwise. For those games that did contain females Dietz found they were portrayed as either needing help from a male (weak and attractive) or sexually aggressive. Beasley and Standley (2002) examined 47 games for gender stereotyping, again finding males to be over represented with a ratio approximately 5:1, male: female characters. Those female characters that were represented tended to be hyper sexualised with scant clothing and large busts. This study considered a cross section of games rated across the board from games rated E for everyone, T for teens and M mature audience according to the Entertainment Software Ratings Board. More recent findings by Martis and Jansz (2004) found through content analysis of twelve games that the number of female characters is increasing in games compared to earlier work such as that of Dietz (1998), and with some females in the leading role such as Lara Croft in Tomb Raider. However, despite the increase of female characters in games, Martis and Jansz found that whatever their role is, the physical representation of women is just as stereotypical and hyper sexualised as previous research suggests (Beasley and Standley, 2002). This is also the case with the Lara Croft character from Tomb Raider. Indeed the images of Lara Croft shown in Figures 1 and 2 show her in a tight fitting, revealing top and short shorts despite carrying two guns. Figure 3 shows the actress Angelina Joie as Lara Croft in the film version of the hit game.

It has also been suggested that the vast majority of female game characters are non-playable characters that cannot be played by the gamer (Miller & Summers, 2007). However, more recent research by Divinch disagrees with this and according to Divinch over 50% of games in most genres have playable female characters, that is, gamers can play as a female within a game (Divinch, 2008). Divinch did however find that there were differences between game genres and the amount of female representation within the games within the genres. Perhaps not surprisingly the game genre with the highest percentage of female characters Divinch found was casual games, a genre that is also popular with female gamers as discussed previously. The term "casual games" is used to describe games that are easy to learn, utilize simple controls and aspire to forgiving gameplay. On the converse, shooter games, which are sub-genres of action game that have the commonality of focusing on the actions of the avatar

Figure 1. Lara Croft in Tomb Raider™
(Source: Downloaded from http://www.wallpaperwell.com/Video_Games/Tomb_Raider/tomb_raider_1440x900_wallpaper_48627)

Figure 2. Lara Croft in Tomb Raider™
(Source: Downloaded from http://www.wallpaperwell.com/ Video_Games/Tomb_Raider/tomb_raider_1440x900_wallpaper_48627)

Figure 3. Angelina Jolie as Lara Croft in the film adaptation of the Tomb Raider™ *game*
(Source: Downloaded from http://www.wallpaperwell.com/ Video_Games/Tomb_Raider/tomb_raider_1440x900_wallpaper_48627)

using some sort of weapon, usually a gun, were found to have the least female representation (Divinch, 2008). The lack of female characters in some game genres, for example in team sport games has been suggested to foster gender inequality by placing women in certain arenas and not others (Bertozzi, 2003). Female representation in games tends to render them as subordinate to male charters. Female characters tend to be stereotypically characterised with the characteristics of beauty, submission, materialism, stupidity and inferiority (Bertozzi, 2003). Having more playable female characters maybe a major factor as to why women gamers make up a large proportion of the casual games industry suggesting a link between representation and female game play.

There has in recent years been an increasing attempt by the games industry to appeal to female gamers and this attempt has led to a change in the demographics of game characters. For instance Burgess et al.'s 2007 study did see a dramatic increase in the number of female characters represented (47% compared to Diez 1998 meagre 9.4%). However despite this improvement in the amount of representation, the representation portrayed is still generally negative. This negative portrayal includes a lack of action and physical appearance, with the hyper sexualisation an essential element of female characters.

BEYOND GAMES: GAME CULTURE

It is not just the games themselves which either underrepresent women or portray women in a negative light, but also game related materials such as magazines, game reviews and game covers. This reinforces and perpetuates the whole games culture as male dominated. According to research by Dill and Thill (2007) popular gaming magazines portray 83% of male game characters as violent. Dill and Thill's research asked teenagers to describe typical male and female game characters and found female characters described as sexually promiscuous, thin with large breast and male characters as powerful, dominant and mean. They suggest these views of masculinity and femininity can impact gamers' views of the roles and abilities of men and women. This could be especially so for younger gamers.

Burgess, Stermer, and Burgess (2007) examined the content of 225 computer games covers for the portrayals of men and women. The study found that although female representation had increased from Dietz (1998) earlier study, gender differences were still evident. For example, male characters were four times more frequently portrayed and were given significantly more game relevant action than female characters. Although female characters appeared less frequently on the covers, when they did appear they were less likely to be the primary character, less likely to be without a male character and the representation of the female characters was more likely to be portrayed as sexy or objectified. Game covers can be viewed by all even if the game rating is not suitable to the observer or the observer is not interested in playing the game making this an important and overlooked area of research on computer games. The cover also provides important information about the game content. 47% of the games analysed included female characters however despite this increase in representation they were more likely to be negatively portrayed. This negative portrayal ranged from a lack of action to their physical portrayal and if a female was a primary character they were more likely to be sharing the spotlight with a male character. Only 18% of females appeared on the cover without a male compared to 56% of males appearing without a female.

There appears to be an inherent masculinity in games and the presumption that gamers are male. Feminine play is marginalised and this marginalisation is influenced by the industry, games and the media (Fron et al, 2007). Indeed game advertisements tend to alienate women through suggesting girls/women don't play games. Games advertisements in women's magazines opens the possibility for broadening the gamer population, however how play is portrayed to women must be considered. Visual media is an important area of consideration since advertisements have been found to influence social identity formation (Mastro, et al., 2008), gender stereotypes (Bandura, 2002), and viewers' perceptions of reality (Gerbner et al., 1994).

Chess (2012) argues that through productivity and self-help with themes such as beauty, family and fitness these advertisements reinforce gendered expectations of how women are expected to play. Play in advertisements of computer games aimed at females is often second to the self-help nature of the game. Chess found that through their advertisements Nindento Wii campaigns target a female audience though the theme of play to bring the family together. Chess suggests that computer games aimed at girls tend to offer productivity over play, self-help over fun and are gendered along the lines of traditional expectations of femininity, adhering to the gender divide in leisure time as discussed in chapter four. According to Chess, Nintendo advertising campaigns aimed at women have played an important role in the construction of the female gamer. Perhaps it could even be argued that they have themselves created a very specific kind of female gamer. This is especially so for the family friendly games Nintendo produces for the family friendly consoles; Wii and DS. It appears from this study on the advertisement of games that advertisements reinforce normative gender roles present throughout the industry and computer games culture. More research on this area of the games industry as well as the wider gaming culture would shed further light onto gender in the wider gaming culture beyond the games themselves and enable a better understanding of gamer choice. Fron et al (2007) suggest game advertisements disenfranchise and alienate women, further contributing to the self-fulfilling prophecy that 'women don't play videogame's.

The role of female characters in games appears to be similar to the gender roles in other media forms such as in children's books (e.g. Ernst, 1995; Fox, 1993). Indeed the underrepresentation of women is not confined to the computer games industry as recent research by McCabe et al on children's books illustrates. McCabe et al (2011) looked at the content of nearly 6000 children's books published from 1900 to 2000 and found female underrepresentation in both human and animal characters throughout the time period of study. The study found males are the central character in 57% of children's books compared to 31% of female central characters. No more than 33% of children's books published in any given year contain central female characters either human or animal, whereas males appear in up to 100%. It is not just the underrepresentation of women but also the sexualisation of women that is an issue. According to a recent American study conducted by Hatton and Trautner (2011) who found through an investigation of the covers of Rolling Stone magazine over the past 43 years that the portrayal of women in the media has become increasingly sexualised over the last few decades whereas this is not true for men. This could mean that computer games are following a general trend that is increasingly sexualising women within the media, and beyond or not including female representation to an equal level as male representation.

THE EFFECTS OF THE SEXIST REPRESENTATION OF FEMALES IN GAMES

Although the games industry and games culture has been criticized for its sexualized representation of women, not much research has taken into account the effects of this exposure. Even if women themselves do not play games the representation of women within games may still have an effect for example through game covers as Burgess et al.'s study purports. It is also reported that women spend a significant amount of time watching males such as brothers and boyfriends play games rather than playing themselves (Sterner et al.,

2006) this observation of the game content may also lead to an impact of the content on the female observer. There is a paucity of research in this area, however early research by Funk and Buchman (1996) suggests that computer game play may be negatively associated with self-esteem in girls; as they found that as time spent playing games increased, girls' self-esteem decreased.

In recent years, psychological research has started to consider the potential effects on both genders. For example Dill, Brown and Collins (2008) found men exposed to gender stereotypical content of women were more tolerant of real-life instances of sexual harassment, indicating a substantial potential and detrimental impact on women. Behm-Morawitz and Mastro (2009) investigated the short term effects of exposure to sexualized female game characters on gender stereotyping and self-concept. The study found that female self-efficacy was affected by playing a sexualized female character, but there was no effect on self-esteem. Interestingly playing the sexualized female character resulted in less favourable attitudes toward women's cognitive capabilities and this was the case no matter the gender of participants; illustrating the potential of games having a wider impact, detrimental to women outside of computer games. These research findings may suggest that computer games influence people's beliefs about women in the real world, supporting Dill et al.'s (2008) findings. Research on the mass media has been found to influence people's attitudes and beliefs regarding gender roles (i.e. Morrison et al, 2004). Bandura's (1986) social cognitive perspective suggests that the media may play an important role in learning about gender norms and values. It has been suggested that the active participation entailed by games increases the likelihood that gamers will learn from the game due to immersion and greater identification (Gentile and Anderson, 2003). The immersion and identification of computer games are reasons why computer games have the potential for making a good environment for learning to occur (Behm-Morawitz & Mastro, 2009). Computer game and learning is a major issue within the games literature and important when discussing the gender divide around serious games. Chapter three will focus on learning and computer games highlighting the impact games could potentially have on gamers. It is apparent that games have the potential to influence a number of things including beliefs, attitudes and gendered expectations.

The impact of stereotypical portrayals of women is highlighted in a study by Davies et al, which shows the negative impact on of these stereotypical portrayals on women's career choice. Davies et al. (2002) conducted a study that investigated women who viewed TV commercials that portrayed women in a stereotypical way compared with women who viewed a commercial that portrayed women in a neutral way. Women in the study who had viewed the stereotypical portrayals indicated a lower interest in maths related careers but had a higher interest in more traditionally female careers. This is an important finding as well as an important area of research as gender stereotyping can have a significant impact on

society as well as individuals as highlighted in the following quote: "gender stereotyping not only limits individual opportunity to progress and access the best life chances, it also limits employers' recruitment pools and contributes to ongoing skills gap in sectors such as engineering, ICT and caring" (EHRC, 2007, p. 17). Therefore this gender stereotyping contributes to the skills gap within the games industry and the underrepresentation of female game developers and game workers in all specialisms within the industry as discussed in detail in chapter six. Research has also found that women who do not categorize themselves in gender stereotypic ways earn more than women who do (Stickney & Konrad, 2007). This is also important and can be linked to the gender pay gap found in male dominated industries which we will discuss in more detail again in chapter six focusing on female game workers.

Research suggests that unrealistic images in the media via television, film and magazines lead to young people desiring difficult to attain bodies (i.e., Posavac et al., 1998). So how bodies are portrayed in games is important (Burgess et al., 2007). In particular the media has been criticised for perpetuating an unrealistic ideal of thinness as attractive (Wilcox & Laird, 2000; Sypeck et al., 2006). We need to understand how games represent females since they are now a significant proportion of the mass media. Martins et al. (2009) used content analysis to look at the representation of the female body in 150 top-selling games in the US. The study found that the more realistic the female characters, and those in games rated for children were thinner than less realistic games and games rated for adults. These are disturbing findings since the realism of games has been found can impact user experience in a number of ways including involvement, aggression and physiological arousal (Ivory & Kalyanaraman, 2007). Therefore, more realistic games may activate body dissatisfaction in females with the idealised thin female body. It is not just the female body that is idealised within games. The ideal muscular male body found in many games has been found to lower the body esteem of male student gamers (Barlett & Harris, 2008). However, as the research suggests, women's representation in games is more persistently sexualised and the negative portrayal has a number of potential negative impacts. Indeed Burrill (2008) suggests computer games enable the construction and performance of masculinity, again emphasising that games are for boys. In a recent report by BBC news (Fletcher, 2012) it would seem that gaming remains a macho environment which extends to sexist language where women are often exposed to abusive language. The Website 'Fat, Ugly or Slutty' posts messages of harassment women receive from other gamers. In the article Fletcher reports an incident were a male player in a gaming competition made offensive comments to a female player, claiming that "sexual harassment is part of the culture." This recent report highlights the need for the games industry to take the representation and treatment of women more seriously.

GENDER, STEREOTYPES AND IDENTITY IN GAMES: THE HYPER SEXUALISED FEMALE CHARACTER

The same behaviours exhibited by men and women are viewed differently. According to Eagly sex roles refer to "socially shared expectations about how men and women should behave and are often examined in terms of agency and communion" (Eagly, 1987, p. 39). Social role theory as proposed by Eagly (1987) suggests that women are expected to be communal, which includes traits such as helpful, nurturing and gentle, whilst men are expected to be agentic, which includes traits such as assertive and confident. According to social role theory if a person of either gender behaves inconsistently or incongruently with their gender role then they will be viewed negatively (Eagly, 1987; Wood & Eagly, 2002; Heilman, 2001). Social role theory is often used to understand the position of women within the workforce for not working in male dominated occupations and in leadership or senior roles as these are viewed as male roles. The inconsistency between leadership roles and female gender role can lead to two kinds of bias; descriptive and prescriptive (Eagly & Karau, 2002; Heilman, 1983, 2001). Descriptive bias results from the lack of fit between the two roles resulting in the notion that women do not have the characteristics for a role such as a leadership role. Prescriptive bias occurs when women adopt masculine characteristics in order to fulfil the role and thus violating her gender role. Williams et al. (2009) investigating gender and online games suggest that "by exploring gendered behaviors and norms in these new and increasingly popular spaces, we can test, refine, and extend our existing theories of gender differences" (p. 701).

As Williams et al highlight gender and computer game research could further our understanding of gender differences. Sex role theory is relevant to gender and computer games since computer games and computer games culture is still viewed as a predominantly male domain. According to Selwyn both men and women view games as a 'particularly male pursuit' (Selwyn, 2007, p. 533). It is also important to consider that many aspects of games such as aggression and violence previously discussed, are not viewed as congruent to feminine gender and therefore not viewed as a leisure pursuit for girls/women (descriptive bias). Prescriptive bias on the other hand occurs when female gamers adopt traditional and expected masculine traits in order to fit into the gaming culture. Recent research by Harvey (2011) supports this view. Harvey found that girls who played hardcore games had their non-normative game play and technical competence described as exceptional with phrases such as "she's the only one," viewed as inferior "she still needs my help" or viewed deviant "she's a tomboy," "she's not like other girls"; suggesting boys view girls that are good at games as 'other'. As previously highlighted numerous studies have found game characters conform to gender stereotypes and female characters in particular are portrayed in a sexual manner (e.g. Downs and Smith, 2010; Martins, et al, 2009; Miller & Summers, 2007). Similarly, gender role attitude is another theory that is potentially relevant to the study of gender and computer games. Gender role attitude refers to the beliefs and expectations about what is appropriate for males and females in terms of behaviour (Gushue & Whitson, 2006). Gender role attitude theory suggests individuals internalize gendered cultural expectations due to external social pressures and the favoured results of gender congruent behaviour which is significant to the representation of women. There is the possibility for games to break gendered stereotypes rather than reinforce them. Online technologies in particular enable men and women to blur their gender roles and experiment with virtual bodies, personalities and identities (Wajcman, 2002). This is particularly so due to computer games avatars which are players in-game representation.

IDENTITY AND THE AVATAR

Avatars are not an escape from our 'self', they are, rather, a longed-for chance of expressing ourselves beyond physical limitations. (Filiciak, 2003, p.100)

There are, as this book aims to illustrate, a number of gender differences in the domain of computer games. Despite these gendered differences, Hayes (2007) argues that computer games are contexts for experimentation with gendered identities and that the complexity of people's identities should be taken into account when looking at women in gaming. Hayes puts forward that an interplay of gender, personal histories and cultural factors will lead to better insights into how games may serve as spaces for the development of new forms of gendered identity. From a similar view point Royse et al. (2007) suggests that female gamers often embody femininity and perform masculinity. According to Royse et al, females create an avatar according to traditionally female norms but with masculine characteristics. Choosing characteristics that are often less available to women in the real, non-virtual world. The avatar is an important expression of identity within a game as illustrated in the quote by Filiciak. Narrative and character development are aspects of games women and girls have been found to feel particularly important to them (Parker & Dromgoole, 2003). Indeed, research by Krotoski (2005) has found that women particularly enjoy designing narrative themselves.

Taylor (2003) argues that women want more choice in how their female avatar will look, which does not necessarily mean they do not want them to appear sexy, but sexy without exaggerated body parts and body parts showing. Although male bodies portrayed in computer games are also exaggerated they are not exaggerated in a sexual manner, but perhaps more symbolic of strength (symbolised through big chest and biceps) whereas as Taylor so rightly points out, large breasts have a fairly one-dimensional meaning (Taylor, 2003). Taylor goes on to express the need for game designers to be more aware of the impact the body has in society and that "they [bodies] become not only places in which we express our identities but, because they are socially constructed, offer or deny particular formulations" (p. 38). It has been suggested that what women gamers want is more gender neutral games (Case, 2004). Culp and Honey (2002) put forward that the industry should create

... less gendered game worlds' that go beyond the dichotomy of gender-focused versus genderless games but allow the player to define how gender is enacted. (Culp & Honey, 2002, as cited in Denner & Campe, 2008, p. 131)

According to recent research by Przybylski et al. (2012), one of the main reason games are so appealing is that gaming allows gamers to try different characteristics, to become their ideal self. Przybylski et al.'s (2012) research found that when gamers acted through their new identity they felt better about themselves. Gamers were found to gain more enjoyment from playing games when there was overlap between their actual self and their ideal self.

We touched briefly on identity in chapter two. Identity is a cognitive construct that represents the psychological importance of a role to a person's self-concept (Stryker & Burke, 1968). People have multiple identities and people can have equal or unequal identification with these roles. Simpson and Carroll (2008) re-viewed 'role' in processes of identity construction and suggest that "roles are intermediary translation devices in the dynamic, social processes of constructing identities" (p. 43). Roles do not become identities but they meditate the meaning-making processes of identity construction. Roles both shape and are shaped by our identities in a dynamic and complex process. The importance of role in identity is evident by the continual usage of the term by individuals to explain their work and non-work activities (Simpson & Carroll, 2008). According to identity theory, the core of identity is the categorisation of the self as an occupant of a particular role and the incorporation of the meanings and expectations that role holds (Stets & Burke, 2000). Identity theorists hypothesise that the higher the salience of an identity relative to other identities incorporated in the self, the greater the probability of behavioural choices in accordance with the expectations attached to that identity (Stryker & Burke, 2000). According to role salience theory, individuals invest more time and energy in roles which are more salient or important to their self-identity or sense of self (Greenhaus & Powell, 2003).

Previous research has found that women tend to underestimate the amount of time they play and do not generally identify as gamers (Lucas & Sherry, 2004; Williams et al., 2009; Yates & Littleton, 2001). In a recent study, Shaw (2012) found that identifying as a gamer intersects with other identities like gender, race, and sexuality. Shaw suggests that negative connotations about gaming lead people to not identify as gamers, and can even lead them to not play computer games. Shaw found that only gender correlated with who identified as a gamer and who did not. Other categories Shaw considered in the study included race, sexuality, religion, education, age and type of gaming platform. All categories influenced and shaped peoples' relationship with gaming, but not to the extent of gender. Gender has been the main way in which representation in games, the industry and gamers has been studied. Shaw suggests that

having not been targeted is a reason as to why race and sexuality is not as salient a category as gender. Shaw found games were viewed as separate from other media and whether people identified as a gamer was affected by whether or not they viewed games negatively. Ong and Tzuo (2011) suggest that games should allow players the ability to customize game characters, which could lead to them challenging gender stereotypes as well as allowing more negotiation between female and male roles and identities. However, Eklund (2011) interviewed heterosexual women who played World of Warcraft in order to gain an understanding of how gender and sexuality is performed within the game. Eklund (2011) found that the rules of the game constrained gendered and sexualised identities.

In particular, virtual worlds have been found to offer players a way to recreate gendered identities (Hayes, 2007). Multiplayer role-playing games offer the most opportunities to do femininity differently online (Kelly et al., 2006). Indeed, Gee (2003) suggests that computer games construct three types of player identity; a virtual identity (the identity of the avatar on the screen), a real world identity (the real life identity of the player), and the player identifies as a projective identity which according to Gee is a combination of the other two identities. Gee suggests that the projective identity involves a double meaning, in that the player both projects their personality into the avatar and at the same time the player is

... seeing the virtual character as one's own project in the making, a creature whom I imbue with a certain trajectory through time

defined by my aspirations for what I want that character to be and become (within the limitations of their capacities of course). (p. 55)

The interplay of player and avatar, according to Gee (2003) creates a powerful media as

... it transcends identification with characters in novels or movies, for instance, because it is both active (the player actively does things) and reflective, in the sense that once the player has made some choices about the virtual character, the virtual character is now developed in a way that sets certain parameters about what the player can do. The virtual character rebounds back on the player and affects his or her future actions. (p. 56)

This last sentence of Gee's quote emphasises the importance of the development of the avatar identity to a players gaming experience. Kelly, Pomerantz, and Currie (2006) from qualitative interviews with sixteen girls in Canada reported that

... online activities allowed them to rehearse different ways of being before trying them out offline, where they might have been reined in for going against perceived expectations for their gender!. (p. 3)

It appears that females in particular can benefit from the gaming experience especially online gaming in virtual worlds were identity is more dynamic and something to be experimented with through the development of, and use of and avatar.

CONCLUSION

We need to understand how games are involved in social relations and peoples sense of self. (Pelletier, 2008, p. 158)

Throughout this book, we hope to have disproved the dominant white, heterosexual, teen gamer image through highlighting current gamer facts and figures, as well as the research and literature in the area. However, despite these facts, figures and previous research findings, it is apparent that the industry designs games for a white, heterosexual, male audience. Female tend to be underrepresented in games (Dill et al., 2005; Williams et al., 2009). This chapter has looked at how female characters are often missing from games, especially as main characters. When females are represented in games, they are often secondary characters and stereotypically represented most often in a hyper-sexualised way. As highlighted, previous research suggests females are often nonessential, passive characters (Dietz, 1998; Haninger & Thompson, 2004), wear revealing and provocative clothing (Beasley & Standley, 2002; Dietz, 1998), and are often portrayed as indulging in sexually suggestive behaviour (Haninger & Thompson, 2004) and with traditionally feminine roles (Ducheneaut et al., 2006). It appears from the research reviewed in this chapter that there are no positive portrayals of women within games. This is a disturbing fact for an industry that is producing games for a more inclusive audience. It may be argued that the games industry wants to keep women as 'other' and by doing so keeping gaming as a predominantly male leisure activity. Within casual games research suggests females are more represented as the main character which is in contrast to studies of more so called 'hard games'. Giving female audiences the casual games genre in order to not completely exclude but rather divide on gendered grounds. Research suggest that games with more male characters attract male players who in turn become game workers who design games with male characters and therefore reproducing the cycle and perpetuating the games industry as a male domain (Lucas & Sherry, 2004; Williams et al., 2009).

There are some games which are more acceptable for women to play for instance The Sims which is based on socialising and building a virtual world. The popularity of this and other casual games do tend to suggest that female roles within computer games are similar to traditional gender roles that women are expected to perform within society. Some researchers suggest games can be empower-

Table 1. Female representation, image and identity in computer games: The key issues

Gender Differences and Reasons for the Gender Divide in Computer Games	Core Issues Involved	How May the Issue be Addressed
Representation of females in games	• Computer games tend to be targeted towards a male audience. • There is a lack of female representation in games especially as active playable characters. • Females in games tend to be nonessential and passive characters. • When females are represented in games they tend to be hyper sexualised. • This hyper sexualisation takes the form of large breasts, tiny waits and little/scant clothing. • Male characters also tend to have unrealistic bodies however this is not sexualised and more in a form that emphasises their physical strength such as large biceps. • Female characters within games are viewed as more helpless and sexually provocative than male characters and they are less likely to be strong and aggressive. • Females are sexually objectified within games and the wider games culture. • Lara Croft hailed as the first female lead action character is also hyper-sexualised and perhaps more for the male than female gamer. • Casual games have more female playable characters than other genres. • The genres with the least female representation are action/adventure and team sport games.	• Game designers need to make games, that are not based on stereotypical ideals of femininity. • More females in the game design workforce could enable games to developed, with less stereotypical views of females. • The greater representation of females in the casual game genre may account for the increase in female participation in this game genre. This could be a message to game developers in other genres especially sport and action games. • There is a need for more gender neutral games.
Identity issues	• Females less likely to identify themselves as gamers than males. • MMORPGs allow experimentation with one's identity in a virtual world. • Development of avatars important to experimenting with gendered identity online and something females in particular are found to enjoy.	• Allow more choice in how a female avatar can look. • Allow gamers to try different identities in a safe environment. This is important to female gamers. • Recognise that a games rules, limit identities.

ing to women (i.e., Peixoto Labre & Duke, 2004; Hayes, 2007) through the ability to allow gamers to act out different identities online. This is appears especially so for online games, with research suggesting this is an appeal in particular to female gamers. More research is needed on the cultural, sexual and political representations in games and how the impact such an influential and important cultural products can have in reproducing and perpetuating stereotypical attitudes amongst players. Shaw and Warf (2009) suggest the affective experience of games on the player is as an important area of research as is representation within games.

Importantly, there is a need to create realistic female characters and diverse characters within games. It is evident that negative portrayals in other media forms can influence attitudes and behaviours which can have a wider impact. For instance, Davies et al.'s (2002) research showed how adverts influenced the career choice of women with regards to maths related careers. As we will discuss in a later chapter games are interactive and have repetitive elements which could make them more influential (Anderson and Bushman, 2001). Therefore, we must question and further understand how the negative portrayals within current games affect players. Research is starting to look at these issues and it is important for research to question the impact of games. For instance research needs to question if negative portrayals of females within games influences women's self-perceptions? If, and perhaps how, computer games influence the developing identities of teens and young adults? As well as to consider the influence and impact other aspects, beyond the games themselves, may have on both consumers and non-consumers of games. These are just a couple of areas future research may consider, there is a general need for more research into the area of gender and computer games especially in terms of how games influence gamers and non-gamers. The next chapters will move away from the computer games and the content of games and move the focus to the computer games industry in terms of the gendered divide in who designs and produces games. The next chapter will look at the previous literature in the area of female game workers providing the reader with knowledge of the issues involved.

REFERENCES

Alwood, E. (1996). *Straight news: Gays, lesbians, & the new media*. New York: Columbia University Press.

Anderson, C. A., & Bushman, B. (2001). Effects of violent video games on aggressive behaviour, aggressive cognition, aggressive affect, psychological arousal, & prosocial behaviour: A meta-analytic reviews of the scientific literature. *Psychological Science*, *12*, 353–359. doi:10.1111/1467-9280.00366 PMID:11554666

Barlett, C. P., & Harris, R. J. (2008). The impact of body emphasizing video games on body image concerns in men & women. *Sex Roles*, *59*, 586–601. doi:10.1007/s11199-008-9457-8

Beasley, B., & Stanley, T. C. (2002). Shirts vs. skins: Clothing as an indicator of gender role stereotyping in video games. *Mass Communication & Society, 5*(3), 279–293. doi:10.1207/S15327825MCS0503_3

Behm-Morawitz, E., & Mastro, D. (2009). The effects of the sexualization of female video game characters on gender stereotyping & female self-concept. *Sex Roles, 61,* 808–823. doi:10.1007/s11199-009-9683-8

Bertozzi, E. (2003). *At stake: Play, pleasure & power in cyberspace.* Retrieved from http://www.egs.edu/library/bertozzi.html

Brand, J. E., Knight, S., & Majewski, J. (2003). *The diverse worlds of computer games: a content analysis of spaces, population, styles & narratives.* Academic Press.

Brown, R., Hal, L., & Holtzer, R. (1997). Gender & video game performance. *Sex Roles, 36*(11/12), 793–812. doi:10.1023/A:1025631307585

B&ura, A. (1986). *Social foundations of thought & action: A social cognitive theory.* Englewood Cliffs, NJ: Prentice Hall.

B&ura, A. (2002). Social cognitive theory of mass communication. In *Media effects: Advances in theory & research* (pp. 121-153). Mahwah, NJ: Erlbaum.

Burgess, M. C., Stermer, S. P., & Burgess, S. R. (2007). Sex, lies, & video games: The portrayal of male & female characters on video game covers. *Sex Roles, 57,* 419–433. doi:10.1007/s11199-007-9250-0

Burrill, D. (2008). *Die tryin': Video games, masculinity, culture.* New York: Peter Lang.

Butler, J. (1990). *Gender trouble: Feminism & the subversion of identity.* London: Routledge.

Carr, D. (2005). Contexts, gaming pleasures, & gendered preferences. *Simulation & Gaming, 36*(4), 464–482. doi:10.1177/1046878105282160

Case, S. (2004). *Women in gaming.* Retrieved from http://www.microsoft.com/windowsxp/games/learnmore/womeningames.mspx

Cassell, J., & Jenkins, H. (1998). *From Barbie to Mortal Kombat: Gender & computer games.* Cambridge, MA: MIT Press.

Chess, S. (2012). *A 36-24-36 cerebrum: Gendering video game play through advertising.* Retrieved from http://www.shiral&.com/Work/advertising_sample.pdf

Children Now. (2001). *Fair play? Violence, gender, & race in video game's.* Retrieved from www.childrennow.org/media/video-games/2001/#race

Chonin, N. (2006, February 5). MMORPG! WOW! TOS! GLBT! Sexual harassment! *San Francisco Chronicle.*

Consalvo, M. (2003a). Hot dates & fairy-tale romances: Studying equality in video games. In *The video game theory reader* (pp. 171–194). London: Routledge.

Consalvo, M. (2003b). *It's a queer world after all: Studying the Sims & sexuality.* New York: GLAAD Centre for the Study of Media & Society.

Consalvo, M. (2007). *Cheating: Gaining advantage in videogames.* Cambridge, MA: MIT Press.

Davies, P. G., Spencer, S. J., Quinn, D. M., & Gerhardstein, R. (2002). Consuming images: How television commercials that elicit stereotype threat can restrain women academically & professionally. *Personality and Social Psychology Bulletin, 28,* 1615–1628. doi:10.1177/014616702237644

De Schutter, B. (2010). Never too old to play: The appeal of digital games to an older audience. *Games & Culture: A Journal of Interactive Media.* doi:10.1177/1555412010364978

Denner, J., & Campe, S. (2008). What games made by girls can tell us. In *Beyond Barbie & Mortal Kombat: New perspectives on gender & gaming* (pp. 129–144). Cambridge, MA: The MIT Press.

Dietz, T. L. (1998). An examination of violence & gender role portrayals in video games: Implications for gender socialization & aggressive behaviour. *Sex Roles, 38,* 425–442. doi:10.1023/A:1018709905920

Dill, K. E., Brown, B. P., & Collins, M. A. (2008). Effects of exposure to sex-stereotyped video game characters on tolerance of sexual harassment. *Journal of Experimental Social Psychology, 44,* 1402–1408. doi:10.1016/j.jesp.2008.06.002

Dill, K. E., Gentile, D. A., Richter, W. A., & Dill, J. C. (2005). Violence, sex, & age in popular video games: A content analysis. In *Featuring females: Feminist analyses of media* (pp. 115–130). Washington, DC: American Psychological Association. doi:10.1037/11213-008

Dill, K. E., & Thill, K. P. (2007). Video game characters & the socialization of gender roles: Young people's perceptions mirror sexist media depictions. *Sex Roles, 57,* 851–864. doi:10.1007/s11199-007-9278-1

Divinch, J. (2008). *The Divinich tapes: Females representation in games across genres, consoles.* Academic Press.

Downs, E., & Smith, S. (2010). Keeping abreast of hypersexuality: A video game character content analysis. *Sex Roles, 62,* 721–733. doi:10.1007/s11199-009-9637-1

Ducheneaut, N., Yee, N., Nickel, E., & Moore, R. J. (2006). Building & MMO with mass appeal: A look at gameplay in World of Warcraft. *Games and Culture, 1*(4), 281–317. doi:10.1177/1555412006292613

Eagly, A. H. (1987). *Sex differences in social behavior: A social role interpretations.* Hillsdale, NJ: Erlbaum.

Eagly, A. H., & Karau, S. J. (2002). Role congruity theory of prejudice toward female leaders. *Psychological Review, 109,* 573–598. doi:10.1037/0033-295X.109.3.573 PMID:12088246

EHRC. (2007). *Gender equality duty: Guidance for public authorities in England March 2007*. London: Equality & Human Rights Commission.

Eklund, L. (2011). Doing gender in cyberspace: the performance of gender by female World of Warcraft players. *Convergence*, *17*(3), 323–342.

Entman, R. M., & Rojecki, A. (2011). *The Black image in the White mind: Media & race in America*. Chicago, IL: University of Chicago Press.

Ernst, S. B. (1995). Gender issues in books for children & young adults. In *Battling dragons: Issues & controversy in children's literature*. Portsmouth, NH: Heinemann.

ESA. (2011). *Video games & the economy*. Retrieved from http://www.theesa.com/gamesindailylife/economy.pdf

Everett, A., & Watkins, S. G. (2008). The power of play: The portrayal & performance of race in video games. In K. Salen (Ed.), *The ecology of games: Connecting youth, games, & learning* (pp. 141–166). Cambridge, MA: The MIT Press.

Faulkner, W., & Lie, M. (2007). Gender in the information society: Strategies of inclusion. *Gender, Technology and Development*, *11*(2), 157–177. doi:10.1177/097185240701100202

Filiciak, M. (2003). Hyper identities: Postmodern identity patterns in massively multiplayer online role-playing games. In *The video game theory reader*. London: Rouledge.

Fletcher, J. (2012). *Sexual harassment in the world of video gaming*. BBC News Magazine.

Fox, M. (1993). Men who weep, boys who dance: The gender agenda between the lines in children's literature. *Language Arts*, *70*(2), 84–88.

Fron, J., Fullerton, T., Morie, J. F., & Pearce, C. (2007). *The hegemony of play*. Paper presented at the Situated Play. New York, NY.

Funk, J. B., & Buchman, D. D. (1996). Playing violent video & computer games & adolescent self-concept. *The Journal of Communication*, *46*(2), 19–32. doi:10.1111/j.1460-2466.1996.tb01472.x

Gee, J. P. (2003). *What video games have to teach us about learning & literacy*. New York: Palgrave Macmillan. doi:10.1145/950566.950595

Gentile, D. A., & Anderson, C. A. (2003). Violent video games: The newest media violence hazard. In D. A. Gentile (Ed.), *Media violence & children*. Westport, CT: Praeger Publishing.

Gerbner, G., Gross, L., Morgan, M., & Signorielli, N. (1994). *Growing up with television: The cultivation perspective*. Hillsdale, NJ: Lawrence Erlbaum.

Gourdin, A. (2005). *Game developers demographics: An exploration of workforce diversity*. International Game Developers Association. Retrieved from http://archives.igda.org/diversity/IGDA_DeveloperDemographics_Oct05.pdf

Graner Ray, S. (2004). *Gender inclusive game design: Expanding the market.* Cambridge, MA: Charles River Media Inc.

Greenhaus, J. H., & Powell, G. N. (2003). When work & family collide: Deciding between competing role demands. *Organizational Behavior and Human Decision Processes, 90,* 291–303. doi:10.1016/S0749-5978(02)00519-8

Gushue, G. V., & Whitson, M. L. (2006). The relationship of ethnic identity & gender role attitudes to the development of career choice goals among Black & Latina girls. *Journal of Counseling Psychology, 53*(3), 379–385. doi:10.1037/0022-0167.53.3.379

Haninger, K., & Thompson, K. M. (2004). Content & ratings of teen-rated video games. *Journal of the American Medical Association, 291,* 856–865. doi:10.1001/jama.291.7.856 PMID:14970065

Hartmann, T., & Klimmt, C. (2006). Gender & computer games: Exploring females' dislikes. *Journal of Computer-Mediated Communication, 11,* 910–931. doi:10.1111/j.1083-6101.2006.00301.x

Harvey, A. (2011). Constituting the player: Feminist techno science, gender, & digital play. *International Journal of Gender. Science & Technology, 3*(1), 170–184.

Hatton, E., & Trautner, M. N. (2011). Equal opportunity objectification? The sexualisation of men & women on the cover of Rolling Stone. *Sexuality & Culture, 15,* 256–278. doi:10.1007/s12119-011-9093-2

Hayes, E. (2007). Gendered identities at play: Case studies of two women playing Morrowind. *Games and Culture, 2*(1), 23–48. doi:10.1177/1555412006294768

Heilman, M. E. (1983). Sex bias in work settings: The lack of fit model. *Research in Organizational Behavior, 5,* 269–298.

Heilman, M. E. (2001). Description & prescription: How gender stereotypes prevent women's ascent up the organizational ladder. *The Journal of Social Issues, 57,* 657–674. doi:10.1111/0022-4537.00234

Hoppes, S., Hally, C., & Sewell, L. (2000). An interest inventory of games for older adults. *Physical & Occupational Therapy in Geriatrics, 18*(2), 71–83. doi:10.1080/J148v18n02_05

Huh, S., & Williams, D. (2010). Dude looks like a lady: Gender swapping in an online game. In W. S. Bainbridge (Ed.), *Online worlds: Convergence of the real & virtual, human-computer interaction series* (pp. 161–174). London: Springer-Verlag. doi:10.1007/978-1-84882-825-4_13

Ivory, J. D. (2006). Still a man's game: Gender representation in online reviews of video games. *Mass Communication & Society, 9*(1), 103–114. doi:10.1207/s15327825mcs0901_6

Ivory, J. D., & Kalanaraman, S. (2007). The effects of technological advancement & violent content in video games on player's feelings of presence, involvement, physiological arousal, & aggression. *The Journal of Communication, 57,* 532–555. doi:10.1111/j.1460-2466.2007.00356.x

Jansz, J., & Martis, R. G. (2007). The Laura phenomenon: Powerful female characters in video games. *Sex Roles*, *56*, 141–148. doi:10.1007/s11199-006-9158-0

Jenson, J., de Castell, S., & Bryson, M. (2003). Girl talk: Gender, equity & identity discourses in a school-based computer culture. *Women's Studies International Forum*, *26*(6), 561–573.

Kafai, Y. (1999). Video game designs by girls & boys: Variability & consistency of gender differences. In M. Kinder (Ed.), *Kids' media culture* (pp. 293–315). Durham, NC: Duke University Press.

Kelly, D. M., Pomerantz, S., & Currie, D. H. (2006). No boundaries? Girls' interactive, online learning about femininities. *Youth & Society*, *38*(1), 3–28. doi:10.1177/0044118X05283482

Kennedy, H. W. (2002). Lara Croft: Feminist icon or cyberbimbo? On the limits of textual analysis. *Game Studies. The International Journal of Computer Game Research*, 2(2).

Kerr, A. (2006). *The business & culture of digital games: Gamework/gameplay*. London: Sage.

Krotoski, A. (2005). Socialising, subversion & the self: Why women flock to massively multiplayer online role playing games. In N. Garrelts (Ed.), *Digital gameplay: Essays on the nexus of game & gamer*. Jefferson, NC: McFarland Press.

Leonard, D. J. (2006). Not a hater, just keepin' it real: the importance of race-& gender-based games studies. *Games and Culture*, *1*(1), 83–88. doi:10.1177/1555412005281910

Leonard, D. J. (2009). Young, black (& brown) & don't give a fuck: Virtual gangstas in the era of state violence. *Cultural Studies. Critical Methodologies*, *9*, 248–272. doi:10.1177/1532708608325938

Leupold, T. (2006). Is there room for 'gaymers' in the gaming industry? *Oakland Tribune*. Retrieved from http://findarticles.com/p/aticles/mi_qn4176/is_20060407/ai_n16142589/

Lucas, K., & Sherry, J. L. (2004). Sex differences in video game play: A communication-based explanation. *Communication Research*, *31*, 499–523. doi:10.1177/0093650204267930

MacCallum-Stewart, E. (2008). Real boys carry girly epics: Normalising gender bending in online games. *Eludamos Journal for Computer Game Culture*, *2*(1), 27–40.

Martins, N., Williams, D. C., Harrison, K., & Ratan, R. A. (2009). A content analysis of female body imagery in video games. *Sex Roles*, *61*, 824–836. doi:10.1007/s11199-009-9682-9

Martins, N., Williams, D. C., Harrison, K., & Ratan, R. A. (2009). A content analysis of female body imagery in video games. *Sex Roles*, *61*, 824–836. doi:10.1007/s11199-009-9682-9

Martis, R. G., & Jansz, J. (2004). *The representation of gender & ethnicity in digital interactive games*. Paper presented at the International Communication Association. New Orleans, LA.

Mastro, D. E., Behm-Morawitz, E., & Kopacz, M. A. (2008). Exposure to television portrayals of Latinos: The implications of aversive racism & social identity theory. *Human Communication Research, 34,* 1–27. doi:10.1111/j.1468-2958.2007.00311.x

McCabe, J., Fairchild, E., Grauerholz, L., Pescosolido, B. A., & Tope, D. (2011). Titles & central characters gender in twentieth-century children's books: Patterns of disparity in titles & central characters. *Gender & Society, 25,* 197. doi:10.1177/0891243211398358

Miller, M., & Summers, A. (2007). Gender differences in video game characters' roles, appearances, & attire as portrayed in video game magazines. *Sex Roles, 57,* 733–742. doi:10.1007/s11199-007-9307-0

Morrison, T. G., Kalin, R., & Morrison, M. A. (2004). Body-image evaluation & image investment among adolescents: A test of sociocultural & social comparison theories. *Adolescence, 39,* 571–592. PMID:15673231

Ochalla, B. (2006). *Boy on boy action: Is gay content on the rise?* Retrieved from http://www.gamasutra.com/features/20061208/ochalla_01.shtml

Ogletree, S. M., & Drake, R. (2007). College students' video game participation & perceptions: Gender differences & implications. *Sex Roles, 56,* 537–542. doi:10.1007/s11199-007-9193-5

Ong, J. I. P. L., & Tzuo, P.-W. (2011). Girls' perceptions of characters' gender roles in digital games: A study in Singapore. *International Journal of Gender. Science & Technology, 3*(3), 620–642.

Palomares, N. A., & Lee, E.-J. (2010). Virtual gender identity: The linguistic assimilation to gendered avatars in computer-mediated communication. *Journal of Language and Social Psychology, 29*(1), 5–23. doi:10.1177/0261927X09351675

Parker, N., & Dromgoole, S. (2003). *ELSPA game vision report: European consumer intelligence report*. London, UK: Entertainment & Leisure Software Publishers Association.

Pearce, C. (2008). The truth about baby boomer gamers: A study of over-forty computer game players. *Games and Culture, 3*(2), 142–174. doi:10.1177/1555412008314132

Peixoto, L. M., & Duke, L. (2004). Nothing like a brisk walk & a sort of demon slaughter to make a girl's night: The construction of the female hero in the Buffy video game. *The Journal of Communication Inquiry, 28*(2), 138–156. doi:10.1177/0196859903261795

Pelletier, C. (2008). Gaming in context: How young people construct their gendered identities in playing & making games. In *Beyond Barbie & Mortal Kombat: New perspectives on gender & gaming* (pp. 145–160). Cambridge, MA: The MIT Press.

Posavac, H. D., Posavac, S. S., & Posavac, E. J. (1998). Exposure to media images of female attractiveness & concern with body weight among young women. *Sex Roles, 38,* 187–201. doi:10.1023/A:1018729015490

Provenzo, E. F. (1991). *Video kids: Making sense of Nintendo.* Cambridge, MA: Harvard University Press.

Przybylski, A. K., Weinstein, N., Murayama, K., Lynch, M. F., & Ryan, R. M. (2012). The ideal self at play: The appeal of video games that let you be all you can be. *Psychological Science, 23*(1), 69–76. doi:10.1177/0956797611418676 PMID:22173739

Royse, P., Lee, J., Undrahbuyan, B., Hopson, M., & Consalvo, M. (2007). Woman & games: Technologies of the gendered self. *New Media & Society, 9,* 555–576. doi:10.1177/1461444807080322

Schroder, A. (2008). We don't want it changed, do we? Gender & sexuality in role-playing games. *Eludamos Journal of Computer Game Culture, 2*(2), 241–256.

Selwyn, N. (2007). Hi-tech=guy-tech? An exploration of undergraduate students' perceptions of information & communication technologies. *Sex Roles, 56,* 525–536. doi:10.1007/s11199-007-9191-7

Sender, K. (2004). *Business, not politics: The making of the gay market.* New York: Columbia University Press.

Shaw, A. (2009). Putting the gay in games: Cultural production & GLBT content in video games. *Games and Culture, 4*(3), 228–253. doi:10.1177/1555412009339729

Shaw, I. G. R., & Warf, B. (2009). *Worlds of affect: Virtual geographies of video games.* Environment & Planning. doi:10.1068/a41284

Sheldon, J. P. (2004). Gender stereotypes in educational software for young children. *Sex Roles, 51*(7-8), 433–444. doi:10.1023/B:SERS.0000049232.90715.d9

Sherry, J. L. (2001). The effects of violent video games on aggression: A meta-analysis. *Human Communication Research, 27*(3), 309–331.

Simpson, B., & Carroll, B. (2008). Reviewing 'role' in processes of identity construction. *Organization, 15*(1), 29–50. doi:10.1177/1350508407084484

Sisler, V. (2008). Digital Arabs: Representation in video games. *European Journal of Cultural Studies, 11*(2), 203–219.

Stets, J. E., & Burke, P. J. (2000). Identity theory & social identity theory. *Social Psychology Quarterly, 63*(3), 224–237. doi:10.2307/2695870

Stickney, L., & Knorad, A. (2007). Gender-role attitudes & earnings: A multinational study of married women & men. *Sex Roles, 57*(11), 801–811. doi:10.1007/s11199-007-9311-4

Stryker, S., & Burke, P. J. (1968). Identity salience & role performance: The relevance of symbolic interaction theory for family research. *Journal of Marriage and the Family*, *30*, 558–564. doi:10.2307/349494

Stryker, S., & Burke, P. J. (2000). The past, present & future of an identity theory. *Social Psychology Quarterly*, *63*(4), 284–297. doi:10.2307/2695840

Sypeck, M. F., Gray, J. J., Etu, S. F., Ahrens, A. H., Mosimann, J. E., & Wiseman, C. V. (2006). Cultural representations of thinness in women: Playboy magazine's depiction of beauty from 1979-1999. *Body Image*, *3*, 229–335. doi:10.1016/j.bodyim.2006.07.001 PMID:18089225

Taub, E. (2006). Nintendo at AAP event to count the grayer gamer. *New York Times*.

Taylor, T. L. (2003). Multiple pleasures: Women & online gaming. *Convergence*, *9*(1), 21–46. doi: doi:10.1177/135485650300900103

Vargas, J. A. (2006, March 11). For gay gamers, a virtual reality checks. *The Washington Post*.

Wajcman, J., & Martin, B. (2002). Narratives of identity in modern management: The corrosion of gender difference? *Social Compass*, *36*(4), 985–1002.

Wilcox, K., & Laird, J. D. (2000). Impact of media images of super-slender women on women's self-esteem: Identification, social comparison, & self perception. *Journal of Research in Personality*, *34*, 278–286. doi:10.1006/jrpe.1999.2281

Williams, D., Consalvo, M., Caplan, S., & Yee, N. (2009). Looking for gender (LFG), gender roles & behaviors among online gamers. *The Journal of Communication*. doi:10.1111/j.1460-2466.2009.01453.x PMID:20161669

Williams, D., Martins, N., Consalvo, M., & Ivory, J. D. (2009). The virtual census: representations of gender, race & age in video games. *New Media & Society*, *11*, 815–834. doi:10.1177/1461444809105354

Williams, M. J., Levy Paluck, E., & Spence-Rodgers, J. (2010). The masculinity of money: Automatic stereotypes predict gender differences in estimated salaries. *Psychology of Women Quarterly*, *34*, 7–20. doi:10.1111/j.1471-6402.2009.01537.x

Wood, E., & Eagly, A. (2002). A cross-cultural analysis of the behaviour of women & men: Implications for the origins of sex differences. *Psychological Bulletin*, *128*, 699–727. doi:10.1037/0033-2909.128.5.699 PMID:12206191

Yates, S., & Littleton, K. (2001). Understanding computer games culture: A situated approach. In *Virtual gender: Technology, consumption & identity* (pp. 103–123). London: Routledge.

KEY TERMS AND DEFINITIONS

Avatar: In computer games, a person creates an avatar to represent themselves on screen. An *avatar* is something that embodies something else.

Female Representation: The representation and portrayal of women within the environment.

Female Underrepresentation: Where there are more men than women within the working environment.

Gender: The state of being male or female (typically used with reference to social and cultural differences rather than biological ones).

Gendered Identity: A person's inner sense of being male or female.

Sexuality: The condition of being characterised and distinguished by your sex.

Chapter 6
Game Workers and the Gender Divide in the Production of Computer Games

ABSTRACT

This chapter discusses working practices prominent in the computer game industry. The chapter provides readers with an understanding of how working practices are gendered, which can deter women from entering into and remaining in the industry. The chapter also provides the reader with a review of the issue of gendered occupational segregation in order to understand the effect this has on individuals, society, male-dominated industries, and the computer game industry, specifically. It considers what impact more female game developers in core content creation roles could potentially have within the industry. The chapter also discusses some qualitative research findings from an international study with women working in the computer game development industry and reviews what attracts women to the industry and the issues they have experienced.

INTRODUCTION

In this chapter, we will discuss the game workers who develop computer games and how and why the gender composition of the computer game workforce is an important consideration when discussing the gendering of computer games. The games industry is an interesting industry as it falls under the umbrella of the wider more established science, engineering and technology sector (SET) and is also part of the creative industries sector. In comparison to the wider SET sector, the games industry is a relatively young industry

DOI: 10.4018/978-1-4666-4534-9.ch006

dating back approximately four decades. The most current available figures report that in the UK women represent just 4% of the computer games industries workforce (Skillset, 2009) which is a 8% decrease from 2006 figures (Skillset, 2006). Similarly low figures have also been reported in the US (Gourdin, 2005) and Canada (Dyer-Witheford & Sharman, 2005). In their study of the computer games workforce in Canada, Dyer-Witheford and Sharman (2005) found that female game workers described the industry as having an 'old boys club' with just 10-15% of Canada's games workforce being female, with very few women at the executive level. Male dominated occupations and industries such as computer games tend to adhere to the male model of work, as indeed do a managerial and senior role, which provides the focus of this chapter. It is not just women who are underrepresented in the computer games industry but also ethnic minorities and disabled people. According to Skillset (2009) less than 4% of computer games employees in the UK are from an ethnic minority background and only 1% of employees classify themselves as disabled according to the terms of the Disability Discrimination Act (DDA). Despite this underrepresentation of other groups within the industry, this chapter will focus solely on gender and female game workers due to the aims and scope of this book.

Underrepresentation of women within the industry can be detrimental to the industry, games culture and equality more generally as we aim to discuss in this chapter. The lack of women and ethnic minorities within the industry has been acknowledged as a possible solution to the skills shortage within the in-

dustry. According to Matthew Jeffery, Head of European Recruitment at Electronic Arts, skills shortages are becoming more common in the gaming industry and measures need to be taken to bring in more new talent. Mathew Jeffrey states that;

Games companies need to broaden out their recruiting scope and attract talent from other new industries and seduce more diverse groups into game teams, particularly women and ethnic minorities. (Skillset, 2008)

It is important for women to have a voice in all areas of the economy and the cultural landscape. The games industry is a particularly important industry as this book highlights throughout. According to Flanagan; 'game makers possess both the most interesting technology and the distribution channels to truly lead the direction of the future' (Flanagan, 2003, p. 359). This quote illustrates how important this industry is especially in terms of technological development and technological usage. The games industry is unique in that it tends to attract a younger workforce. According to a 2005 report conducted by The International Game Developers Association (IGDA), the average age of a game developer is 31, 80% are educated to University level or above and the average years within the industry is 5.4 (Gourdin, 2005). The games industry forms parts of the UK's 'knowledge economy' due to the high level of skills game developers have (Oxford Economics, 2008). According to the Oxford Economics report, in 2008, 69% of the UK industries employees were educated to at least degree level, in comparison to 20% of the UK working age population in the same year. Previous research, on the industries workforce, has found the workforce tends to enjoy the work. For example, game workers in Dyer-Witheford and Sharman's (2005) Canadian study reported that they were satisfied with their jobs and found then challenging and fun. The study also found that cooperation, communication and adaptability to new technology were central skills of the games industry workforce. Training in the industry is on-going in game development studios as highlighted by the upgrade culture discussed in chapter one. In 2005 the IGDA conducted a worldwide online survey of game developers (Gourdin, 2005). The majority of respondents were from the USA, Canada, the UK and Australia. Of the 6,437 responses only 11.5% were female. The majority of respondents agreed that workforce diversity is important to the future success of the game industry. Female respondents agreed more, and more strongly that 'a diverse workforce has a direct impact on the games produced' and that 'diversity is important to the future success of the game industry'.

The computer games industry is a particularly interesting industry as it also forms part of the creative industries sector as well as the wider ICT and SET sectors, viewed as a: "young and rapidly changing technologically driven subsector of the creative industries with significant interactions with the design and software subsectors" (Camicero et al., 2008, p. 37). The creative industry is viewed as appealing to women due to the more relaxed working environment with the ability to be more flexible through practices such as being able to work from home. Recent research by Taylor (2010) explored the experiences of female creative workers in the UK, and found that instead of offering freedom, creative workers tolerate precarious employment for the love of the work. This precarious nature of creative work can result in a number of problems for its workforce, especially women within creative industries especially with regards to maternity leave and childcare (Gill, 2007; McRobbie, 1998). Females represent the majority of creative arts and design students (Pollard et al., 2008) yet a minority in the creative workforce (Freeman, 2007). The precarious nature of employment is perhaps a reason why women are under-represented in the workplace. The aim of this chapter is to look at the workplace for game workers and gain an understanding as to why there are so few women working in this industry. In particular, the chapter will focus on the issues of flexible working and work life balance as previous research, which we will discuss, posits these as major factors for women in this industry and the wider ICT and SET sector. Firstly, we will discuss gendered occupational segregation in the industry.

GENDERED OCCUPATION SEGREGATION: IMPLICATIONS FOR WOMEN, SOCIETY AND THE COMPUTER GAMES INDUSTRY

Gendered occupational segregation refers to the representation that some jobs are viewed as male and traditionally undertaken by men and other jobs are viewed as female jobs and therefore traditionally done by women. The male model of working makes entry into certain occupations unappealing to women and career advancement difficult. Societal expectations play a particularly important role in issues of work life balance, as societal expectations in Western societies regard women as the primary care givers, with the main responsibility for domestic labour. This does not fit with the dominant male model of work. Women tend to be disadvantaged in the workplace, due to prejudice associated with feminine behaviour and what constitutes femininity. Women receive disparate treatment on the basis that masculinity and a masculine culture, is in essence the norm. Women with children or other caring responsibilities find it particularly difficult to maintain a satisfactory work like balance, or work life integration. Gendered occupational segregation exists because in general people tend to choose occupations where their own gender is represented (Miller et al., 2004). Occupational segregation can occur both vertically; concentrating individuals in the lower echelons of an organisation and horizontally; concentrating individuals in particular occupations, making some occupations either 'men's' or 'women's' work.

Gendered occupational segregation is a social phenomenon that persists' despite the growth of female participation in the labour market overall and is proving difficult to eradicate. Previous research has found that women tend to be restricted in their occupational aspirations and choices, even women of high ability (Betz & Fitzgerald, 1987; Chalk et al., 1994). Agriculture, industry (manufacturing) and financial services remain dominated by men, while the service sector (including health, social work and education) remains largely female-dominated (Thewlis, Miller, & Neathey, 2004). Information and communication technology (ICT) and the science, engineering and technology (SET) sectors remain dominated by men in almost all European states (Thewlis et al., 2004). Non-traditional careers are defined as occupations with less than 30% of workers of the same sex (Perrone, 2009). Individuals who assume non-traditional roles as either a career or within the home challenge gender beliefs and often face discrimination and barriers in those roles (Perrone, 2009). Gendered occupational segregation has a negative effect on individuals, businesses and the economy and is therefore an issue to be addressed (Women and Equality Unit, 2005). Gender occupational segregation persists globally including in the UK, USA and across Europe (Prescott & Bogg, 2012).

Occupations are social categories; people within an occupation share things such as preferences and experiences (Weeden & Grusky, 2005). Therefore, occupational categories are an important part of a person's sense of self. Taylor argues that:

... a worker's occupation is imbued with meanings about the identity of the worker and the appropriateness of the worker's role in that occupation - and these meanings can have negative or positive implications for perceptions of interactions and support among workers. (Taylor, 2010, p. 190).

A worker may not necessarily be a minority in an organisation, but they may be within their occupation in that particular organisation, and they will therefore feel the cultural effects of working in a gender incongruent (non-traditional) occupation. Thus, the gender composition of the occupational category regardless of the gender composition of the worker's environment can have an effect on the worker (Taylor, 2010). This is an especially important consideration when looking at female game workers since women can work in the industry in a non-developmental role or in a highly male dominated developmental role and might therefore not experience the same workplace in the same way.

Men and women have been found to experience the workplace differently. The token status of men is beneficial to their careers (often referred to as the glass escalator), a very different outcome to the token status of women, who are discriminated against, have limited career opportunity and often work in a hostile environment (Simpson, 2004). Male teachers and nurses in Simpson's study recognised that their minority status gave them career advantages. Simpson also found that there was also an expectation that men in female dominated careers would want promotion and they were therefore encouraged to improve their chances for promotion through career development. Simpson also found that a lot of 'gender work' is undertaken, in order to restore a masculine identity that has been undermined by the female nature of a job. Simpson found men working in female dominated jobs used a number of strategies to make the job more masculine such as; re-labelling the job, putting emphasis on the more masculine components of the job, and

distancing themselves from feminine components of the job. The strategies used by men in female dominated professions as found by Simpson, reinforce and maintain men as the dominant gender in the workplace/workforce. Men attempt to maintain traditional masculine values through suggesting they do the job better than females; they are more professional or suggesting that it is men's work. These strategies enhance men's career opportunities over women (Cross & Bagilhole, 2002).

It would seem that gender segregation is resilient within the paid labour market, despite changes in society such as globalisation, technological changes, and women's increasing presence within paid labour. Gendered occupational segregation has a detrimental effect on many aspects of women's careers most specifically pay, promotion and career opportunities. The lack of women in the computer games industry, suggests that this gender segregation persists in new industries as well as the older more established ones, despite equal opportunities legislation. It is also apparent that men gain more advantages from their token or minority status compared to women. These advantages include faster promotion, more career opportunities and fewer barriers, suggesting the workplace is still predominately a male domain. This is just a brief overview of gendered occupational segregation to enable readers unfamiliar with the issues some insight as to why we as authors believe it is important for women to be involved in all aspects of the workforce. For a more in-depth discussion of the internal and external factors that can contribute to gendered occupational segregation in the science, engineering and technology sector including the finance sector and construction industry see Prescott and Bogg, 2012. We would now like to turn attention to the computer games industry and the current situation of women working in this male dominated industry.

WOMEN WORKING IN THE COMPUTER GAMES INDUSTRY

Research on women working in the computer games/games industry represents a new and varied area of research for investigating women's career development in new industries and male dominated organisations. Wimmer and Sitnikova (2011) looked at the professional identity of German game workers and found social skills were important due to the team working necessity of the job. Due to the constantly developing technologies, the motivation to develop and learn was essential to the work a finding Dyer–Whiteford and Sharman (2005) also found in their Canadian study. The ideal game worker had a passion for games, followed by high dedication and motivation to work. The most salient reason reported by Wimmer and Sitnikova for game workers to perceive themselves as a part of their profession, was due to their interest in both making and playing games, with an overlap between work and their hobbies. This concept of overlap is echoed by Rapport et al. (2002), in terms of work as primary:

The definition of commitment remains rooted in a traditional concept of the ideal worker as someone for whom work is primary, time to spend at work is unlimited, and the demands

of the family, community and personal life are secondary. (Rapport et al., 2002, p 29, see Shapiro et al., 2008).

Fullerton et al. (2008) argue that more women would be interested in games if more games existed that girls and women liked to play and if work environments could be found that were more supportive of their values and work styles. The authors refer to this as the 'virtuous cycle' "making games that appeal to women and girls attracts more women to work on games, resulting in the creation of more games that appeal to women and girls" (Fullerton et al., 2008, p.141). Research on women working in the games industry is sparse. There is also a paucity of research on women's careers in new industries such as new media, of which the games industry is part. The industry forms part of the creative industries sector as well as the wider ICT and SET sectors, viewed as a "young and rapidly changing technologically driven subsector of the creative industries with significant interactions with the design and software subsectors" (Camicero et al., 2008, p. 37).

The games industry has a pervasive impact upon popular culture, which is influenced by, and influences other media and popular culture including TV, books and films. Despite this, the industry has received little attention from social scientists and there is a paucity of literature in the area. The industry is an important and growing industry with connections with other cultural sectors such as music and film as we have previously highlighted in chapter two. The games industry has accelerated from small firms and individuals programming in their bedrooms to an industry dominated by multinational hardware producers such as Sony and Microsoft (Johns, 2006). According to Johns, the industry has three distinct geographical areas North America, Europe and Japan; producing cultural products distinct to their geographical area. The greatest difference in the nature of games occurs between Japan and the American and European markets. The Japanese games industry is based on comic books, such as Manga, with the games sold in Japan being produced by Japanese producers whereas the other two markets interrelate more (Johns, 2006).

Computer games have become one of the most popular leisure activities for children and adults in Western and Asian societies (Hartmann & Kilmmt, 2006). Additionally, the games industry is a billion-dollar business and its products have become a major part of the media landscape. According to ELSPA (Entertainment and Leisure Software Publishers Association), in 2004 there were a staggering 20.8 million consoles and handheld game consoles in UK homes (Krostoski, 2004). Gaming might be an initial introduction for children to digital technologies and computing. In turn, developing their confidence and skills in their usage; leading to an increased utilisation and interest in a career in computer science and information technology. Although there are some popular discourses which portray computer games as negative, the converse can also be noted, that playing computer games can be associated with some positive outcomes. For example, research has found that in general game

players are more likely to be academically successful, go to University and have better employment prospects (Harris, 2001). Playing games has also been found to help children learn about technologies, mathematics and to play with others (Brand, 2007). However, as Kafai (2006) notes, we need to understand the benefits of learning through games. Kafai also found that regardless of gender, all of the 10-year old children in her research enjoyed making games, which helped them learn. Recently, Hayes (2011) looked at how to engage girls in IT-related learning using The Sims computer game and the virtual world of Teen Second Life. According to Hayes the games start the learning progress, capturing the girls' imagination, enabling them to create and tell stories as well as giving them an understanding of the power of computing. Games introduce girls (and boys) to a wide range of 21st century skills, which may in turn lead them to engaging more in STEM subjects and perhaps choosing a career in STEM. Hayes goes on to list a number of ways games can enhance computational understanding and skills. For example, cheating enables players to gain an understanding of programming language and how codes relate to the game and fan sites enable girls to access mentoring, via more experienced players. We have considered the current situation of women within this industry and discussed why we believe it is important for more females to be attracted to, and remain within the industry. Computer games may be a good way to encourage and attract girls to the industry since gaming can enable the development of IT skills as well as help develop an interest in computers. The next section focuses on segregation within the computer games industry.

GENDERED SEGREGATION IN THE COMPUTER GAMES INDUSTRY

We need an icon that's not Lara Croft! We need our female real-life superstars to go to schools, be interviewed, be in the spotlight, and be exposed. We need initiatives sponsored by big publishers to unapologetically encourage women to enter the games industry, with finances, jobs and in-kind promotion. (E-mail by Aleks Krotowski, as cited in Haines, 2004).

A study by UK based online games magazine MCV found women were segregated within certain roles within the games industry (MCV, 2008). Women within the industry were found as more likely to be working in non-developmental roles such as publishing, marketing, and PR, retail and distribution services, what can be generally classed as traditional female jobs. MCV stated that only 6.9% of developmental roles are filled by women again highlighting the low number of women in core content creation roles. These findings highlight the segregation that occurs within an industry which reinforces women in traditional feminine roles despite working in a male dominant industry (vertical segregation within an industry). Earlier findings in the USA, UK and Canada found the same vertical segregation exists. According to the Gourdin (2005), in the USA when dividing job descriptions by

gender, the only category that comes close to parity is that of 'operations/information technology/human resources'. However, male workers were found to heavily dominate most of the core content creation roles such as production, design, audio, programming and testing. This supports earlier research conducted in the North West of England by Haines (2004), who found that the majority of women in the games industry work in managerial, administrative, marketing and PR roles; with 73% of women working in games, working outside the main jobs of creating games. Haines research found that only 2% of programmers were female, 3% worked in audio, 5% were game designers, 8% production staff and 9% were artists. Similarity in Canada women were found to be disproportionally in administration, marketing and Human Resources (Dyer-Witheford & Sharman, 2005). This segregation, Dyer-Witheford and Sharman (2005) view as a male bias which is limiting the industries market expansion. It would seem that women within the industry have little voice in the content, interaction styles, character representation and the reward systems involved in games (core content creation/developmental roles). All of the core content creation roles affects what is created and how games are perceived. With regards to the wider ICT and SET sectors it has been observed that women tend to work in the softer and less technical areas such as design, rather than the more technical areas such as coding (Poggio, 2000; Panteli et al., 2001). Research would suggest this is also the case within the newer computer games industry, helping to perpetuate and reinforce the industry and the wider ICT/SET sectors as male industries and male domains of both work and play.

According to Kanter (1977) increasing the numbers of women in a working environment will result in a more welcoming working environment for women. However Hirshfield (2010) concluded that more women in a given environment may not necessarily change the dynamics of a male environment, and women may become concentrated and isolated into female-dominated areas and subfields. Previous research on women working in the male dominated games industry seems to support Hirschfield's rather than Kanter's view point. The games industry wants to attract more women to its workforce in the hope of gaining a more diverse gaming audience. However, if future generations of women enter the industry, the industry still may have a gender divide in terms of the roles women occupy. Eccles (1994) suggests that inaccurate and insufficient information about professions is the main reason why young women do not consider or rule out occupations that might fit their self-schema. We posit that the computer games industry could therefore benefit from highlighting the various roles and skills required in the industry as well as the various backgrounds, both educational and occupational, that women who enter the industry come from (Prescott & Bogg, 2011). Another gender difference within the games industry is the disproportionate position of women in senior roles (horizontal segregation). For instance Krotoski (2004) found that only 0.4% of female employees in the UK's

industry are in lead, director or management positions, whilst 1.2% of male employees hold these jobs. Research by Haines (2004), on the other hand, found that nearly a quarter (23%) of senior positions within the twenty UK games companies in her study, were filled by women. However, these senior positions were more often in managerial and marketing roles rather than direct game development roles. Despite the paucity of research in the area, the evidence suggests that both horizontal and vertical segregation exists within the computer games industry as findings from the UK, USA, and Canada suggest. This segregation into specific roles and/or levels can result in women not influencing what games are made and for whom (Prescott & Bogg, 2011). As previously mentioned gendered occupational segregation can have a significant impact on women's careers and lives especially in terms of pay which we would like to now turn our attention too.

THE GENDERED PAY GAP

Gendered occupational segregation is an important issue, especially since segregation into different occupations remains a key factor contributing to the gender gap in earnings (Forth, 2002). According to the Guardian newspaper, British women suffer the largest pay gap in Europe (Revill, 2007) and internationally, women's wages have been found unequal to men's (Weichselbaumer & Winter-Ebmer, 2005). When women are segregated into certain jobs, those jobs usually pay less, have fewer opportunities for progression, less job autonomy, and less authority within an organisation. Earlier research found that women employed in male dominated occupations actually have higher lifetime earnings than women in other occupations (England et al., 1988). Cotter, Hermsen, and Vanneman (2003) in an American study looked at the impact of occupational segregation on gender and race and found that occupational segregation particularly impacted the earnings of African American women. The study found that for all women, higher earnings resulted from working in a male dominated occupation.

As mentioned earlier games development is part of the UK's knowledge industry (Oxford Economics report, 2008). The high skills of the industries developers is reflected in the above average earnings of those employed in the industry, which the report suggests to be £30k per annum, compared to the UK average of £25k per annum. Average UK earnings in 2008 for games professionals ranged from 18k to 80k depending on the role and the number of years' experience (Oxford Economic, 2008). In Canada according to the Vancouver Film School (VFS, 2009) report, game designers and artists earn $25,000 more per annum than average Canadian salaries. The report went on to state that in 2007, salaries for game programmers and producers were double average earnings in Canada. Both reports highlight the monetary gain of working in a developmental role within the industry. The wider ICT industry within the UK has been criticized for having a gender pay gap (Tattersall, Keogh, & Richardson, 2007), with one of the reasons put forward for this pay gap, due to what has been termed 'salary secrets'. There is evidence that

a gender pay gap exists within the industry, in that, women earn on average £7,126 per year less than men (Krotoski, 2004). In America, according to an IGDA (2004) report, women earn an average $9,000 less a year than their male counterparts, despite having worked in the industry for a similar number of years. However, more recent research by the online computer games magazine, MCV in January 2009. MCV (2009) found that, on average women in the games industry earn £2,000 more than their male counterparts, conflicting with previous research in the area.

REASONS FOR FEMALE UNDERREPRESENTATION WITHIN THE INDUSTRY

An educated, technologically competent labour force is the basis of the Canadian industry's growth, but that this creativity is now constrained by sexist hiring patterns and intensifying labour-management tensions. (Dyer-Witheford & Sharman, 2005, p. 188)

Research has found a number of reasons why women are underrepresented in the games industry, especially in the developmental core creation roles. One of the main reasons for the lack of women working in the computer games industry and other male dominated industries and sectors such as ICT and SET is due to the masculine working culture and employment practices that appear persistent in such industries. Dyer-Witheford and Sharman (2005) suggest that the Canadian games industry is constrained by such practices.

Practices inherent to male dominated industries and occupations including the computer games industry include the long hour's culture, the potential need to relocate and the lack of flexible working practices (Prescott & Bogg, 2010). One strategy for increasing the diversity of games is to increase the diversity of those involved in all aspects of game design and production. This is apparent from the research and findings previously discussed throughout the book.

What the games industry needs is to not only increase its diversity, but also change the organisational structures in order to maintain a more diverse workforce (Consalvo, 2008). Combining work with other roles especially motherhood, has been viewed as a major disadvantage to women in the workplace. Family demands may interfere with women's careers, leading them to perhaps refuse overtime, rearrange their working day, or refuse extra work, all of which can be viewed as being less committed to the job. Women have been found to have more work-family conflict than men (Innstrand et al., 2009). Women's extra domestic responsibilities can create work overload, effecting women's experience of work and possibly reducing their career promotional opportunities. These issues are especially prominent for women with or considering having children. It has been acknowledged that there is a lack of women with children working in the games industry as there is in the wider ICT and SET sectors (Deuze et al., 2004; Haines, 2004; Krotoski, 2004; Gourdin, 2005; Consalvo, 2008; Prescott & Bogg, 2010). However, it is unclear from the limited research into women working in the computer games industry whether women who enter the industry do not want children or they do not have children due to their careers.

WORK LIFE BALANCE

Health problems due to working excessive hours, is well documented and women are generally more disadvantaged than men by working long hours. Women working long hours are much more likely to report poor health than men and the physical and psychological effects of stress, generally worse for women than for men (Kodz et al., 2008; Work Life Balance Centre, 2007). The issue of long hours appears to be especially prominent in male dominated occupations, such as the ICT sector (Valenduc et al., 2004) and computer games industry (Consalvo, 2008; Prescott & Bogg, 2010). It has been suggested that the number of hours a person works and a culture of presenteesim (being seen in the work environment) show commitment to your job and your organisation (Simpson 1998; Newell & Dopson, 1996). The long-hour's culture within the gaming industry, has been acknowledged by the International Game Developers Association (IGDA, Quality of Life White Paper, 2004). The paper reports that three out of five developers work 46 hours or more in a normal working week and workers can spend anywhere from 65 to 80 plus hours per week at crunch time. Long hour's is an issue that stems throughout the ICT sector (Valenduc, 2004). Crunch time within the games industry refers to when a game is due to be released, a notorious time for extremely long hours. Crunch time is viewed as being ingrained in the work culture of the industry, with passion viewed as the main reason why employees do the long hours. According to research by Consalvo (2008) the long hours culture and crunch time are the biggest challenges to women in the games industry. Consalvo (2008) suggests that women, like their male counterparts, also have a passion for playing games. It is this passion which although viewed as a necessity to work in game development, may in turn deter women not interested in playing games from entering the industry. Consalvo (2008) viewed passion as problematic in that: 'the ideal worker is constructed as someone possessing a 'passion for games' and that passion is used to help maintain work practices that may ultimately kill the passion' (p. 186). Passion therefore leads to acceptance of long hours; this ultimately can lead to resentment of the working situation. Our research found that the women games developers found crunch time a dreaded, but somehow unavoidable part of the job;

I mean generally the hours are what you would expect, but sometimes it's just madness, those times you just get on with it....One time I remember we hit a major, major problem at the eleventh hour and it was just a period of work, work, work, eating on the job, lots of pizza [laughs], sleep when you could and get on with it. It's not just here though it's the job, its wherever you worked it would happen.

Even the traditional 9 to 5 work role can be problematic for women and men who have to combine work with family responsibilities. This includes those with children or carer commitments. Flexible working has met with some employer resistance; indeed employers show little enthusiasm for employee flexibility, unless they gain benefit (Hyman, Scholarios, & Baldry, 2005). Employers have expressed anxieties and a general reluctance, to introduce flexible work arrangements. This includes concerns that wide availability of flexible working policies will produce an unlimited demand, in addition to fears that some employees will take advantage of such policies, resulting in reduced productivity. Research conducted by Kotz et al. (2008), found that a third of employers reported that women returning from maternity leave, who wanted to reduce their full-time hours to part-time, would not be able to continue in their existing role job or level of seniority. However, there are benefits to employers in introducing flexible working arrangements. Flexible working arrangements facilitate individuals, particularly women to find a better balance, between their needs, their family or carer duties and their work role commitments. In terms of the games industry, this would assist in the retention of trained competent staff. Experienced women for example, may leave due to conflicts between work and home. This is especially the case in relation to our research, where the few women with children cited conflict between home and work and those considering having children felt they might have to leave the industry for more routine and order;

The job is what I always wanted to do, but I really am not sure yet, as to how it would fit in with the demands of family life.

Flexible working can take many forms and can relate to how working hours are organised during the day, week or longer. In the games industry women in particular would benefit from flexible working options, this would aid recruitment and retention. Flexible working can include part time working, such as starting later and finishing earlier enabling parents with childcare responsibilities, time to care for children. Women with children may find term-time working equally beneficial. The reduced annual hours, often would mean unpaid leave during school holidays. However, a benefit is reduction in childcare costs. Flexi-time work is another potential aid for retention, as employees work within essential core periods, and then have some level of flexibility to work the remaining hours. Job-sharing is another flexible option; two employees share one work role. However, this would depend on the feasibility in games development roles. Home-work is another option that may help carers manage work and home roles and therefore assist women in particular. The ability to continue in the work role would be the ideal opportunity to maintain career development during a period of increased family commitments. In addition, finding an appropriate balance during times when non-work commitments may increase, such as childcare or caring responsibilities, retains workers. This will have a significant impact on women, who predominantly assume the care-giving role. An effective method that could potentially increase the number of women in the industry could be the introduction of more flexible working practices such as part time working. Part time work has

been found to be a rarity within the industry (Prescott & Bogg, 2010). We found it was almost accepted by the women, that part time jobs were the exception and rare. As one of the women in our research voiced;

Why aren't there more part time jobs, I don't know, they hardly exist in this Industry], I think bosses think they won't get the work out of you, or the team wouldn't see you as committed.

The lack of part-time working is more detrimental to women's careers, women are more likely than men to work part-time, particularly if they have dependent children (38% of women, compared with 4% of men with dependent children (ONS, 2008). Despite women's increasing participation within the UK workforce, in 2008 almost half of women's jobs were part time, compared with approximately one in six of men's (ONS, 2008). Working part time is often viewed as a solution in managing the coexisting roles of work and motherhood for many women with dependent children having some flexibility and control over your work hours can significantly reduce the negative impact that long hours can have. However, due to the ingrained working conditions of crunch time and the fact that part time work is not common practice within the industry, these issues may therefore deter women from entering, and or remaining in the industry.

Another flexibility issue is the potential need to relocate for one's job. Looking at the professional identity of game workers, Deuze, Martin, and Allen (2007) reported that relocation was a reason as to why the industry is male dominated and does not appeal to women. Indeed, in our research with female game workers, we found more than a quarter of female game workers would not relocate for their work and almost a quarter were unsure if they would (Prescott & Bogg, 2010). According to the Oxford economic report (2008), relocation is also an important issue due to the possible decline of UK games companies and other expensive countries in favour of cheaper countries. For instance, the report suggests that games companies in Canada and Singapore have been targeting individuals from more expensive countries to relocate. In support of the Oxford Economic report (2008) the BBC news in the UK reported on the 8th October 2011 that Britain's games industry is at risk of a brain drain, recommending the industry to nurture its talent in order to prevent people relocating to games companies overseas (Lee, 2011). Of course relocation becomes a more difficult issue for workers with partners, children and/or other caring responsibilities. This can equally be viewed as a gendered issue since research suggests women are more likely to move for their male partner jobs than men will for their female partners job (Bogg, 2007). In the industry, the negative working practices which have a particularly negative impact on attracting and retaining women within the industry include:

- Long-hours culture
- Crunch time
- Flexible working issues
- Potential need to relocate

FEMALE IMPACT: BENEFITS TO THE INDUSTRY AND SOCIETY

Creating and maintaining a more diverse workforce, it seems, could result in game that are more gender inclusive, and that better reflect game play styles and content that would interest a broader population of gamers. (Consalvo, 2008, p. 177)

Sadie Plant (1998) noted that women are an important part of the history of both the use and development of technologies. Sadie Plant was talking about women in the wider ICT sector, however it seems that women have been and still are overlooked in the games industry too. Female developers and designers of early and influential games are often overlooked. Dovey and Kennedy (2006) name three overlooked women; Roberta Williams and Kings Quest (a game produced by Sierra Online), Donna Bailey and Centipede (1981 game for Atari) and Carol Shaw Video Checkers and 3D Tic Tac Toe for Atari, as three early computer game developers. Some women are being recognised for their achievement within the industry. In 2004 the first Interactive British Academy of Film and Television Award (BAFTA) for outstanding new talent was awarded to Paulina Bozek, the producer of Singstar (Krotoski, 2004). In 2004 the annual Women in Games conferences were established in the UK, USA and New Zealand to promote the fact that women play and are involved in the industry. However although the Women in Games conference is viewed positively by the industry is does highlight the minority status of women within the industry.

It is however being recognised that female game teams produce games that appeal to female gamers (Consalvo, 2008; Fullerton et al., 2008). Game design teams that have more women in key design and production roles have produced products female gamers tend to enjoy. For example, Maxis the makers of The Sims, which is one of the top selling PC games of all time and which is estimated to have between 40-50% female player base, has a workforce of 50% female designers and 40% female producers. It has been noted, that The Sims development team has more women than average teams (Fullerton et al., 2008). With reference to The Sims, Jenkins (2001) suggests that the unconscious decisions made by the male and female team at Maxis produce a different game than that made by an all or predominately male design team. Another example is Singstar, which is a game that is social, and competitive. Singstar has sold 15 million units, has a player base of approximately 60% female, and the development team is 33% female with a female executive producer (Bozek, P. Keynote speaker day 1 of the Women in Games 2008 conference, 10-12 September 2008). The industry it seems creates a feedback loop, which affects games content. The main premise of this book is to highlight the need for more women in the production and development of computer games, which could be extremely important for creating more games which females and in turn creating more female gamers interested in computing careers. As reported earlier, findings from the IGDA survey (Gourdin, 2005)

found that the majority of respondents felt that 'a diverse workforce has a direct impact (broad appeal, quality etc.) on games produced'. Female respondents agreed more and more strongly to this statement as they did to the statement 'workforce diversity is important to the future success of the game industry'. There was a difference to these two statements by ethnicity in that non-white respondents compared to white respondents agreed more and more strongly to both statements.

WORKING PRACTICES

There are a number of working practices that are gendered and potentially deter women from entering and remaining in the industry. Our qualitative international research with women artists, producers and programmers from the United Kingdom and the United States found that the women got involved in the industry via friends or family, moved from other entertainment or following Higher education. They enjoyed working in a cutting-edge industry that was challenging, creative, relaxed and fun. In relation to the characteristics needed to progress in the games industry, the women reflected that good self-esteem, being proactive, patient and 'knowing the right' people were important. Many women said that if they were to start their careers again, they would still choose their current career path. Of the women who thought they might leave the industry, their thoughts centred on combining having a family with the hours and limited availability of part time work.

All the women felt the industry would benefit from more women in it and would help change the image of the industry as a male domain and games perceived as 'for the boys only';

At the moment people are 'oh let's make Barbie' or the box pink, ok that's going to appeal to a very small section of little 8 year old girls and until the games industry grows up and realises women aren't a distinct group of people and they are just people, they aren't going to get a handle on it.

The women had mixed views as to whether they felt the industry was becoming more visible and appealing to women. Some felt that it was becoming more appealing and cited reasons such as the quantity of consoles in the home helped increase visibility and accessibility of games to women. The women felt the industry could help by making less gender specific games, and more games that appeal to females;

Well making them less gender specific like at the moment we are talking about making a racing game and we were talking in broad terms of what the reward would be when you win the race and part of the reward would be you get to have these hot chicks in hot pants and that is very gender specific.

Historically before 'Tomb Raider' [computer game] came out people were saying you can't have a woman protagonist, blokes aren't going to want to play that, it's a complete none starter and obviously it turned into a world wide phenomena.

The women thought it was different for women than men working in the computer games industry with views that stated 'you a lot of attention' to 'people are surprised to see me and don't know how to react to me'. The women also felt that generally there was a disparity in the numbers of men and women in the games industry. Reasons given for the disparity between the numbers of men and women in the industry surrounded the perception that men like and play games, therefore men wanted to make games;

Lara Croft [from Tomb Raider game], she is an example of how the guys in the industry see women, and all their characters tend to look like her and it's not until I come onto the characters team, I sort of made the women a little bit less stereotypical, they actually look like a normal looking women, with maybe a little bit of hips and a little midriff. But they are looking more like a woman now than Lara Croft, whose proportions were all wrong and I think that's where you see men being quite sexist and stuff. There is quite a lot of immaturity in them, they seem to be more immature in the games industry, a lot of the guys.

Other reasons cited were that computers were viewed by many as a male domain, women not applying as much as men to join the industry and the perception that generally men were 'naturally' better at maths and physics. Some women felt it was a 'boy's thing' generally and many cited the long hours made it less appealing for women.

Women also felt that girls were not encouraged to do technical things. Interestingly some women felt that being a woman in a predominantly male organisation got them noticed, which could be a positive thing or make them a target for prejudice. The women described how the genders had different approaches to problem solving which were beneficial to the organisation.

In general, our women felt the environments they worked in were masculine to some extent, yet many thought the environment was more 'geeky', than specifically masculine. A small number of women mentioned that pornography and 'inappropriate' materials were standard and that women needed a 'tough skin' to not be offended and 'fit in';

On a stupid point in some companies, they actually have a list of people they have made cry and you get double points if it is a girl.

In relation to personal characteristics to remain in the industry the women cited the need to be willing to work long hours as necessary, to be assertive and get used to working in a male dominated environment. To become 'one of the boys, to fit in' and not be a 'not girlie girl', was a common view;

I was not picked to go on a research trip because the lead wanted to be with his mates and they didn't want a girl there, as they would be wanting to go to strip clubs and stuff.

Men can be immature and sexist in the industry; they like to think all women should be like Lara Croft, women in the industry make the characters less stereotypical and more real.

The women felt that the games industry was still perceived as a male domain and therefore other women would not necessarily view it as a potential career. However, the women felt the games industry was changing and becoming more open to women as a career;

The industry is growing up and becoming more responsible.

CONCLUSION

There has been little research conducted on women who work in the computer games industry with the exception of Haines (2004), Krotoski (2004), and more recently Consalvo (2008). Through a survey and interviews with female game workers, Haines (2004) found that what women in the industry wanted mostly was more encouragement and awareness for young girls to enter the industry and develop a career in gaming. Haines also found that similar to other working environments such as academia, women wanted flexible working hours, mentoring, more role models, more women in senior positions and benefits of interest to women such as childcare as well as more games being developed women like. According to an IGDA (2004) report, more than a third of developers expected to leave the industry within five years and half said they were likely to leave within ten years. The main reasons for this desire to leave the industry by both male and female respondents was due to working practices such as the long hour's culture and the lack of flexible working practices available to employers in the industry. As this chapter has highlighted, these working practices need to acknowledged by the industry and subsequently addressed. There are human resource policies within studies (Gourdin, 2005), however more work needs to be done in this area to address the reasons why women are a minority within the industry. It should also be acknowledged that men would also benefit from human resource policies, which improve the workplace environment and increase employees work life balance as well as women.

It is evident that in the workplace women face a number of barriers that appear to be more prevalent in male dominated occupations and access to leadership roles. Societal expectations and stereotypes play an important

Table 1. Female games workers: The key issues

Gender differences and Reasons for the Gender Divide in Computer Games	Core Issues Involved	How May the Issue be Addressed
Female game workers	• Like the computer games themselves, the games industry is male dominated. • Women are currently underrepresented in all aspects of the computer games industry globally. In the UK it is reported that women represent just 4% of the computer games industries workforce. Similarly low figures are found in other countries. • Working practices within the industry are gendered, deterring women from entering and remaining in the industry. Such gendered working practices include the long hour's culture, the potential need to relocate and the lack of flexible working which are barriers in particular to women with children and other caring responsibilities. • Both vertical and horizontal segregation exists within the industry. Women tend to be concentrated in female roles within the industry such as human resources and administration and they have little representation in the core content creation roles including design and production. Due to the lack of women within the overall industry there is a low representation of females in more senior roles within the industry. • Segregation into specific roles and/or levels can result in women not influencing what games are made and for whom.	• Research on women working in the games industry is sparse. More research is needed to consider the barriers and drivers of women in this male dominated industry. • The industry like the wider ICT and SET sector needs to eradicate the image of being a male domain in order to attract a more gender diverse workforce. • The industry needs to consider ways in how to reduce the effects of the working practices in order to both attract and retain a more diverse workforce. • Promote initiatives such as flexible working. • For retention ask women workers what they need. • Reduce were possible the expectation of long hours as the 'norm' or regular occurrence. • The computer games industry could benefit from highlighting the various roles and skills required in the industry as well as the various backgrounds, both educational and occupational, that people who enter the industry come from. • Women who are in the industry especially those in core content creation roles could act as role models for girls considering a career within the industry.
Female impact of working in the industry	• Females make games that both males and females, but specifically females enjoy playing. • Female game designers and developers are often overlooked for their achievements and contribution to the industry. • Female game designers help produce more gender inclusive games.	• More females playing games could potentially increase the number of females interested in making games. • More female game developers have the potential in making the industry and the games developed attract a more diverse audience. • Female game developers increase the potential impact of the industry. • There is a need for greater gender neutral game design. • There is a need for a more inclusive industry.

part in the careers of men and women. What constitutes appropriate behaviour, based on gender is a theme that runs throughout the literature on gendered occupational segregation and women working in the ICT sector. Women tend to leave the SET sectors throughout education, resulting in a lack of women in the sector workforce. Women in computer games development, face the same issues, resulting in a paucity of women in the sector.

The aim of this chapter was to gain an understanding of the position of women working in the games industry. The chapter also provided the reader with a brief overview of the impact this horizontal and vertical segregation can have to the industry and female game workers. As we have seen, gendered occupational segregation impacts on individuals, especially women, society and the economy, as well as specific industries. As this chapter has shown, more females working within the industry could potentially benefit the industry through the success of games made by female teams and through making games that appeal to a much wider demographic of gamers. The next chapter will discuss the findings from our international research with women working in games development in more detail.

REFERENCES

Betz, N., & Fitzgerald, L. F. (1987). *The career psychology of women*. New York: Academic Press.

Bogg, J. (2007). Dr Jekyll & Ms Hide: Where are the women in science? & what would attract them from other sectors? *Nature, 4470*, 114. doi:10.1038/nj7140-114a

Brand, J. E. (2007). *Interactive Australia 2007: Facts about the Australian computer & video game industry*. Queensland, Australia: Bond University.

Camicero, L., Cardoso, E., Dempster, A., Liu, K., Mould, O., Pezzana, S. P., & Roodhouse, S. (2008). *Game on! A report on the interactive leisure sorftware subsector in London*. London: University of the Arts London.

Chalk, L. M., Meara, N., & Day, J. D. (1994). Possible selves & occupational choices. *Journal of Career Assessment, 2*(4), 364–383. doi:10.1177/106907279400200404

Consalvo, M. (2008). Crunched by passion: women game developers & workplace challenges. In *Beyond Barbie & Mortal Kombat: New perspectives on gender & gaming* (pp. 177–192). Cambridge, MA: The MIT Press.

Cotter, D. A., Hermsen, J. A., & Vanneman, R. (2003). The effects of occupational gender segregation across race. *The Sociological Quarterly, 44*(1), 17–36. doi:10.1111/j.1533-8525.2003.tb02389.x

Cross, S., & Bagilhole, B. (2002). Girls' jobs for the boys? Men, masculinity & non-traditional occupations. *Gender, Work and Organization, 9*(2), 204–226. doi:10.1111/1468-0432.00156

Deuze, M., Martin, C. B., & Alen, C. (2007). The professional identity of gameworkers. *Convergence: The International Journal of Research into New Media Technologies, 13*(4), 335–353. doi:10.1177/1354856507081947

Dovey, J., & Kennedy, H. W. (2006). *Game culture: Computer games as new media*. Berkshire, UK: Open University Press.

Dyer-Whitheford, N., & Sharman, Z. (2005). The political economy of Canada's video & computer game industry. *Canadian Journal of Communication, 20*, 187–210.

Eccles, J. (1994). Understanding women's educational & occupational choices. *Psychology of Women Quarterly, 18*, 585–609. doi:10.1111/j.1471-6402.1994.tb01049.x

England, P., Farkas, G., Kilbourne, B. S., & Dou, T. (1988). Explaining occupational sex segregation & wages: Findings from a model with fixed effects. *American Sociological Review, 53*, 544–558. doi:10.2307/2095848

ESA. (2010). *Entertainment software association fact sheet*. Retrieved from http://www.theesa.com/facts/gamer_data.php

Flanagan, M. (2003). Next level women's digital activism through gaming. In *Digital media revisited: Theoretical & conceptual innovation in digital domains* (pp. 359–388). Cambridge, MA: MIT.

Forth, J. (2002). The gender pay gap: The research evidence. In *Gender research forum*. London: National Institute of Economic & Social Research.

Freeman, A. (2007). *London's creative sector working paper 22*. London: GLA. Retrieved from http://www.london.gov.uk/mayor/economic_unit/docs/wp_22_creative.pdf

Fullerton, T., Fron, J., Pearce, C., & Morie, J. (2008). Getting girls into the game: Towards a virtous cycle. In *Beyond Barbie & Mortal Kombat: New perspectives on gender & gaming* (pp. 161–176). Cambridge, MA: The MIT Press.

Gill, R. (2007). *Technobohemians or the new cybertariat? New media workers in Amsterdam a decade after the web*. Amsterdam: The Institute of Network Cultures.

Gourdin, A. (2005). *Game developers demographics: An exploration of workforce diversity*. International Game Developers Association. Retrieved from http://archives.igda.org/diversity/IGDA_DeveloperDemographics_Oct05.pdf

Haines, L. (2004). *Why are there so few women in games?* Research for Media Training North West September. Retrieved from http://archives.igda.org/women/MTNW_Women-in-Games_Sep04.pdf

Harris, J. (2001). *The effect of computer games on young children -A review of the research*. London: Home Office Research, Development & Statistics Directorate. doi:10.1037/e668282007-001

Hartmann, T., & Klimmt, C. (2006). Gender & computer games: Exploring females' dislikes. *Journal of Computer-Mediated Communication, 11*, 910–931. doi:10.1111/j.1083-6101.2006.00301.x

Hayes, E. (2011). The Sims as a catalyst for girls' IT learning. *International Journal of Gender. Science & Technology, 3*(1), 121–147.

Hirshfield, L. E. (2010). She won't make me feel dumb: Identity threat in a male-dominated discipline. *International Journal of Gender. Science & Technology, 2*(1), 6–24.

Hyman, J., Scholarios, D., & Baldry, C. (2005). Getting on or getting by? Employee flexibility & coping strategies for home & work. *Work, Employment and Society, 19*(4), 705–725. doi:10.1177/0950017005058055

IGDA. (2004). *Quality of life white paper.* International Game Developers Association.

Innstrand, S. T., Langballe, E. M., Falkum, E., Espnes, G. A., & Aasland, O. G. (2009). Gender-specific perceptions of four dimensions of the work/family interaction. *Journal of Career Assessment, 17*(4), 402–416. doi:10.1177/1069072709334238

Jenkins, H. (2001). *From Barbie to Mortal Kombat: Further reflections.* Retrieved from http://culturalpolicy.uchicago.edu/papers/2001-video-games/jenkins.html

Johns, J. (2006). Video games production networks: Value capture, power relations & embeddedness. *Journal of Economic Geography, 6,* 151–180. doi:10.1093/jeg/lbi001

Kafai, Y. B. (2006). Playing & making games for learning: Instructionist & constructionist perspectives for games studies. *Games and Culture, 1*(1), 36–40. doi:10.1177/1555412005281767

Kanter, R. (1977). *Men & women of the corporation.* New York: Basic Books.

Kodz, J., Harper, H., & Dench, S. (2008). *Work-life balance: Beyond the rhetoric.* Institute of Employment Studies.

Krotoski, A. (2004). *Chicks & joysticks: An exploration of women & gaming. Entertainment & Leisure Software Publishers Association.* ELSPA.

Lee, D. (2011). UK 'must act to solve games industry brain drain'. *BBC News Technology.* Retrieved from http://www.bbc.co.uk/news-technology-15188385?

McRobbie, A. (1998). *British fashion design: Rag trade or image industry?* London: Routledge. doi:10.4324/9780203168011

MCV. (2008). *Salary survey.* Retrieved from http://www.mcvuk.com/news/29399/Industry-salary-survey

MCV. (2009). *Women earn more than men in the UK games industry.* Retrieved from http://www.mcvuk.com/news/32964/Women-earn-more-than-men-in-the-UK-games-industry

Miller, L., Neathey, F., Pollard, E., & Hill, D. (2004). *Occupational segregation, gender gaps & skill gaps.* Equal Opportunities Commission.

Newell, H., & Dopson, S. (1996). Muddle in the middle: Organizational restructuring & middle management careers. *Personnel Review, 25*(4), 4–20. doi:10.1108/00483489610123191

ONS. (2008). Statistical bulletin August 2008. In L. F. Statistics (Ed.), *Labour force statistics*. Office for National Statistics.

Oxford Economics. (2008). *The economic contribution of the UK games industry: Final report*. Retrieved from http://www.oef.com/FREE/PDFS/GAMESIMPACT.PDF

Panteli, N., Stack, J., & Ramsay, H. (2001). Gendered patterns in computing work in the late 1990s'. *New Technology, Work and Employment*, *16*(1), 3–16. doi:10.1111/1468-005X.00073

Perrone, K. M., Wright, S. L., & Jackson, Z. V. (2009). Traditional & non-traditional gender roles & work family interface for men & women. *Journal of Career Development*, *36*(1), 8–24. doi:10.1177/0894845308327736

Plant, S. (1998). *Zeros & ones: Digital women & the new technoculture*. London: Fourth Estate.

Poggio, B. (2000). Between bytes ad bricks: Gender culture in work contexts. *Economic and Industrial Democracy*, *21*(3), 381–402. doi:10.1177/0143831X00213006

Pollard, E., Connor, H., & Hunt, W. (2008). *Mapping provision & participation in post-graduate creative art & design*. London: National Arts Learning Network.

Prescott, J., & Bogg, J. (2010). The computer games industry: women's experiences of work role in a male dominated environment. In *Women in engineering, science & technology: Education & career challenges*. Hershey, PA: IGI Global. doi:10.4018/978-1-61520-657-5.ch007

Prescott, J., & Bogg, J. (2011). Segregation in a male dominated industry: Women working in the computer games industry. *International Journal of Gender. Science & Technology*, *3*(1), 205–227.

Prescott, J., & Bogg, J. (2012). *Gendered occupational differences in science, engineering, & technology careers*. Hershey, PA: IGI Global. doi:10.4018/978-1-4666-2107-7

Rapoport, R., Bailyn, L., Fletcher, J. K., & Pruitt, B. H. (2002). *Beyond work-family balance: Advancing gender equity & workplace performance*. San Francisco, CA: Jossey Bass.

Revill, J. (2007, September 9). Pregnancy 'forcing 30,000 out of work' new study reveals British women suffer largest pay gap in Europe. *The Observer*.

Simpson, R. (1998). Presenteeism, power & organisational change: Long hours as a career barrier & the impact on the working lives of women managers. *British Journal of Management Communication Quarterly*, *9*, 37–50.

Simpson, R. (2004). Masculinity at work: The experiences of men in female dominated occupations. *Work, Employment and Society, 18*(2), 349–368. doi:10.1177/09500172004042773

Skillset. (2006). *Skillset: Workforce survey 2006*. London: The Sector Skills Council for the Audio Visual Industries.

Skillset. (2008). Retrieved from http://www.skillset.org/skillset/press/releases/article_6286_1.asp

Skillset. (2009). *2009 employment census: The results of the seventh census of the creative media industries December 2010*. The Sector Skills Council for Creative Media.

Tattersall, A., Keogh, C., & Richardson, H. (2007). *The gender pay gap in the ICT industry*. Salford, UK: University of Salford.

Taylor, C. J. (2010). Occupational sex composition & the gendered availability of workplace support. *Gender & Society, 24*(2), 189–212. doi:10.1177/0891243209359912

Thewlis, M., Miller, L., & Neathey, F. (2004). *Advancing women in the workplace: Statistical analysis*. Manchester, UK: Equal Opportunities Commission.

Valenduc, G., et al. (2004). *Widening women's work in information & communication technology*. European Commission. Retrieved from http://www.ftu-namur.org/fichiers/D12-print.pdf

Vancouver Film School (VFS). (2009). *The game industry now & in the future 2010: Industry facts, trends & outlook*. Vancouver, Canada: Vancouver Film School.

Weeden, K. A., & Grusky, D. B. (2005). The case for a new class map. *American Journal of Sociology, 111*, 141–212. doi:10.1086/428815

Weichselbaumer, D., & Winter-Ebmer, R. (2005). A meta-analysis of the international gender wage gap. *Journal of Economic Surveys, 19*, 483–511. doi:10.1111/j.0950-0804.2005.00256.x

Wimmer, J., & Sitnikova, T. (2011). The professional identity of gameworkers revisited: A qualitative inquiry on the case study of German professionals. In *Proceedings of DiGRA 2011 Conference: Think Design Play*. DiGRA.

Women & Equality Unit. (2005). *Women & men in the workplace*. Equal Opportunities Commission.

Work Life Balance Centre. (2007). *The twenty four seven survey 2007*. Work Life Balance Centre.

KEY TERMS AND DEFINITIONS

Crunch Time: A period of time near the end of the project when exceptionally long hours are required by staff in order to meet deadlines and get the game out on time.

Female Game Workers: Females who work in the computer games industry, especially in the developmental roles more traditionally occupied by men.

Flexible Working: practices that facilitate achieving a satisfactory work-life balance such as part time working and working from home.

Gendered Occupational Segregation: The representation that some jobs are viewed as male and traditionally undertaken by men and other jobs are viewed as female jobs and therefore traditionally done by women.

Horizontal Segregation: A term to refer to men and women undertaking certain jobs. Some jobs are viewed as traditionally male jobs, such as engineering, whereas other jobs are viewed as traditionally female jobs, such as teaching or nursing.

Long Hours: Culture of long hours that may be used to demonstrate career commitment.

Pay Gap: The difference in pay experienced by the genders despite having similar skills and experience to fulfil the roles; women are still at a major disadvantage when it comes to pay.

Vertical Segregation: Women are more likely to be concentrated at the lower end of the career ladder even in jobs that are viewed as traditionally non-female.

Work-Life Balance: The balance between work and other life or role commitments.

Chapter 7
The Experience of Women Game Developers

ABSTRACT

This chapter considers the position of women working in computer games through the voices of over 500 women from the international research. The chapter highlights the problems and opportunities of game work, especially pertinent in attracting and retaining women within the industry. It discusses women's personal experiences of working in the game industry and career factors related to women's experiences working in the computer games industry, including career motivation, person-environment fit, and job satisfaction. The chapter also identifies career factors in the computer game industry, such as career barriers and the drivers that help enhance the careers of women in this and other male-dominated industries.

INTRODUCTION

Throughout our book, we have illustrated the magnitude of the industry, including the industries economic, cultural and technological impact and the previous chapter highlighted the underrepresentation of women in the computer games industry, in both the workforce of the industry generally and within core developmental roles specifically. The computer games industry has a significant impact on the culture, technology and the media landscape and women should be involved in all aspects of the industry, especially games development. Research into the experiences of women working in the games industry and

DOI: 10.4018/978-1-4666-4534-9.ch007

other male dominated sectors, enables those industries to alter working practices in ways that not only attract, but also retain a more diverse workforce. Career motivation, person-environment fit, self-efficacy, self-esteem, work satisfaction, career factors and life issues are all important constructs when looking at the career and career development of women. This chapter will discuss these constructs and the implications for women working in the games industry. The women game developers in this chapter form part of our international research study conducted between 2008 and 2011, more than 500 women shared their experiences of working in the games industry.

CAREER MOTIVATION OF WOMEN IN THE COMPUTER GAMES INDUSTRY

People experience the same work conditions in different ways and can react quite differently to situations based on personal characteristics and attributes. Career motivation is a psychological process enacted from both within the individual, as well as external to the individual. There are two main types of motivation: intrinsic and extrinsic. Intrinsic motivation refers to motivation, due to personal reasons, such as an interest in and enjoyment of an activity. Whereas, extrinsic motivation refers to the individual being motivated by external or instrumental reasons, such as rewards. Thomas, Jansen, and Tymon (1997) suggest that the positive experiences of intrinsic motivation enables individuals to become involved, committed and energised by their work. According to the authors, intrinsic mo-

tivation consists of four components: feelings of meaningfulness, choice, competence and progress. Combined, these four components make up a set of intrinsic rewards deemed necessary to produce and sustain empowerment (Thomas, Jansen, & Tymon, 1997). Intrinsic motivation has been viewed important in career self-management (Quigley & Tymon, 2006). The cognitive evaluation theory put forward by Deci and Ryan (1985) suggest that self-determination and competence are the hallmark of intrinsic motivation. Early theorists of intrinsic and extrinsic motivation tended to view them as opposing constructs. In that, individual intrinsic motivation will decrease to the extent extrinsic motivation increases (Lepper & Greene, 1978). However, there are some theorists who suggest that intrinsic and extrinsic motivation coexist (Deci & Ryan, 1985; Amabile et al., 1994). For instance, Amabile et al. (1994) developed the work preference inventory in order to assess individual differences in both intrinsic and extrinsic motivations of adults and students. They suggested that the main elements of intrinsic motivation are self-determination, competence, task involvement, curiosity, enjoyment, and interest. The main elements of extrinsic motivation are concerns with competition, evaluation, recognition, money or other tangible incentives and constraints by others. We think that both motivations can be strong, salient and stable to the individual and not just due to the social context.

It has been suggested, that women place less importance on career attributes associated with senior/management roles such as money, prestige, advancement and power

(Eddleston et al., 2006). However, results from our research with women games developers would suggest women in the games industry differ. The female game workers were highly motivated by both external (extrinsic motivation) and internal (intrinsic motivation) rewards, indicating women in games do place importance on money, prestige etc. as they do to internal rewards. This is important as despite the games industry being viewed as a male domain, women are still intrinsically motivated by what they do. This finding adds weight to the 'passion for games' premise put forward by Consalvo (2008). This is important for encouraging more women to move into male dominated occupations. Previous work on intrinsic motivation, suggests individuals who are intrinsically motivated become involved, committed and energised by their work (Thomas, Jansen, & Tymon, 1997). It would appear this was the case for the women in our research. Interestingly, intention to stay in the industry in five years time had no significant effect on work motivation. This is an encouraging, yet perhaps a surprising finding, since even for the women who do not wish to remain in the games industry they are still highly motivated. This is especially surprising with regard to intrinsic motivation, as one would expect the 'passion for games' and internal motivations to be impacted if an individual intended to leave the industry (any industry not just the games industry). Some researchers suggest that women place less importance on career attributes associated with senior/management roles such as money, prestige, advancement and power (Eddleston et al., 2006). However, results from our research suggest women in the games industry differ and are highly motivated by both external (extrinsic motivation) and internal (intrinsic motivation) rewards. Interestingly, intention to stay in the industry in five years time had no significant effect on work motivation. This is especially surprising in relation to intrinsic motivation, as one would expect internal motivation to be influenced should an individual intend to leave the industry (any industry not just the games industry). This finding also adds weight to the 'passion for games' premise put forward by Consalvo (2008). According to Consalvo, individuals join the industry because they have a passion for games, which she argues, is the reason why poor working practices, such as long hours remain in the industry. This implies that women working in the more technical areas of the industry are more intrinsically motivated, than women who work in less technical areas. Previous work suggests, individuals intrinsically motivated become involved, committed and energised by their work (Thomas, Jansen, & Tymon, 1997). It would appear this was the case for our women, despite the differences.

PERSON-ENVIRONMENT FIT OF WOMEN IN THE COMPUTER GAMES INDUSTRY

How much an individual matches or fits the environment in which they work is important and is often referred to as person-environment fit. Theoretically, environments will recruit and retain people whose characteristics are congruent to the working environment and people will prefer and persist in environments that are congruent with their vocational personalities. Person-environment fit is defined as the match between the abilities of a person and the demands of a job. Or the needs of a person and what the job provides. Whereas, person-organisation fit refers to how an individual matches an organisations values, beliefs and goals. Holland's career typology theory, emphasises the importance and interdependence of the work environment on individual carer choice. Holland's theory of vocational personalities and work environments was developed to describe, understand and predict the vocational choices people make. The theory is intended to account for the differential attraction of environments for certain types of people. Person-environment fit is of interest to organisational and vocational scholars due to its benefits to employee attitudes and behaviours. Person-environment fit has been positively related to job satisfaction and organisational commitment and negatively related to turnover (O'Reilly et al., 1991). In that satisfied individuals are more committed and less likely to leave. O'Reilly, Chatman and Caldwell (1991) developed an instrument for assessing person-organisation fit; the organisational culture profile (OCP). The authors demonstrated a distinction between person-organisation fit and person-job fit and they suggest that both types of fit have a unique impact on employee issues, such as job satisfaction and intention to leave. Their study found that person-organisation fit predicts job satisfaction, organisational commitment and turnover suggesting the importance of understanding the fit between individual's preferences and organisational

cultures. In a later study, Lauver and Kristof-Brown (2001) further distinguished between employees' perceptions of person-job fit (P-J) and person-organisation fit (P-O). They found that both P–J and P-O fit had an impact on job satisfaction and that P-O fit was a better predictor of intention to leave and suggest that P-O and P-J fit be treated as two distinct constructs.

We found that the majority of female game workers in our research had high job fit, with much less organisational fit. The majority also had high job satisfaction, but less organisational satisfaction. This suggests that female game workers are less satisfied with their organisation, than with their actual job. This is interesting, as it could be argued, that it is the male dominated culture, at the organisational level, that women are most dissatisfied and least congruent with. If women are satisfied and feel they fit well into their chosen job, then perhaps the responsibility lies more at the organisational or perhaps the sector level to understand how better accommodate female employees. More research is needed to understand the influence of organisational culture in the industry and its impact on employees and the working environment. The high levels of job satisfaction found with our women participants, is in contrast to the low levels of job satisfaction Rose (2007) found with ICT professionals. Perhaps professional identity as a game developer or indeed a 'passion for games' does persist within the industry. Furthermore, our analysis revealed that whether or not our women participants intended to stay in the games industry in five years time, had a significant impact on both person-environment fit and satisfaction at work. This confirms previous findings that person-environment fit is related to job satisfaction and intention to stay (O'Reilly et al., 1991). This is important for the games industry, as theoretically organisations recruit and retain people whose characteristics are congruent to the working environment and individuals prefer and persist in environments that are congruent with their vocational personalities (Gottfredson & Duffy, 2008). Lack of opportunities, not enough work life balance and bad working atmosphere were all reasons for the women in our research wanting to leave the industry. Reasons which perhaps suggest organisational, rather than job level issues are to blame.

JOB SATISFACTION OF WOMEN IN THE COMPUTER GAMES INDUSTRY

Job satisfaction may be considered as "a pleasurable or positive emotional state resulting from an appraisal of one's job or job experiences" (Locke, 1976, as cited in Ilies & Judge 2004, p.1300). More simply, job satisfaction is the degree to which individuals like their job (Spector, 1985). There are a variety of facets within the construct of job satisfaction. These involve employees feelings toward different dimensions of their work role and work environment i.e. satisfaction with pay, promotion, co-workers or organisational structure. Satisfaction with ones job or organisation is related to factors such as the job role, the working environment and identifying with organisational goals and objectives. Recently, Weiss (2002) defined job satisfaction as

"positive (or negative) evaluation judgement one makes about one's job or job situation" (as cited in Brief & Weiss, 2002, p. 283). Job satisfaction is viewed as having both cognitive and affective dimensions (Organ & Near, 1985). These dimensions should however, not be considered as in conflict, since moods and emotions experienced in a job may be a cause of job attitudes and an indicator of them (Brief & Weiss, 2002). A variety of personal characteristics have been found to have significant effects on job satisfaction including: gender, race, age, and marital status. Other determinants of job satisfaction have been identified which relate to characteristics of the job. For example, hours of work, size of the organisation, union membership and occupation have a significant effect on self-reported job satisfaction (Shields & Ward, 2001). The length of time an individual has been employed by the organisation has also been found to have an effect on job satisfaction. Increases in job satisfaction are equally associated with role autonomy Low levels of job satisfaction are associated with poor organisational outcomes, such as turnover, poor teamwork and inefficiency (Shields & Ward, 2002). Job satisfaction is therefore important for employee and organisational well being. Although job satisfaction has been well researched in psychology, areas of job satisfaction that still require attention include the relationship between job satisfaction, workplace performance and outside work influences.

Understanding the job satisfaction of employees is an important organisational goal. Many organisational outcomes such as productivity and efficiency are related to employee's levels of job satisfaction (Ellinger et al., 2002). When employees are dissatisfied at work, they are less committed and will often look for opportunities to leave the organisation (Perryman, 2004). Shields and Ward (2001) found that job satisfaction was the single most important determinant of intention to quit. Individuals who reported being very dissatisfied with their job were 65% more likely to report intention to quit, than those who reported being very satisfied. Satisfaction at work has been associated with a number of employment factors such as commitment and intention to leave an organisation or job (Perryman, 2004). In our research we found that, women who intended to stay in the industry had more fit and satisfaction. Intention to remain within the industry is an important issue for the games industry as there has been acknowledgment there is a skills shortage within the industry (Wilson, 2009). Intention to stay is also important in terms of retention issues within the industry. The Oxford Economic (2008) report has suggested that the United Kingdom games industry, is used to recruit workers for their skills and knowledge to other gaming countries. If this is the case, this could be advantageous for other countries and detrimental for the UK games industry.

SELF ISSUES FOR WOMEN IN THE COMPUTER GAMES INDUSTRY

Self-esteem is a personal sense of worthiness that is experienced as positive or negative attitudes directed toward the self, in particular beliefs about being valuable and capable. Branden (1969) defined positive (high) self-esteem as a relationship between the individual's competencies in coping with the fundamental challenges of life and worthiness, in relation to happiness, and doing so consistently over time. In terms of positive (high) self-esteem therefore, self-esteem is related to personal confidence in the potential to learn, make appropriate choices and decisions, and respond positively to change. It is also the experience that: success, achievement, fulfilment and happiness, are right and natural for us. In this respect, self-esteem incorporates: emotional, evaluative, and cognitive components. Self-esteem represents an overall value an individual places on themselves as a person (Judge et al., 1997). The maintenance and enhancement of self-esteem is viewed as a primary motive of human behaviour (Brown & Dutton, 1995). Self-esteem can be seen as an underlying dispositional tendency; trait self-esteem which is long term or as a transient psychological condition; state self-esteem which is short term and situational (Leary & Baumeister, 2000; Hogg & Cooper, 2003). Self-esteem is important in the workplace. To have work and be respected by others in work is central to an individual's well being and to working effectively. High self-esteem individuals have also been found to be more resilient to self image threats they are more likely to savour positive affect (Wood et al., 2003) and they tend to perceive negative feedback more as a challenge than a threat (Seery et al., 2004). Self-efficacy was defined by Bandura (1986) as "people's judgements of their capabilities to organise and execute courses of action required to attain designated types of performances" (Bandura, 1986, p. 391). Central to Bandura's self-efficacy theory is the focus on expectancies for success. Bandura distinguished between two types of expectancy beliefs: outcome expectations; which are beliefs that certain behaviours will lead to certain outcomes and efficacy expectations; the belief about whether one can effectively perform the behaviours necessary for the outcome. Changes in self-efficacy beliefs will lead to changes in occupational interests (Lent et al., 1994). Self-efficacy is important to women's career development especially since according to Betz and Hackett "there exist significant and consistent sex differences in self-efficacy with regards to traditional and non-traditional occupations" (Betz & Hackett, 1981, p. 407). Some suggest that high self-efficacy can have a circular or reciprocal effect, in that, high self-efficacy facilitates performance and successful performance nurtures self-efficacy (Gist and Mitchell, 1992).

Self-efficacy predicts actual performance in a broad range of settings and so raising self-efficacy can have practical consequences for the productivity of individuals in organisations. Once in a job negative beliefs about your abilities may reduce the willingness to take risks, and reduce the desire to be visible, both of which can hinder career progression (Heliman, 1983). Hence self-efficacy is important in the workplace for both men and women. Self-efficacy has been previously associated to people's careers in a number of ways. For example, Van Vuuren, de Jong, and Seydel (2008) found organisational self-efficacy contributed to organisational commitment.

From an American sample, Ton and Hansen (2001), found job satisfaction meditates the relationship between values and interests and they found the same to be true for martial satisfaction. Betz, Borgen, and Harmon (2006) found both personality and vocational confidence contributed to the prediction of occupational group membership. Depending on the occupation, personality or confidences are the most prominent contribution. The majority of studies investigating self-efficacy view high levels of self-efficacy as a positive thing. High self-efficacy is not, however, always a desirable thing. High self-efficacy can create complacency, which in turn decreases performance (Vancouver et al., 2001). However, in response to Vancouver et al.'s findings, Bandura and Locke (2003) concluded that Vancouver et al.'s contradictory findings were due to the experiment itself. Vancouver et al.'s findings do indicate that more research is needed to investigate any possible negative performance outcomes of high self-efficacy.

High self-esteem has been found to increase coping and goal achievement, both of which are valuable within the workplace (Bednar et al., 1989). Inconsistent and contradictory findings have been found between women and men with regards to self-esteem. Some studies have reported males to score higher than females, while other studies have found the converse or identified no differences between the genders (e.g. Tang et al., 2000). In terms of intra-gender differences in self-esteem, career oriented women have been found to have more positive (high) levels of self-esteem, than home oriented women (Tinsley & Faunce, 1980). Also, women possessing positive (high) self-esteem have been found to hold less traditional attitudes than those with less self-esteem. It is considered that this may arise as those women who possess negative (low) self-esteem, also lack the confidence required to assume, or promote, non-traditional roles for themselves and other women (Harrison, Guy, & Lupfer, 1981). In relation to inter-gender variations in self-esteem, positive (high) levels of self-esteem is typically found in those women who are employed in male dominated occupations; however, women tend to underestimate their talents and skills, and their potential future work-related performance.

Self-efficacy has previously been associated to people's careers (van Vuuren, de Jong, & Seydel, 2008) and more recently to pay expectations (Hogue, DuBois, & Fox-Cardamone, 2010). Female participants not willing to relocate also had more self-efficacy than those who were willing to relocate. Self-to theories (Rommes et al., 2007) suggest that self-image and identity construction are important in choosing a profession. Therefore, it could be that women with a higher self-image are more likely to choose a career in a male dominated sector due to the apparent benefits of working in the sector such as pay, status, autonomy (Hogue, DuBois, & Fox-Cardamone, 2010). We found that the majority of game workers had high self-esteem at work and high occupational self-efficacy, suggesting that people who work in the computer games industry have competence and confidence in their ability at work. Previous research has found women in male dominated occupations have higher self-efficacy (Chang, 2003, Fuegen &

Biernat, 2002) which may account for the high competence and confidence for the female participants we identified. Perhaps the women in the industry have high self-efficacy in order to cope in the masculine industry. Previous research has found women in male dominated occupations have higher self-efficacy (Chang, 2003) and women in solo status perform better on masculine tasks (Fuegen & Biernat, 2002), which may account for the high competence and confidence. Our findings also tend to support Long's (1989) view that women in male dominated organisations and industries need high self-efficacy in order to cope with the male dominated environment. This is in contrast to other findings, which suggest women lack confidence in computers (Natale, 2002; Michie & Nelson, 2006).

Self-efficacy is important in the workplace for both men and women. Once in a job, negative beliefs regarding abilities may reduce willingness to take risks and reduce the desire to be visible, both of which can hinder career progression. Self-efficacy has previously been associated to people's careers (van Vuuren, de Jong, & Seydel, 2008) and more recently to pay expectations (Hogue, DuBois, & Fox-Cardamone, 2010). We must remember that self-image and identity construction are important in choosing a profession. Therefore, it could be that women with a higher level of self-image are more likely to be undeterred from choosing a career in a male dominated sector, or due to the apparent benefits of working in these sectors i.e. pay, status, autonomy. Previous research suggests that women in male dominated occupations and industries adopt more masculine traits, as a strategy to cope and be accepted within the male domain (Wajcman, 2007). Long (1989) looked at gender role identity, coping strategies, self-efficacy and stress for women in male-dominated and female-dominated occupations. Long found that women with high masculinity had significantly lower levels of anxiety and strain, higher self-efficacy and coping then low masculinity women. Additionally, low feminine women in non-traditional occupations had higher self-efficacy and greater coping then women with low feminine in traditional occupations. Long suggests that women with high masculine gender role orientation experience less strain and cope more effectively in masculine occupations. This could suggest women with high masculinity are attracted to this and perhaps other male dominated industries as they know they can cope. In addition, Long found that masculinity and self-efficacy were positively correlated and interrelated. We support Long's findings, in that we noted a link between identity, intrinsic motivation and occupational self-efficacy.

Our findings tend to suggest women are perhaps adopting more masculine traits in order to fit into the industry (Prescott & Bogg, 2011). Perhaps women who intend to stay in the industry are either naturally more androgynous or perhaps able to develop androgynous characteristics in order to fit in. It is possible that for those women who intended to leave the industry, gender role identity within the workplace was an issue. Further research is needed to elaborate on these findings and suggestions. We found that role within the industry was important. Lupton (2000) argues that men attempt to realign their gender and oc-

cupational identities, through reconstruction or rationalisation of the nature of their jobs, or by renegotiation of their own conceptions of what it means to be a man. Interestingly, we found age influenced identity, in that, women over 35, had greater masculine identity, than those younger. This poses some interesting questions. Could this mean that masculinity increases in an ageing workforce? Maybe the older generation view masculine traits as important for workplace culture, more so than their younger counterparts. If the latter is the case, then perhaps as the younger generation ages, the masculine concept will become less important in the workforce. Longitudinal research will be of benefit in monitoring this.

CAREER FACTORS OF WOMEN IN THE COMPUTER GAMES INDUSTRY

Promotion was important to the majority of our women, they felt that they were progressing in their careers. This is despite the fact that a third had not been promoted in the past five years. Just over half of the women intended to climb the career ladder and were prepared to make personal sacrifices in order to do so, and nearly half felt that there were not enough opportunities for them to progress in their career. Furthermore, gaining recognition in their field was important to almost all of our women. Our analysis revealed a number of significant findings in relation to attitudes to career barriers and career progression. For example, climbing the career ladder was significantly more important to women who intended to stay in the games industry in five years time, compared to those that did not.

This may possibly suggest a commitment to the industry and perhaps more of a desire or need for progression. Interestingly, the women who did not play computer games in their leisure time, intended to climb the career ladder significantly more than women who did play computer games in their leisure time. This may indicate that for these women, it is not necessarily a passion for games but a passion for their careers and career progression that drives them. A 'passion for games' is therefore not always necessary to be successful in the industry. We also found that women with children intended to climb the career ladder and make personal sacrifices, more so than women without children. This is interesting and may reflect the personal sacrifices women with children in the industry feel they need to make to be successful. Women who intended to stay in the industry in five years time, felt they were progressing in their careers significantly more than women who did not intend to stay. This perception of progression could be an explanation as to why some women intended to stay in the industry and others did not.

In relation to career barriers, findings were contradictory. The majority of women agreed that the glass ceiling exists, yet felt there were no covert barriers to women's achievement, indicating the barriers are overt. Nearly all of the women agreed that some careers are more female friendly than others. Whilst just over half thought women were not well represented within their organisation, the majority agreed that women were not well represented within their profession. This suggests women are represented within the organisation, but much less within the games workers profession. In general, women had a negative view of the career progression of women and recognised that barriers exist, despite feeling they themselves are progressing within their careers. This could be one explanation as to why our women had less fit and satisfaction with their organisation, compared to their jobs. ICT organisations have a flat structure with little hierarchy and can lead to an informal working environment, with short or non-existent career ladders (WWW-ICT, 2009). A lack of formal structures and progression processes can make it particularly difficult for women to gain advancement. Women tend to achieve better in organisations where career paths are clear. Clear organisational structures, especially for progression and advancement, could provide useful support.

LIFE ISSUES FOR WOMEN IN THE COMPUTER GAMES INDUSTRY

It has been suggested that the ICT industry needs to broaden its appeal to a more diverse workforce, through such changes as making part-time work and flexible working more accessible (Griffiths, Moore, & Richardson, 2007). Part-time workers are often penalised in terms of career progression and promotion and the wider ICT industry has been criticised for the lack of part-time work available (Diamond & Whitehouse, 2007). The majority or our women did not have children. This supports findings from research in the wider ICT industry; that women with families are lacking within the sector (WWW-ICT, 2004) and that the games industry tends to favour single people (Deuze et al., 2007). The majority of our women participants worked full-time. Promotion and working hours were related, in that many women expected to have to work long hours in order to succeed. A long hour's culture appears to exist in the games industry with just over three quarters of women reporting a long hour's culture in their organisation. Long hours and crunch time are important issues within the games industry and reducing their impact on employees would be beneficial to the industry. Crunch time could be difficult to eradicate completely, due to restricted budgets, last minute problems and deadlines.

A possible solution could be for organisations to incorporate project management training for leads and managers, to yield greater effectiveness of project timelines and targets. Through more effective project management employee work life balance may possibly be enhanced. It is suggested that the long hours associated with the games industry become perceived as 'occasional', as they would often be in many professional roles, as opposed to 'regular'. Whilst individuals who have a passion for games and gaming enjoy their jobs as the study suggests, there is a growing recognition that achieving a work life balance is of greater importance for many individuals. Women who are the primary carers of children, generally require predictability (mainly regular hours) in order to plan childcare. Improvement in working conditions may lead to women choosing to remain in the industry (for example, after starting a family), increasing the number of women in games development may also have the added benefit of enhancing the image of the games industry, as a potential career for

women. Our findings suggested that despite the women's positive attitude towards their current work life balance, half did feel the number of hours they worked affected their personal relationships and nearly half felt the number of hours worked affected their personal health. To help achieve better work life balance more flexible working practices should be encouraged. To retain women, the industry may need to adapt and evolve common practices to become more family friendly.

CONCLUSION

There have been a number of reasons put forward for the under representation of women within the industry, including the long hours culture (Consalvo, 2008) and the industry's image as a male domain (Graner Ray, 2004). People experience the same work conditions in different ways and can react quite differently to situations based on personal characteristics and attributes. Organisations tend to recruit and retain people whose characteristics are congruent to the working environment. Individuals tend to prefer and remain in environments congruent with their vocational personality or fit. Job satisfaction is influenced by various factors, such as the environment the role takes place in, organisational structure, pay, promotion prospects, co-worker relationships and identifying with organisational goals and objectives. Individual negative beliefs regarding ability can influence self-image and esteem and reduce individual belief in their ability for promotion or progression. Wajcman (2007) suggests that women in male dominated occupations and industries adopt more masculine traits, as a strategy to cope with and be accepted within the male domain.

Men dominate the games industry both as developers and gamers. Research shows women are active gamers, especially with more casual than hard core games. Braithwaite (2010) views the social network site *Facebook* as a catalyst in which women are increasingly becoming more hard core gamers. Our research with women games developers provides a deeper understanding of the attitudes, motivations and aspirations of women who have broken into this male domain. Gaining an understanding of women in the industry may be beneficial in attracting other women to the industry and highlight the industry as a potential career for future generations of women. Encouraging more women into male dominated occupations is one strategy for minimising gendered occupational segregation and the many inequalities that come with it. Taking into account the self-to-prototype matching theory, where professional choice is related to the type of person people think is typical for working in that profession (Hannover & Kessels, 2004) the industry may benefit from increasing its appeal to a wider demographic of female game workers. For instance, although the majority played games in their leisure time, it was apparent that women (and men) do not need to play games for a viable and satisfactory career within the industry. We found a number of positives which may ultimately benefit the industry with many women motivated, satisfied with their job, had good self-esteem and

high occupational self-efficacy. Importantly many intended to remain in the industry in five years time

In terms of attracting more women to the computer games industries workforce, perhaps through emphasising these positive aspects, the games industry could enhance its image as a potential career for women. According to self-to-profession matching theory, people compare what they are good at, what they want from a job and what activities they like, with their (in)correct expectations of a particular profession (Rommes et al., 2007). Indeed, Eccles (1994) suggests that inaccurate and insufficient information about professions is the main reason why young women do not consider or rule out occupations that might fit their self schema. The industry may therefore benefit from highlighting the various roles and skills required in the industry; as well as the various backgrounds, both educational and occupational that women come into the industry from. Over three quarters of the women in our research had previously worked outside of the games industry; the most popular industry participants came from was film and TV, followed by IT and then retail. This information may aide the industry in its future recruitment drives, initiatives and policy implementation.

Research on women in the new industry of computer games is sparse. More understanding of game workers and their working environment, will help organisational researchers understand new industries and possibly how organisational structures are developing. The industry itself has only recently started to receive academic attention. Research investigating working in new media found men and women had different experiences (Gill, 2002). Gill's research included men and women from the games industry but a closer look at how the sexes experience the industry specifically, would be of real advantage to research in this area. Gaining further knowledge of the career structures within computer games organisations may potentially enable organisational researchers to see if there are transparent progression policies in place and if career development is equal to all. Due to the paucity of research looking at women in the games industry, there are a number of future research directions that can be considered. For instance, investigating why women have left the industry would lead to more insight into retention issues and may possibly help the wider ICT and SET sector understand the 'leaky pipeline' which is reported to exist. The findings suggest there are a number of possible areas which warrant further attention.

Understanding why some women choose to work in male dominated occupations would be valuable. Future research may consider investigating why some women are attracted to the games industry and why some women are not. Our research with women games developers has found that women in the industry are highly motivated by both internal and external rewards. These findings pose some interesting questions, For example, is it these motivations alone that attract people to the industry? What other issues come into play? With regard to attraction, a number of questions can be raised. For instance, does the industry attract a certain type of woman or do women have to adapt to its masculine

culture? Equalitarian gender beliefs have been previously correlated with higher self-efficacy and self-esteem (Athrens & O'Brien, 1996). Gaining an understanding of the gender role attitudes of the women in the industry would be an interesting area for future research.

Segregation within the industry and the demographics of the industry both give rise to interesting questions and potential areas of future investigation. For instance, how will this 'young' industry age? Will the industries demographics change in terms of age, children and care responsibilities? If more women within the industry have children, how will attitudes towards such things as relocation and work life balance change? Of particular interest is if women in the industry are not having children due to their careers, or are they postponing child bearing until their careers are established? In relation to flexible working, it would be interesting and extremely useful in terms of policy development and implementation to evaluate women who do work flexibly and the impact this is having on, or they feel it is having on their careers. With regard to grade, will more women in senior roles have an impact on reducing the image of the industry as a male domain? Will more women in senior roles have an impact on environmental changes within the industry, such as those relating to work life balance issues and flexible working practices? How will the industry change with the inevitable increase of Generation Ys entering into it? Also worth considering is if women feel any career barriers can be overcome or not. Did the women expect any barriers before they entered the industry? To what extent would they expect similar barriers in other industries? What strategies do women with families use to cope with crunch time? It would also have been interesting to know what game genres the women in the study worked on and if they are attracted to, or remain in a certain organisation due to the games they make and if the game genres they make has any significance to their attitudes, aspirations or motivations in their job and organisation.

Due to the lack of research into the area of game workers, much more research is needed in all aspects of the industry, its organisational structures, working environment and its employees. Our research with women games developers has shown that female game professionals are a heterogeneous group, from a variety of backgrounds, in a broad range of positions and occupying all levels within the industry. This heterogeneity means female game professionals need for support will vary according to, but not limited to, factors such as age, ethnicity, career stage, domestic responsibilities and the role they occupy within the industry. Several empirical studies have shown that the marginalisation of women from the technological community can have a profound influence on design, technical content and the use of artefacts (Lie, 2003; Lerman et al., 2003). Gender relations have been found to be embedded in the design, meaning and use of ICTs (Wajcman, 2007). Women may have played a part in the history of the development and use of technology (Plant, 1998), but they are not yet fully integrated into its design (Wajcman, 2007). Drawing more women into the design of ICT is not only an equal opportunities issue, but is also crucially about

how the world we live in is designed and for whom. The games industry is part of the wider ICT and SET sectors and has been viewed as a forerunner in the development of technology (Flanagan, 2003). Heeter et al. (2009) used the word 'alien' to refer to the manner in which women are considered in the culture of producing and playing games. The industry has also been criticised for ignoring the needs of minority players such as women (Fron et al., 2007). Female game developers could alter the image of the industry and perhaps help accommodate the needs of minority players.

The games industry needs to improve its appeal to a more diverse workforce, through changes such as making part-time work and flexible working more accessible (Griffiths, Moore & Richardson, 2007). Part-time workers are often penalised in terms of career progression and promotion and the wider ICT industry has been criticised for the lack of part-time work available. Due to the skills shortage, the computer games industry needs to improve its appeal, in order to recruit and retain a more diverse workforce. A workforce with greater diversity has an additional benefit in that in the case of the games industry it has the potential of those making games to develop games, with a greater appeal to a wider and more diverse audience. Men and women have been found to have different play styles and attracting more female developers, may enable more female gamers and vice versa. As according to Fullerton: 'one of the effects of getting women into game design is that they are going to add play patterns' (Fullerton, 2009). Due to this need to attract a wider audience, through a more diverse workforce, the games industry is in a unique position. Perhaps this will lead this industry to pave the way forward, as enhancing its appeal for women and other underrepresented groups, will benefit other male dominated industries in terms of demonstrating a sound business case for change.

We have highlighted a number of areas where the games industry could significantly improve its appeal as a viable career to women. The image of the games industry, like the wider ICT and SET industries, is still very much 'boys work'. However, this image could change with a more diverse workforce and with an increasing number of female gamers world-wide, the industry may then begin to lose its 'for boys only', masculine image. The industry could widen its appeal through an increased awareness of the variety of roles and skills within the industry and through highlighting the benefits and rewards of working in such a creative, competitive and growing industry. The findings from our research with women games developers will hopefully enable the games industry to review its policies and working practices in order to facilitate women and other minority groups within the working environment. So, instead of women 'just fitting in' more can be done to eradicate career barriers and discriminatory work practices to make women feel more comfortable working in the industry.

Table 1. Career factors: Experience of women games developers: The key issues

Career Factors	Core Issues Involved	How May the Issue be Addressed
Recruitment	• Recruitment to industry starts early, need for games that girls and women are interested in. • Improve image of industry to appeal to women. • Work environment. • Environments recruit and retain individuals whose characteristics are congruent to the working environment. • Person-environment fit. • Self-efficacy. • Self-esteem.	• Diversity in games. • Make the workplace women friendly. • Remove barriers to women being recruited to and remaining in the organisation. • Foster a supportive work environment that appeals to women's values and work styles.
Career motivation	• Experience of work environment	• Change environment to foster motivation regardless of gender.
Retention	• Individuals prefer and remain in environments that are congruent with their vocational personalities. • Lack of opportunities. • Not enough work life balance. • Poor working environment. • Job satisfaction. • Work life balance. • Women's career development. • Person-environment fit. • Self-efficacy. • Self-esteem.	• Make the workplace women friendly. • Remove barriers to women being recruited to and remaining in the organisation. • Organisational level issues, to be addressed by management, for change to occur and encourage women to remain in the industry. • Increase flexible working practices. • Identify the barriers and opportunities for job satisfaction.
Organisational business case	• Need to attract a wider games audience. • Need to attract a more diverse workforce.	• Enhance appeal for women and other underrepresented groups.

REFERENCES

Abood, D. A., & Conway, T. L. (1992). Health value & self-esteem as predictors of wellness behaviour. *Health Values*, *16*, 20–26.

Amabile, T. M., Hill, K. G., Hennessey, B. A., & Tighe, E. M. (1994). The work preference inventory: Assessing intrinsic & extrinsic motivational orientations. *Journal of Personality and Social Psychology*, *66*(5), 950–967. doi:10.1037/0022-3514.66.5.950 PMID:8014837

Aronson, K. A., Laurenceau, J. P., Sieveking, N., & Bellet, W. (2005). Job satisfaction as a function of job level. *Administration and Policy in Mental Health*, *32*(3), 285–291. doi:10.1007/s10488-004-0845-2 PMID:15844849

Bandura, A. (1986). *Social foundations of thought & action: A social cognitive theory.* Englewood Cliffs, NJ: Prentice Hall.

Bandura, A., & Locke, E. A. (2003). Negative self-efficacy & goal effects revisited. *The Journal of Applied Psychology*, *88*(1), 87–99. doi:10.1037/0021-9010.88.1.87 PMID:12675397

Bednar, R. L., Wells, M. G., & Peterson, S. R. (1989). *Self-esteem: Paradoxes & innovations in clinical theory & practice.* Washington, DC: American Psychological Association. doi:10.1037/10068-000

Bem, S. L. (1974). The measurement of psychological androgyny. *Journal of Consulting and Clinical Psychology*, *42*(2), 155–162. doi:10.1037/h0036215 PMID:4823550

Betz, N. E., Borgen, F. H., & Harmon, L. W. (2006). Vocational confidence & personality in the prediction of occupational group membership. *Journal of Career Assessment*, *14*(1), 36–55. doi:10.1177/1069072705282434

Betz, N. E., & Hackett, G. (1981). The relationship of career-related self-efficacy expectations to perceived career options in college women & men. *Journal of Counseling Psychology*, *28*(5), 399–410. doi:10.1037/0022-0167.28.5.399

Blyton, P., & Jenkins, J. (2007). *Key concepts in work.* London: Sage.

Branden, N. (1969). *The psychology of self-esteem.* New York: Bantam.

Brief, A. P., & Weiss, H. M. (2002). Organizational behavior: Affect in the workplace. *Annual Review of Psychology*, *53*, 279–307. doi:10.1146/annurev. psych.53.100901.135156 PMID:11752487

Brown, J. A., Woodward, C. A., Shannon, H. S., Cunningham, C. E., Lendrum, B., McIntosh, J., & Rosenbloom, D. (1999). Determinants of job stress & job satisfaction among supervisory & non-supervisory employees in a large Canadian teaching hospital. *Healthcare Management Forum*, *12*, 27–33. doi:10.1016/S0840-4704(10)60688-6 PMID:10538924

Brown, J. D., & Dutton, K. A. (1995). Truth and consequences: the costs & benefits of accurate self-knowledge. *Personality and Social Psychology Bulletin*, *21*, 1288–1296. doi:10.1177/01461672952112006

Cable, D. M., & DeRue, D. S. (2002). The convergent & discriminant validity of subjective fit perceptions. *The Journal of Applied Psychology*, *87*, 1–17. doi:10.1037/0021-9010.87.5.875 PMID:12395812

Cable, D. M., & Judge, T. A. (1996). Person-organization fit, job choice decisions, & organizational entry. *Organizational Behavior and Human Decision Processes*, *67*, 294–311. doi:10.1006/obhd.1996.0081

Campbell, T., Gillaspy, J. A., & Thompson, B. (1997). The factor structure of the bem sex-role inventory (BSRI), confirmatory analysis of long & short forms. *Educational and Psychological Measurement*, *57*(1), 118–124. doi:10.1177/0013164497057001008

Cha, J., Kim, Y., & Kim, T.-Y. (2009). Person-career fit & employee outcomes among research & development professionals. *Human Relations*, *20*(10), 1–30.

Chang, T. F. H. (2003). A social psychological model of women's gender-typed occupational mobility. *Career Development International*, *8*(1), 27–39. doi:10.1108/13620430310459496

Choi, N., & Fugua, D. R. (2003). The structure of the bem sex role inventory: A summary report of 23 validation studies. *Educational and Psychological Measurement*, *63*(5), 872–887. doi:10.1177/0013164403258235

Choi, N., Fuqua, D. R., & Newman, J. L. (2007). Hierarchical confirmatory factor analysis of the bem sex role inventory. *Educational and Psychological Measurement*, *67*(5), 818–832. doi:10.1177/0013164406299106

Choi, N., Fuqua, D. R., & Newman, J. L. (2009). Exploratory & confirmatory studies of the structure of the bem sex role inventory short form with two divergent samples. *Educational and Psychological Measurement*, *69*(4), 696–705. doi:10.1177/0013164409332218

Colley, A., Mulhern, G., Maltby, J., & Wood, A. M. (2009). The short form BSRI: Instrumentality, expressiveness & gender associations among a United Kingdom sample. *Personality and Individual Differences*, *46*, 384–387. doi:10.1016/j.paid.2008.11.005

Connell, J. P., Spencer, M. B., & Aber, J. L. (1994). Educational risk & resilience in African-American youth: Context, self, action, & outcomes in school. *Child Development*, *65*, 493–506. doi:10.2307/1131398 PMID:8013236

Connell, R. (2000). *The men & the boys*. Cambridge, UK: Polity Press.

Consalvo, M. (2008). Crunched by passion: Women game developers & workplace challenges. In *Beyond Barbie & Mortal Kombat: New perspectives on gender & gaming*. London: The MIT Press.

Deci, E. L., & Ryan, R. M. (1985). *Intrinsic motivation & self determination in human behavior*. New York: Plenum. doi:10.1007/978-1-4899-2271-7

Eccles, J. (1994). Understanding women's educational & occupational choices. *Psychology of Women Quarterly*, *18*, 585–609. doi:10.1111/j.1471-6402.1994.tb01049.x

Eddleston, K. A., Veiga, J. F., & Powell, G. N. (2006). Explaining sex differences in managerial career satisfier preferences: The role of gender self-schema. *The Journal of Applied Psychology, 91*(2), 437–450. doi:10.1037/0021-9010.91.2.437 PMID:16551194

Ellinger, A. D., Ellinger, A. E., Yang, B., & Howton, S. W. (2002). The relationship between the learning organization concept & firms' financial performance: An empirical assessment. *Human Resource Development Quarterly, 13,* 5–21. doi:10.1002/hrdq.1010

European Commission. (2004). *Widening women's work in information & communication technology.* WWW-ICT. Retrieved from http://www.ftu-namur.org/fichiers/D12-print.pdf

Fertman, C. I., & Chubb, N. H. (1992). The effects of a psychoeducational program on adolescents' activity involvement, self-esteem, & locus of control. *Adolescence, 27,* 517–526. PMID:1414563

Fuegen, K., & Biernat, M. (2002). Re-examining the effects of solo status for women & men. *Personality and Social Psychology Bulletin, 28,* 913–925.

Fullerton, T., Fron, J., Pearce, C., & Morie, J. (2008). Getting girls into the game: Towards a virtous cycle. In *Beyond Barbie & Mortal Kombat: New perspectives on gender & gaming.* London: The MIT Press.

Gist, M. E., & Mitchell, T. R. (1992). Self-efficacy: A theoretical analysis of its determinants & malleability. *Academy of Management Review, 17,* 183–211.

Gordon, M., & Denisi, A. (1995). A re-examination of the relationship between union membership & job satisfaction. *Industrial & Labor Relations Review, 48,* 222–236. doi:10.2307/2524484

Gottfredson, G. D., & Duffy, R. D. (2008). Using a theory of vocational personalities & work environments to explore subjective well-being. *Journal of Career Assessment, 16*(1), 44–59. doi:10.1177/1069072707309609

Graner Ray, S. (2004). *Gender inclusive game design: Expanding the market.* Cambridge, MA: Charles River Media Inc.

Greene, A. L., & Wheatley, S. M. (1992). I've got a lot to do & I don't think I'll have the time: Gender differences in late adolescents' narratives of the future. *Journal of Youth and Adolescence, 21,* 667–686. doi:10.1007/BF01538738

Hannover, B., & Kessels, U. (2004). Self-to-prototype matching as a strategy for making academic choices: Why high school students do not like maths & science. *Learning and Instruction, 14,* 51–67. doi:10.1016/j.learninstruc.2003.10.002

Harrison, B. G., Guy, R. F., & Lupfer, S. L. (1981). Locus of control & self-esteem as correlates of role orientation in traditional & n-traditional women. *Sex Roles, 7,* 1175–1187. doi:10.1007/BF00287969

Heilman, M. E. (1983). Sex bias in work settings: The lack of fit model. *Research in Organizational Behavior*, *5*, 269–298.

Hogg, M. A., & Cooper, J. (2003). *The SAGE handbook of social psychology*. New Delhi: Sage.

Hogue, M., DuBois, L. Z., & Fox-Cardamone, L. (2010). Gender differences in pay expectations: The role of job intention & self-view. *Psychology of Women Quarterly*, *34*, 215–227. doi:10.1111/j.1471-6402.2010.01563.x

Holt, C. L., & Ellis, J. B. (1998). Assessing the current validity of the bem sex-role inventory. *Sex Roles*, *39*(11/12), 929–941. doi:10.1023/A:1018836923919

IGDA. (2004). *Quality of life white paper*. International Game Developers Association. Retrieved from http://www.igda.org/sites/default/files/IGDA_QualityOfLife_White-Paper.pdf

Ilies, R., & Judge, T. A. (2004). An experience-sampling measure of job satisfaction & its relationships with affectivity, mood at work, job beliefs, & general job satisfaction. *European Journal of Work and Organizational Psychology*, *13*(3), 367–389. doi:10.1080/13594320444000137

Judge, T. A., Locke, E. A., & Durham, C. C. (1997). The dispositional causes of job satisfaction: A core evaluation approach. *Research in Organizational Behavior*, *19*, 151–188.

Korman, A. K. (1966). Self-esteem variable in vocational choice. *The Journal of Applied Psychology*, *50*, 479–486. doi:10.1037/h0024039 PMID:5978041

Latham, G. P., & Pinder, C. C. (2005). Work motivation theory & research at the dawn of the twenty-first century. *Annual Review of Psychology*, *56*, 485–516. doi:10.1146/annurev.psych.55.090902.142105 PMID:15709944

Lauver, K., & Kristof-Brown, A. (2001). Distinguishing between employees' perceptions of person-job & person-organization fit. *Journal of Vocational Behavior*, *59*, 454–470. doi:10.1006/jvbe.2001.1807

Leary, M. R., & Baunmeister, R. (2000). The nature & function of self-esteem: Sociometer theory. In *Advances if experimental social psychology*. San Diego, CA: Academic Press. doi:10.1016/S0065-2601(00)80003-9

Lent, R. W., Brown, S. D., & Hackett, G. (1994). Toward a unifying social cognitive theory of career & academic interest, choice & performance. *Journal of Vocational Behavior*, *45*, 79–122. doi:10.1006/jvbe.1994.1027

Lepper, M., & Greene, D. (1978). Over justification research & beyond: Toward a means-ends analysis of intrinsic & extrinsic motivation. In *The hidden costs of reward*. Hillsdale, NJ: Erlbaum.

Lipinska-Grobelny, A. (2008). Masculinity, femininity, androgyny & work stress. *Medycyna Pracy*, *59*(6), 453–460. PMID:19388459

Lipinska-Grobelny, A., & Wasiak, K. (2010). Job satisfaction & gender identity of women managers & non-managers. *International Journal of Occupational Medicine and Environmental Health*, *23*(2), 161–166. doi:10.2478/v10001-010-0015-6 PMID:20630833

Long, B. C. (1989). Sex-role orientation, coping strategies, & self-efficacy of women in traditional & non traditional occupations. *Psychology of Women Quarterly, 13*, 307–324. doi:10.1111/j.1471-6402.1989.tb01004.x

Lupton, B. (2000). Maintaining masculinity: men who do 'women's work'. *British Journal of Management, 11*, 33–48. doi:10.1111/1467-8551.11.s1.4

Miller, L., Neathey, F., Pollard, E., & Hill, D. (2004). *Occupational segregation, gender gaps & skill gaps*. Equal Opportunities Commission.

O'Reilly, C. A., Chatman, J., & Caldwell, D. F. (1991). People & organizational culture: A profile comparison approach assessing person-organization fit. *Academy of Management Review, 34*(3), 487–516. doi:10.2307/256404

Organ, D. W., & Near, J. P. (1985). Cognitive vs. affect measures of job satisfaction. *International Journal of Psychology, 20*, 241–254.

Ostroff, C. (1992). The relationship between satisfaction, attitudes, & performance: An organizational level analysis. *The Journal of Applied Psychology, 77*(6), 963–974. doi:10.1037/0021-9010.77.6.963

Oxford Economics. (2008). The economic contribution of the UK games industry: Final report. *Oxford Economics*. Retrieved from http://www.oxfordeconomics.com/publication/open/222646

Perryman, R. D. (2004). *Healthy attitudes: Quality of working life in the London NHS, 2000-2002*. Retrieved from http://www.employment-studies.co.uk/pubs/summary.php?id=404

Powell, G. N., & Greenhaus, J. H. (2010). Sex, gender & the work-to-family interface: Exploring negative & positive interdependencies. *Academy of Management Journal, 53*(3), 513–534. doi:10.5465/AMJ.2010.51468647

Prescott, J., & Bogg, J. (2011). Segregation in a male dominated industry: Women working in the computer games industry. *International Journal of Gender. Science & Technology, 3*(1), 205–227.

Prescott, J., & Bogg, J. (2012). Re-evaluating the BEM sex role inventory (BSRI): A factor analysis of the BSRI. *Assessment and Development Matters, 3*(2), 28–31.

Quigley, N. R., & Tymon, W. G. (2006). Toward an integrated model of intrinsic motivation & career self-management. *Career Development International, 11*(6), 522–543. doi:10.1108/13620430610692935

Ravaldi, C., Vannacci, A., Bolognesi, E., Mancini, S., Faravelli, C., & Ricca, V. (2006). Gender role, eating disorder symptoms, & body image concern in ballet dancers. *Journal of Psychosomatic Research, 61*(4), 529–535. doi:10.1016/j.jpsychores.2006.04.016 PMID:17011362

Rigotti, T., Schyns, B., & Mohr, G. (2008). A short version of the occupational self-efficacy scale: structural & construct validity across five countries. *Journal of Career Assessment*, *16*(2), 238–255. doi:10.1177/1069072707305763

Robie, C., Ryan, A. M., Schmieder, R. A., Parra, L. F., & Smith, P. C. (1998). The relation between job level & job satisfaction. *Group & Organization Management*, *23*, 470–495. doi:10.1177/1059601198234007

Robins, R. W., Hendin, H. M., & Trzesniewki, K. H. (2001). Measuring global self-esteem: Construct validation of a single-item measure & the Rosenberg self-esteem scale. *Personality and Social Psychology Bulletin*, *27*(2), 151–161. doi:10.1177/0146167201272002

Rommes, E., Overbeek, G., Scholte, R., Engles, R., & De Kemp, R. (2007). I'm not interested in computers': Gender-based occupational choices of adolescents. *Information Communication and Society*, *10*(3), 299–319. doi:10.1080/13691180701409838

Rosenberg, M. (1965). *Society & adolescent self-image*. Princeton, NJ: Princeton University Press.

Rusticus, S. A., Hubley, A. M., & Zumbo, B. D. (2004). Cross-national comparability of the rosenberg self-esteem scale. In *Proceedings of 112th Convention of the American Psychological Association*. Honolulu, HI: APA.

Saks, A. M., & Ashforth, B. E. (1997). A longitudinal investigation of the relationship between job information sources, applicant sources, applicant perceptions of fit, & work outcomes. *Personnel Psychology*, *50*(2), 395–426. doi:10.1111/j.1744-6570.1997.tb00913.x

Schyns, B., & von Collani, G. (2002). A new occupational self-efficacy scale & its relations to personality constructs & organisational variables. *European Journal of Work and Organizational Psychology*, *11*, 219–241. doi:10.1080/13594320244000148

Seery, M. D., Blasccovich, J., Weisbuch, M., & Vick, S. B. (2004). The relationship between self-esteem level, self-esteem stability, & cardiovascular reactions to performance feedback. *Journal of Personality and Social Psychology*, *87*, 133–145. doi:10.1037/0022-3514.87.1.133 PMID:15250798

Shields, M. A., & Ward, M. (2001). Improving nurse retention in the national health service in England: The impact of job satisfaction on intentions to quit. *Journal of Health Economics*, *20*, 677–701. doi:10.1016/S0167-6296(01)00092-3 PMID:11558644

Skillset. (2009). *2009 employment census: The results of the seventh census of the creative media industries December 2009*. The Sector Skills Council for Creative Media.

Spector, P. E. (1985). Measurement of human service staff satisfaction: Development of the job satisfaction survey 1. *American Journal of Community Psychology*, *13*(6), 693–713. doi:10.1007/BF00929796 PMID:4083275

Spencer, S. J., Josephs, R. A., & Steele, C. M. (1993). Low self-esteem: The uphill struggle for self integrity. In *Self-Esteem: The puzzle of low self-regard*. New York: Plenum Press. doi:10.1007/978-1-4684-8956-9_2

Tang, T. L., Singer, M. G., & Roberts, S. (2000). Employees' perceived organizational instrumentality: An examination of the gender differences. *Journal of Managerial Psychology*, *15*(5), 378–406. doi:10.1108/02683940010337112

Thomas, K. W., Jansen, E., & Tymon, W. G. Jr. (1997). Navigating in the realm of theory: An empowering view of construct development. In *Research in organizational change & development*. Greenwich, CT: JAI Press.

Tinsley, D. J., & Faunce, P. S. (1980). Enabling, facilitating & precipitating factors associated with women's career orientation. *Journal of Vocational Behavior*, *17*, 183–194. doi:10.1016/0001-8791(80)90003-2

Ton, M.-T. N., & Hansen, J.-I. C. (2001). Using a person-environment fit framework to predict satisfaction & motivation in work & marital roles. *Journal of Career Assessment*, *9*(4), 315–331. doi:10.1177/106907270100900401

Twenge, J. M. (1997). Changes in masculine & feminine traits over time: a meta-analysis. *Sex Roles*, *36*(5/6), 305–325. doi:10.1007/BF02766650

van Vuuren, M., de Jong, M. D. T., & Seydel, E. R. (2008). Contributions of self & organisational efficacy expectations to commitment a fourfold typology. *Employee Relations*, *30*(2), 142–156. doi:10.1108/01425450810843339

Vancouver, J. B., Thompson, C. M., & Williams, A. A. (2001). The changing signs in the relationships between self-efficacy, personal goals & performance. *Journal of Applied Psychology of Women Quarterly*, *86*, 605–620. doi:10.1037/0021-9010.86.4.605 PMID:11519645

Wajcman, J. (2007). From women & technology to gendered technoscience. *Information Communication and Society*, *10*(3), 287–298. doi:10.1080/13691180701409770

Whitley, B. E. (1988). Masculinity, femininity, & self-esteem: A multi trait-multi method analysis. *Sex Roles*, *18*(7/8), 419–431. doi:10.1007/BF00288393

Wilcox, C., & Francis, L. L. (1997). Beyond gender stereotyping: Examining the validity of the bem sex-role inventory among 16 to 19 year old females in England. *Personality and Individual Differences*, *23*(1), 9–13. doi:10.1016/S0191-8869(97)00026-3

Williams, S., & Cooper, C. L. (1998). Measuring occupational stress: Development of the pressure management indicator. *Journal of Occupational Health Psychology*, *3*(4), 306–321. doi:10.1037/1076-8998.3.4.306 PMID:9805279

Wood, J. V., Heimpel, S. A., & Michela, J. L. (2003). Savoring versus dampening: Self-esteem differences in regulating positive effect. *Journal of Personality and Social Psychology*, *85*, 566–580. doi:10.1037/0022-3514.85.3.566 PMID:14498791

KEY TERMS AND DEFINITIONS

Career Motivation: A psychological process enacted from both within the individual as well as external to the individual.

Female Game Workers: Females who work in the computer games industry, especially in the developmental roles more traditionally occupied by men.

Flexible Working: Practices that facilitate achieving a satisfactory work life balance such as part time working and working from home.

Job Satisfaction: The degree to which individuals enjoy their job.

Person-Environment Fit: How much an individual matches or fits the environment in which they work is important and is often referred to as person-environment fit. Theoretically, environments will recruit and retain people whose characteristics are congruent to the working environment, and people will prefer and persist in environments that are congruent with their vocational personalities.

Self Esteem: A personal sense of worthiness that is experienced as positive or negative attitudes directed toward the self, in particular, beliefs about being valuable and capable.

Self-Efficacy: People's judgement about their capability to undertake a task or a performance.

Work Life Balance: The balance between work and other life or role commitments.

Chapter 8
Issues Career Women Face

ABSTRACT

This chapter considers the issues women generally face in their careers and in particular in ICT and SET careers. The chapter discusses the barriers women can face in their careers and the drivers that can enable women to advance and progress in their careers. This discussion includes a review of mentoring and networking and illustrates the gender divide in access to mentors and networking opportunities. The chapter also considers work-life balance issues, which are particularly important for women working in male-dominated occupations and industries. It considers women's lack of visibility in male-dominated occupations and industries and discusses the leaky pipeline and the factors that can aide retention and plug the pipeline for women.

INTRODUCTION

You will be amused that when Mr. Dulles said goodbye to me this morning he said 'I feel I must tell you that when you were appointed I thought it terrible and now I think your work here has been fine!' So, against the odds the women inch forward, but I'm rather old to be carrying on the fight. (Eleanor Roosevelt to Joseph Lash, February 13, 1946)

Career women face a number of issues in the workplace, this is particularly the case for women working in science, engineering and technology (SET) where women remain outnumbered by men. This can have far reaching implications for recruitment and retention. Servon and Visser (2011) found from their research with 2,493 women in SET careers in the private sector that 23% of participants felt that women in their roles were held in

DOI: 10.4018/978-1-4666-4534-9.ch008

low regard, particularly in the Engineering and Technology sector. Worryingly, over 50% of the women reported experiencing sexual harassment at work. A third of the women reported feeling extremely isolated at work and many felt that they were not progressing in their career. This would suggest that the 'leaky pipeline' is as active as it is in the academic sector. Our own research would support Servon and Visser's (2011) findings, as feelings of stagnation and isolation, suggest there may be a lack of women to aspire to in similar roles and potentially a lack of mentoring or support networks. In addition, due to the gendering of certain occupations and roles, feelings of 'not fitting in' may encourage women to adopt masculine traits in order to better 'fit in'. As we have suggested throughout this book, throughout the SET industries, in both the public and private sector in order to successfully recruit and retain women, the culture of the organisation must evolve to accommodate women. This chapter will focus on the issues facing women in the workplace, whilst they are not all unique to SET, they all have a powerful influence on the progression of women in male dominated occupations.

CAREER BARRIERS AND DRIVERS

The issue of gender bias and its implications in the world of work is ongoing. Women continue to be disadvantaged and can remain invisible in the workplace when it comes to recognition for achievement. Research has demonstrated that women's scientific achievements are often undervalued and unrewarded. For example, Lincoln et al. (2012) analyzed the composition of award committees, given by 13 societies from science, technology, engineering, and medicine (STEM), and found that women made up only 19.5% of the average award committee. They found that while awards to women increased by 78.5% between 2000 to 2010, women won only 10% of research-based awards and were more successful in gaining service awards (32%) or teaching awards (37%). Interestingly, men were more than eight times likely, to win a scholarly award and almost three times more likely to win a young investigator award. We support the researchers conclusions, in that as women were much more successful in gaining service and scholarship awards than men, there appears a perception that scientific scholars are men and women teachers or service providers and potentially incongruent with the scientist role. Such gender bias is notable and may be institutionally gendered in terms of what roles women and men play in science as we have discussed throughout this book. Implicit bias in award, selection and nomination committees requires consideration and potentially training of members to avoid unconscious bias. This would equally be of benefit in job selection and promotion committees.

Lack of women is reflected in academic writing, it is apparent that women authors are missing from leading publications, where it can influence dissemination of results, the impact of the research and career progression. This includes writing in leading scientific journals. For example, recently Conley and

Stadmark (2012) found that less women than men are invited to write articles in the *News and Views* section of *Nature* and *Perspectives in Science* Journals. This has two critical outcomes, firstly women are less visible in the leading science journals as having a contribution to make and secondly publication in the leading scientific journals is particularly useful for career progression, potentially disadvantaging women researchers. *Nature* has attempted to increase the number of published female authors previously, unfortunately this was after it was found that less women published in the *Insight* section. Following Conley and Stadmark's (2012) findings in *Nature*, we can expect that that the number of women authors will increase in this section.

Women can be disadvantaged in the workplace through socialisation, for example, women often speak less when outnumbered in groups, as is the case in male dominated occupations. This is a particular issue, particularly for SET careers. Karpowitz et al. (2012) reported that women tended to speak significantly less than their proportional representation, less than 75 percent of the time that men spoke. This is important as it may influence self-efficacy, should those in the minority feel undermined or marginalised, viewing themselves as un-influential in the group. Karpowitz et al. (2012) observed 94 groups of at least five people. They found that on average the groups discussed issues for 25 minutes, before reaching a decision. Importantly, when women were more involved, the researchers noted that unique and helpful

perspectives were included in the discussion. We will now consider gender bias, stereotypes and attitude.

GENDER BIAS AND STEREOTYPES

No, I have never wanted to be a man. I have often wanted to be more effective as a woman, but I have never felt that trousers would do the trick! (Eleanor Roosevelt, If You Ask Me, 1940)

Gender stereotypes can influence our emotions. For example in attributions made when individuals make mistakes. In recent research, Thoroughgood, Sawyer and Hunter (2012) assessed to what extent our emotions regarding leaders are influenced by gendered stereotypes in the workplace. The researchers used email fictional scenarios to ask participants to rate how competent they perceived a male or female leader to be. Interestingly, the leader was depicted as working in a gendered industry. The masculine industry was construction and the feminine nursing. Participants were presented with three different scenarios. The first involved the leaders making task-based errors, such as badly managing resources. The second involved relationship errors, such as losing their temper. The final scenario contained no errors committed. Over 300 individuals took part in the research; they were predominantly female students and were asked to rate how competent they thought the leader was for in performing tasks and relationships at work. Participants also rated how much they would want to work for the fictional leader.

Gender stereotyping might lead us to predict that women leaders would be viewed more negatively for relationship errors and men for task-based errors. This could even be much worse in gendered industries such as nursing or construction, or equally science, ICT and computer games. The rationale for this being that such behaviour violates gender role expectations, relating to competency, women being perceived as better at relationships the emotional side of work and men perceived as better at work based tasks, the getting things done side of work. Interestingly, Thoroughgood et al. found that whilst making errors generally led to lower ratings, attitudes were influenced by the industry. Men received a much greater number of negative judgements than women, in the construction industry. The authors report that regardless of gender, men and women need to be competent across domains, to be an effective leader. However, we would caution, that as the participants were students and subsequently a restricted age range, this could have influenced the findings. For example perception as to if many women actually work in the construction industry, this could have lead to attitude bias in how participants responded.

In a recent study by Moss-Racusin et al. (2012), men and women scientists were found to commit gender bias. The study tested scientist's reactions to men and women job applicants, with equal qualifications. The researchers used a randomized double-blind study design, to test scientists' attitudes to job applicants. The academic scientists were given application documents from a student applying for a lab manager position. Half the scientists were given the application with a male name attached, and half were given the same application with a female name attached. The applications were all identical; all that was changed was the applicants' name, to present them as man or woman. Interestingly, but perhaps unsurprisingly, the women applicants were rated lower than men for competence to do undertake the role applied for, the likelihood the scientist would recruit them to the role and if the scientist would be willing to act as mentor, if the applicant got the role. Importantly, both male and female scientists rated the female applicants lower, indicating that both men and women scientists were found to commit gender bias. The starting salaries that the scientists stated they would offer the applicants also varied, with the women applicants offered $26,507.94, compared to the $30,238.10 offered to the men. This implies that women, as much as men may consciously or unconsciously have an attitudinal bias towards women. Such prejudice may arise from societal stereotypes. A woman may read a job advertisement and consider carefully what she is capable of, whereas a man may have more confidence in their abilities. It appears that the scientists used what appeared to be reasonable justification as to why they rated the women as less competent, without resorting to any sexist language, yet still entrenched attitudes biased opinion! Using language can be powerful as indicating lack of competency appears reasonable justification as opposed to sexual bias. Should such subtle gender bias not be recognised, being informed you are not 'good enough', may be perceived by a woman as true, a fact and influence self-efficacy and confidence to apply for future roles. The authors stated that:

If faculty express gender biases, we are not suggesting that these biases are intentional or stem from a conscious desire to impede the progress of women in science. Past studies indicate that people's behaviour is shaped by implicit or unintended biases, stemming from repeated exposure to pervasive cultural stereotypes that portray women as less competent.

To overcome implicit bias, self-awareness is required to challenge behaviour, hopefully as the media highlights such issues, individuals will start to question their own and their colleagues' behaviour.

However, the lack of women in SET careers starts early, in the gendered beliefs among schoolchildren that science subjects are for the 'boys'. There have been some attempts to challenge stereotypes in children, for example Mattel™ who manufacturer the Barbie doll, brought out a 'Computer Engineer Barbie', who came with a pink laptop. Betz and Sekaquaptewa (2012) in a United States study found that science role models who appear 'girlie' can be negative in encouraging girls to be interested in science and maths subjects, due to perceiving 'girlie scientists' as incompatible. In their study, 144 girls with an average age of 11.5 years were given magazine style items to read, in two slightly different scenarios. One had 3 female undergraduates, who were successful in science subjects and appeared with makeup, pink clothes and said

they liked reading fashion magazines. After reading the magazines, the girls who before reading, had stated they had little interest in science subjects, reported even less interest to study science in the future and had less belief in their own abilities. Girls who read the alternative version, with 3 female undergraduates, who were successful in science subjects but not wearing pink clothes or appearing overtly girlie reported more interest and belief in ability. To test if this was due to 'girlie' female scientists being perceived as difficult to emulate, the authors tested 42 more schoolgirls, after reading the 'girlie' version they again reported that 'girlie' female scientists were less attainable. Of particular concern was the fact that the girls uninterested in science said that being good at science and being 'girlie' don't go together. The researchers felt this may be due to rigid stereotypes about gender and scientists. Obviously, as children age viewpoints change, however, this is an important finding as children may select to opt out of science subjects (and choose other non-science alternatives in school) in their early teens, reducing their options for Higher Education and science careers.

Female role models are important in challenging stereotypes, in particular women established in SET careers with the visibility and profile to inspire.

SENIOR WOMEN, PROFILE AND VISIBILITY

A woman is like a teabag, only in hot water do you realise how strong she is. - Nancy Regan (1981)

In high profile senior roles women are lacking, for example, in the United Kingdom, the Guardian newspaper (Khaleeli, 2012), interviewed two former women senior leaders from the television industry. Caroline Thomson, former chief operating officer at the British Broadcasting Corporation (BBC), resigned from the corporation after being unsuccessful in achieving the 'top job' of director general of the BBC, a post never held by a woman. The second interviewee was Dawn Airey, former chief executive of the Channel 5 television corporation in the United Kingdom. The interview focused on if a woman would ever be head of the BBC. During the interview Dawn Airey lamented the lack of women at the top:

If you go through the big [cultural] institutions in the UK, how many are run by women? It's not just about being competent and running the business efficiently, and with vision. These institutions should be representing society – to not have women running a least a third of them does beg a lot of questions. We also know that there is a lot of narcissism in appointments. People tend to appoint candidates similar to themselves, so you always have to ask who is making these decisions. It's also about informal networks. Men are better, generally, at networking, and spend more time with each other socially. Women think if they do a job well, it is sufficient, but that's not always the case.

Caroline Thomson felt strongly that women brought different qualities to the workplace and their role within a work team:

In my early career, because it was unusual to be a woman when I started, I spent a lot of time arguing that women were exactly the same as men. But, now I think women bring something different in their approach. And I think teams with a good balance of men and women are more effective. Men can bring a lot of dynamism and self-promotion, and women can bring a lot of can-do culture and are good at working with others.

Both women also commented on the lack of visibility of senior women and women as leaders. Caroline Thompson commented that:

Ageism and sexism is a deep issue for a lot of broadcasters, not just the BBC. Mark Thompson [former Director-General of the BBC] felt very strongly about it and pushed hard for more older women. It's wrong to assume all men don't care about these things. But I think having more senior women executives would help, because there are older men on screen and it does seem like a double standard.

Horrifyingly, Caroline Thompson noted an event that happened to her only a few years ago

It is a young industry. I remember my 50th birthday party and at the time we had a big campaign to make sure producers acknowledged older audiences, so there were big posters around saying, remember 40% of people over 50 have sex once a week. I did not know whether to be pleased or horrified! Broadcasting can be very inward-looking and it leads to this herd mentality. It's not just about presenters – if a format works, everyone, then commissions things that are similar.

For women working in Radio, 'Sound Women' a support and lobby group are working to get women better represented on the radio. It is therefore encouraging that, the person who did get the job Thompson applied for, the BBC, director general, George Entwistle, issued a call for the gender imbalance of the morning prime-time, BBC Radio 4 Today program to change in his first week in post. The Guardian newspaper reported that fewer than one in five people appearing on the Radio 4 Today programme were women. An average of 18.5% of reporters and guests appearing on Today were women. This was measured over a four-week period in June and July, 2012 and has slightly increased from the 16.6% recorded over a similar period in 2011 when the Guardian first analysed the Today program. The Guardian stated that the percentage is lower than the proportion of United Kingdom female judges or Members of Parliament. Encouragingly, in the first full week after Entwistle's comments, women contributors and guests rose to an average of 24%. The BBC acknowledged in the Sabbagh et al. (2012), article that there was a gender imbalance, yet felt they had little control over the issue:

Everyone can agree there should be better gender balance in the media including Today but, like all broadcasters, we have to reflect the world as it is. It's a fact there are fewer women than men at senior levels in business, politics and world affairs. That is bound to be reflected in our output.

This would appear at face value a realistic 'world view', yet we would suggest urge organisations to look harder, in order for women's voices to be heard and counteract gendered perceptions.

To aid recruitment and retention, the presence of senior women is important, such as presence on company boards. Gender diversity on boards is critical to sustaining performance and companies appear to recognise the importance of appointing diverse directors in terms of age and expertise. However, one crucial area is often overlooked, that of gender diversity. Women are underrepresented on Boards, for example only 16% in the United States and 14% in the European Union. European figures indicate that whilst the percentage of women in FTSE 100 companies increased to 12.5% in 2010, this was only a 5.5% increase from 2000. The percentage of women directors does vary by European country. The Scandinavian countries have the most, in excess of 20+% women board members; the United Kingdom, Ireland, and Netherlands 10% to 12.5%; Germany, France, Luxembourg, and Belgium 7.5% to 9.7%; and the Mediterranean countries such as Spain, Italy, and Greece 2% to 6.5%. There are several benefits to appointing more women on boards. In Fortune-500 companies ranked by the number of women board directors, those in the highest quartile in 2009, reported a 42% greater return on sales and a 53% higher return on equity than other companies. Research suggests that companies with at least three women directors deal more effectively with risk and focus on long-term priorities (Joy et al., 2012). There is a link between the presence of women on boards and organisational reputation. Several rating agencies and investment funds, such as CalP-ERS and PAX World, use the extent of gender diversity as one of their investment criteria. Furthermore, operational performance and share prices in FTSE listed companies are higher in companies where women comprise more than 20% of board members. Research (McKinsey, 2012) has proven a positive correlation between a company's performance and the proportion of women serving on its executive board. The research found that companies with the highest level of gender diversity in the most senior management roles outperform in their sector, in return on equity, operating results and stock price growth. Female directors can act as role models to other female employees and improve female recruitment.

Interestingly research has found that women are more likely to be appointed to very senior positions in organisations that are in crisis. Ryan et al. (2011), used hypothetical situations to determine how participants would choose to fill a position, such as company finance director or politician. The research asked participants to choose between two very similar candidates, who differed in gender. If the information in relation to the position was described as being within a stable environment, such as a successful growing organisation, or a winnable political seat, men and women were equally likely to be chosen. However, when information indicated that there was a difficult situation, with a high chance of failure, a woman was more likely to be selected. Indeed, women leaders were preferred when the situation was actively precarious. This would suggest that within stable organisations, stereotypical masculine leadership traits are desirable, such as being assertive, competitive and forthright. However, in crisis-situations leaders more stereotypical feminine traits, such as being considerate, thoughtful, understanding and creative are thought desirable, perhaps even perceived as necessary, for an organisation to survive in unstable times. This concept has been termed the 'glass cliff' due to the potential negative repercussions for the woman leader. Ryan et al. (2011) report that women chief executive officers (CEOs) generally have shorter tenure. This may relate to their appointment during a crisis-situation and resulting negative consequences.

If women are to occupy senior roles in greater numbers, then perceptions have to change. Senior women in any industry are role models for women in industry and visibility assists in the recruitment of young women. Encouraging the belief of 'I could do that' increase self-efficacy, which is important for career motivation and success.

THE LEAKY PIPELINE TO SENIORITY

In relation to the leaky pipeline, a report by the UK Resource Centre for Women in SET and Royal Society (2012) has revealed that only 12% of third year female PhD students want a career in academia. The findings from the study indicate that experience of the structures, cultures, environments and practices of scientific research plays a crucial role in influencing the career choices of research students (see Table 1). The research

Table 1. Key findings of the UK Resource Centre for Women in SET and Royal Society research with chemistry Ph.D students (2012)

A greater number of female Ph.D students had:
- Been advised in negative terms of the challenge they would face, due to their gender
- Been deeply affected by what might be termed 'standard supervision issues' (e.g. enjoying little pastoral care and having to cope with a supervisor who lacks interpersonal/management skills)
- Been uncomfortable with the culture of their research group (about working patterns, time and expectations and the level of competition between group members), especially where the culture was particularly 'macho'
- Believed academic careers were too consuming, solitary and not sufficiently collaborative
- Believed that doctoral research process is filled with frustration, pressure and stress
- Believed that the short-term contract aspect of post-doctoral work could not be reconciled with other aspects of their life, particularly relationships and family
- Believed they would need to make sacrifices in relation to femininity and motherhood to succeed in academia
- Developed concerns about poor, although normal experimental success rates and apprehensive as to what this may infer to others about their skills and competence
- Encountered significant supervision issues, which they felt powerless to resolve
- Experienced a lack of integration with their research group, isolation and exclusion
- Viewed competition for a permanent academic post was too fierce for them to compete successfully

identified factors, which relate to the doctoral study experience, and deter a larger proportion of women than men from remaining in research beyond their PhD. It was found that women scientists leave academia in far greater numbers than men due to the characteristics of academic careers viewed as unappealing, the impediments they believe they will encounter are disproportionate to the rewards and the sacrifices they believe that they will have to make are great. The report suggests that chemistry PhDs and academic careers are modelled on masculine models, which does not support women PhD students or inspire them to remain in research in the long term.

The report states that at the beginning of their studies, 72% of women expressed an intention to pursue careers as researchers and 61% of men expressed the same intention. By the third year, the proportion of men planning careers in research fell to 59%, for the women, the number fell dramatically to 37%. The majority of women (88%) and men (79%) did not want to pursue an academic career.

Issues such as funding for research projects and job security were an issue for both genders, but greater numbers of women viewed academic careers as too consuming, solitary and unnecessarily competitive. Unfortunately, in terms of role models, female students cited the fact that female professors were often perceived as having masculine characteristics, such as aggression and competitiveness, and were often childless. Furthermore, female students were often informed that due to their gender, they would encounter problems. These issues are pertinent throughout any SET Ph.D studies. The culture of the University as an organisation, the culture of a career in SET, in conjunction with ingrained stereotypes, attributions and bias remains to be addressed or an academic career will remain desirable to a reduced talent pool. There is a therefore a business case for addressing these issues within organisations and professional bodies.

ASPIRING TO SENIORITY

Although women make up roughly half of the workforce, far fewer women than men reach senior management and leadership positions. While the business case for gender diversity at all levels is compelling, progress has been glacial. (The Institute of Leadership and Management, 2011, p. 1)

Research by (ILM, 2011), with a large United Kingdom sample of 2,960 practising leaders and managers (49% men and 51% women) found that there was a disparity in the career ambitions of women managers, when compared to men. The ILM reported that women are more likely to limit their ambitions to the lower management levels, with less women, when compared to men, expecting to reach a senior management position, such as director. Furthermore, the ILM research found that the female managers reported lower career confidence (50%), than men (30%). Importantly, 50% of the women reported feelings of self-doubt, compared to 31% of the men. In terms of looking to the future senior managers, a significant disparity was identified. Only 15% of women under 30 expected to reach director level, within ten years. However, almost double the number of male managers (27%), under 30, expected to reach director level, within ten years. Of particular note in the ILM research was the fact that almost half (47%) of the women managers were in favour of quotas to increase female representation on boards, whereas only a quarter of the male participants were.

To develop women as leaders, the management company McKinsey have been running a leadership project, since 2008. The project aims to learn what drives and sustains successful female leaders. The philosophy is to assist young women navigate their careers to a successful leadership role. The project involves interviewing successful women leaders, from diverse fields, globally. Based on this project, a leadership model has been developed (Barsh et al., 2008). The model comprises five interrelated dimensions:

1. **Meaning:** The individual finding their strengths and using them to work in the service of an inspiring purpose
2. **Managing Energy:** The individual knowing where their energy comes from and how to manage it
3. **Positive Framing:** Adopting a more constructive way for the individual to view their world, to expand their horizons, to gain resilience to progress in negative times.
4. **Connecting:** Identifying who can help growth, building stronger relationships, increasing sense of belonging
5. **Engaging:** The individual becoming self-reliant, confident, accepting opportunities and collaborating with others.

The Centered Leadership Model (Barsh et al., 2008), has been specifically developed for women and is based on their needs and experiences. However, the authors note it is suitable to develop men. Barsh et al. (2008), distinguish that centred leadership emphasises the role of positive emotions. The model relates to the physical, intellectual, emotional and spiritual strength that drives personal achievement.

In terms of developing women, the ILM noted that reassessment in the workplace was required for women to attain leadership posts in greater numbers:

We know that women are more hesitant than men when applying for new positions. While men are willing to take greater risks when applying for stretching jobs, women are more risk averse, preferring to apply for roles where they are satisfied they meet the job description. In the long term, though, gender equality calls for a more fundamental reassessment and rewiring of work and the workplace. We need to move away from the traditional ideal of the hierarchical, male breadwinner leadership. (ILM, pg 10, 2011)

The ILM report and McKinsey research certainly resonates with our research findings, in that low confidence is related to ambition, in that self-efficacy or belief of attaining a senior leadership role will influence career ambition and applications for promotion. Mentoring has a key role to play in developing self-confidence, aspiration and leadership development. Employers have a key role in identifying successful leaders to mentor to female managers. Women need encouragement and advice to develop their networks for career growth.

MENTORING

The lack of women in certain professions, particularly SET professions is well documented (i.e. Bebbingham, 2002; Vinnecombe & Singh, 2003; Ogden, McTavish & McKean, 2006). Mentoring can be an important factor for women's progression. Formal mentoring programs match mentors and mentees, designate minimum time commitments and monitor relationships. Informal mentoring relationships tend to develop spontaneously, in that a mentee is able to choose their own mentor. Many authors suggest women lack equal access to adequate informal mentoring, due to the lack of senior women and role models and men preferring to mentor men (i.e. Bussy-Jones et al., 2006). Mentoring may exist throughout much of an individual career. There has been some criticism of mentoring in that it is ineffective, whilst it is different to informal mentoring, it can grow different but valuable relationships. Formal mentoring relationships can be very effective and can aid workforce retention. Organisations that instigate formal mentoring programs can recruit, retain, promote and develop their employees. This is of particular benefit to women working in males dominated occupations. Our research found that women cited a lack of mentoring opportunities as a barrier to their progression. Some of the women in our research cited that it was access to a mentor that was the issue:

I mean it about the time really, unless you know someone really good, that you look up to, then its do your research to find someone and then if you do [approach them], chances are they are too busy.

Researchers have found a number of drawbacks with traditional mentoring, especially for women and ethnic minorities. One of the problems for women and people from ethnic minorities is the availability of suitable mentors and potential role models (i.e. Anderson, 2005; Bussy-Jones et al., 2006). If formal mentoring is not as effective and thus, not as beneficial as informal mentoring, then women are disadvantaged within organizations, which in turn may influence career progression. Women do not necessarily need to be mentored by women to have a successful mentoring relationship, but perhaps the lack of senior women is a hindrance to many women's careers. Turban, Thomas, and Lee (2002), found gender did not affect the mentoring received although they did find that people were more likely to be in a relationship with those perceived similar to themselves. E-mentoring is also possible, it allows flexibility, beneficial to women with children and childcare responsibilities, who might have more difficulty accessing a mentor. Mentoring can build confidence (Anderson, 2005), improve career motivation and career self-efficacy (Day & Allen, 2004) and reduce work/home conflict (Nielson, Carlson, & Lankau, 2001). Allen et al. 2004 conducted a meta-analysis of the career benefits of mentees. They found that mentees were more satisfied with their career, believed they would advance in their careers, were more committed to their careers and had a greater intention to stay in their current organisation than the non-mentored individuals. Interestingly, the meta-analysis concluded that mentees had greater salary growth, more promotions and more job satisfaction than those not mentored.

Mentoring is a dynamic and complex relationship that has the potential for personal and professional development (Barker, 2006). Mentoring can be defined as an activity in which an individual with advanced knowledge or experience actively provides assistance and support to enhance the career development of an individual with less knowledge and experience. Kram (1985) suggested there are five specific career functions which mentors can provide, sponsorship, coaching, protection, challenging assignments and exposure (visibility). However, Fowler and O'Gorman (2005), suggest Kram's protection function, in the current work climate, is not required by mentees. Mentoring provides career development and a psychosocial function. The career development function enables mentee's to learn and develop, there are five specific career functions which mentors can provide for mentees: sponsorship, coaching, protection, challenging assignments, and exposure (visibility). The psychosocial function highlights the interpersonal aspects to mentoring in order to enhance the competence, self-efficacy, personal and professional development of the mentee.

Some researchers argue that women who have mentors gain access to resources and senior managers through their mentor, enabling career progression (Vinnecombe & Singh, 2003; Robinson & Cannon 2005). Alternatives to traditional mentoring exist such as e-mentoring, this allows flexibility and is particularly beneficial to women with care responsibilities or those with no identifiable mentor in their work location (Whiting & de Janasz, 2004). Gender differences between mentors have been reported, with male mentors providing mentees with greater career mentoring and female mentors providing greater psychosocial mentoring. The greatest amount of psychosocial mentoring occurred between female mentors and female mentees and the least amount between female mentor and male mentee. Allen and Eby (2004) suggested that female mentors may empathise more with female mentees due to discriminatory barriers in the workplace. Some researchers suggest that traditional male dominance, prevents female mentor/male mentee relationships (O'Neill and Blake-Beard, 2002; Robinson & Cannon, 2005). Allen et al. (2004) conducted a meta analysis of the career benefits of mentoring to mentees. The Meta analysis found that mentored people were more satisfied with their career, believed they would advance in their careers, were more committed to their careers and had a greater intention to stay in their current organization, than non-mentored employees. In addition, there are psychosocial benefits from mentoring, such as confidence building and personal growth (Anderson, 2005; Hayden, 2006). In addition, Day and Allen (2004) found that individuals who are mentored have more career motivation and career self-efficacy. Nielson, Carlson, and Lankau (2001), found another potential benefit to mentoring in that it can be a source of social support and reduce any stress due to conflicts between work and home. The study found it is important for both men and women to have a supportive mentor who shares the same work/life balance values as them. Baugh and Fagenson-Eland's (2005), study of mentors and mentees in three technology firms in America revealed that mentees perceived that they gained more career and psychosocial support when their mentor worked in the same employment setting, compared to mentees whose mentors worked in a different employment setting. From their findings Baugh and Fagenson-Eland's, suggest that mentors in different organizations cannot offer their men-tees the same level of sponsorship, coaching, protection, challenging assignments, visibility and exposure or the psychosocial elements of mentoring as mentors within their organization can provide. Therefore, they suggest that if an individual wants to progress within the organization they are currently in then they should seek a mentor within that same organization. The key positive and negative aspects of mentoring are detailed in Table 2.

NETWORKING

Women can be restricted in the workplace due to their lack of involvement and use of networks. There are two main types of networks formal (prescribed) and informal (emergent). Formal networks are formally prescribed relationships among functionally defined groups that exist for accomplishing some organizational task (Ibarra, 1993; Hetty van Emmerik et al., 2006). According to McGuire (2000), formal networks are more likely to be public, official and have clear boundaries, with

Table 2. Positive and negative aspects to mentoring

Positives
Psychosocial benefits.
Career progression benefits.
Supportive role.
Increase confidence.
The sharing of ideas and knowledge.
Negatives
Time consuming.
Relationships - forced or attached to a bad mentor are problematic.
Individuals perceiving that they may need extra support.

identifiable membership. Informal networks on the other hand, tend to be more personal, voluntary and have more fluid boundaries with participation not officially governed nor recognized (McGuire, 2000). Durbin (2011) highlights the importance of differentiating between formal and informal networks. According to Durbin (2011), senior women have limited access to informal networks. Research suggests that men form informal networks, (what have been termed 'old boys' networks') which enables career progression and support. Old boy's networks are exclusively male and established through such commonly shared activities and interests as golf, football and pubs (Linehan, 2001). These networks exclude women by their nature of shared activity and similarity of members. Forret and Dougherty (2004) explored the relationship between involvement in networking behaviours and both objective and perceived career success outcomes. Study findings indicated that some types of networking behaviour related to career outcomes. Five different types of networking behaviours were used in the study: maintaining external contacts, socializing, engaging in professional activities, participating in community activities, and increasing internal visibility. Increasing internal visibility and engaging in professional activities significantly influenced career success outcomes. The authors suggest that it is important to distinguish among networking behaviours and their relationship to career outcomes, when researching networks. Furthermore, the study supports previous research surrounding the gendered nature of network benefits, as it found that gender differences influence the

utility of networking behaviour, as a career-enhancing strategy. The authors argue that networks were more beneficial to the career progression of males than of females. In particular, the study found gender differences within networking behaviour, especially for internal visibility and professional activities. They found that men, to a greater extent than women, received benefits from increased visibility, with more promotions. With regard to professional activities, being involved in professional activities was positive for men, but could be negative for women. Suggesting men's professional activities are valued more highly by organizations.

Women engage more than men in both formal and informal networking, yet men are more skilled at utilizing networks then women (i.e. Hetty van Emmerik et al., 2006). These findings support that of Singh et al. (2007), who found men were more adept that women at seeking out key people to network with. Networking is creating a system of information, contact and support which may be crucial for career success and advancement. In her detailed study of networking of UK women 'girlfriends in high places' McCarthy (2004), found numerous benefits to networking. McCarthy argues that networks are able to provide clues as to how to spread information, enabling learning, and build trust and solidarity throughout an organization, while providing individuals with an outlet for pursuing personal development and career advancement. McCarthy (2004) suggests that women still perceive the 'Old Boy Network' to be a significant barrier to career progression. Reasons for women's exclusion from this network include socialization and 'male bonding' activities that strengthen reciprocal behaviours amongst men. The unequal division of childcare and housework which significantly falls to the responsibility of women, consequently results in women having less time to participate in 'out of hours' networking activities. The ability to make contacts and then to cultivate those contacts into business relationships has rapidly become a core competency in the workplace, with employers benefiting in a variety of ways from their employee's social networks. Researchers have argued that women are hindered in their careers, due to the inequality in accessing social capital (Timberlake, 2005). This inequality provides fewer opportunities for women to develop and fully utilize networks and contacts disadvantaging both women and organizations. Some researchers go so far as to suggest, that networks may reproduce patriarchy rather than erode it (Bierema, 2005).

Benefits to women only networks are evident throughout the literature, such as women only IT training programs (Rommes, Faulkner, & Van Slooten, 2005). This suggests women benefit from positive role models, encouragement and support. Although women's networks present an option to informal male networks, not all women are in support of them. McGuire (2000), found women did not want to be labelled radical or feminist. 'Mothers meetings' is another negative way in which women only networks can be viewed (Perriton, 2006). Pini, Brown, and Ryan's (2004) Australian study of women mayors revealed that women were divided, in their views regarding women only networks.

One group expressed support for women's networking, a second group was critical of women organizing in such a way and a third group expressed ambivalence about the value of women's networks. Pini, Brown, and Ryan (2004) suggest women only networks are only a short-term strategy to target discrimination, with a long term agenda for organizational and social change that includes diverse networking and engaging with male dominated networks.

WORK/LIFE BALANCE

Work/life balance has been the subject of intense debate and cited as one of the most important considerations for graduates when choosing an employer (Personnel Today, 2010; Lyon & Woodward, 2004). Health problems as a result of working excessive hours are well documented (Kotz et al., 2003, Burn, 2002). Research evidence confirms that women are generally more disadvantaged than men by working long hours. Indeed, women working long hours are much more likely than those who do not work long hours, to report poor health (Hyman & Summers, 2003; Kodz et al., 2003; Gareis & Barnett, 2002). There is an association between life satisfaction and occupational status; men and women in professional jobs report higher levels of life satisfaction than those in skilled or unskilled jobs (Schoon et al., 2005). However, organisations where long hours are the norm are potentially restrictive for women, as women tend to remain responsible for domestic and caring responsibilities outside work. This may in part of the explain why women are more likely than men to be dissatisfied and suffer the most due to working long hours.

The number of women entering traditionally male dominated careers is increasing. Understanding of how work/life balance should work is crucial for appropriate adoption and implementation of practices such as flexible working (Hyman & Summer, 2003). In addition, some research has noted a range of anxieties employers have expressed and reluctance to introducing flexible work arrangements (Hyman et al., 2005; Kodz et al., 2002). This includes concerns that wide availability of flexible working policies will produce an unlimited demand, in addition to fears that some employees will take advantage of such policies, resulting in reduced productivity and a detriment to services. Research conducted by Kotz et al. (2002) confirmed that 35 per cent of employers said that women returning from maternity leave wanting to change from full-time to part-time working, would not be able to return to their existing job and level of seniority. Traditional working hours may present problems for employees who have to combine work and family responsibilities. There are benefits therefore in introducing flexible working arrangements that permit individuals to find a better balance between home and work. Table 3 details the benefits and options for flexible working.

Perhaps the overarching obstacle to achieving work/life balance in games development is the long hours' culture. Long hours are often regarded as necessary, especially at 'crunch time' and some research suggests that using strategies for maintaining a work/life balance can be damaging to ones career (Drew

Table 3. Flexible working benefits and options

Types of Flexible Working
Flexible working could be taken as working full time, with flexibility in relation to timing of the hours, through flexible working time or a personalised annualised hours contract.
Working reduced hours such as shorter days or less days a week, part year working, term-time working, job sharing
Working either full or reduced hours at home
Taking a career break
Types of Reasons for Flexible Working
Care of pre-school children
Care of school age children
Care of elderly and dependant relatives
Personal disability
Recovery from a prolonged illness
Preparation for retirement
Time to develop new skills
Commitment to charity or volunteer work
Benefits for the Employee Can Include
Better balance of work and home commitments
Increased quality of life
Reduced Stress
Greater job satisfaction
Ability to remain in role
Ability to maintain career development
Benefits for the Organisation can Include
Retention of trained and valuable staff
Increased productivity
Decreased absence
Increased motivation
Viewed as valuing diversity
Improve recruitment
Improve retention
Retain and develop employees

& Murtagh, 2005; Hyman et al., 2005). Working long hours is common in the United Kingdom, the United States, Australia and Japan. Factors for working long hours include volume of work, organisational initiatives, project based working, a greater emphasis on customer focus and staff shortages. In games development, as with other specialist roles, there is the additional issues of the need for the specialist, to work to a deadline such as 'crunch time'. The culture of the organisation, influences the expectations of managers and colleagues as to if a long hours culture is accepted, especially if 'presenteeism' is valued as a sign of commitment to work. Given the increasing numbers of women entering traditionally male dominated professions, urgent consideration is required as to how careers can be reconciled with work life balance and the needs of workers.

CONCLUSION

To aid recruitment and retention, the presence of senior women is important, such as presence on company boards. Gender diversity on boards is critical to sustaining performance and companies appear to recognise the importance of appointing diverse directors in terms of age and expertise. Female directors can act as role models to other female employees and improve female recruitment. Research has found that women are more likely to be appointed to very senior positions in organisations that are in crisis. This would suggest that within stable organisations, stereotypical masculine leadership traits are desirable, such as being assertive, competitive and forthright. However, in crisis-situations leaders more stereotypical feminine traits, such as being considerate, thoughtful, understanding and creative are thought desirable, perhaps even

perceived as necessary, for an organisation to survive in unstable times. This concept has been termed the 'glass cliff' due to the potential negative repercussions for the woman leader.

Women are more likely to limit their ambitions to the lower management levels, with less women, when compared to men, expecting to reach a senior management position, such as director. In relation to the leaky pipeline, a report by the UK Resource Centre for Women in SET and Royal Society (2012) has revealed that only 12% of third year female PhD students want a career in academia. The findings from the study indicate that experience of the structures, cultures, environments and practices of scientific research plays a crucial role in influencing the career choices of research students. The lack of women in SET careers starts early, in the gendered beliefs among schoolchildren that science subjects are for the 'boys'. There have been some attempts to challenge stereotypes in children. Betz and Sekaquaptewa (2012), in a United States study, found that science role models who appear 'girlie' can be negative in encouraging girls to be interested in science and maths subjects, due to perceiving 'girlie scientists' as incompatible.

Work/life balance has been the subject of intense debate and cited as one of the most important considerations for graduates when choosing an employer. The number of women entering traditionally male dominated careers is increasing. Understanding of how work/life balance should work is crucial for appropriate adoption and implementation of practices such as flexible working. Health problems as a result of working excessive hours are well documented. Perhaps the overarching obstacle to achieving work/life balance in games development is the long hours' culture. Long hours are often regarded as necessary, especially at 'crunch time' and some research suggests that using strategies for maintaining a work/life balance can be damaging to ones career. Gender stereotypes can influence our emotions. For example in attributions made when individuals make mistakes. Women, as much as men, may consciously or unconsciously have an attitudinal bias towards women. Such prejudice may arise from societal stereotypes. To overcome implicit bias, self-awareness is required to challenge behaviour, hopefully as the media highlights such issues, individuals will start to question their own and their colleagues' behaviour.

Equity within scientific research has increased in recent decades. It could be argued that women today have the same range of opportunities as men; however, we feel there is still a long way to go to achieve gender parity. Indeed, Barsh and Yee (2011) suggest that in relation to organisational change, 70% of transformation efforts fail and that support for the most senior staff and a comprehensive plan to achieve change and entrenched behaviours is required for success. Gender, analysis should be encouraged, for example in

Table 4. Issues women face: The key issues

Issues Women Face	Core Issues Involved	How May the Issue be Addressed
Recruitment	• Implicit bias in award, selection and nomination committees. • Improve image of industry to appeal to women. • Work environment. • Environments recruit and retain individuals whose characteristics are congruent to the working environment. • Person-environment fit. • Self-efficacy. • Self-esteem.	• Training of selection group members to avoid unconscious bias. • Ensure women are represented in adequate numbers on promotion, job, prize committees etc. • Check for implicit bias in criteria for awards and nominations and research assessment type RAE exercises. • Make the workplace women friendly. • Remove barriers to women being recruited to and remaining in the organisation. • Foster a supportive work environment that appeals to women's values and work styles.
Career motivation	• Experience of work environment. • Women are less visible in the leading science journals.	• Recognise the contribution women can make in publication in the leading scientific journals is particularly useful for career progression. • Make the environment one that fosters motivation regardless of gender.
Retention	• Individuals prefer and remain in environments that are congruent with their vocational personalities. • Lack of opportunities. • Not enough work life balance. • Poor working environment. • Job satisfaction. • Work life balance. • Women's career development. • Person-environment fit. • Self-efficacy and self-esteem.	• Remove barriers to women being recruited to and remaining in the organisation. • Make the workplace women friendly. • Organisational level issues, to be addressed by management, for change to occur and encourage women to remain in the industry. • Increase flexible working practices. • Identify the barriers and opportunities for job satisfaction.

relation to conferences examining by gender invited speakers, round table speakers, workshop facilitators and invited participants. In high profile senior roles women are lacking. Senior women in any industry are role models for women in industry and visibility assists in the recruitment of young women. Some researchers argue that women who have mentors gain access to resources and senior managers through a mentor, enabling career progression. Culture change is required to address the issues raised in this chapter and repair the 'leaky pipeline' in SET. In the next chapter, we will highlight the key issues in relation to improving the position of women in the SET sectors.

REFERENCES

Allen, T. D., & Eby, L. T. (2004). Factors related to mentor reports of mentoring functions provided: Gender & relational characteristics. *Sex Roles*, *50*(12), 129–139. doi:10.1023/B:SERS.0000011078.48570.25

Allen, T. D., Lentz, E., & Day, R. (2006). Career success outcomes associated with mentoring others. *Journal of Career Development*, *32*(3), 272–285. doi:10.1177/0894845305282942

Allen, T. D., Poteet, M. L., Eby, L. T., Lentz, E., & Lima, L. (2004). Career benefits associated with mentoring for protégés: A meta-analysis. *The Journal of Applied Psychology*, *89*(1), 127–136. doi:10.1037/0021-9010.89.1.127 PMID:14769125

Anderson, D. R. (2005). The importance of mentoring programs to women's career advancement in biotechnology. *Journal of Career Development*, *32*(1), 60–73. doi:10.1177/0894845305277039

Barker, E. R. (2006). Mentoring – A complex relationship. *Journal of the American Academy of Nurse Practitioners*, *18*, 56–61. doi:10.1111/j.1745-7599.2006.00102.x PMID:16460411

Barsh, J., Cranston, S., & Craske, R. A. (2008). *Centered leadership: How talented women thrive: A new approach to leadership can help women become more self-confident & effective business leaders report*. Retrieved from http://www.mckinseyquarterly.com/Centered_leadership_How_talented_women_thrive_2193

Barsh, J., & Yee, L. (2011). *Unlocking the full potential of women in the US economy*. Retrieved from http://www.mckinsey.com/client_service/organization/latest_thinking/unlocking_the_full_potential

Baugh, S., & Fagenson-Eland, E. A. (2005). Boundaryless mentoring: An exploratory study of the functions provided by internal versus external organizational mentors. *Journal of Applied Social Psychology*, *35*(5), 939–955. doi:10.1111/j.1559-1816.2005.tb02154.x

Bebbington, D. (2002). Women in science, engineering & technology: A review of the issues. *Higher Education Quarterly*, *56*(4), 360. doi:10.1111/1468-2273.00225

Betz, D., & Sekaquaptewa, D. (2012). My fair physicist? Feminine math & science role models demotivate young girls. *Social Psychological & Personality Science, 3*(6), 738–746. doi:10.1177/1948550612440735

Bierema, L. L. (2005). Women's networks: A career development intervention or impediment? *Human Resource Development International, 8*(2), 207–224. doi:10.1080/13678860500100517

Bussey-Jones, J., Bernstein, L., Higgins, S., Malebranche, D., Paranjape, A., & Genao, I. et al. (2006). Repaving the road to academic success: The IMeRge (internal medicine research group at emory), approach to peer mentoring. *Academic Medicine, 81*(7), 674–677. doi:10.1097/01.ACM.0000232425.27041.88 PMID:16799297

Conley, D., & Stadmark, J. (2012). Gender matters: A call to commission more women writers. *Nature, 488*(7413), 590. doi:10.1038/488590a PMID:22932370

Day, R., & Allen, T. D. (2004). The relationship between career motivation & self-efficacy with protégé career success. *Journal of Vocational Behavior, 64*, 72–91. doi:10.1016/S0001-8791(03)00036-8

Drew, E., & Murtagh, E. M. (2005). Work/life balance: Senior management champions or laggards? *Women in Management Review, 20*(4), 262–278. doi:10.1108/09649420510599089

Durbin, S. (2011). Creating knowledge through networks: A gender perspective. *Gender, Work and Organization, 18*, 90–112. doi:10.1111/j.1468-0432.2010.00536.x

Fowler, J.L & O'Gorman. (2005). Mentoring functions: A contemporary view of the perceptions of mentees & mentors. *British Journal of Management, 16*, 51–57. doi:10.1111/j.1467-8551.2005.00439.x

Gareis, K. C., & Barnett, R. C. (2002). Under what conditions do long hours affect psychological distress: A study of full-time & reduced-hours female doctors. *Work and Occupations, 29*(4), 483–497. doi:10.1177/0730888402029004005

Hayden, J. (2006). Mentoring: Help with climbing the career ladder. *Health Promotion Practice, 7*(3), 289–292. doi:10.1177/1524839906289269 PMID:16760239

Hetty Van Emmerik, I. J., Euwema, M. C., Geschiere, M., & Schouten, M. F. A. G. (2006). Networking your way through the organization: Gender differences in the relationship between network participation & career satisfaction. *Women in Management Review, 21*(1), 54–66. doi:10.1108/09649420610643411

Hyman, J., Scholarios, D., & Baldry, C. (2005). Getting on or getting by? Employee flexibility & coping strategies for home & work. *Work, Employment and Society, 19*(4), 705–725. doi:10.1177/0950017005058055

Hyman, J., & Summers, J. (2003). Lacking balance? Work-life employment practices in the modern economy. *Personnel Review, 33*(4), 418–429. doi:10.1108/00483480410539498

Ibarra, H. (1993). Personal networks of women & minorities in management: A conceptual framework. *Academy of Management Review, 18*(1), 56–87.

ILM. (2011). *Ambition & gender at work.* Institute of Leadership & Management. Retrieved from www.i-l-m.com

Joy, L., Carter, N., Wagner, H. M., & Narayanan, S. (2012). *The bottom line: Corporate performance & women's representation on boards.* Retrieved from www.catalyst.org/file/139/bottom%20line%202.pdf

Karpowitz, C. F., Mendelberg, T., & Shaker, L. (2012). Gender inequality in deliberative participation. *The American Political Science Review, 106*(3), 533. doi:10.1017/S0003055412000329

Khaleeli, H. (2012). *Will a woman ever run the BBC?* Retrieved from http://www.guardian.co.uk/commentisfree/2012/sep/28/will-a-woman-ever-run-bbc

Kodz, J., Davis, S., Lain, D., Strebler, M., Rick, J., Bates, P., et al. (2002). *Work-life balance: Beyond the rhetoric. institute of employment studies, report 384.* Retrieved from http://www.employment-studies.co.uk/summary/summary.php?id=384

Kram, K. E. (1985). *Mentoring at work: Developmental relationships in organizational life.* Glenview, IL: Scott Foresman.

Lincoln, A. E., Pincus, S., Koster, J. B., & Leboy, P. S. (2012). The Matilda effect in science: Awards & prizes in the US, 1990s & 2000s. *Social Studies of Science, 42*(2), 307. doi:10.1177/0306312711435830 PMID:22849001

Linehan, M. (2001). Networking for female managers career development. *Journal of Management Development, 20*(10), 823–829. doi:10.1108/EUM0000000006237

Lyon, D., & Woodward, A. E. (2004). Gender & time at the top cultural constructions of time in high-level careers & homes. *European Journal of Women's Studies, 11*(2), 205–221. doi:10.1177/1350506804042096

McCarthy, H. (2004). *Girlfriends in high places: How women's networks are changing the workplace.* London: Demos.

McGuire, G. M. (2000). Gender, race, ethnicity & networks: The factors affecting the status of employees network members. *Work and Occupations, 27*(4), 501–523. doi:10.1177/0730888400027004004

McKinsey. (2012). *Women matter report, 2012.* Retrieved from http://www.mckinsey.com/features/women_matter

Meager, N., Anxo, D., Gineste, S., Trinczek, R., & Pamer, S. (2003). *Working long hours: A review of the evidence*. Retrieved from http://www.dti.gov.uk/er/emar/errs16vol1.pdf

Moss-Racusin, C. A., Dovidio, J. F., Brescoll, V. L., Graham, M. J., & Handelsman, J. (2012). Science faculty's subtle gender biases favour male students. In *Proceedings of the National Academy of Sciences of the United States of America*. PNAS. doi:10.1073/pnas.1211286109

Nielson, T. R., Carlson, D. S., & Lankau, M. J. (2001). The supportive mentor as a means of reducing work-family conflict. *Journal of Vocational Behavior*, *59*, 364–381. doi:10.1006/jvbe.2001.1806

O'Neill, R. M., & Blake-Beard, S. D. (2002). Gender barriers to the female mentor – male protégé relationship. *Journal of Business Ethics*, *37*, 51–63. doi:10.1023/A:1014778017993

Ogden, S. M., McTavish, D., & McKean, L. (2006). Clearing the way for gender balance in the management of the UK financial services industry. *Women in Management Review*, *21*(1), 40–53. doi:10.1108/09649420610643402

Perriton, L. (2006). *Does woman + a network = career progression?* Retrieved from http://eprints.whiterose.ac.uk/2419/1/perritonl2_Leadership._Does_woman_plus_a_network_equal_career_success.pdf

Personnel Today. (2010, April 16). Graduates look for work life balance. *Personnel Today*.

Pini, B., Brown, K., & Ryan, C. (2004). Women-only networks as a strategy for change? A case study from local government. *Women in Management Review*, *19*(6), 286–292. doi:10.1108/09649420410555051

Robinson, J. D., & Cannon, D. L. (2005). Mentoring in the academic medical setting: The gender gap. *Journal of Clinical Psychology*, *12*(3), 265–270.

Rommes, E., Faulkner, W., & Van Slooten, I. (2005). Changing lives: The case for women-only vocational technology training revisited. *Journal of Vocational Education and Training*, *57*(3), 293–318. doi:10.1080/13636820500200288

Ryan, M. K., Haslam, S. A., Hersby, M. D., & Bongiorno, R. (2011). Think crisis-think female: The glass cliff & contextual variation in the think manager-think male stereotype. *The Journal of Applied Psychology*, *96*(3), 470–484. doi:10.1037/a0022133 PMID:21171729

Schoon, I., Hansson, L., & Salmela-Aro, K. (2005). Combining work & family life: Life satisfaction among married & divorced men & women in Estonia, Finland, & the UK. *European Psychologist*, *10*(4), 309–319. doi:10.1027/1016-9040.10.4.309

Servon, L., & Visser, M. (2011). Progress hindered: The retention & advancement of women in science, engineering & technology careers. *Human Resource Management Journal*, *21*(3), 272–284. doi:10.1111/j.1748-8583.2010.00152.x

SET & Royal Society. (2012). *Report: The chemistry PhD: The impact on women's retention*. UK Resource Centre for Women in SET & the Royal Society of Chemistry. Retrieved from http://www.biochemistry.org/Portals/0/SciencePolicy/Docs/Chemistry%20Report%20For%20Web.pdf

Singh, V., Vinnicombe, S., & Terjesen, S. (2007). Women advancing onto the corporate board. In *Handbook of women in business & management*. London: Edward Elgar.

Thoroughgood, C. N., Sawyer, K. B., & Hunter, S. T. (2012). Real men don't make mistakes: Investigating the effects of leader gender, error type, & the occupational context on leader error perceptions. *Journal of Business and Psychology, 1*(27), 889–227.

Timberlake, S. (2005). Social capital & gender in the workplace. *Journal of Management Development, 24*(1), 34–44. doi:10.1108/02621710510572335

Turban, D. B., Thomas, W. D., & Lee, F. K. (2001). Gender, race & perceived similarity effects in developmental relationships: The moderating role of relationship duration. *Journal of Vocational Behavior, 61*, 240–262. doi:10.1006/jvbe.2001.1855

Vinnicombe, S., & Singh, V. (2003). Locks & keys to the boardroom. *Women in Management Review, 18*(6), 325–333. doi:10.1108/09649420310491495

Whiting, V. R., & de Janasz, S. C. (2004). Mentoring in the 21st century: Using the internet to build skills & networks. *Journal of Management Education, 28*(3), 275–293. doi:10.1177/1052562903252639

KEY TERMS AND DEFINITIONS

Barriers: Barriers that may prevent an individual from progressing in their career.

Gender: The state of being male or female (typically used with reference to social and cultural differences rather than biological ones).

Mentoring: Where an individual is provided with a mentor in a more senior position to help guide, advise, and provide general support within the workplace in order to aid career progression and advancement of the mentee.

Networking: There are two main types of networks: formal (prescribed) and informal (emergent). Formal networks are formally prescribed relationships among functionally defined groups that exist for accomplishing some organizational task. Informal networks, on the other hand, tend to be more personal, voluntary, and have more fluid boundaries with participation not officially governed nor recognized.

Chapter 9
Reflections for the Future

ABSTRACT

This chapter considers the careers of women more generally, not just of those in the computer game industry. The chapter considers ways forward and how the workplace can be improved to help women's careers. This includes identifying career factors and considering a number of psychological constructs, such as stereotypes and solo status. It considers the position of women in senior management and leadership positions, explores how women are disadvantaged in the workforce, and provides the reader with an understanding of the issue of time and how this impacts the careers of women due to the long hours culture associates with many careers, especially male-dominated careers. Finally, the chapter looks at how organisational practices can support women in the workforce.

INTRODUCTION

Career aspirations are important to consider when looking at women's advancement and career development. Early research by Carr (1997) found health issues associated with career aspirations, in that women who had not achieved their career goals had lower levels of 'purpose of life' and higher levels of depression than women who felt they had achieved their earlier goals. Mayrhofer et al. (2005) put forward that career aspiration is a form of self-selection since individual self-select success is dependent on personal strengths and weaknesses. Career aspirations are influenced by many factors including

DOI: 10.4018/978-1-4666-4534-9.ch009

gender, socioeconomic status, race, parent's occupation, educational level and expectations (Domenico & Jones, 2006).

Implicit stereotypes have been found to impact gender differences in estimated salaries; with money and wealth viewed as masculine (Williams et al., 2010). Bendl and Schmidt (2010) suggest that although the glass ceiling is still a useful metaphor, they also argue that the glass firewall is perhaps a more useful metaphor. The authors put forward that the glass firewall metaphor captures the complexity, fluidity and heterogeneity of discrimination in contemporary organizations. This captures the 'invisibility' and multifaceted nature of barriers to women within the workplace. Wilson-Kovacs, Ryan, and Haslam (2006) examined the concept of the glass cliff to explain what happens to women as they advance in senior positions. The glass cliff is a metaphor used to refer to mainly women in leadership positions, which tend to be risky and precarious. The study looked at women in the UK's private IT sector and found the concept of the glass cliff useful when looking at retention and the lack of women in executive positions, within the sector. There is also evidence of a glass cliff in politics (Ryan, Haslam, & Kulich, 2010). Other ways in which women are marginalized may be due to organizational structures or cultures.

Gendered occupational segregation has a detrimental effect on many aspects of women's careers most specifically pay, promotion and career opportunities. As we have discussed throughout this book, gender inequalities are apparent in the workforce and echoed at the most senior levels. In the United Kingdom women comprise more than half of the senior workforce (57%), yet at the most senior levels, only 24% of chief executives are female. In terms of pay, difference are found at all levels. The Fawcett Society (2012), campaigns for gender equality and believes that a dedicated women's employment strategy is required. The Fawcett Society report a 15 percent difference in the pay of men and women. However, there are sector differences, with a 13.2% gender pay gap in the public sector and 20.4% gender pay gap in the private sector. The Chartered Management Institute (CMI, 2012), conduct a National Management Salary Survey yearly, in the United Kingdom. The 2011/2012 data was collected from 38,843 employees, from junior manager to board level and reported that women senior managers face a lifetime pay gap of £423,390 less over their lifetimes, than men who follow identical career paths. The Chartered Management Institute have also reported that women managers now earn £14,689 a year less than their male counterparts, with female directors earning an average basic salary of £127,257, compared with a male director's average salary of £141,946. Cash bonuses were also considerably less. The average for a male executive was £7,496, compared with £3,726 for a female executive. Of particular concern, was the fact that women are more likely to be made redundant than men. The CMI reported that between Aug 2011 and Aug 2012, 4.3 per cent of female executives, compared with 3.2 per cent of male executives, and 7.4 per cent of female directors compared with 3.1 per cent of male directors, were made redundant. The number of women losing their jobs has almost doubled, since the last survey of 2010/2011 data (CMI, 2012). Due to the economic downturn, redundancies are unfortunately commonplace. However, the CMI finding lead to the conclusion that inequity exists, with more senior women, than men potentially retiring early, disengaging from the labour market or seeking new employment. New employment, may well be below the level the individual is qualified for and possibly part-time, due to availability of employment.

It would seem that gender segregation is resilient within the paid labour market, despite changes in society such as globalisation, technological change, and women's increasing presence within paid labour. Gendered occupational segregation is an important issue, especially since segregation into different occupations remains a key factor contributing to the gender gap in earnings. Gender Segregation can occur both vertically; concentrating individuals in the lower echelons of an organization and horizontally; concentrating individuals in particular occupations, making some occupations either 'men's' or 'women's' work. The glass ceiling is a term often used to refer to the vertical segregation of women since it is women who tend to experience this form of segregation the most. In America, the Institute for Women's Policy Research (IWPR) suggested that progress towards gender integration in the workforce was made during the 1970's and 1980's, but little progress has been made since the 1990's (Hegewisch et al., 2010). Women remain predominantly in occupations with lower pay, lower prestige and status and lower security. It is argued that gendered cultural beliefs constrain the career aspirations and preferences of men and women (Correll, 2010). However, work identity for both men and women is central to individual identity and work is becoming an increasingly important element in women's lives (Simpson, 2004; Tinklin et al., 2005). Women in male dominated occupations have been found to receive less support than men, with more support received when in mixed gender occupations. In contrast, men receive high levels of support in female dominated occupations. Men in female dominated occupations report that their minority status is an advantage in terms of hiring and promotion opportunities. Hultin (2003) found that men who work in typically female occupations have substantially better prospects of promotion and career progression, than their similarly qualified female counterparts. Research suggests that in general men in female dominated occupations progress more than women in male or female dominated occupations. It is apparent that men and women experience the workplace differently. For example, men gain more advantages from their token or minority status compared to women, notably the glass escalator. These advantages include faster promotion, more career opportunities and fewer barriers, suggesting the workplace is still predominately a male domain. Being a minority is an advantage for men but a disadvantage for women (Taylor, 2010). This chapter will consider the multifaceted issues in relation to careers of women.

CAREER FACTORS AND GENDERED STEREOTYPES

Throughout the SET sector, there is a need to move away from gendered stereotypes concerning abilities and appropriate career choices based on gender. Stereotype influences starts early. For example, Chatard et al. (2007), suggest that even being reminded of gender stereotypes can distort students' memories of their prior exam performance. A study with 73 high school students of both genders demonstrated that students who more strongly endorsed gender stereotypes in relation to maths and the arts, subsequently showed more biased recall of their past exam performance. The *girls* with strong stereotypes *underestimated their past math performance*, *boys* with strong stereotypes *underestimated their past arts performance*. In a second study, with 64 high school students, the researchers asked one group of students to rate their agreement with gender based statements, such as 'Men are gifted in mathematics' and 'Women are gifted in the arts', prior to rating their own abilities. The other group, rated their own performance, prior to rating the gender based stereotype statements. All students were then asked to recall their past exam performance. Interestingly, girls, who read the stereotypes first, underestimated their actual past maths exam performance and overestimated their arts performance. However, the boys overestimated their maths performance. Furthermore, Nosek et al. (2009) conducted international research on gender-science stereotypes and gender differences in school-science test scores. The researchers gathered data online to record the implicit beliefs about gender and science amongst more than half a million people in 34 different countries. The study used male related words and science related words to identify bias and found that individuals associate the male and science categories. Crucially, 70% of participants exhibited an implicit stereotype, by associating science with males, much more than females. The researchers also evaluated science test scores recorded in 1999 and 2003 for children aged approximately 12 years and found a correlation with the implicit stereotype scores. In the countries with more stereotype beliefs held about gender and science, girls tended to under-perform at science, compared to boys. This suggests that if a culture holds an implicit belief that women are not associated with science, this can influence girls' and women's science performance.

If girls continue to be influenced by gender stereotypes, they will be less likely to consider a career in SET, as they will underestimate their potential success. Through more gender inclusive socialization within schools and within the home children will reject stereotypes and want to pursue a wide range of careers and help in the eradication of gendered occupational segregation. It is apparent that girls need to be encouraged to become drivers of technology, through knowledge of how computers work, as well as computer use. It is especially pertinent that children are taught the value of computer science and technology in today's society. The situation within schools is not confined to computer science and technology. It extends to attracting girls to pursue science and engineering subjects, to develop their interest at an early age. Globally according to the Program for International Student Assessment (PISA, 2006), both genders at age fifteen place an equal value on science, however at university level the discrepancy between the genders opting for science and technology subjects is more noticeable. Gaming might be an initial introduction for children to digital technologies, developing confidence and usage skills (Brand, 2007). This may lead to an interest in a career in computer science and information technology. However, if as Case (2004) suggests that what women gamers want, is more gender neutral games, this must be considered. More women in games development would be beneficial in developing games women want to play, in the way they want to play. The games industry wants to attract more women to its workforce in the hope of gaining a more diverse audience.

However, if future generations of women are to enter the SET sector, a gender divide in terms of the roles women occupy may still be apparent. Banks and Milestone (2011) put forward that new forms of work, such as the digital new media sector, tend to keep some of the gender discriminations and inequalities of the old economy. For example, women in the games industry have similar demographics to those found in the wider SET sector, for example, young, single and childless. In the technology sector, women working in the games industry tend to be concentrated within the more traditionally feminine roles. The games industry could widen its appeal through an increased awareness of the variety of roles and skills within the industry and

through highlighting the benefits and rewards of working in such a creative, competitive and growing industry. Women should be involved in all aspects of the industry, especially games development, due to the massive impact the industry has on culture, technology and the media landscape today. Watt (2008) uses the term pipeline when considering women across the STEM sector, the pipeline starts in secondary school through the workforce. According to Watt, "consideration of gender difference and gendered influences at each of these critical points in the pipeline, is key to interventions designed to promote women's participation" (p. 4). We tend to agree with Watt, in that the pipeline comes more into effect during secondary school education and is considerably more noticeable at university level and beyond. After all, secondary school is the point when children have developed identities, likes/dislikes and formed opinions of the world, including what industries, occupations and professions they may or may not identify and feel they will fit into, as well as have the ability to succeed (rightly or wrongly) in. Lagesen (2007) looked at strategies to include women into computer science and found that the most successful strategy was a direct effort to increase the relative number of women, combined with efforts to make the women feel welcome and appreciated. It is apparent from UK and USA data, that a leaky pipeline' exists, with an increasing number of women dropping out of SET, the higher they climb, through the higher education system This results in less women available to move into SET employment, especially at a higher level. According to the Office for National Statistics

Labor Force Statistics (ONS, 2009), computer and related activities employ 514,000 people, of which, 22% are women. There has been a general decline in female participation within the IT industry in the UK, with only 22% of IT workers being female in 2004 as opposed to 50% in 1960. Women in this sector tend to be more strongly represented in the lower echelons. For example, the Labor Force Statistics (ONS, 2009) found that 30% of women were IT operations technicians, only 15% were ICT managers and 11% IT strategy and planning professionals. Women have been found as being better educated than men but are located in the lower status and lower pay areas of the industry (Faulkner, 2001).

Despite the adoption of equal opportunities policies and various campaigns worldwide to attract women into SET careers. In technology for example, women are leaving the industry in large numbers (Burns et al., 2007). Tattersall et al. (2007) found that women are still discriminated against, in terms of pay and promotion opportunities when they take time out of work for maternity leave (Valenduc et al., 2004) report. Wickham et al., (2008) in a study of software firms in Ireland, found that often women had to choose between career and motherhood, due to inflexible practices. ICT organizations often have a flat management structure with little hierarchy. Flat organizations lead to an informal working environment but career ladders can be short or nonexistent. A lack of formal structures and progression processes can make if particularly difficult for women to gain advancement, it has been argued that women tend to achieve better in organizations where career paths are clear.

The ICT industry does not generally support part-time working or other flexible working arrangements for either gender, which has more of an impact on women with children. Research suggests that women differ in their reasons for choosing a career in ICT. Teague (2002), through interviews with fifteen female professionals working in computing careers found that the women choose their computing careers for a variety of reasons. Reasons included the influence of others, ability and liking of math's and/or problem solving. Kidd and Green (2006) studied the careers of UK research scientists and found that the factors explaining career commitment and intention to remain in the profession were similar for men and women. Suggesting that gender in itself does not explain women leaving the profession. Interestingly, Kid and Green also found that parenthood and relationship status had no direct relationship with work attitudes, career commitment or intention to leave science.

Trauth, Quesenberry, and Huang (2008) argue that there are different cultural influences on women in IT, which are related to differences in nationality and ethnicity. For example, a recurrent theme in the literature on women's underrepresentation in the ICT sector is the issue of parenthood that according to Trauth et al. is experienced differently by women across various cultures. For James and Cardador (2007), women's cognitions and beliefs about technology and science are more negative than men's, resulting in a disinterest in the employment sector. One reason for this disinterest in computers is the long hours that have become standard (Fullerton et al., 2008). Another reason relates to the identity of women within the industry. Women are asked to exchange aspects of their gender identity for a masculine version and forsake their femininity without this de-gendering process occurring in men. According to Bury (2011), female ICT professionals in hybrid roles felt they "identified as female geeks connected to childhood tomboyism and involves a complex negotiation of normative masculine and feminine identities, a process that both challenges and reinforces gender norms" (p. 33). Butler (1990) first put forward that when a person identifies with a gender, they identify with a set of norms. Femininity is measured against the hegemonic masculine ideal. Singh and Allen (2007) found that women rate their abilities lower and report lower confidence than men do in computer related tasks.

Stereotypes play an important part within the industry. Harries and Wilkinson (2004) investigated first year Canadian University students perceptions of twelve information occupations. Computer engineer and lawyer received the highest prestige rating and librarians the lowest. The study found that the presence of more women in an occupation had a negative impact on the prestige of the profession, the salary it attracts, the education required to enter it and the degree of computing knowledge required. Ahuja (2002) found social factors such as gender stereotyping, role models, parental support, and structural factors such as access to technology and teacher support, influence women's entry and performance in IT careers. In addition, being the only woman in a group heightens gender stereotypes and can result in stereotypical task performance. Furthermore, if an individual is

the only one in his or her social category, in a group, they have solo status, such as being the only woman in a group. Solo status has been related to reduced performance (Sekaquaptewa & Thompson, 2003), and Fuegen and Biernat (2002) found that women with solo status can perform better on masculine tasks, as they try to avoid a feminine stereotype and 'fit in'. Stereotyping is one of the issues that the UK government is looking at. In 2012, the UK Government, Commons Select Committee for Business, Innovation and Skills announced a new inquiry into Women in the Workplace. They invited the public and interested groups to contribute their thoughts via the Internet. Due to the level of interest on the topic, the Commons extended the deadline for evidence until the end of 2012. The Committee asked for views on the following questions (Business, Innovation and Skills, 2012):

- Do the Gender Equality Duty and the Equality Act go far enough in tackling *inequalities*, such as gender pay gap and job segregation, between men and women in the workplace?

- How should the *gender stereotyping* prevalent in particular occupations, for example in engineering, banking, construction, and the beauty industry, be tackled?

- How successful is the voluntary code of conduct (a recommendation of the Davies Report) which addresses gender diversity and best practice, covering relevant search criteria and processes relating to *FTSE board level appointments*?

- To what extent should investors take into account the *percentage of women on boards*, when considering company reporting and appointments to the board?
- What has been the impact of the *current economic crisis on female employment* and wage levels?
- What more should be done to promote *part-time work at all levels* of the workplace and to ensure that both women and men have opportunities to gain senior positions within an organization while working part time?
- What steps should be taken to provide *greater transparency on pay and other issues*, such as workforce composition?
- Why are there still so few *women in senior positions on boards*, and what are the benefits of having a greater number?
- To what extent have the *recommendations* in Lord Mervyn Davies' Report "Women on Board" (Davis, 2011) been acted upon?

All important points to challenge behaviour and support change. The last question relates to the Davis report (2011), that urged FTSE 100 companies to double the percentage of women on Boards by 2015, to 25%. The Davies Report (2011) noted:

Government must reserve the right to introduce more prescriptive alternatives if the recommended business-led approach does not achieve significant change. (Davies, 2011, p. 2)

In 2010, women made up only 12.5% of the members of the Corporate Boards of FTSE 100 companies. This was up from 9.4% in 2004. The latest 2012 figures show they now make up 15%, yet there are still 11 companies in the FTSE 100 with all-male Boards. There is considerable variation in progress across countries. In particular, the Scandinavian countries of Norway, Sweden and Finland have made good progress, for example, Norway has achieved 40% of women on Boards. This is attributed to the fact that in 2003, Norway passed a compulsory quota law requiring a minimum 40 per cent of Board members to be of women. International data indicates gender and Board membership issues (Table 1). The 30% Club hope that the European Commission will not vote for the Draft EU Directive to impose a 40 percent quota on listed company boards. The club formed in 2010 and champions gender diversity on boards. The club suggests that quotas can actually be harmful to the development of diversity. The 30% Club suggest an alternative to quotas is a voluntary approach and that this will have a more beneficial impact in organizations (The 30% Club, 2012). However, for the majority of organizations, it remains how much candidates fit the values, norms and behaviours of existing Board members, as the criteria for Board acceptance.

Boards require contributions from individuals with a variety of viewpoints, including gender to bring a balanced holistic viewpoint to board decision making. Research by Doldor et al. (2012) suggests that at the current rate of change, it will over 70 years to

Table 1. Percentage of women on boards

Area	Date	Action	Sanctions	% Women on Boards
Australia	2010	Companies listed on ASX are required to disclose proportion of women on boards and publish objectives for gender diversity.	Government statement that companies will face legal and financial penalties.	10.9%
EU	2011	EU Commission VP believes quotas may be necessary if companies do not take voluntary action. VP has stated 30% of supervisory board positions by 2015 (and 40% by 2020) should be the objective.	VP talked of 'credible legal sanctions'.	9.6% (industrialised Europe)
US	2009	SEC introduced code requiring disclosure of nomination committees' diversity considerations in appointing candidates.	-	11.4%

Source: from Women on Boards: A Statistical Review by Country, Region, Sector and Market Index; Governance Metrics International.

achieve gender balance in the FTSE 100 company boardrooms. Furthermore, Doldar et al. (2012) noted that only 32 per cent of FTSE 100 companies, disclosed the number of women directors on their Boards. To function well Boards must share information, with critical debate and good interpersonal dynamics. However, boards can perpetuate 'old boy's clubs'. Gender stereotypes create biased perceptions regarding competence and suitability for top level corporate roles. This influences considerations as to suitability for such roles. Often such stereotypical views are based on a distinct lack of factual evidence. For example, Singh et al. (2008), found that women Board directors, were more likely to hold MBA degrees, have multiple sector experience (private, public, voluntary, governmental) and have international experience. To develop the pipeline and increase the overall pool of women qualified to serve at board level, companies need to identify women within the organization with board-level qualities. Furthermore, initiatives must be in place for women to progress, with bar-

riers to progression identified. This would include reviewing institutional policies and processes to ensure they are equitable and transparent, address flexible working, mentoring and networking opportunities and identifying cultural issues within the organization that may be impeding the progress of women, such as training to address bias and stereotypes, surrounding women's capacity. Gender, time and work-life balance issues will now be discussed.

GENDER AND TIME

Work life balance issues have become proliferate in the literature on women's careers and the career development of women. A culture of long hours' is associated with many male dominated sectors, such as ICT and this has a dramatic impact on women's career progression and work life balance (Valenduc et al., 2004). It is apparent from the SET industries, that a long hours culture is a dominant feature and a main reason women, especially those with or wanting children, leave the sector.

The long hour's culture and the lack of gaining a sufficient work life balance are a major cause of the leaky pipeline across the sector. The sector is notorious for its long hours culture and this may indeed prevent many women from considering and being attracted to entering a career in the sector. Therefore the need to reduce the long hours culture in many industries such as ICT is important as is increasing flexible working practices that do not impact on career progression and development, will help increase gender diversity. Women are still, in the main, responsible for the majority of domestic labour and childcare (Raskin, 2006). Even when they work from home, women combine work with childcare (Noonan et al., 2007; De Ruijter & Van der Lippe, 2007).

A major reason for women's lack of progress in the workplace has been due to their continuing responsibility for caring and domestic work. Predominantly, women remain responsible for the majority of domestic matters (Bird & Schnurman-Crook, 2005). Married women devote approximately twice as much time to housework than married men (Bianchi et al., 2002, as cited in Cunningham, 2007). Askari et al. (2010) found women expect inequality in their relationships; they expect to do more childcare and household chores. Cunningham (2007) found that husbands of women with more employment experience, perform more housework than husbands of women with shorter employment histories. Schultheiss (2009) suggests that mothering needs to be conceptualized as work in order for it to be valued. Lovejoy and Stone (2011) conducted

interviews with 54 stay-at-home mothers who previously worked in professional or managerial jobs. The research revealed that most of the women planned to pursue alternative careers, mostly in female-dominated professions on their return to work. Research has also found that women with advance degrees were three times more likely than men to opt out of the labour force, mainly for family responsibilities (Baker, 2002). Both of these studies highlight the effect having a family can have on the careers of many women. In work with a research element, it is often time available for research that is impacted upon by care and family responsibilities. In the United Kingdom, an analysis of the research assessment exercise (RAE), in academia was conducted (HERA, 2009). The aim of the research was to investigate if disability, age, sex, ethnicity and nationality were related to selection of staff for inclusion in the 2008 Research Assessment Exercise (RAE 2008). It examined the question of whether the process of selecting staff was unbiased, or whether some staff were disadvantaged. It was found that men were submitted in greater numbers for the RAE, 2008. This was particularly evident in the elite Russell group Universities (these are the top 20 UK research Universities), where women comprised 19% to 39%, of those entered for the RAE (Bogg, 2011). The report noted it its key points that:

Point 89: "As with RAE2001, having accounted for other measurable factors, differences between selection of men and women continue to be observed over the age range 30-50 despite the changes between RAE2001 and RAE2008 to promote equal opportunities in the RAE." (HERA, 2009, Pg 24)

Point 90: "Bibliometric evidence from the 2006 report is consistent with the suggestion that lower selection rate of women in the 30-50 age range was due to a lower proportion of women having a research record that leads them to be selected, rather than bias in the selection process. While this behaviour may be linked to selection bias resulting from age and gender, it could equally be a result of deeply rooted inequalities in the research careers of men and women." (HERA, 2009, pg 24)

Research by Lubinski and Benbow (2006) found gender differences in the number of hour's people were willing to work, which they argue impacts the career success of women, since men are willing to work more hours per week due to less domestic and caring responsibilities. Working long hours is often associated with masculine organizational norms and hours worked has been found to be a causal variable, which affects income attainment (O'Neill & O'Reilly, 2010). Through an examination of professional computing employment in Australia, Diamond, and Whitehouse (2007) found a stronger long hour's culture in the private compared to the public sector. Furthermore, part-time work was a rarity in both sectors. They also found that men and women respond differently to workplace constraints. For example, females with children were more likely to move into

areas were hours could be maintained and be made more predictable. Part- time work presents specific challenges, such as the need for stimulating assignments, a lack of networking opportunities and information exchange were all predominant features. Part time work is associated with a lack of career opportunities (Crompton et al., 2003). For example, Tomlinson and Durban (2010) found that the careers of female managers stalled when the women moved from full to part time work. Knights and Richards (2003) suggested that many women have restricted time for career building for progression compared to their male counterparts. Part-time work can assist women accommodate career and family, however for professional women equal access to career development opportunities is required for progression.

GENDER AND SUPPORT

A climate that supports employee growth, empowerment, participation and professional development is required for growth. This can be achieved via training, mentoring and equitable pay for all employees. This is likely to be associated with a positive public image, attracting employees and retaining staff. There remain inaccurate perceptions in relation to women in SET careers such as the perception that women do not possess natural leadership qualities (Crolla et al., 2011). This may in part be due to personality and the influence of gender. Personality is important in terms of career interests, career self-efficacy, performance and satisfaction. It influences openness to new experiences, as anxiety is a major component of avoidance and extraversion and risk taking a component of approaching new experiences and learning. Looking at the relationship between personality types and vocational interests, Dilchert (2007) found that highly extraverted individuals are more interested in managerial and leadership positions. Dilchert (2007) found that individuals with managerial interests, especially high profile leadership tend to score the lowest on agreeableness compared to the other traits. A proactive personality has been found to be related to job satisfaction, in an investigation into women's proactive personality and entrepreneurial intentions, Gupta and Bhawe (2007) found proactive women had significantly higher entrepreneurial intentions and were more were more affected by stereotype threat, than less proactive women. Stereotype threat, is when individuals are aware of stereotypes related to their social group and believe they may be judged by these stereotypes. This can lead to vulnerability to the threat of the stereotype. Stereotype threat can lead to a decrease in performance as the individual disengages from the stereotyped task. Self-efficacy is also relevant, Van Vuuren, de Jong, and Seydel (2008) found self-efficacy contributed to organizational commitment. Betz, Borgen, and Harmon (2006) found both personality and vocational confidence contributed to the prediction of occupational group membership. Personality, confidence and interest have relevance to occupational choice, with the relevance of the importance of each variable differing depending on the occupation (Betz, Borgen, & Harmon, 2006).

The processes of gender related self-efficacy and self-esteem are complex, multifaceted and heterogeneous. A positive self-concept especially in terms of positive or high self-esteem and self-efficacy appears to be advantageous for women in the workplace, especially those working in male dominated occupations and industries. However, neither self-efficacy or self-esteem are static phenomena, both can change depending on domain, experiences and over the lifespan. Research suggests that self-esteem and self-efficacy are distinct yet related constructs (Hogue, DuBois, & Fox-Cardamone, 2010). Both are, however viewed as aspects of a persons' self-concept and important for women (and men) in the workplace despite research suggesting gender differences within the concepts. Hogue, DuBois, and Fox-Cardamone (2010) found that self-efficacy is one aspect of the self-concept that moderates the impact of gender and gender stereotypes, on pay expectations, whereas self-esteem does not. This indicates that the self-concept is important and can have differing influences. Having a woman as a role model can certainly help a women believe barriers can be overcome. For example, Lockwood (2006) asked students to read a fictional newspaper account of an outstanding professional, who had excelled in the same field that they aspired to work in. However, some of the students read an account of a woman professional while others read about a man. Lockwood found that female students' who read an account of a woman professional, rated themselves more positively, than female students who read about a man. By contrast, male students who read about a man as a role model did not rate themselves any more positively than male students who read about a female role model. In a second study, students were asked to name a real person who was their role-model in their career ambitions. Lockwood found that 63% of female students chose a woman, 76% of male students chose a man. Crucially, 27% of female students who named a female role-model stated they were inspired by the gender-related barriers that must have been overcome by their role-model. The male students stated that gender was not a factor in their choice. This indicates that women, as role-models, to other women, can function as inspiration by demonstrating gender barriers can be overcome, to achieve work role success

Generational differences are also important to consider due to the changing nature of the working environment, especially newer industries such as digital media and computer games. Research suggests that these newer industries attract a younger workforce (Prescott & Bogg, 2010; Deuze et al., 2007; Gourdin, 2005). In recent years, generational differences have been a pertinent focus of work related performance. Generally, those born between 1943 and 1964 are referred to as baby boomers (boomers), those born between 1965 and 1981 as Generation X and those born after 1982 as Generation Y. The current workforce has at least three, possibly four generations in it, which can cause conflict. According to Gelston (2008), workforce relations between the generations is at a low, with major issues centring round the use of technology and work ethics. Generation X (1965 – 1981),

have been reported as cynical, pessimistic and individualistic in the workplace (Smola & Sutton, 2002). They are viewed as less loyal to their organization and more committed to their own careers. They value work life balance more than their generational predecessors. Generation X are the first generation to successfully embrace workplace change (Sayers, 2007). Generation X women working in technology, found that personal fulfilment was intrinsically connected to professional success and that this generation of women wanted support in terms of mentors, opportunities for promotion and more flexibility to achieve a work life balance (Feyerherm & Vick, 2005). For the generation that has grown up with technology and the digital age, Generation Y (1982-present), are viewed as driven, demanding, highly confident and highly socialized . Generation Y have been found to have higher self esteem, narcissism, anxiety and depression, whilst having a lower need for social approval and more external locus of control (Twenge & Campbell, 2008). Generation Y however, has been found to be less independent than previous generations, requiring more structure, guidance and feedback (Feiertag & Berge, 2008). Generational differences highlight the evolution of the workplace and change in what is considered appropriate and important. There is an increasing importance attached to work life balance, particularly in younger generations of workers, this must be considered in the context of SET careers and career development. Throughout our working culture, the issue of reducing working hours and increasing more gender and family friendly working practices will help reduce and perhaps one day eliminate gendered occupational segregation.

Organizational practices, which positively support women and increase psychological health would seem to be a logical extension given the association of positive employment experiences with psychological well-being (Burke, 2003; Nelson & Burke, 2002). Career success can be either subjective or objective (Ng, Eby, Sorensen, & Feldman, 2005). Objective career success is usually measured through things such as highest level attained, highest salary earned, and professional honours. Subjective career successes on the other hand are typically attitudes, emotions or perception of how the individual feels about their accomplishments, which previous researchers have measured via job satisfaction, organizational commitment and professional identity (Feldman & Ng, 2007). Women and men tend to use different kinds of measures for assessing their own career success. Men tend to use objective measures, such as grade and salary, whereas women more subjective measures, such as work/life satisfaction (Powell & Butterfield, 2003).

CONCLUSION

Women face a variety of barriers within the labour market in terms of career progression and advancement. Several barriers emerge repeatedly in the literature and numerous studies (i.e., Arfken, Bellar, & Helms, 2004; McCathy, 2004; Allen, 2005) suggest the following barriers to women's career pro-

gression; limited networking opportunities, limited access to mentors and role models, limited flexibility and child care provision, general discrimination, gender segregation of the workforce and higher values placed on masculine attributes. This unfair treatment influences career advancement opportunities and also increases stress and reduces wellbeing at work (Perrewe & Nelson, 2004). Today women still perceive the 'old boys' network' to be a significant barrier to career progression. Women tend to be excluded from these networks and consequently forgo the benefits and reciprocal behaviours (Vinnicombe, Singh, & Kumra, 2004). Developing women's networks can be an effective strategy for overcoming some obstacles to diversity because they challenge the invisible structures women face at work (McCarthy, 2004). Bain and Cummings (2000) suggest that programs to intensify networking and to provide mentoring and support have been shown to compensate for the dissatisfaction women academics experience as they wait for their chance to move up in academia.

Research has suggested that male characteristics are more desirable than female characteristics in the workforce especially in senior management and leadership roles (Willemson, 2002). However female managers who behave in a masculine way can be perceived negatively. Women do not generally reach higher levels of management across workforce sectors in large numbers, and those that do are often segregated into certain industries, such as, healthcare (Arfken, Bellar, & Helms, 2004). Stereotyping leads to the concept of leadership as masculine and this can lead to a bias against female candidate's promotion to a leadership post. This is more so when the female works in an industry incongruent with her gender role. Interestingly, the study found that female and older participants showed more prejudice than men and younger participants. Research suggests that stereotypically masculine characteristics and behaviours are the most desired in management and leadership roles, however, some researchers now suggest individuals with more androgynous characteristics make the best managers/leaders. In addition, women in senior positions are often framed within the context of advancement for business, rather than being morally right and fair. However, research has found that gender-neutral attributes are perceived as being most associated with that of a successful manager (Willemson, 2002). Eagly and Carli (2007) have suggested that the segregated nature of teams and networks in organizations exposes

Table 2. The ABC model of key steps for change

Aim: Identify *senior influential champions* that will *promote change* within the organization and *challenge traditional male-centred management viewpoints, promote gender equity* as a key business aim, to assist in recruitment and retention of women.   **Business:** Case for change, *promote the rationale, develop the policies and processes* within the organization to assist in changing behaviour and practices that potentially restrict women's development, such as the promotion process.   **Capacity Building:** *Training and development based on local/organizational need, establish the evidence base,* the *data* collected in relation to gender inequity *is irrefutable* and an excellent point to instigate change, *monitor the data as evidence of change. Ask the women employees what they want and need*!

(Bogg, 2012)

Table 3. The key issues

Issues Women Face	Core Issues Involved	How May the Issue be Addressed
Gender and stereotypes	• Cultural and societal expectations based on gender. • Stereotypes of what is gender congruent behaviour. • Lack of women with children within the industries (role models/mentors). • Lack of female role models/ mentors.	• Encourage women and girls to enter male dominated disciplines and careers. • Encourage females in senior roles to act as mentors/role models and help future generations of women. • Eradicate gender based stereotypes, such as the 'think manager, think male' stereotype. • Highlight the diversity of skills and roles within certain sectors, and industries. • Develop more appropriate recruitment and retention strategies appropriate for a more diverse workforce.
Gender and time	• Lack of networking opportunities. • Long hours culture. • Lack of flexible working practices.	• Increase awareness of the benefits of networking. • Investigate the advantages of digital networking opportunities. • Support women through mentoring and networking opportunities. • Review current polices relating to hours of work and flexible working practices. • Encourage the uptake of flexible working practices. • Employ strategies to help reduce the long hours culture.
Gender and support	• Lack of women in senior. • Positions. • Lack of transparent pay. • Lack of clear/transparent promotion opportunities. • Self-efficacy and Self esteem.	• Transparency in pay and promotional structures. • Develop retention strategies, to address the leaky pipeline, such as those related to work life balance issues. • Encourage women to apply for management/senior positions Promote gender equality in the workplace at all levels from recruitment to retention.

women to old-boys networks, competitive behaviours, a long-hours culture and the use of informal events. Informal events often relate to activities considered more masculine, such as football or golf. This can perpetuate exclusive organizational cultures, where to fit, is to be masculine. Such cultures make it difficult for women to build relationships to ascend to the Boardroom or 'fit' once in the Boardroom. Research has suggested that women are more likely to excel in organizations that emphasise gender equity and value both feminine and masculine characteristics in their workers (Bajo & Dickson, 2002).

Supportive organizational practices for women demonstrate good business practice and lead to positive outcomes such as improved job satisfaction and identity with and commitment to the organization (Wang, Lawler, & Shi, 2010). Women describing more supportive organizational practices also indicated greater job and career satisfaction, higher levels of psychological well-being and increased organizational identity and commitment (Burke, Burgess, & Fallon, 2005). Family friendly policies positively relate to organizational commitment. Flexible working practices can facilitate the reconciliation between paid work and home life, whilst contributing to equality and diversity. Flexible working is important in challenging a masculine culture of long hours and helps women to reconcile work and family commitments. Women describing more supportive organizational practices also indicate more job and career satisfaction; higher levels of psychological well-being and increased organizational identity and commitment (Ng & Burke, 2005).

Women who perceive supportive organizational practices, indicate greater career satisfaction, higher levels of psychological well-being and increased organizational identity and commitment (Burke, Burgess, & Fallon, 2005). A climate that supports employee growth, empowerment, participation and professional development via training, mentoring and equitable pay for all employees is likely to be associated with a positive public image, and will attract employees and retain staff. The following model is a useful for considering the key steps for change. It contains the issues any organization should consider, when trying to change a culture to become more gender inclusive (Table 2). Table 3 presents the key issues raised in this chapter. The next and final chapter of our book presents out final thoughts and conclusions.

REFERENCES

Ahuja, M. K. (2002). Women in the information technology profession: A literature review, synthesis & research agenda. *European Journal of Information Systems*, *11*, 20–34. doi:10.1057/palgrave.ejis.3000417

Allen, I. (2005). Women doctors & their careers: What now? *British Medical Journal*, *331*, 569–572. doi:10.1136/bmj.331.7516.569 PMID:16150771

Arfken, D. E., Bellar, S. L., & Helms, M. H. (2004). The ultimate glass ceiling revisited: The presence of women on corporate boards. *Journal of Business Ethics*, *50*, 177–186. doi:10.1023/B:BUSI.0000022125.95758.98

Askari, S. F., Liss, M., Erchull, M. J., Staebell, S. E., & Axelson, S. J. (2010). Men want equality, but women don't expect it: Young adults' expectations for participation in household & child care chores. *Psychology of Women Quarterly, 34*, 243–252. doi:10.1111/j.1471-6402.2010.01565.x

Bain, O., & Cummings, W. (2000). Academe's glass ceiling: Societal, professional-organizational, & institutional barriers to the career advancement of academic women. *Comparative Education Review, 44*(4), 493–514. doi:10.1086/447631

Bajo, L. M., & Dickson, M. W. (2002). Perceptions of organizational culture & women's advancement in organizations: A cross-cultural examination. *Sex Roles, 45*, 399–414. doi:10.1023/A:1014365716222

Baker, J. G. (2002). The influx of women into legal professions: an economic analysis. *Monthly Labor Review, 125*(8), 14–24.

Banks, M., & Milestone, K. (2011). Individualization, gender & cultural work. *Gender, Work and Organization, 18*(1), 73–89. doi:10.1111/j.1468-0432.2010.00535.x

Bendl, R., & Schmidt, A. (2010). From 'glass ceilings' to 'firewalls' - Different metaphors for describing discrimination. *Gender, Work and Organization, 17*(5), 612–634. doi:10.1111/j.1468-0432.2010.00520.x

Betz, N. E., Borgen, F. H., & Harmon, L. W. (2006). Vocational confidence & personality in the prediction of occupational group membership. *Journal of Career Assessment, 14*(1), 36–55. doi:10.1177/1069072705282434

Bird, G. W., & Schnurman-Crook, A. (2005). Professional identity & coping behaviors in dual-career couples. *Family Relations, 54*(1), 145–160. doi:10.1111/j.0197-6664.2005.00012.x

Bogg, J. (2010). *Gender, the RAE 2008 & the Russell group universities*. Paper presented at the Nature Journal Conference. London, UK.

Bogg, J. (2012). *The ABC model of key steps for change*. Liverpool, UK: University of Liverpool.

Brand, J. E. (2007). *Interactive Australia 2007: Facts about the Australian computer & video game industry*. Queensland, Australia: Bond University.

Burke, R. J. (2003). Hospital restructuring, workload, & nursing staff satisfaction & work experiences. *The Health Care Manager, 22*(2), 99–107. doi:10.1097/00126450-200304000-00003 PMID:12785546

Burke, R. J., Burgess, Z., & Fallon, B. (2005). Organizational practices supporting women & their satisfaction & well-being. *Women in Management Review, 21*(5), 416–425. doi:10.1108/09649420610676217

Burns, B., Griffiths, M., Moore, K., & Richardson, H. (2007). *Disappearing women: North West ICT final report*. Salford, UK: Salford University.

Bury, R. (2011). She's geeky: The performance of identity among women working in IT. *International Journal of Gender. Science & Technology, 3*(1), 33–53.

Business, I., & the Skills Committee. (2012). *Women in the workplace*. Retrieved from http://www.parliament.uk/business/committees/committees-a-z/commons-select/business-innovation-&-skills/inquiries/women-in-the-workplace

Butler, J. (1990). *Gender trouble: Feminism & the subversion of identity*. London: Routledge.

Carr, D. (1997). The fulfilment of career dreams at midlife: Does it matter for women's mental health? *Journal of Health and Social Behavior, 38*, 331–344. doi:10.2307/2955429 PMID:9425778

Case, S. (2004). *Women in gaming*. Retrieved from http://www.microsoft.com/windowsxp/games/learnmore/womeningames.mspx

Chartered Management Institute. (2012). *National management salary survey results*. Retrieved from http://www.managers.org.uk/practical-support/management-community/professional-networks/2012-national-management-salary-survey

Chatard, A., Guimond, S., & Selimbegovic, L. (2007). How good are you in math? The effect of gender stereotypes on students' recollection of their school marks. *Journal of Experimental Social Psychology, 43*, 1017–1024. doi:10.1016/j.jesp.2006.10.024

30% Club. (2012). *30% club underlines belief that quotas are harmful to ongoing gender debate*. Retrieved from http://www.30percentclub.org.uk

Correll, S. J. (2010). Gender & the career choice process: The role of biased self-assessment. *American Journal of Sociology, 106*(6), 1691–1730. doi:10.1086/321299

Crolla, E., O'Sullivan, H., & Bogg, J. (2011). Gender & medical leadership: Student perceptions & implications for developing future leaders in primary & secondary care - A pilot study. *Journal of Primary Care & Community Health, 2*(4), 225–228. doi:10.1177/2150131911409413 PMID:23804838

Crompton, R., Dennet, J., & Wigfield, A. (2003). *Organizations, careers & caring*. Retrieved from http://www.jrf.org.uk/sites/files/jrf/n33.pdf

Cunningham, M. (2007). Influences of women's employment on the gendered division of household labor over the life course: Evidence from a 31-year panel study. *Journal of Family Issues, 28*(3), 422–444. doi:10.1177/0192513X06295198 PMID:18458763

Cunningham, M. (2007). Influences of women's employment on the gendered division of household labor over the life course: evidence from a 31-year panel study. *Journal of Family Issues, 28*(3), 422–444. doi:10.1177/0192513X06295198 PMID:18458763

Davies, M. (2011). *Women on boards*. Retrieved from http://www.bis.gov.uk/assets/biscore/business-law/docs/w/11-745-women-onboards

De Ruijter, E., & Van der Lippe, T. (2007). Effects of job features on domestic outsourcing as a strategy for combining paid & domestic work. *Work and Occupations, 34*(2), 205–230. doi:10.1177/0730888406296510

Deuze, M., Martin, C. B., & Alen, C. (2007). The professional identity of gameworkers. *Convergence: The International Journal of Research into New Media Technologies, 13*(4), 335–353. doi:10.1177/1354856507081947

Diamond, C., & Whitehouse, G. (2007). Gender, computing & the organization of working time: Public/private comparisons in the Australian context. *Information Communication and Society, 10*(3), 320–337. doi:10.1080/13691180701409879

Dilchert, S. (2007). Peaks & valleys: Predicting interests in leadership & managerial positions from personality profiles. *International Journal of Selection and Assessment, 15*(3), 317–334. doi:10.1111/j.1468-2389.2007.00391.x

Doldor, E., Vinnicombe, S., Gaughan, M., & Sealy, R. (2012). *Gender diversity on boards: The appointment process & the role of executive search firms*. Equality & Human Rights Commission. Retrieved from http://www.equalityhumanrights.com/uploaded_files/research/rr85_final.pdf

Domenico, D. M., & Jones, K. H. (2006). Career aspirations of women in the 20th century. *Journal of Career & Technical Education, 22*(2), 1–7.

Eagly, A. H., & Carli, L. L. (2007). Women & the labyrinth of leadership. *Harvard Business Review, 85*(9), 63–71. PMID:17972496

Faulkner, W. (2001). The technology question in feminism: A view from feminist technology studies. *Women's Studies International Forum, 24*(1), 79–95. doi:10.1016/S0277-5395(00)00166-7

Fawcett Society. (2012). *Fawcett warns of a 'backwards step' on equal pay*. Retrieved from http://fawcettsociety.org.uk/index.asp?PageID=1289

Feiertag, J., & Berge, Z. L. (2008). Training generation N: How educators should approach the net generation. *Education + Training, 50*(6), 457–464. doi:10.1108/00400910810901782

Feldman, D. C., & Ng, T. W. H. (2007). Careers: Mobility, embeddedness, & success. *Journal of Management, 33*(3), 350–377. doi:10.1177/0149206307300815

Feyerherm, A., & Vick, Y. H. (2005). Generation X women in high technology: Overcoming gender & generational challenges to succeed in the corporate environment. *Career Development International, 10*(3), 216–227. doi:10.1108/13620430510598337

Fuegen, K., & Biernat, M. (2002). Re-examining the effects of solo status for women & men. *Personality and Social Psychology Bulletin, 28*, 913–925.

Fullerton, T., Fron, J., Pearce, C., & Morie, J. (2008). Getting girls into the game: Towards a virtuous cycle. In *Beyond Barbie & Mortal Kombat: New perspectives on gender & gaming*. Cambridge, MA: The MIT Press.

Gelston, S. (2008). *Gen Y, gen X & the baby boomers: Workplace generation wars*. Retrieved from http://www.cio.com

Gourdin, A. (2005). *Game developers demographics: An exploration of workforce diversity*. International Game Developers Association. Retrieved from http://archives.igda.org/diversity/IGDA_DeveloperDemographics_Oct05.pdf

Gupta, V. K., & Bhawe, N. M. (2007). The influence of proactive personality & stereotype threat on women's entrepreneurial intentions. *Journal of Leadership & Organizational Studies*, *13*(4), 73–85. doi:10.1177/1071791 9070130040901

Harries, R., & Wilkinson, M. A. (2004). Situating gender: students' perceptions of information work. *Information Technology & People*, *17*(1), 71–86. doi:10.1108/09593840410522189

Hegewisch, A., Liepmann, H., Hayes, J., & Hartmann, H. (2010). *Separate & not equal? Gender segregation in the labor market & the gender wage gap*. Washington, DC: Institute for Women's Policy Research. doi:10.1037/e686432011-001

HERA. (2009). *Selection of staff for inclusion in RAE2008*. Retrieved from http://www.hefce.ac.uk/media/hefce1/pubs/hefce/2009/0934/09_34.pdf

Hogue, M., DuBois, L. Z., & Fox-Cardamone, L. (2010). Gender differences in pay expectations: The role of job intention & self-view. *Psychology of Women Quarterly*, *34*, 215–227. doi:10.1111/j.1471-6402.2010.01563.x

Hultin, M. (2003). Some take the glass escalator, some hit the glass ceiling? Career consequences of occupational sex segregation. *Work and Occupations*, *30*(1), 30–61. doi:10.1177/0730888402239326

James, K., & Cardador, J. (2007). Cognitions about technology & science: A measure & its relevance to career decisions. *Journal of Career Assessment*, *15*(4), 463–482. doi:10.1177/1069072707305766

Kidd, J. M., & Green, F. (2006). The careers of research scientists: Predicators of three dimensions career commitment & intention to leave science. *Personnel Review*, *35*(3), 229–251. doi:10.1108/00483480610656676

Knights, D., & Richards, W. (2003). Sex discrimination in UK academia. *Gender, Work and Organization*, *10*(2), 213–238. doi:10.1111/1468-0432.t01-1-00012

Lockwood, P. (2006). Someone like me can be successful: Do college students need same-gender role models? *Psychology of Women Quarterly*, *30*, 36–46. doi:10.1111/j.1471-6402.2006.00260.x

Lovejoy, M., & Stone, P. (2011). Opting back In the influence of time at home on professional women's career redirection after opting out. *Gender, Work and Organization*, 1–23.

Lubinski, D., & Benbow, C. P. (2006). Study of mathematically precocious youth after 35 years: Uncovering antecedents for the development of math-science expertise. *Perspectives on Psychological Science*, *1*, 316–345. doi:10.1111/j.1745-6916.2006.00019.x

Mayrhofer, W., Steyrer, J., Meyer, M., Strunk, G., Schiffinger, M., & Iellatchitch, A. (2005). Graduates career aspirations & individual characteristics. *Human Resource Management Journal*, *15*(1), 38–56. doi:10.1111/j.1748-8583.2005.tb00139.x

McCarthy, M. (2004). Girlfriends in high places: How women's networks are changing the workplace. *Demos (Mexico City, Mexico)*.

Nelson, D. L., & Burke, R. J. (2000). Women executives: Health, stress & success. *The Academy of Management Executive*, *14*(2), 107–121.

Ng, E. S. W., & Burke, R. J. (2005). Person–organization fit & the war for talent: does diversity management make a difference? *International Journal of Human Resource Management*, *16*(7), 1195–1210. doi:10.1080/09585190500144038

Ng, T. W. H., Eby, L. T., Sorensen, K. L., & Feldman, D. C. (2005). Predictors of objective & subjective career success: A meta-analysis. *Personnel Psychology*, *58*, 367–408. doi:10.1111/j.1744-6570.2005.00515.x

Noonan, M. C., Estes, S. B., & Glass, J. L. (2007). Do workplace flexibility policies influence time spent in domestic labor? *Journal of Family Issues*, *28*(2), 263–288. doi:10.1177/0192513X06292703

Nosek, B., Smyth, F., Sriram, N., Lindner, N., Devos, T., & Ayala, A. … Greenwald, A. (2009). National differences in gender-science stereotypes predict national sex differences in science & math achievement. *Proceedings of the National Academy of Sciences, 106* (26), 10593-10597.

O'Neill, O. A., & O'Reilly, C. A. (2010). Careers as tournaments: the impact of sex & gendered organizational culture preferences on MBAs' income attainment. *Journal of Organizational Behavior*, *31*, 856–876. doi:10.1002/job.641

ONS. (2009). *Statistical bulletin August 2009*. London: Office for National Statistics.

Perrewe, P. L., & Nelson, D. L. (2004). Gender & career success: The facilitative role of political skill. *Organizational Dynamics*, *33*(4), 366–378. doi:10.1016/j.orgdyn.2004.09.004

PISA. (2006). *Science competencies for tomorrow's world*. The Programme for International Student Assessment. Retrieved from http://www.oecd.org/dataoecd/15/13/39725224.pdf

Powell, G. N., & Butterfield, D. A. (2003). Gender, gender identity, & aspirations to top management. *Women in Management Review*, *18*(1/2), 88–96. doi:10.1108/09649420310462361

Prescott, J., & Bogg, J. (2010). The computer games industry: women's experiences of work role in a male dominated environment. In *Women in engineering, science & technology: Education & career challenges*. Hershey, PA: IGI Global. doi:10.4018/978-1-61520-657-5.ch007

Raskin, P. M. (2006). Women, work & family: Three studies of roles & identity among working mothers. *The American Behavioral Scientist*, *49*(10), 1354–1381. doi:10.1177/0002764206286560

Ryan, M. K., Haslam, A., & Kulich, C. (2010). Politics & the glass cliff: Evidence that women are preferentially selected to contest hard-to-win seats. *Psychology of Women Quarterly*, *34*, 56–64. doi:10.1111/j.1471-6402.2009.01541.x

Sayers, R. (2007). The right staff from X to Y: Generational change & professional development in future academic libraries. *Library Management, 28*(8/9), 474–487. doi:10.1108/01435120710837765

Schultheiss, D. E. P. (2009). To mother or matter: can women do both? *Journal of Career Development, 36*(1), 25–48. doi:10.1177/0894845309340795

Sekaquaptewa, D., & Thompson, M. (2003). Solo status, stereotype threat, & performance expectancies: Their effects on women's performance. *Journal of Experimental Social Psychology, 39*, 68–74. doi:10.1016/S0022-1031(02)00508-5

Simpson, R. (2004). Masculinity at work: The experiences of men in female dominated occupations. *Work, Employment and Society, 18*(2), 349–368. doi:10.1177/09500172004042773

Singh, K., & Allen, K. R. (2007). Women in computer-related majors: A critical synthesis of research & theory from 1994 to 2005. *Review of Educational Research, 77*(4), 500–533. doi:10.3102/0034654307309919

Singh, V., Terjesen, S., & Vinnicombe, S. (2008). Newly appointed directors in the boardroom: How do women & men differ? *European Management Journal, 26*(1), 48–58. doi:10.1016/j.emj.2007.10.002

Smola, K. W., & Sutton, C. D. (2002). Generational differences: Revisiting generational work values for the new millennium. *Journal of Organizational Behavior, 23*, 363–382. doi:10.1002/job.147

Tattersall, A., Keogh, C., & Richardson, H. (2007). *The gender pay gap in the ICT industry*. Manchester, UK: University of Salford.

Taylor, C. J. (2010). Occupational sex composition & the gendered availability of workplace support. *Gender & Society, 24*(2), 189–212. doi:10.1177/0891243209359912

Teague, J. (2002). Women in computing: What brings them to it, what keeps them in it? *SIGCSE Bulletin, 34*(2), 17–158. doi:10.1145/543812.543849

Tinklin, T., Croxford, L., Ducklin, A., & Frame, B. (2005). Gender & attitudes to work & family roles: The views of young people at the millennium. *Gender and Education, 17*(2), 129–142. doi:10.1080/09540250420003011429

Tomlinson, J., & Durbin, S. (2010). Female part-time managers work-life balance, aspirations & career mobility. *Equality, Diversity & Inclusion. International Journal (Toronto, Ont.), 29*(3), 255–270.

Trauth, E. M., Quesenberry, J. L., & Huang, H. (2008). A multicultural analysis of factors influencing career choice for women in the information technology workforce. *Journal of Global Information Management, 16*(4), 1–23. doi:10.4018/jgim.2008100101

Twenge, J. M., & Campbell, S. M. (2008). Generational differences in psychological traits & their impact on the workplace. *Journal of Managerial Psychology, 23*(8), 862–877. doi:10.1108/02683940810904367

Valenduc, G., et al. (2004). *Widening women's work in information & communication technology*. European Commission. Retrieved from http://www.ftu-namur.org/fichiers/D12-print.pdf

Van Vuuren, M., de Jong, M. D. T., & Seydel, E. R. (2008). Contributions of self & organizational efficacy expectations to commitment a fourfold typology. *Employee Relations*, *30*(2), 142–156. doi:10.1108/01425450810843339

Vinnicombe, S., Singh, V., & Kumra, S. (2004). *Making good connections: Best practice for women's corporate networks*. Cranfield University School of Management.

Wang, P., Lawler, J. J., & Shi, K. (2010). Implementing family-friendly employment practices in banking industry: Evidences from some African & Asian countries. *Journal of Occupational and Organizational Psychology*.

Watt, H. M. G. (2008). What motivates females & males to pursue sex-stereotyped careers? In *Gender & occupational outcomes: Longitudinal assessments of individual, social, & cultural influences*. Washington, DC: American Psychological Association. doi:10.1037/11706-003

Wickham, J., Collins, G., Greco, L., & Browne, J. (2008). Individualization & equality: Women's careers & organizational form. *Organization*, *15*(2), 211–231. doi:10.1177/1350508407086581

Willemsen, T. M. (2002). Gender typing of the successful manager - A stereotype reconsidered. *Sex Roles*, *46*, 385–391. doi:10.1023/A:1020409429645

Williams, M. J., Levy Paluck, E., & Spence-Rodgers, J. (2010). The masculinity of money: Automatic stereotypes predict gender differences in estimated salaries. *Psychology of Women Quarterly*, *34*, 7–20. doi:10.1111/j.1471-6402.2009.01537.x

Wilson-Kovacs, A. M., Ryan, M., & Haslam, A. (2006). The glass-cliff: women's career paths in the UK private IT sector. *Equal Opportunities International*, *25*(8), 674–687. doi:10.1108/02610150610719137

KEY TERMS AND DEFINITIONS

Career Aspirations: A person's aspiration to progress within a career.

Gender: The state of being male or female (typically used with reference to social and cultural differences rather than biological ones).

Pay: Referred to in terms of the gender pay gap within the computer games industry and the SET sector.

Work Life Balance: The balance between work and other life or role commitments.

Chapter 10
Final Thoughts and Concluding Comments

ABSTRACT

In the final concluding chapter, the authors review the key concepts discussed throughout the book. This includes the multiplicity of interacting factors that influence the gendering of computer games. They consider how computer games are gendered through game content and play and how the production of games is equally gendered and this male perspective in the design of games leads to the underrepresentation of women within games.

INTRODUCTION

The computer games industry is a major entertainment and leisure activity for many children and adults across the globe. The games industry is firmly established as a major feature of the contemporary media landscape in many parts of the world. As we have highlighted throughout this book, the industry is big business and has a significant impact in terms of both its economic and cultural im-

pact on society today. The cultural impact of the industry and the games they produce is of particular relevance when considering the gender divide in computer games since games influence today's culture and media landscape. Throughout this book we have highlighted why the issue of gender and computer games is a pertinent and important issue, as well as a timely issue. A number of recent developments and technological advances have significantly impacted gaming in who plays games and

DOI: 10.4018/978-1-4666-4534-9.ch010

where they play them. Firstly, the Internet and the emergence of online multi-players means that gamers do not need a gaming console but can play games through a PC, as well as allowing gamers to play against one another and collaborate in team games with players around the world. Secondly the emergence of wireless platforms, enabling players to play games on mobile phones (smartphones) and other handheld gaming devices. We have aimed to give readers an overview of key areas to consider in assessing gender and computer games. Importantly, we wanted to highlight the multifaceted factors involved in perpetuating and reinforcing the image that computer games are a male domain. This is especially so when considering who develops and produces computer games as well as the content of games which we argue in support of other researchers that one influences the other. In that, the content of games influences who is interested in playing computer games, which influences who desires to work in the industry, which in turn influences the content of the games, all based on gender assumptions.

We have demonstrated how a multiplicity of interacting factors influences the gendering of computer games. From the consumption to the production of games females are viewed as 'other', and outside of the mainstream computer games industry and gaming culture. The objective of the book was to provide the reader with a broad overview of how computer games are gendered at the detriment of girls and women reinforcing and perpetuating the view that computer games, as technology is viewed, a male domain. In particular, the book has considered how computer games are gendered through the content of the actual game, how games are played, where they are played and the reasons for playing them. The book has also considered how the production of games is also gendered and this perpetuates the industry and games as male since games are produced with not only a male audience in mind but also designed from a male perspective and view point. It is this male perspective in the design of games that has led to the underrepresentation of women within games as well as the hyper sexualisation of females in games, potentially leading to less female gamers and an underrepresentation of female game workers. The main premise of this book has been to consider the ways in which computer games are gendered and consider how this gendering may be addressed in order to close the gap between the gendered digital divide of games.

It would seem there is possibly a large gap which exists between the public's perception of computer games and what the research suggests. Jenkins (2008) reported eight myths about computer games which included that children are the primary market for computer games, almost no girls play computer games, computer games are not a meaningful form of expression and computer game play is socially isolating. The literature reviewed within this book tends to confirm that these four myths of the eight put forward by Jenkins are indeed myths. Although women are increasingly becoming gamers, playing more games and more often, it is apparent that female are not anywhere near being equally represented in the computer games industries workforce. Therefore, men are still designing games for both males and females with little input from a female perspective. With the massive growth of the global gaming audience and the advances in technology as well as creative possibilities, the games industry offers a wide range of interesting career opportunities. However these opportunities are currently appealing more to males than females. Despite legislation over the past 40 years, gender disparities in certain occupations remain. It appears that a number of issues run throughout the industry which contribute to the underrepresentation of women. Factors such as the long hour's culture associated with the industry, the lack of flexible working available, the lack of females, especially females with families within the industry and thus the lack of role models, as well as the image of the industry as masculine, contributes to the low representation of women. However it may not just be workforce issues at play resulting in the low representation of women within the industry. As we have highlighted throughout all aspects of computer games and computer games culture is gendered and in turn this impacts on not only the image of computer games as being form males only but also that the industry is a male domain and as a result many women may not view the industry as a viable career.

THE NEW INDUSTRY OF COMPUTER GAMES: NEW INDUSTRY SAME OLD ISSUES

Although the focus of this book has not been solely on the computer games industry in terms of who designs the games, this is a recurrent

theme throughout the book and an important area to consider separately from the other issues raised. The issue of who designs and develops games is a recurrent theme since we believe that who designs technology, in this instance computer games, influences and impacts dramatically on not only what and how technology is designed but also in who it is designed for. Why women are underrepresented in certain careers has been a pertinent question for career researchers and scholars interested in gender equality issues for decades. Researchers have been particularly interested in the lack of women in computing and information and communication technology (ICT) careers for which the computer games industry fall under the umbrella of.

For the wider ICT sector, the geeky image and the unsocial nature of computer related work are barriers to women's participation. Overt sexism and discrimination is not as evident within the sector, however our research findings suggest it can still exist. It appears that gender segregation persists in new industries, as well as the older more established ones such as science, engineering and finance (Prescott & Bogg, 2012). What is apparent from the computer games industry is that gendered occupational segregation exists, and persists in this relatively new industry and the culture does not generally appeal to or support women in the workplace. Like the more established science, engineering and technology sector (SET), this new industry has many of the same issues including the long hour's culture, inflexible working practices and a lack of women with children in the industry. Women in the industry tend to be concentrated within the more traditional less technical roles, which are the non-content creation roles such as human resources, marketing and administration roles. Therefore when discussing underrepresentation of women within the industry, one must be aware that it is not just increasing women in the industry as a whole that is important, but also increasing women's participation in all areas and occupations, within the industry, in order for true gender equity.

Although women have made progress into male dominated careers, it is apparent and evidenced by the gendered segregation within this relatively new industry that gender differences persist. Not only are women less likely to choose a career in computers and computer games, they are also more likely to leave if they do. Gendered occupational segregation is an issue for both gender equality and essential in addressing the skills shortage in certain occupations such as computer games. Throughout this book, other issues in particular race and ethnicity have been considered as we are aware that other demographics, not just women, face barriers within the workplace and other social institutions. It is costly for any industry to under utilise the full pool of talent available, it is also costly for sectors to lose talent, knowledge, skills and experience, through not attracting or retaining a diverse workforce. Women can bring a different perspective and voice and should be included and involved at all levels within the computer games industry. The computer games industry makes a significant impact socially and economically and both males and females should be equally be involved in producing and being a part of this impact.

GENERATIONAL DIFFERENCES

Generational differences are also important to consider due to the changing nature of the working environment, especially newer industries such as digital media and computer games. Research suggests that these newer industries attract a younger workforce (Prescott & Bogg, 2010; Deuze et al., 2007; Gourdin, 2005). In recent years, generational differences have been a pertinent focus of work related performance. A generation is a group of people or cohort that share birth years and experiences as they move through life. Individuals within a generation are influenced in their developmental years by a variety of critical factors. Critical factors include, social, economic, and political events, significant to that generation. This sharing of similar experiences leads people within a generation to develop similar values, opinions, and life experiences which distinguishes them from other generations (Kupperschmidt, 2000; Smola & Sutton, 2002; Gursoy, Maier, & Chi, 2008; D'Amato & Herfeldt, 2008). Although there is some slight ambiguity concerning the date ranges of the generational cohorts, it is generally accepted that, those born between 1943 and 1964 are referred to as baby boomers (boomers), those born between 1965 and 1981 as Generation X (Xers) and those born after 1982 as Generation Y (Yers).

The current workforce has at least three, possibly four generations in it, which can cause conflict (Gelston, 2008). A number of work related differences have been reported to exist between the generations resulting in conflict. For instance, boomers (1943–1964), it is claimed, value job security and a stable working environment; they are loyal to their organization, are idealistic, optimistic and driven (Kupperschmidt, 2000). Boomers also tend to be associated with the adage, 'live to work' (Sayers, 2007). Generation Xers (1965 – 1981) on the other hand, tend to be viewed as cynical, pessimistic and individualistic (Kupperschmidt, 2000; Smola & Sutton, 2002). They are viewed as less loyal to their organization and more committed to their own careers. They also value work life balance more than their generational predecessors (Smola & Sutton, 2002). Research looking at Generation X women working in technology, found that personal fulfilment was intrinsically connected to professional success and that this generation of women wanted support in terms of mentors, opportunities for promotion and more flexibility to achieve a work life balance (Feyerherm & Vick, 2005). For the generation that has grown up with technology and the digital age, Generation Y (1982-present), are viewed as driven, demanding, highly confident and highly socialized (Smola & Sutton, 2002). Generation Yers have also been found to have higher self esteem, narcissism, anxiety and depression, whilst having a lower need for social approval and more external locus of control (Twenge & Campbell, 2008). Generational differences highlight the evolution of the workplace and change in what is considered appropriate and important. There is an increasing importance attached to work life balance, particularly in younger generations of workers, this must be considered in the context of SET careers and career development. This is especially so

in new technology careers such as computer games. Chapter three looked at the influence new technology has on learning and the expectations of the Net Generation which must also be bore in mind when considering the workforce and the career factors that can influence the careers of women such as those discussed in chapters eight and nine.

OUR STUDY FINDINGS

Women face a number of barriers which hinder their career choices and career progression, this is especially so for women working in male dominated occupations and careers. For instance, Eagly and Carli (2003) found women in male dominated organizations, suffered from gender stereotypes more than women in more gender neutral or female dominated organizations. This does not appear to be the case for men working in female dominated occupations, who often gain from working in gender incongruent industries. Although there is some research that suggests men are penalized for not adhering to gender norms (Heilman et al., 2004; Heilman & Okimoto, 2007), but not to the same extent as women.

As we have already acknowledged the computer games industry is part of the wider ICT and SET sectors and is a major forerunner in the development of technology (Flanagan, 2003). In the current, digital age the computer games industry is an important industry for academic study. Several empirical studies have shown that the marginalisation of women from the technological community can have a profound influence on design, technical content and the use of artefacts (i.e. Lie,

2003; Lerman, Oldenziel, & Mohun, 2003). Embedded in the design, meaning and use of ICTs are gender relations (Wajcman, 2007). As we acknowledged, women have played a part in the history of the development and use of technology (Plant, 1998) and computer games, but they are not yet fully integrated into the design of technology (Wajcman, 2007). Variability in gendering, by place, nationality, ethnicity, sexuality and generation exists and thus, women's experience of ICT is equally diverse and this must also be recognised. Heeter et al. (2009) used the word 'alien' to refer to the manner in which women who produce computer games are viewed. Female game developers could alter the image of the industry and perhaps help accommodate the needs of minority players. Chapter seven provided an in-depth discussion of the main findings from our research on female game developers. There is a paucity of research in the area of the experiences of women working in male dominated occupations, industries and sectors especially in the new industry of computer game development. We hope to add to this area of research by providing a voice of female game workers in our study who discuss their experiences of working in this highly male dominated industry.

Our research found that the industry could widen its appeal through increasing awareness of the roles and skills available within the industry. The computer games and wider ICT industries would benefit from advertising that a degree in computer science is not always necessary; individuals may come to work in technology related industries, via other disciplines as our findings suggest. The industry could

also increase its appeal through highlighting the benefits and rewards of working in such a creative, competitive and growing industry. This would include monetary gain, being part of an innovative industry and having a role in helping to develop and shape the technology of the future. The industry needs to review their policies and working practices in order to facilitate women and other minority groups within the working environment. Instead of women 'just fitting in' more can be done to eradicate career barriers and discriminatory work practices to make women feel more comfortable working in the industry.

The games industry would benefit from a more diverse workforce since this has the potential of making games with more appeal to a wider and more diverse audience. Men and women have been found to have different play styles and attracting more female developers, may enable more female gamers and vice versa. According to Fullerton, "one of the effects of getting women into game design is that they are going to add play patterns" (Edge online, 2009). Due to this desire to attract a wider audience, the games industry occupies a unique position. Perhaps this unique position will lead the industry to enhance its appeal to women and other underrepresented groups. Research shows women are active gamers, especially with more casual than hard-core games. Braithwaite (2010) views Facebook as a catalyst in which women are increasingly becoming more hard-core gamers. The games industry could significantly improve its appeal as a viable career to women. Firstly, the image of the games industry, like the wider ICT and SET industries, is still very much 'boys work'. However, this image could change with a more diverse workforce. Increasing the number of female gamers could help change the overall activity to be viewed as more inclusive, helping to shed its 'for boys only', masculine image. The current digital age may lead more girls and women to engage technology as users, which in turn may lead them to develop an interest in how computers and technology works leading to a potential interest in a technological or computing career.

The major issues relating to the gendering of computer games are provided in Table 1. The table indicates the core issues involved, for each of the reasons given, the chapter the issues are discussed in and suggestions on how to address the issues. Our suggestions link to Tables 2 and 3, which provide Industry and game development recommendations.

GUIDING MESSAGE: THE GENDERED DIVIDE IN COMPUTER GAMES AND GAMING CULTURE

In the preface, we describe both the need for and purpose of this book – an interdisciplinary, literature review of the multifaceted issues related to the gendered digital divide in computer games. The book represents our story from a predominantly social psychological perspective on the multifaceted issues, important when considering gender and computer games. In particular our emphasis has been on the computer games industry through a look at quantitative and qualitative research findings from our research investigating the reasons for the underrepresentation of women within this industry and also to give readers

an insight into what women who work in the industry have to say about their experiences. Although we have tended to focus on the production of computer games we hope to have brought insight to readers with regards to the gendered consumption of computer games especially in terms of the content of the games and the wider gaming culture. Despite legislation over the past 40 years, gender disparities in certain occupations remain. It appears that a number of issues run throughout the industry which contribute to the underrepresentation of women. Factors such as the long hour's culture associated with the industry, the lack of flexible working available, the lack of females, especially females with families within the industry and thus the lack of role models, as well as the image of the industry as masculine, contributes to the low representation of women. However it may not just be workforce issues at play resulting in the low representation of women within the industry. As we have highlighted throughout all aspects of computer games and computer games culture is gendered and in turn this impacts on not only the image of computer games as being form males only but also that the industry is a male domain and as a result many women may not view the industry as a viable career.

There are a number of issues involved in the gendering of computer games and many of these issues interrelate as well as often perpetuating each other. The book chapters, consider all aspects of computer games and gaming culture which illustrate their role in the gendering of computer games. One of the main premises of this book is to highlight the

Table 1. The core issues

Gender Differences and the Reason for the Gendered Digital Divide in Computer Games	Core Issues Involved	Discussed in the Following Chapters	How May the Issue be Addressed
Macho culture Male/masculine image of the industry Male/masculine image of the computer games	• Stereotypes of what is gender congruent behaviour. • Cultural and societal expectations based on gender. • Social role theory. • Women concentrated in certain occupations within the industry. • Image of computer games and technology is male.	Chapters 1, 5, and 6	• Encourage women and girls to enter the games industry workforce, especially in core content creation roles. • There is a need for more female role models to encourage female students to pursue education and careers in computing and computer gaming. • Provide more support for female students to engage with computing and technology. • Eradicate gender based stereotypes such as the image that computers and computer games are for 'boys only'. • Highlight the diversity of roles and skills required within the games industry. • Highlight the benefits of working in this industry such monetary benefits; it is viewed as fun work and part of both the knowledge and creative industries. • Highlight the benefits of working in a creative, interesting and rewarding industry
Gender divide in technology	• Access to, usage of, contribution to, and representation within technology is gendered. • Technology viewed as male. • Stereotypes of what is gender congruent behaviour. • Cultural and societal expectations based on gender. • Social role theory.	Chapters 1 and 2	
How computer games are gendered	• Leisure is gendered. • Game space is gendered in terms of ownership, accesses and usage. • Game content; a lack of females in games, the hyper sexualisation of females and the subordinate position of females within games. • Casual games viewed as female games. • Differences in play styles, motivations and game preferences. • Female professional games is viewed as subordinate.	Chapters 1, 2, 3, 4 and 5	

continued on following page

Table 1. Continued

Gender Differences and the Reason for the Gendered Digital Divide in Computer Games	Core Issues Involved	Discussed in the Following Chapters	How May the Issue be Addressed
Work pressures - Masculine work environment	• Lack of women within the industry. • Long hours culture. • Lack of flexible working practices. • Lack of women with children within the industry (role models/mentors).	Chapters 6, 7 and 8	• Increase girls/women's self-efficacy and self esteem in male dominated disciplines and environments by making them more female inclusive. • Review current polices relating to hours of work and flexible working practices. • Encourage the uptake of flexible working practices. • Employ strategies to help reduce the long hours culture. • Make long hours and crunch time a rarity rather than the norm. • Develop staff in project management skills in order to help reduce the long hours needed as deadlines approach. • Encourage the workforce to be more accepting to the needs of women with children and other caring responsibilities. • Encourage the workforce to have a work life balance.
Career path	• Lack of women in senior position/management. • Lack of transparent pay. • Lack of clear/transparent promotion opportunities.	Chapters 6, 7, 8 and 9	• Transparency in pay and promotional structures. • Encourage women to enter the industry and climb the career ladder within the industry. • Help plug the leaky pipeline through developing retention strategies such those related to work life balance issues. • Support women in senior positions through mentoring and networking opportunities. • Encourage women to apply for management/senior positions. • Support female mentees for promotion into senior roles. • Promote gender equality in the workplace at all levels from recruitment to retention.

interplay of different aspects of computer games which helps maintain and perpetuate the gendered digital divide in computer games. Throughout this book and the issues discussed, it is apparent that people experience computer game differently and that neither women nor men are homogenized groups, but that previous findings suggest a number of distinct gender based difference. For instance in chapter four we consider the difference in play styles, motivations for playing games and indeed differences in game preferences between the genders. This chapter also highlighted issues which relate and influence play such as space and leisure time which, as we have shown, are both gendered and directly

and indirectly influence what, why and when games are played. By taking into account how females are represented within computer game as well as the wider gaming culture, we are able to gain an understanding as to why females view the industry and gaming as male. Indeed the portrayal of females as we have discussed in chapter five emphasizes why many view games designed by males as being based on male fantasies and portraying an idealized femininity. However it must be bore in mind that not all games have these overtly and hyper sexualised representation. Indeed as mentioned the Nindendo consoles of the Wii and DS have a more inclusive game design and thus have moved away from these

Table 2. Key industry issues and recommendations

Industry Issues	
The Gender Divide	• The image of technology needs to change to incorporate a female view. • The increasing use of technology is making technology more inclusive. However, major gender differences exist to the detriment of females. More is required to reduce this gendered gap especially with regard to confidence and self-efficacy. • This fast moving industry needs to take into account the skill needs of it employers. This is especially important in retaining a female workforce. • Female game workers should be encouraged to retain after maternity leave and given the support to update or regain their skills needed for their role. • There is a need to reduce the gender digital divide through education initiatives that focus on getting girls to the same confidence level with ICT as boys. • Initiatives need to be more widely available and include a number of digital technologies used in everyday lives in order to help reduce this gap. • Girls/women should be equally encouraged to engage with technology.
Impact of Females Working in the Industry	• The industry like the wider ICT and SET sector needs to eradicate the image of being a male domain in order to attract a more gender diverse workforce. • The industry needs to consider ways in how to reduce the effects of the working practices in order to both attract and retain a more diverse workforce. • Promote initiatives such as flexible working. • For retention ask women workers what they need. • Reduce were possible the expectation of long hours as the 'norm' or regular occurrence. • The computer games industry could benefit from highlighting the various roles and skills required in the industry as well as the various backgrounds, both educational and occupational, that people who enter the industry come from. • Women who are in the industry especially those in core content creation roles could act as role models for girls considering a career within the industry. • More females playing games could potentially increase the number of females interested in making games. • More female game developers have the potential in making the industry and the games developed attract a more diverse audience. • Female game developers increase the potential impact of the industry. • There is a need for greater gender neutral game design. • Research on women working in the games industry is sparse. More research is needed to consider the barriers and drivers of women in this male dominated industry.
Recruitment	• Training of selection group members to avoid unconscious bias. • Ensure women are represented in adequate numbers on promotion, job, prize committees etc. • Check for implicit bias in criteria for awards and nominations and research assessment type RAE exercises. • Make the workplace women friendly. • Remove barriers to women being recruited to and remaining in the organisation. • Foster a supportive work environment that appeals to women's values and work styles.
Career Motivation	• Recognise the contribution women can make in publication in the leading scientific journals is particularly useful for career progression. • Make the environment one that fosters motivation regardless of gender.
Retention	• Remove barriers to women being recruited to and remaining in the organisation. • Make the workplace women friendly. • Organisational level issues, to be addressed by management, for change to occur and encourage women to remain in the industry. • Increase flexible working practices. • Identify the barriers and opportunities for job satisfaction.

Table 3. Key game development and play issues and recommendations

Game Development and Play Issues	
	Game Development and Play Issues
Gaming Gendered Spaces	• Gaming is a gendered leisure activity. There is a need for gaming to be a more accepted leisure activity for females. • Parents need encouragement to enable girls within the home to have equal access to computer gaming technology. • Encourage females to play games on alternative platforms and spaces, such as mobile phones and social networking sites, to increase female participation. • Virtual games spaces allow female gamers the space to compete free from their gender, reducing stereotypical behaviour in game play. This should be encouraged and acknowledged as a benefit to game play. • Research suggests girls only initiatives help improve girls' interest in, and usage of technologies such as computer games.
Motivation for Game Play	• More understanding is needed of the difference in game play and what attracts both male and female gamers to play computer games. • More understanding of what makes games fun and is fun for different demographics. • The sexual division of labour within the home in terms of domestic and childcare responsibilities leads to women having less leisure time then males. This is a pertinent issue and one that extends beyond computer game play. • The increase in family friendly games is making games more social and increasing female participation in the leisure pursuit. However more games need to be made which are gender neutral in all genres. • It should be recognized that there is not a single woman and therefore not a single game genre for women despite women preferring causal games. • To reduce the gender dichotomy it should be recognised that 'casual gamers' can be as equally committed to their preferred games as so called 'hardcore gamers' are. • Women play a wide variety of game genres and we believe more women making games will increase the different types of games made, with different play styles, attracting a much wider and diverse audience. • Games of all genres need to appeal to a more inclusive gamer audience. • Game developers should be making good games for all.
Female Representation in Games	• Game designers need to make games, that are not based on stereotypical ideals of femininity. • More females in the game design workforce could enable games to developed, with less stereotypical views of females. • The greater representation of females in the casual game genre may account for the increase in female participation in this game genre. This could be a message to game developers in other genres especially sport and action games. • There is a need for more gender neutral games. • Allow more choice in how a female avatar can look. • Allow gamers to try different identities in a safe environment. This is important to female gamers. • Recognise that a games rules, limit identities.
Computer Games	• Due to the association of violence and games with masculinity, the masculine dominance of computer games and the computer games culture is perpetuated and reinforced through games considered 'mainstream' by the industry and hard core gamers. • The benefits of playing games could help reduce the gender gap in spatial cognition. • Future research on computer games needs to take into account gender differences. • If the image of computer games became more gender neutral, perhaps females would receive as equal parental mediation as their male counterparts. • Family friendly games are increasing the demographic diversity of gamers. • Parental attitude is important and can have a huge impact on a child's game playing. • More guidance is needed to enable parents to make informed choices regarding their children's game play. • Women play games and if this was more widely acknowledged then this would help reduce the male image of computer games.

continued on following page

Table 3. Continued

Game Development and Play Issues	
Learning Games	• Using games in the classroom may reduce the gendered digital divide. • In order for the gendered divide to close, those who use, and advocate the use of computer games in the learning environment must be aware of gendered issues, associated with computer games and other forms of technology. • Emphasise that games provide players the opportunity to use role play to learn and develop. • Computer games for learning, should focus on any students unfamiliar with game technologies. • Be aware that some students may be less confident in playing computer games. • Extra support provided to students as necessary. • Ensure no student is disadvantaged, through using technology in learning.

negative female portrayals. However what is interesting about both the Wii and DS consoles is that they are not viewed as hardcore gaming systems like Microsoft's Xbox and Sony's Playstation are viewed. Nindendo could therefore be viewed as having designed the female gamer by firstly advertising to females and secondly making games more females would and indeed do like. However in attracting a more gender inclusive gamer market, females who play games on these consoles are viewed as a different type of gamer, outside of the mainstream, hard core gamer section and into the causal gamer which many view as not real gamers.

Chapters one, two and three have shown how important computer games and the computer games industry is in terms of the media landscape today both in terms of the economic and cultural impact of computer games. The purpose of these three chapters is to highlight to the reader why they gender divide within computer games is such an important and timely issue. Chapter one provided an insight into computer games and considered whether computer games are good or bad. Our premise in writing this book is that computer games are a good leisure and entertainment activity, which have a potential of providing a number of skills such as increasing pro social behaviour, providing technology skills and increasing visuo-spatial skills. Chapter one highlighted some of the negative issues that have been raised previously; mainly the violent and aggressive content of games. Chapter two focused on providing the reader with facts and figures about the industry with the aim of providing an overview of the current situation with regard to computer games and the computer games industry as well as highlighting the situation of female gamers. Whereas chapter three focused on serious games and how games are increasingly being considered or used in none entertainment ways; in the main education and learning, as well as health promotion and behaviour change. The purpose of discussing how games are used or could potentially be used beyond leisure and entertainment is again to emphasize the impact that computer games are having in society beyond the individual gamer experience. This look into serious games may not initially have a gendered focus, however as we have shown, the gendering of computer games extends beyond the games themselves and include a number of differences including gender differences with regard to attitudes towards, confidence in, and self-efficacy issues in computer games. Therefore using serious games to aide learning, behaviour change or health promotion may be a different experience for females than males and non-gamers than gamers. All of these gender issues need considering when considering the gendering of computer games. We advocate the use of serious games however caution as well as more research is needed investigating the different experiences of using game for non-leisure, non-entertainment purposes between different demographics especially different genders.

There is also the issue of access and image. There is a distinct lack of females within games, as indeed there are in other media forms. Furthermore, we need to question what kind of representation of females should be in games. Chapter six looked at the underrepresentation of women working in the computer games industry, highlighting to the reader factors contributing to this underrepresentation. Chapter seven focused on our own research of women who currently work in this male dominated industry, providing a voice for female game workers and highlighting their experiences. Men dominate the games industry both as developers and gamers. Research shows women are active gamers, especially with more casual than hard core games. Women should be involved in all aspects of the industry, especially games development, due to the numerous benefits that the industry can offer. Our research with women games developers highlights how highly motivated women in the industry are. Career motivation, person-environment fit, self-efficacy, self-

esteem, work satisfaction, career factors and life issues are all important constructs when looking at the career and career development of women. Research into the experiences of women working in the games industry and other male dominated sectors enables those industries to alter working practices in ways that not only attract, but also retain a more diverse workforce.

In chapters eight and nine, we focused on how gendered segregation and its related issues persist. We discussed the fact that equity within scientific research has increased in recent decades and how it could be argued that women today have the same range of opportunities as men. However, we feel there is still a long way to go to achieve gender parity. Senior women in any industry are role models for women in industry and visibility assists in the recruitment of young women. Some researchers argue that women who have mentors gain access to resources and senior managers through a mentor, enabling career progression. Work/life balance has been the subject of intense debate and cited as one of the most important considerations for graduates when choosing an employer. The number of women entering traditionally male dominated careers is increasing. Understanding of how work/life balance should work is crucial for appropriate adoption and implementation of practices such as flexible working. Health problems as a result of working excessive hours are well documented. We have highlighted how gender stereotypes can influence our emotions and suggested that prejudice may arise from societal stereotypes. In order to overcome implicit bias, self- awareness is required to challenge behaviour, hopefully as the media highlights such issues, individuals will start to question their own and their colleagues' behaviour. Tables 2 and 3 highlight our key issues and recommendations for reducing the gendered digital divide in computer games.

THE WAY FORWARD: FUTURE RESEARCH QUESTIONS

The real world just doesn't offer up as easily the carefully designed pleasures, the thrilling challenges, and the powerful social bonding afforded by virtual environments. Reality doesn't motivate us as effectively. Reality isn't engineered to maximize our potential. Reality wasn't designed from the bottom up to make us happy. (McGonigal, 2011, p. 3)

The quote by Jane McGonigal adds to our understanding of, and emphasizes again why computer games are such an influential and powerful medium today. We believe this industry to be an interesting, developing and an industry worthy of increasingly more academic interest. Previous academic research tended to focus on the un-healthiness of gaming; aggressive behaviour, lack of physical activity, addiction and the reinforcement of gender stereotypes. More recently we have seen a shift in research that is considering the benefits and positive outcomes of playing games in the advent of pro social games and gaming. Indeed, a number of the highly regarded and influential TED talks have focused on the advantages of games. For example Gabe Zichermann talked on how games make

kids smarter and Ali Carr-Chellman discussed how gaming can be used to re-engage boys in learning.

Throughout our book, we have highlighted how computer games are gendered. Strategies for addressing the problems need to come from a variety of standpoints and perspectives, this is especially so because the gendering to computer games is complex and at all levels. In order to devise better solutions we need a richer knowledge of the complex, multifaceted issues in order to gain successful solutions, which was our hope in writing this book. Throughout this book, we have seen how the male dominance of the computer games industry and the computer gaming culture impacts on female in a number of ways including but not limited to game play, motivation, interests, image, access to and use of computer games. Having a greater understanding as to why some women choose to work in this male dominated industry is valuable for devising solutions on attracting more women into certain occupations and industries. There are many areas for future research in relation to the gendering of computer games. For instance do male dominated industries attract a certain type of woman or do women have to adapt to its masculine culture? This may indicate whether male dominated occupations/industries attract women with more masculine or androgynous identity, or if adopting masculine traits is used to cope with the working environment, as the research on women in leadership/senior roles tends to suggest. For retention, the most prominent question for further research would be to evaluate the effect of long hours and crunch time has on both women and men in the sector. Addressing long hours worked, may potentially aide recruitment and retention initiatives, especially for women with, or planning children. Qualitative follow up, investigating the women who planned to leave the sector and why, would also facilitate recruitment and retention strategies. Employers need to increase the attractiveness of IT careers and promoting knowledge may enhance their desirability and increase workplace diversity. Future research should focus on factors contributing to the development of a successful career for women in IT, a life span approach may be useful to determine gender role attitude and the opportunities and barriers experienced longitudinally. In relation to flexible working, it would be interesting and extremely useful for policy development to evaluate women who work flexibly and the impact this is having on their careers. Other interesting questions pertinent to the ICT and computer games industry focus on the changing workforce, generation Y and technological development. The digital age may influence how women view computers, technology and ultimately careers in these areas. Digital networking and mentoring opportunities may increasingly become beneficial to women's career development. Networking through social networking tools such as *Twitter* and *LinkedIn* may enable women to overcome many of the barriers of more face-to-face, traditional networking and mentoring methods.

In order to meet growing demands it is important for countries to capitalise on the full potential of its available workforce and utilise women, especially in IT related careers. Encouraging more women into male domi-nated occupations is a strategy for reducing gendered occupational segregation and the inequalities that accompany it. More women in senior roles will influence the image of the industry and aid recruitment. One of the major issues we have highlighted is the underrepresentation of women working in the development of computer games and we have used our research with female game workers to exemplify the issues. It will be interesting to revisit in ten years time the same issues and consider what has changed.

I've been here 5 years but I'm not sure if I'll be here in five years time, no, no, I'd like to be but I want a family at some point, before its too late, so maybe not, but we will see. (Female games developer)

REFERENCES

Brathwaite, B. (2010). *Women in games: From famine to Facebook*. Retrieved from http://www.huffingtonpost.com/brenda-brathwaite/women-in-games-from-famin_b_510928.html

D'Amato, A. (2008). Learning orientation, organizational commitment and talent retention across generations: A study of European managers. *Journal of Managerial Psychology*, *23*(8), 929–953. doi:10.1108/02683940810904402

Deuze, M., Martin, C. B., & Alen, C. (2007). The professional identity of gameworkers. *Convergence: The International Journal of Research into New Media Technologies*, *13*(4), 335–353. doi:10.1177/1354856507081947

Eagly, A. H., & Carli, L. L. (2003). The female leadership advantage: An evaluation of the evidence. *The Leadership Quarterly, 14,* 807–834. doi:10.1016/j.leaqua.2003.09.004

Edge Online. (2009). Retrieved from http://www.edge-online.com/features/gdc-we-need-more-women-games

Feyerherm, A., & Vick, Y. H. (2005). Generation X women in high technology: Overcoming gender and generational challenges to succeed in the corporate environment. *Career Development International, 10*(3), 216–227. doi:10.1108/13620430510598337

Flanagan, M. (2003). Next level women's digital activism through gaming. In *Digital media revisited: Theoretical and conceptual innovation in digital domains* (pp. 359–388). Cambridge, MA: MIT.

Gourdin, A. (2005). *Game developers demographics: An exploration of workforce diversity.* International Game Developers Association.

Gursoy, D., Maier, T. A., & Chi, C. G. (2008). Generational differences: An examination of work values and generation gaps in the hospitality workforce. *International Journal of Hospitality Management, 27,* 448–458. doi:10.1016/j.ijhm.2007.11.002

Heeter, C., Egidio, R., Mishra, P., Winn, B., & Winn, J. (2009). Alien games: Do girls prefer games designed by girls? *Games and Culture, 4*(1), 74–100. doi:10.1177/1555412008325481

Heilman, M. E., & Okimoto, T. G. (2007). Why are women penalized for success at male tasks? The implied communality deficit. *The Journal of Applied Psychology, 92,* 81–92. doi:10.1037/0021-9010.92.1.81 PMID:17227153

Heilman, M. E., Wallen, A. S., Fuchs, D., & Tamkins, M. M. (2004). Penalties for success: Reactions to women who succeed at male gender-typed tasks. *The Journal of Applied Psychology, 89,* 416–427. doi:10.1037/0021-9010.89.3.416 PMID:15161402

Jenkins, H. (2006). *Fans, bloggers, and gamers: Exploring participatory culture.* New York: NYU Press.

Kupperschmidt, B. R. (2000). Multigeneration employees: Strategies for effective management. *The Health Care Manager, 19*(1), 65–76. doi:10.1097/00126450-200019010-00011 PMID:11183655

Lerman, N. E., Oldenziel, R., & Mohun, A. P. (2003). *Gender and technology: A reader.* Baltimore, MD: John Hopkins University Press.

Lie, M. (2003). *He, she and IT revisited: New perspectives on gender and the information society.* Oslo, Norway: Gyldenhal Akademisk.

McGonigal, J. (2011). *Reality is broken: Why games make us better and how they can change the world.* New York: Penguin Press.

Plant, S. (1998). *Zeros and ones: Digital women and the new technoculture.* London: Fourth Estate.

Prescott, J., & Bogg, J. (2010). The computer games industry: Women's experiences of work role in a male dominated environment. In *Women in engineering, science and technology: Education and career challenges.* Hershey, PA: IGI Global. doi:10.4018/978-1-61520-657-5.ch007

Prescott, J., & Bogg, J. (2012). *Gendered occupational differences in science, engineering, and technology careers.* Hershey, PA: IGI Global. doi:10.4018/978-1-4666-2107-7

Sayers, R. (2007). The right staff from X to Y: Generational change and professional development in future academic libraries. *Library Management, 28*(8/9), 474–487. doi:10.1108/01435120710837765

Smola, K. W., & Sutton, C. D. (2002). Generational differences: Revisiting generational work values for the new millennium. *Journal of Organizational Behavior, 23,* 363–382. doi:10.1002/job.147

Twenge, J. M., & Campbell, S. M. (2008). Generational differences in psychological traits and their impact on the workplace. *Journal of Managerial Psychology, 23*(8), 862–877. doi:10.1108/02683940810904367

Wajcman, J. (2007). From women and technology to gendered technoscience. *Information Communication and Society, 10*(3), 287–298. doi:10.1080/13691180701409770

APPENDIX: ONLINE RESOURCES

We have provided a list of online resources which readers may find useful in gaining further information on the issues of women and computer games and the wider ICT sector. The list is not complete; it will hopefully be a good starting guide for those interested in gaining further information and wanting to become more involved.

Computer Games Sites for Women/Girls

The following is a list of online resources that specifically looks at girls/women and computer games.

- Computer club 4 girls – http://www.cc4g.net/

Computer Clubs for Girls (CC4G) is a new kind of club full of interesting things to do. It's exclusively for 10 to 13 year old girls.

- http://girlgamers.co.uk/about/

GirlGamers.co.uk is a dedicated girl gaming site. So if you're female and you love playing video games, then you've come to the right place.

- Frag Dolls – http://www.fragdolls.com/us/

The Frag Dolls are a group of girl gamers whose site includes their individual blogs, a forum, and a calendar of events, including opportunities to play against one or more of the Frag Dolls in online games.

- Mary-Margaret.com – http://www.mary-margaret.com/Public/Home/index.cfm

The Mary-Margaret Network encompasses a diverse clientele in the games, electronic media, and entertainment industries. We place outstanding candidates - from individual contributors to C-level executives - in positions in every department: from art to engineering, production to sales, and graphics to operations. Since 1996, our focus on superior service to employers and candidates has earned us an unsurpassed reputation for recruitment services and career management.

- IGDA Women in games development – http://archives.igda.org/women/

Extensive list of resources and links at the International Game Developers Association 'Women in Games Development' Special Interest Group.

- Thumbbandits – http://thumbbandits.com/

Thumb Bandits is a Gaming Community for both male and female gamers, however the site is heavily slanted towards Women Gamers, the Games Industry Re Women Gamers, Female Gaming within Academia and many interest pieces on / about women.

- Women gamers.com – http://www.womengamers.com/

Because women do play! A Website aimed at women who play computer games.

- WIGI – http://www.womeningamesinternational.org/

Women in Games International works to promote the inclusion and advancement of women in the global games industry. We believe diversifying the game development, media, academic and publishing workplace results in not only a more equitable space, but better products. Women In Games International advocates for issues important to both women and men in the game development industry, including a better work/life balance and healthy working conditions.

Computer Games Sites for Gay Gamers

- Gay gamer net – http://gaygamer.net/
- The gay gamer – http://www.thegaygamer.com/

Computer Games Sites for Older Gamers

- The older gamers.com – http://www.theoldergamers.com/
- Mature gamer – http://www.maturegamer.co.uk/
- Mature video gamer.com – http://www.maturevideogamer.co.uk/
- The older gamer.com forum, a forum for gamers aged over 25 – http://www.theoldergamers.com/forum/

Serious Games

There is an abundance of serious games on the market today, here are some useful Website .

- Games for Change – http://www.gamesforchange.org/
- Persuasive Games – http://www.persuasivegames.com/
- Mission to Learn – http://www.missiontolearn.com/2009/09/more-learning-games-for-change/
- Epistemic Games – http://epistemicgames.org/eg/

ICT Related Resources

- Anita Borg Institute – http://www.anitaborg.org

California-based organization, whose mission is to increase the impact of women on technology and to increase the positive impact of technology on women's lives. Formerly called the Institute for Women and Technology, it now bears the name of its distinguished founder, Anita Borg. The site includes information about its initiatives and links to related sites.

- Association for Women in Computing – http://www.awc-hq.org

Information about the AWC, links to local chapters and related sites.

- BCS Women's Forum – http://www.bcs.org/category/8630

This Website from the British Computing Society focuses on issues concerning women's participation in information technology. The aim is to stimulate "dialogue and discussion about the policies and practices in IT and using them to make IT a place that is inclusive." The site offers profiles of women in IT, statistics and research, annotated links to related groups and organizations, and the opportunity to participate in online discussion forums.

- Binary Girl – http://www.binarygirl.com

This Web site, "where girls and technology click," aims to "share knowledge with those interested in learning more about technology through an interactive community of women."

- Computer Girl – http://www.computergirl.us/

Started by Stanford undergraduate Amy Wu, the Computer Girl site is designed "to bridge the gap between young women in high school and the computer world." It offers abundant resources: Web sites, articles, role models, statistics, job categories, summer camp listings, and more. It also provides a place where students can ask questions about the field of computer science [e.g., the job market, salaries, finding mentors, scholarships, work/life balance, etc.].

- Center for Women and Information Technology – http://www.umbc.edu/cwit/

Established to encourage women's and girls' greater involvement with information technology, the Center offers many resources on its Web site, including extensive news coverage of women and IT, announcements of relevant conferences and calls for papers, a bibliography of books about women and IT, a huge collection of Web-based syllabi for women- and gender-related courses, Internet resources dealing with women and IT, and more.

- Committee on the Status of Women in Computing Research (CRA-W) – http://cra-w.org/

Site includes a number of useful annotated links to sites/events/statistics of particular interest to women interested in computer science.

- Cyber Grrl – www.cybergrrl.com

A site for women interested in technology with the slogan: 'inspiring, informing and celebrating women'

- Digital Sisters – http://www.digital-sistas.org

Digital Sisters has been created "to promote and provide technology education and enrichment for young girls and women of color." The Web site provides information about relevant events, news, educational resources, reports and statistics, and links to related sites.

- Dot Diva – www.dotdiva.org.

A site for women with the philosophy that computing can make a better world.

- Exploring Gender and Technology – http://www.gse.harvard.edu/~wit/exploring/index. htm

"This site presents current research, perspectives, and innovative approaches to the gender gap in technology collected from secondary research." It offers statistics, case studies, a video, online discussion, an annotated bibliography, and annotated links for educators and for girls.

- Girl Geeks – http://www.girlgeeks.org/

GirlGeeks aims to encourage women to develop their careers in technology.

- Girl Geek Dinners – http://girlgeekdinners.com/

Hold local events to bring women together to educate each other over dinner. A number of girl geek organizations exist through the world including Canada, USA, Australia, Japan, Indian and throughout Europe.

- Girly Geekdom – http://girlygeekdom.com/

'GirlyGeekdom hopes to bring fun, exciting and inspirational content along with relevant news and information from the Science, Technology and Engineering industry'.

- Girl Start – http://www.girlstart.org/

Girlstart is a non-profit organization created to empower girls to excel in math, science, and technology. Resources, information and games available on the Website.

- Girltech – http://www.girlstech.douglass.rutgers.edu/

Girlstech explains and demonstrates a framework to evaluate electronic resources (Web sites, CD-ROMs, and games) for girls and young women to encourage and increase their involvement in the sciences and technology.

- Girl Tech – http://www.girltech.com/

Girl Tech's mission is to enhance girls' lives and foster their use of technology by bringing to market technology-enhanced lifestyle electronics just for girls ages 8-12. These products are designed with girls' play preferences in mind, addressing issues that are important to them such as privacy and communication.

- Interactive selection – http://www.interactiveselection.com/women.asp - interactive selection support WiG (women in games) and look to recruit women in the games industry. They have a specific site for women- http://www.womeningamesjobs.com/
- GirlGamers.co.uk
- Rapunsel – http://www.rapunsel.org/

"Realtime, applied programming for under-represented students' early literacy (RAPUNSEL) is Rapunsel is single-player dance game designed to teach computer programming to 10-12 year olds. The project was started with the goal of empowering young girls to learn programming as a way of addressing the critical shortage of women in technology related careers and degree programs. By giving players the opportunity to explore coding through scaffolded challenges in a playful world, we hope to empower young people to learn about computer science. It is a cross platform, downladable game created in the Torque game engine."

- The National Center for Women and IT – www.ncwit.org/

The NCWIT works to increase diversity in IT and computing. NCWIT believes that greater diversity will create a larger and more competitive workforce, and will foster the design of technology that is as broad and innovative as the population it serves. NCWIT focuses on improving diversity across the entire spectrum: K-12 through college education, and on to academic, corporate and entrepreneurial careers.

- Web Grrls – http://www.Webgrrls.com

Webgrrls is an online & offline networking organization of professional women focusing on propelling our careers & businesses forward by *leveraging the power of women*, *technology*, and *tools* that help us succeed. For over 15 years Webgrrls has been at the forefront of the women's movement online. We're an online & offline networking organization of professional women focusing on propelling our careers & businesses forward by *leveraging the power of women*, *technology*, and *tools* that help us succeed.

- Whyville – http://www.whyville.net/top/gates.html

Whyville is an imaginative Web site that aims to help elementary, middle, and high school students (boys and girls) understand and enjoy science. It differs from most science education sites in its use of avatars, games, computer simulation and modelling, a Whyville newspaper, and interactivity among Whyville participants.

- Women and Girls Tech Up – http://www.techup.org/index.html

Online zine grew out of an 18-month private collaborative online meeting of 16 small organizations for women and girls. To encourage women and girls - and the organizations which serve them - to use technology to share ideas, opinions, support, creativity and political action. The project was co-sponsored by The Women's Foundation and The Electronic Frontier Foundation, and funded by Pacific Bell.

- Women in Technology – http://www.womenintech.com/

A Hawaii-based organization that seeks to improve the "economic quality of life for women by encouraging them into higher-paying technology occupations." Women in Technology has developed a number of initiatives to achieve this goal, some aimed at middle- and high school students, others at college students and women in the workforce. The Web site includes information about all the initiatives, along with resource articles, scholarship information, a calendar of events, and extensive links to related sites.

- Women in Technology – http://www.womenintechnology.co.uk/

At womenintechnology.co.uk we are committed to increasing the number of women working and achieving in the UK's technology profession. We provide a complete recruitment service, offer a dedicated online IT job board, regularly host networking events, run personal development and career orientated training courses and provide in-depth information about key matters affecting the IT industry and the people who work within it.

- Zoey's Room - A Tech Know Community for Girls – http://www.zoeysroom.com/

"Zoey's room is an online community for girls ages 10-14, a place where girls can go to explore math, science and technology in a fun, safe and creative environment." Zoey's room offers an online collaborative community, a chance to communicate with Zoey in her chat room, Fab Female role model online chats, a place to showcase girls' creative work, and hands on challenges that lead to big prizes such as digital cameras.

Related References

To continue our tradition of advancing information science and technology research, we have compiled a list of recommended IGI Global readings. These references will provide additional information and guidance to further enrich your knowledge and assist you with your own research and future publications.

Abrams, S. S. (2010). The dynamics of video gaming: Influences affecting game play and learning. In P. Zemliansky, & D. Wilcox (Eds.), *Design and implementation of educational games: Theoretical and practical perspectives* (pp. 78–91). Hershey, PA: Information Science Reference. doi:10.4018/978-1-61520-781-7.ch006

Achtenhagen, L., & Johannisson, B. (2013). Games in entrepreneurship education to support the crafting of an entrepreneurial mindset. In S. de Freitas, M. Ott, M. Popescu, & I. Stanescu (Eds.), *New pedagogical approaches in game enhanced learning: Curriculum integration* (pp. 20–37). Hershey, PA: Information Science Reference. doi:10.4018/978-1-4666-3950-8.ch002

Akcaoglu, M. (2013). Using MMORPGs in classrooms: Stories vs. teachers as sources of motivation. In Y. Baek, & N. Whitton (Eds.), *Cases on digital game-based learning: Methods, models, and strategies* (pp. 15–24). Hershey, PA: Information Science Reference.

Al-Jenaibi, B. (2011). Gender issues in the diversity and practice of public relations in the UAE case study of P.R. male managers and female P.R. practitioners. *International Journal of E-Politics*, 2(3), 35–56. doi:10.4018/jep.2011070104

Albert, L. J., Hill, T. R., & Venkatsubramanyan, S. (2011). Effects of perceiver / target gender and social networking presence on web-based impression formation. *International Journal of E-Politics*, 2(2), 55–73. doi:10.4018/jep.2011040104

Albert, L. J., Hill, T. R., & Venkatsubramanyan, S. (2012). Gender differences in social networking presence effects on web-based impression formation. In C. Romm Livermore (Ed.), *Gender and social computing: Interactions, differences and relationships* (pp. 200–220). Hershey, PA: Information Science Publishing.

Albuquerque, O., & Moreira, G. G. (2011). The contribution of videogames to anti-social attitudes and behaviours amongst youngsters. In M. Cruz-Cunha, V. Varvalho, & P. Tavares (Eds.), *Business, technological, and social dimensions of computer games: Multidisciplinary developments* (pp. 237–251). Hershey, PA: Information Science Reference. doi:10.4018/978-1-60960-567-4.ch015

Aldrich, C., & DiPietro, J. C. (2011). An overview of gaming terminology: Chapters I – LXXVI. In I. Management Association (Ed.), Gaming and simulations: Concepts, methodologies, tools and applications (pp. 24-44). Hershey, PA: Information Science Reference. doi: doi:10.4018/978-1-60960-195-9.ch102

Alkhattabi, M., Neagu, D., & Cullen, A. (2012). User perceptions of information quality in e-learning systems: A gender and cultural perspective. In R. Pande, & T. Van der Weide (Eds.), *Globalization, technology diffusion and gender disparity: Social impacts of ICTs* (pp. 138–145). Hershey, PA: Information Science Reference. doi:10.4018/978-1-4666-0020-1.ch012

Anagnostou, K. (2011). How has the internet evolved the videogame medium? In M. Cruz-Cunha, V. Varvalho, & P. Tavares (Eds.), *Business, technological, and social dimensions of computer games: Multidisciplinary developments* (pp. 448–462). Hershey, PA: Information Science Reference. doi:10.4018/978-1-60960-567-4.ch027

Anderson, B. (2010). MMORPGs in support of learning: Current trends and future uses. In R. Van Eck (Ed.), *Gaming and cognition: Theories and practice from the learning sciences* (pp. 55–81). Hershey, PA: Information Science Reference. doi:10.4018/978-1-61520-717-6.ch003

Appiah, O., & Elias, T. (2011). Race-specific advertising on commercial websites: Effects of ethnically ambiguous computer generated characters in a digital world. In M. Eastin, T. Daugherty, & N. Burns (Eds.), *Handbook of research on digital media and advertising: User generated content consumption* (pp. 161–179). Hershey, PA: Information Science Reference.

Arroyo-Palacios, J., & Romano, D. M. (2010). Bio-affective computer interface for game interaction. *International Journal of Gaming and Computer-Mediated Simulations*, *2*(4), 16–32. doi:10.4018/jgcms.2010100102

Asbell-Clarke, J., Edwards, T., Rowe, E., Larsen, J., Sylvan, E., & Hewitt, J. (2012). Martian boneyards: Scientific inquiry in an MMO game. *International Journal of Game-Based Learning*, *2*(1), 52–76. doi:10.4018/ijgbl.2012010104

Bachvarova, Y., & Bocconi, S. (2014). Games and social networks. In T. Connolly, T. Hainey, E. Boyle, G. Baxter, & P. Moreno-Ger (Eds.), *Psychology, pedagogy, and assessment in serious games* (pp. 204–219). Hershey, PA: Information Science Reference.

Balachandar, A., & Gurusamy, R. (2012). Conflict segments of women employees of IT sector in India: Its relevance with the demographic profile. *International Journal of Human Capital and Information Technology Professionals*, *3*(1), 42–53. doi:10.4018/jhcitp.2012010104

Balzac, S. R. (2010). Reality from fantasy: Using predictive scenarios to explore ethical dilemmas. In K. Schrier, & D. Gibson (Eds.), *Ethics and game design: Teaching values through play* (pp. 291–310). Hershey, PA: Information Science Reference. doi:10.4018/978-1-61520-845-6.ch018

Baranowski, T., O'Connor, T., Hughes, S., Beltran, A., Baranowski, J., & Nicklas, T. … Buday, R. (2013). Smart phone video game simulation of parent-child interaction: learning skills for effective vegetable parenting. In S. Arnab, I. Dunwell, & K. Debattista (Eds.), Serious games for healthcare: Applications and implications (pp. 247-264). Hershey, PA: Medical Information Science Reference. doi: doi:10.4018/978-1-4666-1903-6.ch012

Barlow, M. (2011). Game led HCI improvements. In M. Cruz-Cunha, V. Varvalho, & P. Tavares (Eds.), *Business, technological, and social dimensions of computer games: Multidisciplinary developments* (pp. 126–145). Hershey, PA: Information Science Reference. doi:10.4018/978-1-60960-567-4.ch009

Bates, M. (2013). The ur-real sonorous envelope: Bridge between the corporeal and the online technoself. In R. Luppicini (Ed.), *Handbook of research on technoself: Identity in a technological society* (pp. 272–292). Hershey, PA: Information Science Reference.

Belfo, F. (2011). Business process management in the computer games industry. In M. Cruz-Cunha, V. Varvalho, & P. Tavares (Eds.), *Business, technological, and social dimensions of computer games: Multidisciplinary developments* (pp. 383–400). Hershey, PA: Information Science Reference. doi:10.4018/978-1-60960-567-4.ch023

Ben, E. R. (2012). Gendering professionalism in the internationalization of information work. In R. Pande, & T. Van der Weide (Eds.), *Globalization, technology diffusion and gender disparity: Social impacts of ICTs* (pp. 51–69). Hershey, PA: Information Science Reference. doi:10.4018/978-1-4666-0020-1.ch005

Berzsenyi, C. (2014). Writing to meet your match: Rhetoric and self-presentation for four online daters. In H. Lim, & F. Sudweeks (Eds.), *Innovative methods and technologies for electronic discourse analysis* (pp. 210–234). Hershey, PA: Information Science Reference.

Bevc, T. (2010). Models of politics and society in video games. In P. Zemliansky, & D. Wilcox (Eds.), *Design and implementation of educational games: Theoretical and practical perspectives* (pp. 47–64). Hershey, PA: Information Science Reference. doi:10.4018/978-1-61520-781-7.ch004

Bhatnagar, K. (2013). Supply chain management and the other half. In I. Association (Ed.), *Supply chain management: Concepts, methodologies, tools, and applications* (pp. 106–120). Hershey, PA: Business Science Reference.

Bishop, J. (2010). Increasing capital revenue in social networking communities: Building social and economic relationships through avatars and characters. In S. Dasgupta (Ed.), *Social computing: Concepts, methodologies, tools, and applications* (pp. 1987–2004). Hershey, PA: Information Science Reference. doi:10.4018/978-1-60960-100-3.ch509

Bishop, J. (2011). Increasing capital revenue in social networking communities: Building social and economic relationships through avatars and characters. In I. Management Association (Ed.), Virtual communities: Concepts, methodologies, tools and applications (pp. 1720-1737). Hershey, PA: Information Science Reference. doi: doi:10.4018/978-1-60960-100-3.ch509

Bishop, J. (2013). The psychology of trolling and lurking: The role of defriending and gamification for increasing participation in online communities using seductive narratives. In J. Bishop (Ed.), *Examining the concepts, issues, and implications of internet trolling* (pp. 106–123). Hershey, PA: Information Science Reference. doi:10.4018/978-1-4666-2803-8.ch009

Black, E. W., Ferdig, R. E., DiPietro, J. C., Liu, F., & Whalen, B. (2011). Visual analyses of the creation of avatars. In R. Ferdig (Ed.), *Discoveries in gaming and computer-mediated simulations: New interdisciplinary applications* (pp. 284–300). Hershey, PA: Information Science Reference. doi:10.4018/978-1-60960-565-0.ch016

Blasko, D. G., Lum, H. C., White, M. M., & Drabik, H. B. (2014). Individual differences in the enjoyment and effectiveness of serious games. In T. Connolly, T. Hainey, E. Boyle, G. Baxter, & P. Moreno-Ger (Eds.), *Psychology, pedagogy, and assessment in serious games* (pp. 153–174). Hershey, PA: Information Science Reference.

Blomqvist, M. (2010). Absent women: Research on gender relations in IT education mediated by Swedish newspapers. In S. Booth, S. Goodman, & G. Kirkup (Eds.), *Gender issues in learning and working with information technology: Social constructs and cultural contexts* (pp. 133–149). Hershey, PA: Information Science Reference. doi:10.4018/978-1-61520-813-5.ch008

Boa-Ventura, A. (2012). Virtual worlds and behavioral change: Overcoming time/ space constraints and exploring anonymity to overcome social stigma in the case of substance abuse. In N. Zagalo, L. Morgado, & A. Boa-Ventura (Eds.), *Virtual worlds and metaverse platforms: New communication and identity paradigms* (pp. 271–286). Hershey, PA: Information Science Reference.

Boivie, I. (2010). Women, men and programming: Knowledge, metaphors and masculinity. In S. Booth, S. Goodman, & G. Kirkup (Eds.), *Gender issues in learning and working with information technology: Social constructs and cultural contexts* (pp. 1–24). Hershey, PA: Information Science Reference. doi:10.4018/978-1-61520-813-5.ch001

Booth, S., & Wigforss, E. (2010). Approaching higher education: A life-world story of home-places, workplaces and learn-places. In S. Booth, S. Goodman, & G. Kirkup (Eds.), *Gender issues in learning and working with information technology: Social constructs and cultural contexts* (pp. 173–191). Hershey, PA: Information Science Reference. doi:10.4018/978-1-61520-813-5.ch010

Braun, P. (2011). Advancing women in the digital economy: eLearning opportunities for meta-competency skilling. In I. Management Association (Ed.), Global business: Concepts, methodologies, tools and applications (pp. 1978-1990). Hershey, PA: Business Science Reference. doi:doi:10.4018/978-1-60960-587-2.ch708

Bryant, J. A., & Drell, J. (2010). Family fun and fostering values. In K. Schrier, & D. Gibson (Eds.), *Ethics and game design: Teaching values through play* (pp. 167–180). Hershey, PA: Information Science Reference. doi:10.4018/978-1-61520-845-6.ch011

Buraphadeja, V., & Dawson, K. (2011). Exploring personal myths from the Sims. In I. Management Association (Ed.), Gaming and simulations: Concepts, methodologies, tools and applications (pp. 1750-1762). Hershey, PA: Information Science Reference. doi: doi:10.4018/978-1-60960-195-9.ch705

Byrd, M. Y. (2012). Critical race theory: A framework for examining social identity diversity of Black women in positions of leadership. In C. Scott, & M. Byrd (Eds.), *Handbook of research on workforce diversity in a global society: Technologies and concepts* (pp. 426–439). Hershey, PA: Business Science Reference. doi:10.4018/978-1-4666-1812-1.ch025

Carneiro, M. G. (2011). Artificial intelligence in games evolution. In M. Cruz-Cunha, V. Varvalho, & P. Tavares (Eds.), *Business, technological, and social dimensions of computer games: Multidisciplinary developments* (pp. 98–114). Hershey, PA: Information Science Reference. doi:10.4018/978-1-60960-567-4.ch007

Chandra, S., Gruber, T., & Lowrie, A. (2012). Service recovery encounters in the classroom: Exploring the attributes of professors desired by male and female students. *International Journal of Technology and Educational Marketing*, *2*(2), 1–19. doi:10.4018/ijtem.2012070101

Chandra, S., Gruber, T., & Lowrie, A. (2013). Service recovery encounters in the classroom: Exploring the attributes of professors desired by male and female students. In P. Tripathi, & S. Mukerji (Eds.), *Marketing strategies for higher education institutions: Technological considerations and practices* (pp. 219–239). Hershey, PA: Business Science Reference.

Chen, K., Chen, J. V., & Ross, W. H. (2010). Antecedents of online game dependency: The implications of multimedia realism and uses and gratifications theory. *Journal of Database Management*, *21*(2), 69–99. doi:10.4018/jdm.2010040104

Chen, K., Chen, J. V., & Ross, W. H. (2012). Antecedents of online game dependency: The implications of multimedia realism and uses and gratifications theory. In K. Siau (Ed.), *Cross-disciplinary models and applications of database management: Advancing approaches* (pp. 176–208). Hershey, PA: Information Science Reference.

Chiu, M. (2013). Gaps between valuing and purchasing green-technology products: Product and gender differences. *International Journal of Technology and Human Interaction*, 8(3), 54–68. doi:10.4018/jthi.2012070106

Cicchirillo, V. (2010). Online gaming: Demographics, motivations, and information processing. In M. Eastin, T. Daugherty, & N. Burns (Eds.), *Handbook of research on digital media and advertising: User generated content consumption* (pp. 456–479). Hershey, PA: Information Science Reference. doi:10.4018/978-1-60566-792-8.ch023

Concha, A. S. (2012). Filipino cyborg sexualities, chatroom masculinities, self-ascribed identities, ephemeral selves. In R. Pande, & T. Van der Weide (Eds.), *Globalization, technology diffusion and gender disparity: Social impacts of ICTs* (pp. 211–224). Hershey, PA: Information Science Reference. doi:10.4018/978-1-4666-0020-1.ch018

Conger, S. (2011). Web 2.0, virtual worlds, and real ethical issues. In I. Management Association (Ed.), *Virtual communities: Concepts, methodologies, tools and applications* (pp. 226-238). Hershey, PA: Information Science Reference. doi: doi:10.4018/978-1-60960-100-3.ch117

Costin, Y. (2012). Adopting ICT in the mompreneurs business: A strategy for growth? In C. Romm Livermore (Ed.), *Gender and social computing: Interactions, differences and relationships* (pp. 17–34). Hershey, PA: Information Science Publishing.

Costin, Y. (2013). Adopting ICT in the mompreneurs business: A strategy for growth? In I. Association (Ed.), *Small and medium enterprises: Concepts, methodologies, tools, and applications* (pp. 322–339). Hershey, PA: Business Science Reference.

Coverdale, T. S., & Wilbon, A. D. (2013). The impact of in-group membership on e-loyalty of women online shoppers: An application of the social identity approach to website design. *International Journal of E-Adoption*, 5(1), 17–36. doi:10.4018/jea.2013010102

Cox, A. D., Eno, C. A., & Guadagno, R. E. (2012). Beauty in the background: A content analysis of females in interactive digital games. *International Journal of Interactive Communication Systems and Technologies*, 2(2), 49–62. doi:10.4018/ijicst.2012070104

Cozza, M. (2010). Gender and technology: Mind the gap! In A. Hallin, & T. Karrbom-Gustavsson (Eds.), *Organizational communication and sustainable development: ICTs for mobility* (pp. 256–274). Hershey, PA: Information Science Reference.

Cramer, J., & Crocco, M. S. (2010). Women and technology, upon reflection: Linking global women's issues to the digital gender divide in urban social studies education. In J. Yamamoto, J. Kush, R. Lombard, & C. Hertzog (Eds.), *Technology implementation and teacher education: Reflective models* (pp. 184–202). Hershey, PA: Information Science Reference. doi:10.4018/978-1-61520-897-5.ch011

Deale, D. F., Key, S. S., Regina, M., & Pastore, R. (2012). Women and gaming. *International Journal of Gaming and Computer-Mediated Simulations*, 4(1), 86–89. doi:10.4018/jgcms.2012010105

Devyatkov, V., & Alfimtsev, A. (2011). Human-computer interaction in games using computer vision techniques. In M. Cruz-Cunha, V. Varvalho, & P. Tavares (Eds.), *Business, technological, and social dimensions of computer games: Multidisciplinary developments* (pp. 146–167). Hershey, PA: Information Science Reference. doi:10.4018/978-1-60960-567-4.ch010

Dhar-Bhattacharjee, S., & Takruri-Rizk, H. (2011). Gender segregation and ICT: An Indo-British comparison. *International Journal of E-Politics*, 2(1), 45–67. doi:10.4018/jep.2011010104

Driouchi, A. (2013). Women empowerment and ICTs in developing economies. In *ICTs for health, education, and socioeconomic policies: Regional cases* (pp. 146–164). Hershey, PA: Information Science Reference. doi:10.4018/978-1-4666-3643-9.ch007

Dubbels, B. (2013). Gamification, serious games, ludic simulation, and other contentious categories. *International Journal of Gaming and Computer-Mediated Simulations*, 5(2), 1–19. doi:10.4018/jgcms.2013040101

Duin, H., Hauge, J. B., Hunecker, F., & Thoben, K. (2011). Application of serious games in industrial contexts. In M. Cruz-Cunha, V. Varvalho, & P. Tavares (Eds.), *Business, technological, and social dimensions of computer games: Multidisciplinary developments* (pp. 331–347). Hershey, PA: Information Science Reference. doi:10.4018/978-1-60960-567-4.ch020

Dunn, R. A. (2013). Identity theories and technology. In R. Luppicini (Ed.), *Handbook of research on technoself: Identity in a technological society* (pp. 26–44). Hershey, PA: Information Science Reference.

Durbin, S. (2010). SET women and careers: A case study of senior female scientists in the UK. In A. Cater-Steel, & E. Cater (Eds.), *Women in engineering, science and technology: Education and career challenges* (pp. 232–254). Hershey, PA: Engineering Science Reference. doi:10.4018/978-1-61520-657-5.ch011

Ellcessor, E., & Duncan, S. C. (2011). Forming the guild: Star power and rethinking projective identity in affinity spaces. *International Journal of Game-Based Learning*, 1(2), 82–95. doi:10.4018/ijgbl.2011040106

Elwell, M. G. (2011). Questing for standards: Role playing games in second life. In M. Cruz-Cunha, V. Varvalho, & P. Tavares (Eds.), *Business, technological, and social dimensions of computer games: Multidisciplinary developments* (pp. 81–97). Hershey, PA: Information Science Reference. doi:10.4018/978-1-60960-567-4.ch006

Erdör, M. (2012). Developments in e-entrepreneurship in Turkey and a case study of a startup company founded by a woman entrepreneur. *International Journal of E-Entrepreneurship and Innovation*, 3(4), 47–52. doi:10.4018/jeei.2012100104

Ertl, B., Helling, K., & Kikis-Papadakis, K. (2012). The impact of gender in ICT usage, education and career: Comparisons between Greece and Germany. In C. Romm Livermore (Ed.), *Gender and social computing: Interactions, differences and relationships* (pp. 98–119). Hershey, PA: Information Science Publishing.

Essid, J. (2011). Playing in a new key, in a new world: Virtual worlds, millennial writers, and 3D composition. In A. Cheney, & R. Sanders (Eds.), *Teaching and learning in 3D immersive worlds: Pedagogical models and constructivist approaches* (pp. 169–184). Hershey, PA: Information Science Reference. doi:10.4018/978-1-60960-517-9.ch010

Eveleth, D. M., & Eveleth, A. B. (2010). Team identification, team performance and leader-member exchange relationships in virtual groups: Findings from massive multi-player online role play games. *International Journal of Virtual Communities and Social Networking*, 2(1), 52–66. doi:10.4018/jvcsn.2010010104

Falcão, T. (2012). Structures of agency in virtual worlds: Fictional worlds and the shaping of an in-game social conduct. In N. Zagalo, L. Morgado, & A. Boa-Ventura (Eds.), *Virtual worlds and metaverse platforms: New communication and identity paradigms* (pp. 192–205). Hershey, PA: Information Science Reference.

Farmer, L. S. (2011). Gaming in adult education. In V. Wang (Ed.), *Encyclopedia of information communication technologies and adult education integration* (pp. 687–706). Hershey, PA: Information Science Reference.

Farmer, L. S. (2011). Gender impact on adult education. In V. Wang (Ed.), *Encyclopedia of information communication technologies and adult education integration* (pp. 377–395). Hershey, PA: Information Science Reference.

Farmer, L. S., & Murphy, N. G. (2010). eGaming and girls: Optimizing use in school libraries. In R. Van Eck (Ed.), Interdisciplinary models and tools for serious games: Emerging concepts and future directions (pp. 306-332). Hershey, PA: Information Science Reference. doi: doi:10.4018/978-1-61520-719-0.ch013

Fatma, S. (2013). ICT in Arab education: Issues and challenges. In F. Albadri (Ed.), *Information systems applications in the Arab education sector* (pp. 136–147). Hershey, PA: Information Science Reference.

Feinberg, J. R., Schewe, A. H., Moore, C. D., & Wood, K. R. (2013). Puttering, tinkering, building, and making: A constructionist approach to online instructional simulation games. In R. Hartshorne, T. Heafner, & T. Petty (Eds.), *Teacher education programs and online learning tools: Innovations in teacher preparation* (pp. 417–436). Hershey, PA: Information Science Reference.

Felicia, P., & Pitt, I. (2011). Harnessing the emotional potential of video games. In I. Association (Ed.), *Instructional design: Concepts, methodologies, tools and applications* (pp. 1282–1299). Hershey, PA: Information Science Reference. doi:10.4018/978-1-60960-503-2.ch511

Ferri, G. (2013). Rhetorics, simulations and games: The ludic and satirical discourse of molleindustria. *International Journal of Gaming and Computer-Mediated Simulations*, 5(1), 32–49. doi:10.4018/jgcms.2013010103

Fitz-Walter, Z., Tjondronegoro, D., & Wyeth, P. (2013). Gamifying Everyday activities using mobile sensing. In D. Tjondronegoro (Ed.), *Tools for mobile multimedia programming and development* (pp. 98–114). Hershey, PA: Information Science Reference.

Fogel, G. K., & Lewis, L. F. (2012). Target marketing and ethics: Brand advertising and marketing campaigns. In E. Carayannis (Ed.), *Sustainable policy applications for social ecology and development* (pp. 214–231). Hershey, PA: Information Science Reference. doi:10.4018/978-1-4666-1586-1.ch016

Forman, A. E., Baker, P. M., Pater, J., & Smith, K. (2011). Beautiful to me: Identity, disability, and gender in virtual environments. *International Journal of E-Politics*, 2(2), 1–17. doi:10.4018/jep.2011040101

Forman, A. E., Baker, P. M., Pater, J., & Smith, K. (2012). The not so level playing field: Disability identity and gender representation in second life. In C. Romm Livermore (Ed.), *Gender and social computing: Interactions, differences and relationships* (pp. 144–161). Hershey, PA: Information Science Publishing.

Fox, J., & Ahn, S. J. (2013). Avatars: Portraying, exploring, and changing online and offline identities. In R. Luppicini (Ed.), *Handbook of research on technoself: Identity in a technological society* (pp. 255–271). Hershey, PA: Information Science Reference.

Freier, N. G., & Saulnier, E. T. (2011). The new backyard: Social and moral development in virtual worlds. In K. Schrier, & D. Gibson (Eds.), *Designing games for ethics: Models, techniques and frameworks* (pp. 179–192). Hershey, PA: Information Science Reference.

Friedman, A., Hartshorne, R., & VanFossen, P. (2010). Exploring guild participation in MMORPGs and civic leadership. In Y. Baek (Ed.), *Gaming for classroom-based learning: Digital role playing as a motivator of study* (pp. 176–204). Hershey, PA: Information Science Reference. doi:10.4018/978-1-61520-713-8.ch011

Gabriels, K., Bauwens, J., & Verstrynge, K. (2012). Second life, second morality? In N. Zagalo, L. Morgado, & A. Boa-Ventura (Eds.), *Virtual worlds and metaverse platforms: New communication and identity paradigms* (pp. 306–320). Hershey, PA: Information Science Reference.

García-Gómez, A. (2013). Technoself-presentation on social networks: A gender-based approach. In R. Luppicini (Ed.), *Handbook of research on technoself: Identity in a technological society* (pp. 382–398). Hershey, PA: Information Science Reference.

Ghosh, A. (2012). Leveraging sexual orientation workforce diversity through identity deployment. In C. Scott, & M. Byrd (Eds.), *Handbook of research on workforce diversity in a global society: Technologies and concepts* (pp. 403–424). Hershey, PA: Business Science Reference. doi:10.4018/978-1-4666-1812-1. ch024

Ghuman, D., & Griffiths, M. (2012). A cross-genre study of online gaming: Player demographics, motivation for play, and social interactions among players. *International Journal of Cyber Behavior, Psychology and Learning, 2*(1), 13–29. doi:10.4018/ijcbpl.2012010102

Gilbert, S. (2010). Ethics at play: Patterns of ethical thinking among young online gamers. In K. Schrier, & D. Gibson (Eds.), *Ethics and game design: Teaching values through play* (pp. 151–166). Hershey, PA: Information Science Reference. doi:10.4018/978-1-61520-845-6.ch010

Goeke, R. J., Hogue, M., & Faley, R. H. (2010). The impact of gender and experience on the strength of the relationships between perceived data warehouse flexibility, ease-of-use, and usefulness. *Information Resources Management Journal, 23*(2), 1–19. doi:10.4018/irmj.2010040101

Gomes, T., & Carvalho, A. A. (2011). The pedagogical potential of MMOG: An exploratory study including four games and their players. In M. Cruz-Cunha, V. Varvalho, & P. Tavares (Eds.), *Computer games as educational and management tools: Uses and approaches* (pp. 103–121). Hershey, PA: Information Science Reference. doi:10.4018/978-1-60960-569-8.ch007

Gómez, M. C., García, A. V., Llorente, A. M., Dávila, P. A., & Sepúlveda, P. Z. (2013). Gender violence experiences of urban adult indigenous women: Case study. In F. García-Peñalvo (Ed.), *Multiculturalism in technology-based education: Case studies on ICT-supported approaches* (pp. 79–99). Hershey, PA: Information Science Reference.

Griffiths, M., Hussain, Z., Grüsser, S. M., Thalemann, R., Cole, H., Davies, M. N., & Chappell, D. (2011). Social interactions in online gaming. *International Journal of Game-Based Learning, 1*(4), 20–36. doi:10.4018/ijgbl.2011100103

Griffiths, M., Hussain, Z., Grüsser, S. M., Thalemann, R., Cole, H., Davies, M. N., & Chappell, D. (2013). Social interactions in online gaming. In P. Felicia (Ed.), *Developments in current game-based learning design and deployment* (pp. 74–90). Hershey, PA: Information Science Reference.

Griffiths, M., & Richardson, H. (2010). Against all odds, from all-girls schools to all-boys workplaces: Women's unsuspecting trajectory into the UK ICT sector. In S. Booth, S. Goodman, & G. Kirkup (Eds.), *Gender issues in learning and working with information technology: Social constructs and cultural contexts* (pp. 99–112). Hershey, PA: Information Science Reference. doi:10.4018/978-1-61520-813-5.ch006

Grimes, G., & Bartolacci, M. (2010). Second life: A virtual world platform for profiling online behavior for network and information security education? An initial investigation. *International Journal of Interdisciplinary Telecommunications and Networking, 2*(4), 60–64. doi:10.4018/jitn.2010100105

Gulz, A., & Haake, M. (2010). Challenging gender stereotypes using virtual pedagogical characters. In S. Booth, S. Goodman, & G. Kirkup (Eds.), *Gender issues in learning and working with information technology: Social constructs and cultural contexts* (pp. 113–132). Hershey, PA: Information Science Reference. doi:10.4018/978-1-61520-813-5.ch007

Gunraj, A., Ruiz, S., & York, A. (2011). Power to the people: Anti-oppressive game design. In K. Schrier, & D. Gibson (Eds.), *Designing games for ethics: Models, techniques and frameworks* (pp. 253–274). Hershey, PA: Information Science Reference.

Gupta, M., Jin, S., Sanders, G. L., Sherman, B. A., & Simha, A. (2012). Getting real about virtual worlds: A review. *International Journal of Virtual Communities and Social Networking*, *4*(3), 1–46. doi: doi:10.4018/jvcsn.2012070101

Guth, J., & Wright, F. (2010). "We don't have the key to the executive washroom": Women's perceptions and experiences of promotion in academia. In A. Cater-Steel, & E. Cater (Eds.), *Women in engineering, science and technology: Education and career challenges* (pp. 159–182). Hershey, PA: Engineering Science Reference. doi:10.4018/978-1-61520-657-5.ch008

Guthrie, R. A., Soe, L., & Yakura, E. K. (2011). Support structures for women in information technology careers. *International Journal of E-Politics*, *2*(1), 30–44. doi:10.4018/jep.2011010103

Gwee, S., San Chee, Y., & Tan, E. M. (2011). The role of gender in mobile game-based learning. *International Journal of Mobile and Blended Learning*, *3*(4), 19–37. doi:10.4018/jmbl.2011100102

Gwee, S., San Chee, Y., & Tan, E. M. (2013). The role of gender in mobile game-based learning. In D. Parsons (Ed.), *Innovations in mobile educational technologies and applications* (pp. 254–271). Hershey, PA: Information Science Reference.

Hackbarth, G., Dow, K. E., Wang, H., & Johnson, W. R. (2010). Changing attitudes toward women IT managers. *International Journal of Information Systems and Social Change*, *1*(3), 28–44. doi:10.4018/jissc.2010070103

Hackbarth, G., Dow, K. E., Wang, H., & Johnson, W. R. (2012). Changing attitudes toward women IT managers. In J. Wang (Ed.), *Societal impacts on information systems development and applications* (pp. 114–129). Hershey, PA: Information Science Reference. doi:10.4018/978-1-4666-0927-3.ch008

Halder, D., & Jaishankar, K. (2012). Cyber laws for preventing cyber crimes against women in Canada. In *Cyber crime and the victimization of women: Laws, rights and regulations* (pp. 82–94). Hershey, PA: Information Science Reference.

Halder, D., & Jaishankar, K. (2012). Cyber space regulations for protecting women in UK. In *Cyber crime and the victimization of women: Laws, rights and regulations* (pp. 95–104). Hershey, PA: Information Science Reference.

Halder, D., & Jaishankar, K. (2012). Definition, typology and patterns of victimization. In *Cyber crime and the victimization of women: Laws, rights and regulations* (pp. 12–39). Hershey, PA: Information Science Reference.

Halder, D., & Jaishankar, K. (2012). Etiology, motives, and crime hubs. In *Cyber crime and the victimization of women: Laws, rights and regulations* (pp. 40–54). Hershey, PA: Information Science Reference.

Halder, D., & Jaishankar, K. (2012). Introduction. In *Cyber crime and the victimization of women: Laws, rights and regulations* (pp. 1–11). Hershey, PA: Information Science Reference.

Halder, D., & Jaishankar, K. (2012). Legal treatment of cyber crimes against women in USA. In *Cyber crime and the victimization of women: Laws, rights and regulations* (pp. 69–81). Hershey, PA: Information Science Reference.

Halder, D., & Jaishankar, K. (2012). Women's rights in the cyber space and the related duties. In *Cyber crime and the victimization of women: Laws, rights and regulations* (pp. 55–68). Hershey, PA: Information Science Reference.

Hamari, J., & Järvinen, A. (2011). Building customer relationship through game mechanics in social games. In M. Cruz-Cunha, V. Varvalho, & P. Tavares (Eds.), *Business, technological, and social dimensions of computer games: Multidisciplinary developments* (pp. 348–365). Hershey, PA: Information Science Reference. doi:10.4018/978-1-60960-567-4.ch021

Hartshorne, R., VanFossen, P. J., & Friedman, A. (2012). MMORPG roles, civic participation and leadership among generation Y. *International Journal of Gaming and Computer-Mediated Simulations*, *4*(1), 55–67. doi:10.4018/jgcms.2012010103

Harwood, T. (2012). Emergence of gamified commerce: Turning virtual to real. *Journal of Electronic Commerce in Organizations*, *10*(2), 16–39. doi:10.4018/jeco.2012040102

Heeter, C., Lee, Y., Magerko, B., & Medler, B. (2011). Impacts of forced serious game play on vulnerable subgroups. *International Journal of Gaming and Computer-Mediated Simulations*, *3*(3), 34–53. doi:10.4018/jgcms.2011070103

Heeter, C., Lee, Y., Magerko, B., & Medler, B. (2013). Impacts of forced serious game play on vulnerable subgroups. In R. Ferdig (Ed.), *Design, utilization, and analysis of simulations and game-based educational worlds* (pp. 158–176). Hershey, PA: Information Science Reference. doi:10.4018/978-1-4666-4018-4.ch010

Heeter, C., Magerko, B., Medler, B., & Fitzgerald, J. (2011). Game design and the challenge-avoiding, self-validator player type. In R. Ferdig (Ed.), *Discoveries in gaming and computer-mediated simulations: New interdisciplinary applications* (pp. 49–63). Hershey, PA: Information Science Reference. doi:10.4018/978-1-60960-565-0.ch004

Heeter, C., Sarkar, C. D., Palmer-Scott, B., & Zhang, S. (2012). Engineering sociability: Friendship drive, visibility, and social connection in anonymous co-located local wi-fi multiplayer online gaming. *International Journal of Gaming and Computer-Mediated Simulations*, *4*(2), 1–18. doi:10.4018/jgcms.2012040101

Heider, D., & Massanari, A. L. (2010). Friendship, closeness and disclosure in second life. *International Journal of Gaming and Computer-Mediated Simulations*, *2*(3), 61–74. doi:10.4018/jgcms.2010070104

Heitmann, M., & Tidten, K. (2011). New business models for the computer gaming industry: Selling an adventure. In M. Cruz-Cunha, V. Varvalho, & P. Tavares (Eds.), *Business, technological, and social dimensions of computer games: Multidisciplinary developments* (pp. 401–415). Hershey, PA: Information Science Reference. doi:10.4018/978-1-60960-567-4.ch024

Heo, M., & Spradley-Myrick, L. M. (2012). Girls and computers - Yes we can!: A case study on improving female computer confidence and decreasing gender inequity in computer science with an informal, female learning community. In I. Management Association (Ed.), Computer engineering: Concepts, methodologies, tools and applications (pp. 1126-1143). Hershey, PA: Engineering Science Reference. doi: doi:10.4018/978-1-61350-456-7.ch504

Hewahi, N. M., & Baraka, A. M. (2012). Emotion recognition model based on facial expressions, ethnicity and gender using backpropagation neural network. *International Journal of Technology Diffusion*, *3*(1), 33–43. doi:10.4018/jtd.2012010104

Hewett, S. (2011). Using video games to improve literacy levels of males. In I. Association (Ed.), *Instructional design: Concepts, methodologies, tools and applications* (pp. 192–206). Hershey, PA: Information Science Reference. doi:10.4018/978-1-60960-503-2.ch115

Hicks, D. (2014). Technology, gender, and professional identity. In *Technology and professional identity of librarians: The making of the cybrarian* (pp. 128–147). Hershey, PA: Information Science Reference.

Hobbs, R., & Rowe, J. (2011). Creative remixing and digital learning: Developing an online media literacy learning tool for girls. In I. Management Association (Ed.), Gaming and simulations: Concepts, methodologies, tools and applications (pp. 971-978). Hershey, PA: Information Science Reference. doi: doi:10.4018/978-1-60960-195-9.ch405

Hoffman, E. (2010). Sideways into truth: Kierkegaard, Philistines, and why we love sex and violence. In K. Schrier, & D. Gibson (Eds.), *Ethics and game design: Teaching values through play* (pp. 109–124). Hershey, PA: Information Science Reference. doi:10.4018/978-1-61520-845-6.ch008

Hoffmann, E. M. (2010). Women in computer science in Afghanistan. In S. Booth, S. Goodman, & G. Kirkup (Eds.), *Gender issues in learning and working with information technology: Social constructs and cultural contexts* (pp. 48–63). Hershey, PA: Information Science Reference. doi:10.4018/978-1-61520-813-5.ch003

Hsu, C. (2010). Exploring the player flow experience in e-game playing. *International Journal of Technology and Human Interaction, 6*(2), 47–64. doi:10.4018/jthi.2010040104

Huang, J., & Aaltio, I. (2010). Social interaction technologies: A case study of Guanxi and women managers' careers in information technology in China. In T. Dumova, & R. Fiordo (Eds.), *Handbook of research on social interaction technologies and collaboration software: Concepts and trends* (pp. 257–269). Hershey, PA: Information Science Reference.

Hughes, G. (2010). Queen bees, workers and drones: Gender performance in virtual learning groups. In S. Booth, S. Goodman, & G. Kirkup (Eds.), *Gender issues in learning and working with information technology: Social constructs and cultural contexts* (pp. 244–254). Hershey, PA: Information Science Reference. doi:10.4018/978-1-61520-813-5.ch014

Igun, S. E. (2010). Gender and national information and communication technology (ICT) policies in Africa. In E. Adomi (Ed.), *Handbook of research on information communication technology policy: Trends, issues and advancements* (pp. 208–221). Hershey, PA: Information Science Reference. doi:10.4018/978-1-61520-847-0.ch013

Igun, S. E. (2013). Gender and national information and communication technology (ICT) policies in Africa. In B. Maumbe, & J. Okello (Eds.), *Technology, sustainability, and rural development in Africa* (pp. 284–297). Hershey, PA: Information Science Reference. doi:10.4018/978-1-4666-3607-1.ch018

Ikolo, V. E. (2010). Gender digital divide and national ICT policies in Africa. In E. Adomi (Ed.), *Handbook of research on information communication technology policy: Trends, issues and advancements* (pp. 222–242). Hershey, PA: Information Science Reference. doi:10.4018/978-1-61520-847-0.ch014

Ikolo, V. E. (2013). Gender digital divide and national ICT policies in Africa. In I. Association (Ed.), *Digital literacy: Concepts, methodologies, tools, and applications* (pp. 812–832). Hershey, PA: Information Science Reference.

Ionescu, A. (2012). ICTs and gender-based rights. *International Journal of Information Communication Technologies and Human Development, 4*(2), 33–49. doi:10.4018/jicthd.2012040103

Ionescu, A. (2013). Cyber identity: Our alter-ego? In R. Luppicini (Ed.), *Handbook of research on technoself: Identity in a technological society* (pp. 189–203). Hershey, PA: Information Science Reference.

Ionescu, A. (2013). ICTs and gender-based rights. In J. Lannon, & E. Halpin (Eds.), *Human rights and information communication technologies: Trends and consequences of use* (pp. 214–234). Hershey, PA: Information Science Reference.

Irving, C. J., & English, L. M. (2011). Women, information and communication technologies, and lifelong learning. In V. Wang (Ed.), *Encyclopedia of information communication technologies and adult education integration* (pp. 360–376). Hershey, PA: Information Science Reference.

Jarmon, L. (2010). Homo virtualis: Virtual worlds, learning, and an ecology of embodied interaction. *International Journal of Virtual and Personal Learning Environments, 1*(1), 38–56. doi:10.4018/jvple.2010091704

Jayasingh, S., & Eze, U. C. (2012). Analyzing the intention to use mobile coupon and the moderating effects of price consciousness and gender. *International Journal of E-Business Research, 8*(1), 54–75. doi:10.4018/jebr.2012010104

Jenson, J., & de, C. S. (2010). Gender and digital gameplay: Theories, oversights, accidents, and surprises. In D. Kaufman & L. Sauvé (Eds.), *Educational gameplay and simulation environments: Case studies and lessons learned* (pp. 96–105). Hershey, PA: Information Science Reference. doi:10.4018/978-1-61520-731-2.ch006

Johnson, R. D. (2011). Gender differences in e-learning: Communication, social presence, and learning outcomes. *Journal of Organizational and End User Computing, 23*(1), 79–94. doi:10.4018/joeuc.2011010105

Johnson, V. (2012). The gender divide: Attitudinal issues inhibiting access. In R. Pande, & T. Van der Weide (Eds.), *Globalization, technology diffusion and gender disparity: Social impacts of ICTs* (pp. 110–119). Hershey, PA: Information Science Reference. doi:10.4018/978-1-4666-0020-1.ch009

Jyothi, P. (2012). Challenges faced by women: BPO sector. In R. Pande, & T. Van der Weide (Eds.), *Globalization, technology diffusion and gender disparity: Social impacts of ICTs* (pp. 147–155). Hershey, PA: Information Science Reference. doi:10.4018/978-1-4666-0020-1.ch013

Kafai, Y. B., Fields, D., & Searle, K. A. (2010). Multi-modal investigations of relationship play in virtual worlds. *International Journal of Gaming and Computer-Mediated Simulations, 2*(1), 40–48. doi:10.4018/jgcms.2010010104

Kallay, J. (2010). Rethinking genre in computer games: How narrative psychology connects game and story. In R. Van Eck (Ed.), *Interdisciplinary models and tools for serious games: Emerging concepts and future directions* (pp. 30–49). Hershey, PA: Information Science Reference. doi:10.4018/978-1-61520-719-0.ch002

Kallergi, A., & Verbeek, F. J. (2014). Playful interfaces for scientific image data: A case for storytelling. In K. Blashki, & P. Isaias (Eds.), *Emerging research and trends in interactivity and the human-computer interface* (pp. 471–489). Hershey, PA: Information Science Reference.

Karl, K., Peluchette, J., & Schlagel, C. (2010). A cross-cultural examination of student attitudes and gender differences in Facebook profile content. *International Journal of Virtual Communities and Social Networking, 2*(2), 11–31. doi:10.4018/jvcsn.2010040102

Kaul, A., & Kulkarni, V. (2010). Gender and politeness in Indian emails. In R. Taiwo (Ed.), *Handbook of research on discourse behavior and digital communication: Language structures and social interaction* (pp. 389–410). Hershey, PA: Information Science Reference. doi:10.4018/978-1-61520-773-2.ch025

Ke, F., Yildirim, N., & Enfield, J. (2012). Exploring the design of game enjoyment through the perspectives of novice game developers. *International Journal of Gaming and Computer-Mediated Simulations, 4*(4), 45–63. doi:10.4018/jgcms.2012100104

King, E. (2013). Possibility spaces: Using the Sims 2 as a sandbox to explore possible selves with at-risk teenage males. In P. Felicia (Ed.), *Developments in current game-based learning design and deployment* (pp. 169–187). Hershey, PA: Information Science Reference.

Kirkup, G. (2010). Gendered knowledge production in universities in a web 2.0 world. In S. Booth, S. Goodman, & G. Kirkup (Eds.), *Gender issues in learning and working with information technology: Social constructs and cultural contexts* (pp. 231–243). Hershey, PA: Information Science Reference. doi:10.4018/978-1-61520-813-5.ch013

Kirkup, G., Schmitz, S., Kotkamp, E., Rommes, E., & Hiltunen, A. (2010). Towards a feminist manifesto for e-learning: Principles to inform practices. In S. Booth, S. Goodman, & G. Kirkup (Eds.), *Gender issues in learning and working with information technology: Social constructs and cultural contexts* (pp. 255–274). Hershey, PA: Information Science Reference. doi:10.4018/978-1-61520-813-5.ch015

Koh, E., Liu, N., & Lim, J. (2012). Gender and anonymity in virtual teams: An exploratory study. In C. Romm Livermore (Ed.), *Gender and social computing: Interactions, differences and relationships* (pp. 1–16). Hershey, PA: Information Science Publishing.

Kongmee, I., Strachan, R., Pickard, A., & Montgomery, C. (2012). A case study of using online communities and virtual environment in massively multiplayer role playing games (MMORPGs) as a learning and teaching tool for second language learners. *International Journal of Virtual and Personal Learning Environments*, 3(4), 1–15. doi:10.4018/jvple.2012100101

Koo, G., & Seider, S. (2010). Video games for prosocial learning. In K. Schrier, & D. Gibson (Eds.), *Ethics and game design: Teaching values through play* (pp. 16–33). Hershey, PA: Information Science Reference. doi:10.4018/978-1-61520-845-6.ch002

Kumari, B. R. (2012). Gender, culture, and ICT use. In R. Pande, & T. Van der Weide (Eds.), *Globalization, technology diffusion and gender disparity: Social impacts of ICTs* (pp. 36–50). Hershey, PA: Information Science Reference. doi:10.4018/978-1-4666-0020-1.ch004

Kwok, N. W., & Khoo, A. (2011). Gamers' motivations and problematic gaming: An exploratory study of gamers in World of Warcraft. *International Journal of Cyber Behavior, Psychology and Learning*, 1(3), 34–49. doi:10.4018/ijcbpl.2011070103

Kwok, N. W., & Khoo, A. (2013). Gamers' motivations and problematic gaming: An exploratory study of gamers in World of Warcraft. In R. Zheng (Ed.), *Evolving psychological and educational perspectives on cyber behavior* (pp. 64–81). Hershey, PA: Information Science Reference.

Lamoreaux, K., & Varghese, D. (2012). Deliberate leadership: Women in IT. In I. Management Association (Ed.), Computer engineering: Concepts, methodologies, tools and applications (pp. 1381-1402). Hershey, PA: Engineering Science Reference. doi: doi:10.4018/978-1-61350-456-7.ch601

Lankoski, P., Johansson, A., Karlsson, B., Björk, S., & Dell'Acqua, P. (2011). AI design for believable characters via gameplay design patterns. In M. Cruz-Cunha, V. Varvalho, & P. Tavares (Eds.), *Business, technological, and social dimensions of computer games: Multidisciplinary developments* (pp. 15–31). Hershey, PA: Information Science Reference. doi:10.4018/978-1-60960-567-4.ch002

Laosethakul, K., Leingpibul, T., & Coe, T. (2010). Investigation into gender perception toward computing: A comparison between the U.S. and India. *International Journal of Information and Communication Technology Education*, 6(4), 23–37. doi:10.4018/jicte.2010100103

Laosethakul, K., Leingpibul, T., & Coe, T. (2012). Investigation into gender perception toward computing: A comparison between the U.S. and India. In L. Tomei (Ed.), *Advancing education with information communication technologies: Facilitating new trends* (pp. 305–319). Hershey, PA: Information Science Reference.

Lawrence, H. R. (2013). Women's roles: Do they exist in a technological workforce? In S. Wang, & T. Hartsell (Eds.), *Technology integration and foundations for effective leadership* (pp. 57–69). Hershey, PA: Information Science Reference.

Lin, T., Wu, Z., Tang, N., & Wu, S. (2013). Exploring the effects of display characteristics on presence and emotional responses of game players. *International Journal of Technology and Human Interaction*, 9(1), 50–63. doi:10.4018/jthi.2013010104

Linares, K., Subrahmanyam, K., Cheng, R., & Guan, S. A. (2011). A second life within second life: Are Virtual world users creating new selves and new lives? *International Journal of Cyber Behavior, Psychology and Learning*, 1(3), 50–71. doi:10.4018/ijcbpl.2011070104

Linares, K., Subrahmanyam, K., Cheng, R., & Guan, S. A. (2013). A second life within second life: Are virtual world users creating new selves and new lives? In R. Zheng (Ed.), *Evolving psychological and educational perspectives on cyber behavior* (pp. 205–228). Hershey, PA: Information Science Reference.

Livermore, C. R., & Somers, T. M. (2011). Gender, power, and edating. *International Journal of E-Politics*, 2(2), 74–88. doi:10.4018/jep.2011040105

Lorentz, P. (2012). Is there a virtual socialization by acting virtual identities? Case study: The Sims. In N. Zagalo, L. Morgado, & A. Boa-Ventura (Eds.), *Virtual worlds and metaverse platforms: New communication and identity paradigms* (pp. 206–218). Hershey, PA: Information Science Reference.

Losh, S. C. (2013). American digital divides: Generation, education, gender, and ethnicity in American digital divides. In I. Association (Ed.), *Digital literacy: Concepts, methodologies, tools, and applications* (pp. 932–958). Hershey, PA: Information Science Reference.

Ludi, S. (2012). Educational robotics and broadening participation in STEM for underrepresented student groups. In B. Barker, G. Nugent, N. Grandgenett, & V. Adamchuk (Eds.), *Robots in K-12 education: A new technology for learning* (pp. 343–361). Hershey, PA: Information Science Reference. doi:10.4018/978-1-4666-0182-6.ch017

Lund, K., Lochrie, M., & Coulton, P. (2012). Designing scalable location based games that encourage emergent behaviour. *International Journal of Ambient Computing and Intelligence*, *4*(4), 1–20. doi: doi:10.4018/jaci.2012100101

Ma, M., & Oikonomou, A. (2010). Network architectures and data management for massively multiplayer online games. *International Journal of Grid and High Performance Computing*, *2*(4), 40–50. doi:10.4018/jghpc.2010100104

Macgregor, R., Hyland, P. N., & Harvey, C. (2012). The effect of gender on associations between driving forces to adopt ICT and benefits derived from that adoption in medical practices in Australia. In C. Romm Livermore (Ed.), *Gender and social computing: Interactions, differences and relationships* (pp. 120–142). Hershey, PA: Information Science Publishing.

Macgregor, R., Hyland, P. N., & Harvey, C. (2013). The effect of gender on associations between driving forces to adopt ICT and benefits derived from that adoption in medical practices in Australia. In I. Association (Ed.), *Small and medium enterprises: Concepts, methodologies, tools, and applications* (pp. 1186–1207). Hershey, PA: Business Science Reference.

MacGregor, R. C., Hyland, P. N., & Harvie, C. (2011). The effect of gender on perceived benefits of and drivers for ICT adoption in Australian medical practices. *International Journal of E-Politics*, *2*(1), 68–85. doi:10.4018/jep.2011010105

Maguire, K. C. (2011). Is it a boy or a girl? Anonymity and gender in computer-mediated interactions. In I. Management Association (Ed.), Virtual communities: Concepts, methodologies, tools and applications (pp. 1590-1610). Hershey, PA: Information Science Reference. doi: doi:10.4018/978-1-60960-100-3.ch501

Mano, R. S. (2013). Gender effects on managerial communication and work performance. *International Journal of Cyber Behavior, Psychology and Learning*, *3*(2), 34–46. doi:10.4018/ijcbpl.2013040103

Manuel, A. (2010). The career challenge of the gendered academic research culture: Can internet technologies make a difference? In A. Cater-Steel, & E. Cater (Eds.), *Women in engineering, science and technology: Education and career challenges* (pp. 255–279). Hershey, PA: Engineering Science Reference. doi:10.4018/978-1-61520-657-5.ch012

Marache-Francisco, C., & Brangier, E. (2014). The gamification experience: UXD with a gamification background. In K. Blashki, & P. Isaias (Eds.), *Emerging research and trends in interactivity and the human-computer interface* (pp. 205–223). Hershey, PA: Information Science Reference.

Marciano, A. (2011). The role of internet newsgroups in the coming-out process of gay male youth: An Israeli case study. In E. Dunkels, G. Franberg, & C. Hallgren (Eds.), *Youth culture and net culture: Online social practices* (pp. 222–241). Hershey, PA: Information Science Reference.

Maree, D. J., & Maree, M. (2010). Factors contributing to the success of women working in science, engineering and technology (SET) careers. In A. Cater-Steel, & E. Cater (Eds.), *Women in engineering, science and technology: Education and career challenges* (pp. 183–210). Hershey, PA: Engineering Science Reference. doi:10.4018/978-1-61520-657-5.ch009

Martin, S. (2012). Exploring identity and citizenship in a virtual world. *International Journal of Virtual and Personal Learning Environments*, *3*(4), 53–70. doi:10.4018/jvple.2012100105

Martins, H. F. (2012). The use of a business simulation game in a management course. In M. Cruz-Cunha (Ed.), *Handbook of research on serious games as educational, business and research tools* (pp. 693–707). Hershey, PA: Information Science Reference. doi:10.4018/978-1-4666-0149-9.ch035

Masrom, M., & Ismail, Z. (2010). Women access to computers and internet: A Malaysian perspective. In A. Cater-Steel, & E. Cater (Eds.), *Women in engineering, science and technology: Education and career challenges* (pp. 211–231). Hershey, PA: Engineering Science Reference. doi:10.4018/978-1-61520-657-5.ch010

Mattingly, D. J. (2012). Indian women working in call centers: Sites of resistance? In R. Pande, & T. Van der Weide (Eds.), *Globalization, technology diffusion and gender disparity: Social impacts of ICTs* (pp. 156–168). Hershey, PA: Information Science Reference. doi:10.4018/978-1-4666-0020-1.ch014

McDaniel, R., & Fiore, S. M. (2010). Applied ethics game design: Some practical guidelines. In K. Schrier, & D. Gibson (Eds.), *Ethics and game design: Teaching values through play* (pp. 236–254). Hershey, PA: Information Science Reference. doi:10.4018/978-1-61520-845-6.ch015

McDonald, J., Loch, B., & Cater-Steel, A. (2010). Go WEST - Supporting women in engineering, science and technology: An Australian higher education case study. In A. Cater-Steel, & E. Cater (Eds.), *Women in engineering, science and technology: Education and career challenges* (pp. 118–136). Hershey, PA: Engineering Science Reference. doi:10.4018/978-1-61520-657-5.ch006

McKinnell Jacobson, C. (2011). Virtual worlds and the 3-D internet. In I. Management Association (Ed.), Virtual communities: Concepts, methodologies, tools and applications (pp. 1855-1879). Hershey, PA: Information Science Reference. doi: doi:10.4018/978-1-60960-100-3.ch520

McLean, L., & Griffiths, M. D. (2013). Gamers' attitudes towards victims of crime: An interview study using vignettes. *International Journal of Cyber Behavior, Psychology and Learning*, *3*(2), 13–33. doi:10.4018/ijcbpl.2013040102

Mellström, U. (2010). New gender relations in the transforming IT-industry of Malaysia. In S. Booth, S. Goodman, & G. Kirkup (Eds.), *Gender issues in learning and working with information technology: Social constructs and cultural contexts* (pp. 25–47). Hershey, PA: Information Science Reference. doi:10.4018/978-1-61520-813-5.ch002

Mena, R. J. (2014). The quest for a massively multiplayer online game that teaches physics. In T. Connolly, T. Hainey, E. Boyle, G. Baxter, & P. Moreno-Ger (Eds.), *Psychology, pedagogy, and assessment in serious games* (pp. 292–316). Hershey, PA: Information Science Reference.

Mendes, R. (2010). Glass ceilings in Portugal? An analysis of the gender wage gap using a quantile regression approach. *International Journal of Human Capital and Information Technology Professionals*, *1*(2), 1–18. doi:10.4018/jhcitp.2010040101

Miller, K. B. (2013). Gaming as a woman: Gender difference issues in video games and learning. In S. D'Agustino (Ed.), *Immersive environments, augmented realities, and virtual worlds: Assessing future trends in education* (pp. 106–122). Hershey, PA: Information Science Reference.

Milolidakis, G., Kimble, C., & Grenier, C. (2011). A practice-based analysis of social interaction in a massively multiplayer online gaming environment. In M. Cruz-Cunha, V. Varvalho, & P. Tavares (Eds.), *Business, technological, and social dimensions of computer games: Multidisciplinary developments* (pp. 32–48). Hershey, PA: Information Science Reference. doi:10.4018/978-1-60960-567-4.ch003

Mitgutsch, K. (2011). Playful learning experiences: Meaningful learning patterns in players' biographies. *International Journal of Gaming and Computer-Mediated Simulations*, *3*(3), 54–68. doi:10.4018/jgcms.2011070104

Modesto, F. A. (2012). Virtual worlds innovation with open wonderland. In M. Cruz-Cunha (Ed.), *Handbook of research on serious games as educational, business and research tools* (pp. 250–268). Hershey, PA: Information Science Reference. doi:10.4018/978-1-4666-0149-9.ch013

Mora-García, A. M., & Merelo-Guervós, J. J. (2012). Evolving bots' ai in Unreal. In A. Kumar, J. Etheredge, & A. Boudreaux (Eds.), *Algorithmic and architectural gaming design: Implementation and development* (pp. 134–157). Hershey, PA: Information Science Reference. doi:10.4018/978-1-4666-1634-9.ch007

Moro, M. M., Weber, T., & Freitas, C. M. (2012). Women in Brazilian CS research community: The state-of-the-art. In I. Management Association (Ed.), Computer engineering: Concepts, methodologies, tools and applications (pp. 1824-1839). Hershey, PA: Engineering Science Reference. doi: doi:10.4018/978-1-61350-456-7.ch801

Mörtberg, C., & Elovaara, P. (2010). Attaching people and technology: Between E and government. In S. Booth, S. Goodman, & G. Kirkup (Eds.), *Gender issues in learning and working with information technology: Social constructs and cultural contexts* (pp. 83–98). Hershey, PA: Information Science Reference. doi:10.4018/978-1-61520-813-5.ch005

Mosca, I. (2013). From fiction to reality and back: Ontology of ludic simulations. *International Journal of Gaming and Computer-Mediated Simulations*, *5*(1), 13–31. doi:10.4018/jgcms.2013010102

Moseley, A. (2012). An alternate reality for education? Lessons to be learned from online immersive games. *International Journal of Game-Based Learning*, *2*(3), 32–50. doi:10.4018/ijgbl.2012070103

Moseley, A. (2014). A case for integration: Assessment and games. In T. Connolly, T. Hainey, E. Boyle, G. Baxter, & P. Moreno-Ger (Eds.), *Psychology, pedagogy, and assessment in serious games* (pp. 342–356). Hershey, PA: Information Science Reference.

Murphy, J., & Zagal, J. (2011). Videogames and the ethics of care. *International Journal of Gaming and Computer-Mediated Simulations*, *3*(3), 69–81. doi:10.4018/jgcms.2011070105

Mutaza, S., & Sami, L. K. (2012). Gender aspects in the use of ICT in information centres. In R. Pande, & T. Van der Weide (Eds.), *Globalization, technology diffusion and gender disparity: Social impacts of ICTs* (pp. 129–137). Hershey, PA: Information Science Reference. doi:10.4018/978-1-4666-0020-1.ch011

Nezlek, G., & DeHondt, G. (2011). Gender wage differentials in information systems: 1991 – 2008 a quantitative analysis. *International Journal of Social and Organizational Dynamics in IT*, *1*(1), 13–29. doi:10.4018/ijsodit.2011010102

Nezlek, G., & DeHondt, G. (2013). Gender wage differentials in information systems: 1991 – 2008 a quantitative analysis. In B. Medlin (Ed.), *Integrations of technology utilization and social dynamics in organizations* (pp. 31–47). Hershey, PA: Information Science Reference.

Ng, E. M. (2011). Exploring the gender differences of student teachers when using an educational game to learn programming concepts. In P. Felicia (Ed.), *Handbook of research on improving learning and motivation through educational games: Multidisciplinary approaches* (pp. 550–566). Hershey, PA: Information Science Reference. doi:10.4018/978-1-60960-495-0.ch026

Nikolaos, P. (2013). A conceptual "cybernetic" methodology for organizing and managing the e-learning process through [D-] CIVEs: The case of "second life". In P. Renna (Ed.), Production and manufacturing system management: Coordination approaches and multi-site planning (pp. 242-277). Hershey, PA: Engineering Science Reference. doi: doi:10.4018/978-1-4666-2098-8.ch013

Nitsche, M. (2012). The players' dimension: From virtual to physical. In N. Zagalo, L. Morgado, & A. Boa-Ventura (Eds.), *Virtual worlds and metaverse platforms: New communication and identity paradigms* (pp. 181–191). Hershey, PA: Information Science Reference.

Nordlinger, J. (2010). Virtual ethics: Ethics and massively multiplayer online games. In K. Schrier, & D. Gibson (Eds.), *Ethics and game design: Teaching values through play* (pp. 102–108). Hershey, PA: Information Science Reference. doi:10.4018/978-1-61520-845-6.ch007

Nsibirano, R., Kabonesa, C., & Madanda, A. (2012). Gender symbolism and technology uptake: A literature review. In R. Pande, & T. Van der Weide (Eds.), *Globalization, technology diffusion and gender disparity: Social impacts of ICTs* (pp. 120–127). Hershey, PA: Information Science Reference. doi:10.4018/978-1-4666-0020-1.ch010

Okafor, C., & Amalu, R. (2012). Motivational patterns and the performance of entrepreneurs: An empirical study of women entrepreneurs in south-west Nigeria. *International Journal of Applied Behavioral Economics*, *1*(1), 29–40. doi: doi:10.4018/ijabe.2012010103

Okdie, B. M., Guadagno, R. E., Petrova, P. K., & Shreves, W. B. (2013). Social influence online: A tale of gender differences in the effectiveness of authority cues. *International Journal of Interactive Communication Systems and Technologies*, *3*(1), 20–31. doi:10.4018/ijicst.2013010102

Ortiz, J. A. (2011). Knowing the game: A review of videogames and entertainment software in the United States - Trends and future research opportunities. In M. Cruz-Cunha, V. Varvalho, & P. Tavares (Eds.), *Business, technological, and social dimensions of computer games: Multidisciplinary developments* (pp. 293–311). Hershey, PA: Information Science Reference. doi:10.4018/978-1-60960-567-4.ch018

Ortiz de Gortari, A. B., Aronsson, K., & Griffiths, M. (2011). Game transfer phenomena in video game playing: A qualitative interview study. *International Journal of Cyber Behavior, Psychology and Learning*, *1*(3), 15–33. doi:10.4018/ijcbpl.2011070102

Orvalho, V. C., & Orvalho, J. (2011). Character animation: Past, present and future. In M. Cruz-Cunha, V. Varvalho, & P. Tavares (Eds.), *Business, technological, and social dimensions of computer games: Multidisciplinary developments* (pp. 49–64). Hershey, PA: Information Science Reference. doi:10.4018/978-1-60960-567-4.ch004

Özdemir, E. (2012). Gender and e-marketing: The role of gender differences in online purchasing behaviors. In C. Romm Livermore (Ed.), *Gender and social computing: Interactions, differences and relationships* (pp. 72–86). Hershey, PA: Information Science Publishing. doi:10.4018/978-1-4666-1598-4.ch044

Pande, R. (2012). Gender gaps and information and communication technology: A case study of India. In R. Pande, & T. Van der Weide (Eds.), *Globalization, technology diffusion and gender disparity: Social impacts of ICTs* (pp. 277–291). Hershey, PA: Information Science Reference. doi:10.4018/978-1-4666-0020-1.ch022

Pande, R. (2013). Gender gaps and information and communication technology: A case study of India. In I. Association (Ed.), *Digital literacy: Concepts, methodologies, tools, and applications* (pp. 1425–1439). Hershey, PA: Information Science Reference.

Pannicke, D., Repschläger, J., & Zarnekow, R. (2011). Business opportunities in social virtual worlds. In M. Cruz-Cunha, V. Varvalho, & P. Tavares (Eds.), *Business, technological, and social dimensions of computer games: Multidisciplinary developments* (pp. 432–447). Hershey, PA: Information Science Reference. doi:10.4018/978-1-60960-567-4.ch026

Parker, J. R., & Becker, K. (2013). The simulation-game controversy: What is a ludic simulation? *International Journal of Gaming and Computer-Mediated Simulations*, *5*(1), 1–12. doi:10.4018/jgcms.2013010101

Phelps, D. (2010). What videogames have to teach us about screenworld and the humanistic ethos. In K. Schrier, & D. Gibson (Eds.), *Ethics and game design: Teaching values through play* (pp. 125–149). Hershey, PA: Information Science Reference. doi:10.4018/978-1-61520-845-6.ch009

Poggi, A. (2011). Enhancing online games with agents. In M. Cruz-Cunha, V. Varvalho, & P. Tavares (Eds.), *Business, technological, and social dimensions of computer games: Multidisciplinary developments* (pp. 65–80). Hershey, PA: Information Science Reference. doi:10.4018/978-1-60960-567-4.ch005

Pole, A. (2012). Would Elizabeth Cady Stanton blog?: Women bloggers, politics, and political participation. In C. Romm Livermore (Ed.), *Gender and social computing: Interactions, differences and relationships* (pp. 183–199). Hershey, PA: Information Science Publishing.

Poster, W. R. (2012). The case of the U.S. mother / cyberspy / undercover Iraqi militant: Or, how global women have been incorporated in the technological war on terror. In R. Pande, & T. Van der Weide (Eds.), *Globalization, technology diffusion and gender disparity: Social impacts of ICTs* (pp. 247–260). Hershey, PA: Information Science Reference. doi:10.4018/978-1-4666-0020-1.ch020

Pragnell, C., & Gatzidis, C. (2012). Addiction in World of Warcraft: A virtual ethnography study. In H. Yang, & S. Yuen (Eds.), *Handbook of research on practices and outcomes in virtual worlds and environments* (pp. 54–74). Hershey, PA: Information Science Publishing.

Prakash, N. (2012). ICT and women empowerment in a rural setting in India. In R. Pande, & T. Van der Weide (Eds.), *Globalization, technology diffusion and gender disparity: Social impacts of ICTs* (pp. 15–24). Hershey, PA: Information Science Reference. doi:10.4018/978-1-4666-0020-1.ch002

Prescott, J., & Bogg, J. (2010). The computer games industry: Women's experiences of work role in a male dominated environment. In A. Cater-Steel, & E. Cater (Eds.), *Women in engineering, science and technology: Education and career challenges* (pp. 138–158). Hershey, PA: Engineering Science Reference. doi:10.4018/978-1-61520-657-5.ch007

Prescott, J., & Bogg, J. (2013). Career development, occupational choice, and organizational culture: Societal expectations, constraints, and embedded practices. In *Gendered occupational differences in science, engineering, and technology careers* (pp. 136–165). Hershey, PA: Information Science Reference.

Prescott, J., & Bogg, J. (2013). Career promoters: A gender divide. In *Gendered occupational differences in science, engineering, and technology careers* (pp. 216–238). Hershey, PA: Information Science Reference.

Prescott, J., & Bogg, J. (2013). Engendered workplace segregation: Work is still essentially a male domain. In *Gendered occupational differences in science, engineering, and technology careers* (pp. 1–25). Hershey, PA: Information Science Reference.

Prescott, J., & Bogg, J. (2013). Final thoughts and concluding comments. In *Gendered occupational differences in science, engineering, and technology careers* (pp. 239–263). Hershey, PA: Information Science Reference.

Prescott, J., & Bogg, J. (2013). Male dominated industries: Jobs for the boys. In *Gendered occupational differences in science, engineering, and technology careers* (pp. 26–63). Hershey, PA: Information Science Reference.

Prescott, J., & Bogg, J. (2013). Progression aspirations and leadership. In *Gendered occupational differences in science, engineering, and technology careers* (pp. 192–215). Hershey, PA: Information Science Reference.

Prescott, J., & Bogg, J. (2013). Self, career, and gender issues: A complex interplay of internal/external factors. In *Gendered occupational differences in science, engineering, and technology careers* (pp. 79–111). Hershey, PA: Information Science Reference.

Prescott, J., & Bogg, J. (2013). Stereotype, attitudes, and identity: Gendered expectations and behaviors. In *Gendered occupational differences in science, engineering, and technology careers* (pp. 112–135). Hershey, PA: Information Science Reference.

Prescott, J., & Bogg, J. (2013). The computer games industry: New industry, same old issues. In *Gendered occupational differences in science, engineering, and technology careers* (pp. 64–77). Hershey, PA: Information Science Reference.

Prescott, J., & Bogg, J. (2013). Work life balance issues: The choice, or women's lack of it. In *Gendered occupational differences in science, engineering, and technology careers* (pp. 167–191). Hershey, PA: Information Science Reference.

Preston, J. A., Chastine, J., O'Donnell, C., Tseng, T., & MacIntyre, B. (2012). Game jams: Community, motivations, and learning among jammers. *International Journal of Game-Based Learning*, 2(3), 51–70. doi:10.4018/ijgbl.2012070104

Quan, J. J., Dattero, R., Galup, S. D., & Dhariwal, K. (2011). The determinants of information technology wages. *International Journal of Human Capital and Information Technology Professionals*, 2(1), 48–65. doi:10.4018/jhcitp.2011010104

Quesenberry, J. L. (2012). Re-examining the career anchor model: An investigation of career values and motivations among women in the information technology profession. In R. Pande, & T. Van der Weide (Eds.), *Globalization, technology diffusion and gender disparity: Social impacts of ICTs* (pp. 169–183). Hershey, PA: Information Science Reference. doi:10.4018/978-1-4666-0020-1.ch015

Quick, J. M., Atkinson, R. K., & Lin, L. (2012). Empirical taxonomies of gameplay enjoyment: Personality and video game preference. *International Journal of Game-Based Learning*, 2(3), 11–31. doi:10.4018/ijgbl.2012070102

Quick, J. M., Atkinson, R. K., & Lin, L. (2012). The gameplay enjoyment model. *International Journal of Gaming and Computer-Mediated Simulations*, 4(4), 64–80. doi:10.4018/jgcms.2012100105

Raditloaneng, W. (2012). Gender equality as a development factor in the application of ICT for agro-forestry. In R. Lekoko, & L. Semali (Eds.), *Cases on developing countries and ICT integration: Rural community development* (pp. 123–133). Hershey, PA: Information Science Reference.

Rafi, M. S. (2010). The sociolinguistics of SMS ways to identify gender boundaries. In R. Taiwo (Ed.), *Handbook of research on discourse behavior and digital communication: Language structures and social interaction* (pp. 104–111). Hershey, PA: Information Science Reference. doi:10.4018/978-1-61520-773-2.ch006

Rajesh, M. N. (2012). Virtual tourism as a new form of oppression against women. In R. Pande, & T. Van der Weide (Eds.), *Globalization, technology diffusion and gender disparity: Social impacts of ICTs* (pp. 200–209). Hershey, PA: Information Science Reference. doi:10.4018/978-1-4666-0020-1.ch017

Rambo, K., & Liu, K. (2011). Culture-sensitive virtual e-commerce design with reference to female consumers in Saudi Arabia. In B. Ciaramitaro (Ed.), *Virtual worlds and e-commerce: Technologies and applications for building customer relationships* (pp. 267–289). Hershey, PA: Business Science Reference.

Ratan, R. (2013). Self-presence, explicated: Body, emotion, and identity extension into the virtual self. In R. Luppicini (Ed.), *Handbook of research on techno-self: Identity in a technological society* (pp. 322–336). Hershey, PA: Information Science Reference.

Reimann, D. (2012). Shaping interactive media with the sewing machine: Smart textile as an artistic context to engage girls in technology and engineering education. In I. Management Association (Ed.), *Computer engineering: Concepts, methodologies, tools and applications* (pp. 1342-1351). Hershey, PA: Engineering Science Reference. doi:doi:10.4018/978-1-61350-456-7.ch517

Reiners, T., & Wood, L. C. (2013). Immersive virtual environments to facilitate authentic education in logistics and supply chain management. In Y. Kats (Ed.), *Learning management systems and instructional design: Best practices in online education* (pp. 323–343). Hershey, PA: Information Science Reference. doi:10.4018/978-1-4666-3930-0.ch017

Rensfeldt, A. B., & Riomar, S. (2010). Gendered distance education spaces: "Keeping women in place"? In S. Booth, S. Goodman, & G. Kirkup (Eds.), *Gender issues in learning and working with information technology: Social constructs and cultural contexts* (pp. 192–208). Hershey, PA: Information Science Reference. doi:10.4018/978-1-61520-813-5.ch011

Resmi, A. T., & Kamalanabhan, T. J. (2013). Confirmatory factor analysis and alternate test models for impression management in SMEs: A gender based study. *International Journal of Information Systems and Supply Chain Management, 6*(2), 72–87. doi:10.4018/jisscm.2013040106

Rhima, T. E. (2010). Gender and ICT policy. In E. Adomi (Ed.), *Frameworks for ICT policy: Government, social and legal issues* (pp. 164–181). Hershey, PA: Information Science Reference. doi:10.4018/978-1-61692-012-8.ch011

Rodrigues, R. G., Pinheiro, P. G., & Barbosa, J. (2012). Online playability: The social dimension to the virtual world. In M. Cruz-Cunha (Ed.), *Handbook of research on serious games as educational, business and research tools* (pp. 391–421). Hershey, PA: Information Science Reference. doi:10.4018/978-1-4666-0149-9.ch021

Romm-Livermore, C., Somers, T. M., Setzekorn, K., & King, A. L. (2012). How e-daters behave online: Theory and empirical observations. In C. Romm Livermore (Ed.), *Gender and social computing: Interactions, differences and relationships* (pp. 236–256). Hershey, PA: Information Science Publishing.

Rommes, E. (2010). Heteronormativity revisited: Adolescents' educational choices, sexuality and soaps. In S. Booth, S. Goodman, & G. Kirkup (Eds.), *Gender issues in learning and working with information technology: Social constructs and cultural contexts* (pp. 150–172). Hershey, PA: Information Science Reference. doi:10.4018/978-1-61520-813-5.ch009

Rosas, O. V., & Dhen, G. (2012). One self to rule them all: A critical discourse analysis of French-speaking players' identity construction in World of Warcraft. In N. Zagalo, L. Morgado, & A. Boa-Ventura (Eds.), *Virtual worlds and metaverse platforms: New communication and identity paradigms* (pp. 337–366). Hershey, PA: Information Science Reference.

Rose, L. (2012). Social networks, online technologies, and virtual learning: (Re)structuring oppression and hierarchies in academia. In N. Ekekwe, & N. Islam (Eds.), *Disruptive technologies, innovation and global redesign: Emerging implications* (pp. 266–279). Hershey, PA: Information Science Reference. doi:10.4018/978-1-4666-0134-5.ch014

Rowan, L., & Bigum, C. (2011). Reassembling the problem of the under-representation of girls in IT courses. In A. Tatnall (Ed.), *Actor-network theory and technology innovation: Advancements and new concepts* (pp. 208–222). Hershey, PA: Information Science Reference.

Russo, M. R., & Bryan, V. C. (2013). Technology, the 21st century workforce, and the construct of social justice. In V. Wang (Ed.), *Handbook of research on technologies for improving the 21st century workforce: Tools for lifelong learning* (pp. 56–75). Hershey, PA: Information Science Publishing.

Saadé, R. G., Kira, D., & Otrakji, C. A. (2012). Gender differences in interface type task analysis. *International Journal of Information Systems and Social Change, 3*(2), 1–23. doi:10.4018/jissc.2012040101

Sadowska, N. M. (2010). Commerce and gender: Generating interactive spaces for female online user. In T. Dumova, & R. Fiordo (Eds.), *Handbook of research on social interaction technologies and collaboration software: Concepts and trends* (pp. 245–256). Hershey, PA: Information Science Reference.

Salminen-Karlsson, M. (2010). Computer courses in adult education in a gender perspective. In S. Booth, S. Goodman, & G. Kirkup (Eds.), *Gender issues in learning and working with information technology: Social constructs and cultural contexts* (pp. 209–230). Hershey, PA: Information Science Reference. doi:10.4018/978-1-61520-813-5.ch012

San Chee, Y., Gwee, S., & Tan, E. M. (2011). Learning to become citizens by enacting governorship in the statecraft curriculum: An evaluation of learning outcomes. *International Journal of Gaming and Computer-Mediated Simulations*, 3(2), 1–27. doi:10.4018/jgcms.2011040101

Sánchez-Apellániz, M., Núñez, M., & Charlo-Molina, M. J. (2012). Women and globalization. In C. Wankel, & S. Malleck (Eds.), *Ethical models and applications of globalization: Cultural, socio-political and economic perspectives* (pp. 119–140). Hershey, PA: Business Science Reference.

Sappleton, N. (2011). Overcoming the segregation/stereotyping dilemma: Computer mediated communication for business women and professionals. *International Journal of E-Politics*, 2(2), 18–36. doi:10.4018/jep.2011040102

Sappleton, N. (2012). Overcoming the segregation/stereotyping dilemma: Computer mediated communication for business women and professionals. In C. Romm Livermore (Ed.), *Gender and social computing: Interactions, differences and relationships* (pp. 162–182). Hershey, PA: Information Science Publishing.

Sauvé, L., Villardier, L., & Probst, W. (2010). Online multiplayer games: A powerful tool for learning communication and teamwork. In D. Kaufman, & L. Sauvé (Eds.), *Educational gameplay and simulation environments: Case studies and lessons learned* (pp. 175–194). Hershey, PA: Information Science Reference. doi:10.4018/978-1-61520-731-2.ch012

Sawyer, B. (2011). Research essay: What will serious games of the future look like? *International Journal of Gaming and Computer-Mediated Simulations*, 3(3), 82–90. doi:10.4018/jgcms.2011070106

Schulz, H. M., & Eastin, M. S. (2010). An opportunity for in-game ad placement: The history of the video game industry interpreted through the meaning lifecycle. In M. Eastin, T. Daugherty, & N. Burns (Eds.), *Handbook of research on digital media and advertising: User generated content consumption* (pp. 480–490). Hershey, PA: Information Science Reference. doi:10.4018/978-1-60566-792-8.ch024

Sedehi, H., & Baleani, F. (2012). Business interactive game business interactive game (BIG): An innovative game to support enterprise management training. In M. Cruz-Cunha (Ed.), *Handbook of research on serious games as educational, business and research tools* (pp. 859–872). Hershey, PA: Information Science Reference. doi:10.4018/978-1-4666-0149-9.ch044

Sefyrin, J. (2010). "For me it doesn't matter where I put my information": Enactments of agency, mutual learning, and gender in IT design. In S. Booth, S. Goodman, & G. Kirkup (Eds.), *Gender issues in learning and working with information technology: Social constructs and cultural contexts* (pp. 65–82). Hershey, PA: Information Science Reference. doi:10.4018/978-1-61520-813-5.ch004

Sell, A., de Reuver, M., Walden, P., & Carlsson, C. (2012). Context, gender and intended use of mobile messaging, entertainment and social media services. *International Journal of Systems and Service-Oriented Engineering*, 3(1), 1–15. doi:10.4018/jssoe.2012010101

Seth, N., & Patnayakuni, R. (2012). Online matrimonial sites and the transformation of arranged marriage in India. In C. Romm Livermore (Ed.), *Gender and social computing: Interactions, differences and relationships* (pp. 272–295). Hershey, PA: Information Science Publishing.

Sevo, R., & Chubin, D. E. (2010). Bias literacy: A review of concepts in research on gender discrimination and the U.S. context. In A. Cater-Steel, & E. Cater (Eds.), *Women in engineering, science and technology: Education and career challenges* (pp. 21–54). Hershey, PA: Engineering Science Reference. doi:10.4018/978-1-61520-657-5.ch002

Shaw, A. (2011). Toward an ethic of representation: Ethics and the representation of marginalized groups in videogames. In K. Schrier, & D. Gibson (Eds.), *Designing games for ethics: Models, techniques and frameworks* (pp. 159–177). Hershey, PA: Information Science Reference.

Shin, N., Norris, C., & Soloway, E. (2011). Mobile gaming environment: Learning and motivational effects. In P. Felicia (Ed.), *Handbook of research on improving learning and motivation through educational games: Multidisciplinary approaches* (pp. 467–481). Hershey, PA: Information Science Reference. doi:10.4018/978-1-60960-495-0.ch022

Shirk, S., Arreola, V., Wobig, C., & Russell, K. (2012). Girls' e-mentoring in science, engineering, and technology based at the University of Illinois at Chicago women in science and engineering (WISE) program. In I. Management Association (Ed.), Computer engineering: concepts, methodologies, tools and applications (pp. 1144-1163). Hershey, PA: Engineering Science Reference. doi: doi:10.4018/978-1-61350-456-7.ch505

Sicart, M. (2010). Values between systems: Designing ethical gameplay. In K. Schrier, & D. Gibson (Eds.), *Ethics and game design: Teaching values through play* (pp. 1–15). Hershey, PA: Information Science Reference. doi:10.4018/978-1-61520-845-6.ch001

Simão de Vasconcellos, M., & Soares de Araújo, I. (2013). Massively multiplayer online role playing games for health communication in Brazil. In K. Bredl, & W. Bösche (Eds.), *Serious games and virtual worlds in education, professional development, and healthcare* (pp. 294–312). Hershey, PA: Information Science Reference. doi:10.4018/978-1-4666-3673-6.ch018

Simkins, D. (2010). Playing with ethics: Experiencing new ways of being in RPGs. In K. Schrier, & D. Gibson (Eds.), *Ethics and game design: Teaching values through play* (pp. 69–84). Hershey, PA: Information Science Reference. doi:10.4018/978-1-61520-845-6.ch005

Stacey, P., & Nandhakumar, J. (2011). Emotional journeys in game design teams. In M. Cruz-Cunha, V. Varvalho, & P. Tavares (Eds.), *Business, technological, and social dimensions of computer games: Multidisciplinary developments* (pp. 220–236). Hershey, PA: Information Science Reference. doi:10.4018/978-1-60960-567-4.ch014

Staines, D. (2010). Videogames and moral pedagogy: A neo-Kohlbergian approach. In K. Schrier, & D. Gibson (Eds.), *Ethics and game design: Teaching values through play* (pp. 35–51). Hershey, PA: Information Science Reference. doi:10.4018/978-1-61520-845-6.ch003

Starosky, P., & Pereira, M. D. (2013). Role-playing game as a pedagogical proposition for story co-construction: A Brazilian experience with deaf individuals in an educational context. In C. Gonzalez (Ed.), *Student usability in educational software and games: Improving experiences* (pp. 274–292). Hershey, PA: Information Science Reference.

Steinkuehler, C., & Johnson, B. Z. (2011). Computational literacy in online games: The social life of mods. In R. Ferdig (Ed.), *Discoveries in gaming and computer-mediated simulations: New interdisciplinary applications* (pp. 218–231). Hershey, PA: Information Science Reference. doi:10.4018/978-1-60960-565-0.ch012

Surgevil, O., & Özbilgin, M. F. (2012). Women in information communication technologies. In C. Romm Livermore (Ed.), *Gender and social computing: Interactions, differences and relationships* (pp. 87–97). Hershey, PA: Information Science Publishing.

Švelch, J. (2010). The good, the bad, and the player: The challenges to moral engagement in single-player avatar-based video games. In K. Schrier, & D. Gibson (Eds.), *Ethics and game design: Teaching values through play* (pp. 52–68). Hershey, PA: Information Science Reference. doi:10.4018/978-1-61520-845-6.ch004

Swain, C. (2011). Culturally responsive games and simulations. In I. Management Association (Ed.), Gaming and simulations: Concepts, methodologies, tools and applications (pp. 1298-1312). Hershey, PA: Information Science Reference. doi: doi:10.4018/978-1-60960-195-9.ch504

Swim, J., & Barker, L. (2012). Pathways into a gendered occupation: Brazilian women in IT. *International Journal of Social and Organizational Dynamics in IT*, 2(4), 34–51. doi:10.4018/ijsodit.2012100103

Takruri-Rizk, H., Sappleton, N., & Dhar-Bhattacharjee, S. (2010). Progression of UK women engineers: Aids and hurdles. In A. Cater-Steel, & E. Cater (Eds.), *Women in engineering, science and technology: Education and career challenges* (pp. 280–300). Hershey, PA: Engineering Science Reference. doi:10.4018/978-1-61520-657-5.ch013

Tan, S., Baxa, J., & Spackman, M. P. (2010). Effects of built-in audio versus unrelated background music on performance in an adventure role-playing game. *International Journal of Gaming and Computer-Mediated Simulations*, 2(3), 1–23. doi:10.4018/jgcms.2010070101

Tara, S., & Ilavarasan, P. V. (2012). Western work worlds and altering approaches to marriage: An empirical study of women employees of call centers in India. In R. Pande, & T. Van der Weide (Eds.), *Globalization, technology diffusion and gender disparity: Social impacts of ICTs* (pp. 262–276). Hershey, PA: Information Science Reference. doi:10.4018/978-1-4666-0020-1.ch021

Teixeira, P. M., Félix, M. J., & Tavares, P. (2012). Playing with design: The universality of design in game development. In M. Cruz-Cunha (Ed.), *Handbook of research on serious games as educational, business and research tools* (pp. 217–231). Hershey, PA: Information Science Reference. doi:10.4018/978-1-4666-0149-9.ch011

Teng, C., Jeng, S., Chang, H. K., & Wu, S. (2012). Who plays games online? The relationship between gamer personality and online game use. *International Journal of E-Business Research*, 8(4), 1–14. doi:10.4018/jebr.2012100101

Terry, A., & Gomez, R. (2012). Gender and public access ICT. In R. Gomez (Ed.), *Libraries, telecentres, cybercafes and public access to ICT: International comparisons* (pp. 51–64). Hershey, PA: Information Science Publishing.

Thacker, S., & Griffiths, M. D. (2012). An exploratory study of trolling in online video gaming. *International Journal of Cyber Behavior, Psychology and Learning*, 2(4), 17–33. doi:10.4018/ijcbpl.2012100102

Thomas, D. I., & Vlacic, L. B. (2011). Human and virtual beings as equal collaborative partners in computer games. In M. Cruz-Cunha, V. Varvalho, & P. Tavares (Eds.), *Computer games as educational and management tools: Uses and approaches* (pp. 23–51). Hershey, PA: Information Science Reference. doi:10.4018/978-1-60960-569-8.ch003

Toprac, P., & Abdel-Meguid, A. (2011). Causing fear, suspense, and anxiety using sound design in computer games. In M. Grimshaw (Ed.), *Game sound technology and player interaction: Concepts and developments* (pp. 176–191). Hershey, PA: Information Science Reference.

Tran, B. (2012). Gendered technology-based organizations: A view of the glass cliff through the window of the glass ceiling. In D. Jemielniak, & A. Marks (Eds.), *Managing dynamic technology-oriented businesses: High-tech organizations and workplaces* (pp. 253–272). Hershey, PA: Business Science Reference. doi:10.4018/978-1-4666-1836-7.ch015

Tran, B. (2014). Rhetoric of play: Utilizing the gamer factor in selecting and training employees. In T. Connolly, T. Hainey, E. Boyle, G. Baxter, & P. Moreno-Ger (Eds.), *Psychology, pedagogy, and assessment in serious games* (pp. 175–203). Hershey, PA: Information Science Reference.

Trauth, E. M., Quesenberry, J. L., & Huang, H. (2010). Factors influencing career choice for women in the global information technology workforce. In M. Hunter, & F. Tan (Eds.), *Technological advancement in developed and developing countries: Discoveries in global information management* (pp. 23–48). Hershey, PA: Information Science Reference.

Trepte, S., Reinecke, L., & Behr, K. (2011). Playing myself or playing to win? Gamers' strategies of avatar creation in terms of gender and sex. In R. Ferdig (Ed.), *Discoveries in gaming and computer-mediated simulations: New interdisciplinary applications* (pp. 329–352). Hershey, PA: Information Science Reference. doi:10.4018/978-1-60960-565-0.ch019

Tu, C., Yen, C., & Blocher, M. (2011). A study of the relationship between gender and online social presence. *International Journal of Online Pedagogy and Course Design*, *1*(3), 33–49. doi:10.4018/ijopcd.2011070103

Tyagi, A. (2011). Virtual reality and identity crisis—: Implications for individuals and organizations. In K. Malik, & P. Choudhary (Eds.), *Business organizations and collaborative web: Practices, strategies and patterns* (pp. 202–218). Hershey, PA: Information Science Reference. doi:10.4018/978-1-60960-581-0.ch013

Umarov, I., & Mozgovoy, M. (2012). Believable and effective AI agents in virtual worlds: Current state and future perspectives. *International Journal of Gaming and Computer-Mediated Simulations*, *4*(2), 37–59. doi:10.4018/jgcms.2012040103

Ursyn, A. (2014). Challenges in game design. In *Computational solutions for knowledge, art, and entertainment: Information exchange beyond text* (pp. 413–428). Hershey, PA: Information Science Reference.

Uzun, L., Ekin, M. T., & Kartal, E. (2013). The opinions and attitudes of the foreign language learners and teachers related to the traditional and digital games: Age and gender differences. *International Journal of Game-Based Learning*, *3*(2), 91–111. doi:10.4018/ijgbl.2013040106

van de Laar, B., Reuderink, B., Bos, D. P., & Heylen, D. (2010). Evaluating user experience of actual and imagined movement in BCI gaming. *International Journal of Gaming and Computer-Mediated Simulations*, *2*(4), 33–47. doi:10.4018/jgcms.2010100103

van der Weide, T. (2012). A digital (r)evolution to the information age. In R. Pande, & T. Van der Weide (Eds.), *Globalization, technology diffusion and gender disparity: Social impacts of ICTs* (pp. 1–14). Hershey, PA: Information Science Reference. doi:10.4018/978-1-4666-0020-1.ch001

Velazquez, M. (2013). "Come fly with us": Playing with girlhood in the world of pixie hollow. In Y. Baek, & N. Whitton (Eds.), *Cases on digital game-based learning: Methods, models, and strategies* (pp. 1–14). Hershey, PA: Information Science Reference.

Veltri, N. F., Webb, H. W., & Papp, R. (2010). GETSMART: An academic-industry partnership to encourage female participation in science, technology, engineering and math careers. In A. Cater-Steel, & E. Cater (Eds.), *Women in engineering, science and technology: Education and career challenges* (pp. 56–77). Hershey, PA: Engineering Science Reference. doi:10.4018/978-1-61520-657-5.ch003

Vikaros, L., & Degand, D. (2010). Moral development through social narratives and game design. In K. Schrier, & D. Gibson (Eds.), *Ethics and game design: Teaching values through play* (pp. 197–215). Hershey, PA: Information Science Reference. doi:10.4018/978-1-61520-845-6.ch013

Voulgari, I., & Komis, V. (2011). Collaborative learning in massively multiplayer online games: A review of social, cognitive and motivational perspectives. In P. Felicia (Ed.), *Handbook of research on improving learning and motivation through educational games: Multidisciplinary approaches* (pp. 370–394). Hershey, PA: Information Science Reference. doi:10.4018/978-1-60960-495-0.ch018

Wakunuma-Zojer, K. J. (2012). Gender and ICT policy for development and empowerment: A critique of a national ICT policy. In I. Management Association (Ed.), *Regional development: Concepts, methodologies, tools, and applications* (pp. 1005-1027). Hershey, PA: Information Science Reference. doi: doi:10.4018/978-1-4666-0882-5.ch510

Wallgren, L. G., Leijon, S., & Andersson, K. M. (2013). IT managers' narratives on subordinates' motivation at work: A case study. In A. Mesquita (Ed.), *User perception and influencing factors of technology in everyday life* (pp. 282–297). Hershey, PA: Information Science Reference.

Weber, R., & Shaw, P. (2009). Player types and quality perceptions: A social cognitive theory based model to predict video game playing. *International Journal of Gaming and Computer-Mediated Simulations*, *1*(1), 66–89. doi:10.4018/jgcms.2009010105

Wei, Z., & Kramarae, C. (2012). Women, big ideas, and social networking technologies: Hidden assumptions. In R. Pande, & T. Van der Weide (Eds.), *Globalization, technology diffusion and gender disparity: Social impacts of ICTs* (pp. 70–82). Hershey, PA: Information Science Reference. doi:10.4018/978-1-4666-0020-1.ch006

Weiss, A., & Tettegah, S. (2012). World of race war: Race and learning in World of Warcraft. *International Journal of Gaming and Computer-Mediated Simulations*, *4*(4), 33–44. doi:10.4018/jgcms.2012100103

White, G. (2010). Increasing the numbers of women in science. In A. Cater-Steel, & E. Cater (Eds.), *Women in engineering, science and technology: Education and career challenges* (pp. 78–95). Hershey, PA: Engineering Science Reference. doi:10.4018/978-1-61520-657-5.ch004

White, M. M. (2012). Designing tutorial modalities and strategies for digital games: Lessons from education. *International Journal of Game-Based Learning*, *2*(2), 13–34. doi:10.4018/ijgbl.2012040102

Winter, A. (2010). The smart women – Smart state strategy: A policy on women's participation in science, engineering and technology in Queensland, Australia. In A. Cater-Steel, & E. Cater (Eds.), *Women in engineering, science and technology: Education and career challenges* (pp. 1–20). Hershey, PA: Engineering Science Reference. doi:10.4018/978-1-61520-657-5.ch001

Wolfenstein, M. (2013). Digital structures and the future of online leadership. In S. D'Agustino (Ed.), *Immersive environments, augmented realities, and virtual worlds: Assessing future trends in education* (pp. 257–279). Hershey, PA: Information Science Reference. doi:10.4018/978-1-4666-4502-8.ch096

Woodfield, R. (2012). Gender and employability patterns amongst UK ICT graduates: Investigating the leaky pipeline. In R. Pande, & T. Van der Weide (Eds.), *Globalization, technology diffusion and gender disparity: Social impacts of ICTs* (pp. 184–199). Hershey, PA: Information Science Reference. doi:10.4018/978-1-4666-0020-1.ch016

Yakura, E. K., Soe, L., & Guthrie, R. (2012). Women in IT careers: Investigating support for women in the information technology workforce. In C. Romm Livermore (Ed.), *Gender and social computing: Interactions, differences and relationships* (pp. 35–49). Hershey, PA: Information Science Publishing.

York, A. M., & Nordengren, F. R. (2013). E-learning and web 2.0 case study: The role of gender in contemporary models of health care leadership. In H. Yang, & S. Wang (Eds.), *Cases on formal and informal e-learning environments: Opportunities and practices* (pp. 292–313). Hershey, PA: Information Science Reference.

Yost, E., Handley, D. M., Cotten, S. R., & Winstead, V. (2010). Understanding the links between mentoring and self-efficacy in the new generation of women STEM scholars. In A. Cater-Steel, & E. Cater (Eds.), *Women in engineering, science and technology: Education and career challenges* (pp. 97–117). Hershey, PA: Engineering Science Reference. doi:10.4018/978-1-61520-657-5.ch005

Youngs, G. (2012). Globalization, information and communication technologies, and women's lives. In R. Pande, & T. Van der Weide (Eds.), *Globalization, technology diffusion and gender disparity: Social impacts of ICTs* (pp. 25–34). Hershey, PA: Information Science Reference. doi:10.4018/978-1-4666-0020-1.ch003

Zhang, S., Jiang, H., & Carroll, J. M. (2010). Social identity in Facebook community life. *International Journal of Virtual Communities and Social Networking*, 2(4), 64–76. doi:10.4018/jvcsn.2010100105

Zhao, Y., Wang, W., & Zhu, Y. (2010). Antecedents of the closeness of human-avatar relationships in a virtual world. *Journal of Database Management*, 21(2), 41–68. doi:10.4018/jdm.2010040103

Zutshi, A., & Creed, A. (2010). ICT and gender issues in the higher education of entrepreneurs. *International Journal of E-Entrepreneurship and Innovation*, 1(1), 42–59. doi:10.4018/jeei.2010010103

Compilation of References

30% Club. (2012). *30% club underlines belief that quotas are harmful to ongoing gender debate*. Retrieved from http://www.30percentclub.org.uk

Aarseth, E. (2001). Computer game studies, year one. *Game Studies*, *1*(1), 1–10.

Aarseth, E. (2004). Genre trouble: Narrativism & the art of simulation. In *First person: New media as story, performance, & game* (pp. 45–55). Cambridge, MA: The MIT Press.

Abood, D. A., & Conway, T. L. (1992). Health value & self-esteem as predictors of wellness behaviour. *Health Values*, *16*, 20–26.

Agarwal, R., & Krarhanna, E. (2002). Time flies when you are having fun: cognitive absorption & beliefs about information technology usage. *Management Information Systems Quarterly*, *24*(4), 665–694. doi:10.2307/3250951

Ahuja, M. K. (2002). Women in the information technology profession: A literature review, synthesis & research agenda. *European Journal of Information Systems*, *11*, 20–34. doi:10.1057/palgrave.ejis.3000417

Allen, I. (2005). Women doctors & their careers: What now? *British Medical Journal*, *331*, 569–572. doi:10.1136/bmj.331.7516.569 PMID:16150771

Allen, T. D., & Eby, L. T. (2004). Factors related to mentor reports of mentoring functions provided: Gender & relational characteristics. *Sex Roles*, *50*(12), 129–139. doi:10.1023/B:SERS.0000011078.48570.25

Allen, T. D., Lentz, E., & Day, R. (2006). Career success outcomes associated with mentoring others. *Journal of Career Development*, *32*(3), 272–285. doi:10.1177/0894845305282942

Allen, T. D., Poteet, M. L., Eby, L. T., Lentz, E., & Lima, L. (2004). Career benefits associated with mentoring for protégés: A meta-analysis. *The Journal of Applied Psychology*, *89*(1), 127–136. doi:10.1037/0021-9010.89.1.127 PMID:14769125

Alwood, E. (1996). *Straight news: Gays, lesbians, & the new media*. New York: Columbia University Press.

Amabile, T. M., Hill, K. G., Hennessey, B. A., & Tighe, E. M. (1994). The work preference inventory: Assessing intrinsic & extrinsic motivational orientations. *Journal of Personality and Social Psychology*, *66*(5), 950–967. doi:10.1037/0022-3514.66.5.950 PMID:8014837

Anderson, C. A., Beerkowitz, L., Donnerstein, E., Huesmann, R. L., Johnson, J., & Linz, D. et al. (2003). The influence of media violence on youth. *Psychological Science in the Public Interest*, *4*, 81–110.

Anderson, C. A., & Bushman, B. (2001). Effects of violent video games on aggressive behaviour, aggressive cognition, aggressive affect, psychological arousal, & prosocial behaviour: A meta-analytic reviews of the scientific literature. *Psychological Science*, *12*, 353–359. doi:10.1111/1467-9280.00366 PMID:11554666

Anderson, C. A., & Dill, K. E. (2000). Video games & aggressive thoughts, feelings, and behavior in the laboratory & in life. *Journal of Personality and Social Psychology*, *78*(4), 772–790. doi:10.1037/0022-3514.78.4.772 PMID:10794380

Anderson, D. R. (2005). The importance of mentoring programs to women's career advancement in biotechnology. *Journal of Career Development*, *32*(1), 60–73. doi:10.1177/0894845305277039

Anderson, N., Lankshear, C., Timms, C., & Courtney, L. (2008). Because it's boring, irrelevant & I don't like computers: Why high school girls avoid professionally-oriented ICT subjects. *Computers & Education, 50,* 1304–1318. doi:10.1016/j.compedu.2006.12.003

Angelo, J. (2004). *New study reveals that women over 40 who play online games spend more time playing than male or teenage gamers.* Business Wire.

Arfken, D. E., Bellar, S. L., & Helms, M. H. (2004). The ultimate glass ceiling revisited: The presence of women on corporate boards. *Journal of Business Ethics, 50,* 177–186. doi:10.1023/B:BUSI.0000022125.95758.98

Aronson, K. A., Laurenceau, J. P., Sieveking, N., & Bellet, W. (2005). Job satisfaction as a function of job level. *Administration and Policy in Mental Health, 32*(3), 285–291. doi:10.1007/s10488-004-0845-2 PMID:15844849

Ashton, D. (2011). Upgrading the self: Technology & the self in the digital games perpetual innovation economy. *Convergence, 17*(3), 307–321.

Askari, S. F., Liss, M., Erchull, M. J., Staebell, S. E., & Axelson, S. J. (2010). Men want equality, but women don't expect it: Young adults' expectations for participation in household & child care chores. *Psychology of Women Quarterly, 34,* 243–252. doi:10.1111/j.1471-6402.2010.01565.x

Assad, O., Hermann, R., Lilla, D., Mellies, B., Meyer, R., & Shevach, L. et al. (2011). Motion-based games for Parkinson's disease patients. *Lecture Notes in Computer Science, 6972,* 47–58. doi:10.1007/978-3-642-24500-8_6

B&ura, A. (1986). *Social foundations of thought & action: A social cognitive theory.* Englewood Cliffs, NJ: Prentice Hall.

B&ura, A. (2002). Social cognitive theory of mass communication. In *Media effects: Advances in theory & research* (pp. 121-153). Mahwah, NJ: Erlbaum.

Bain, O., & Cummings, W. (2000). Academe's glass ceiling: Societal, professional-organizational, & institutional barriers to the career advancement of academic women. *Comparative Education Review, 44*(4), 493–514. doi:10.1086/447631

Bajo, L. M., & Dickson, M. W. (2002). Perceptions of organizational culture & women's advancement in organizations: A cross-cultural examination. *Sex Roles, 45,* 399–414. doi:10.1023/A:1014365716222

Baker, J. G. (2002). The influx of women into legal professions: an economic analysis. *Monthly Labor Review, 125*(8), 14–24.

Balance Blackboard Blog. (2008). *Wii fit advertising killing.* Retrieved from http://www.balanceboardblog.com/2008/04/analyst-wii-fit-advertising-killing.html

Bandura, A. (1977). *Social learning theory.* New York: General Learning Press.

Bandura, A. (1986). *Social foundations of thought & action: A social cognitive theory.* Englewood Cliffs, NJ: Prentice Hall.

Bandura, A., & Locke, E. A. (2003). Negative self-efficacy & goal effects revisited. *The Journal of Applied Psychology, 88*(1), 87–99. doi:10.1037/0021-9010.88.1.87 PMID:12675397

Banks, M., & Milestone, K. (2011). Individualization, gender & cultural work. *Gender, Work and Organization, 18*(1), 73–89. doi:10.1111/j.1468-0432.2010.00535.x

Barker, E. R. (2006). Mentoring – A complex relationship. *Journal of the American Academy of Nurse Practitioners, 18,* 56–61. doi:10.1111/j.1745-7599.2006.00102.x PMID:16460411

Barlett, C. P., & Harris, R. J. (2008). The impact of body emphasizing video games on body image concerns in men & women. *Sex Roles, 59,* 586–601. doi:10.1007/s11199-008-9457-8

Barsh, J., & Yee, L. (2011). *Unlocking the full potential of women in the US economy.* Retrieved from http://www.mckinsey.com/client_service/organization/latest_thinking/unlocking_the_full_potential

Barsh, J., Cranston, S., & Craske, R. A. (2008). *Centered leadership: How talented women thrive: A new approach to leadership can help women become more self-confident & effective business leaders report.* Retrieved from http://www.mckinseyquarterly.com/Centered_leadership_How_talented_women_thrive_2193

Bartholow, B. D., & Anderson, C. A. (2002). Effects of violent video games on aggressive behavior: Potential sex differences. *Journal of Experimental Social Psychology, 38*(3), 283–290. doi:10.1006/jesp.2001.1502

Baugh, S., & Fagenson-Eland, E. A. (2005). Boundaryless mentoring: An exploratory study of the functions provided by internal versus external organizational mentors. *Journal of Applied Social Psychology, 35*(5), 939–955. doi:10.1111/j.1559-1816.2005.tb02154.x

Beasley, B., & Stanley, T. C. (2002). Shirts vs. skins: Clothing as an indicator of gender role stereotyping in video games. *Mass Communication & Society, 5*(3), 279–293. doi:10.1207/S15327825MCS0503_3

Bebbington, D. (2002). Women in science, engineering & technology: A review of the issues. *Higher Education Quarterly, 56*(4), 360. doi:10.1111/1468-2273.00225

Bednar, R. L., Wells, M. G., & Peterson, S. R. (1989). *Self-esteem: Paradoxes & innovations in clinical theory & practice*. Washington, DC: American Psychological Association. doi:10.1037/10068-000

Behm-Morawitz, E., & Mastro, D. (2009). The effects of the sexualization of female video game characters on gender stereotyping & female self-concept. *Sex Roles, 61*, 808–823. doi:10.1007/s11199-009-9683-8

Bem, S. L. (1974). The measurement of psychological androgyny. *Journal of Consulting and Clinical Psychology, 42*(2), 155–162. doi:10.1037/h0036215 PMID:4823550

Bendl, R., & Schmidt, A. (2010). From 'glass ceilings' to 'firewalls' - Different metaphors for describing discrimination. *Gender, Work and Organization, 17*(5), 612–634. doi:10.1111/j.1468-0432.2010.00520.x

Bennerstedt, U., Ivarsson, J., & Linderoth, J. (2011). *How gamers manage aggression: Situating skills in collaborative computer games*. Computer-Supported Collaborative Learning. doi:10.1007/s11412-011-9136-6

Bennett, D., & Bruner, C. (2000). The role of gender in the design of electronic learning environments for children. *Tech Learning's Well-connected Educator Journal, 21*.

Bertozzi, E. (2003). *At stake: Play, pleasure & power in cyberspace*. Retrieved from http://www.egs.edu/library/bertozzi.html

Bertozzi, E., & Lee, S. (2010). Not just fun & games: Digital play, gender and attitudes towards technology. *Women's. Studies in Communications, 30*(2), 179–204.

Betz, D., & Sekaquaptewa, D. (2012). My fair physicist? Feminine math & science role models demotivate young girls. *Social Psychological & Personality Science, 3*(6), 738–746. doi:10.1177/1948550612440735

Betz, N. E., Borgen, F. H., & Harmon, L. W. (2006). Vocational confidence & personality in the prediction of occupational group membership. *Journal of Career Assessment, 14*(1), 36–55. doi:10.1177/1069072705282434

Betz, N. E., & Hackett, G. (1981). The relationship of career-related self-efficacy expectations to perceived career options in college women & men. *Journal of Counseling Psychology, 28*(5), 399–410. doi:10.1037/0022-0167.28.5.399

Betz, N., & Fitzgerald, L. F. (1987). *The career psychology of women*. New York: Academic Press.

Bierema, L. L. (2005). Women's networks: A career development intervention or impediment? *Human Resource Development International, 8*(2), 207–224. doi:10.1080/13678860500100517

Bird, G. W., & Schnurman-Crook, A. (2005). Professional identity & coping behaviors in dual-career couples. *Family Relations, 54*(1), 145–160. doi:10.1111/j.0197-6664.2005.00012.x

Blyton, P., & Jenkins, J. (2007). *Key concepts in work*. London: Sage.

Boellstorff, T. (2008). *Coming of age in Second Life: An anthropologist explores the virtually human*. Princeton, NJ: Princeton University Press.

Bogg, J. (2010). *Gender, the RAE 2008 & the Russell group universities*. Paper presented at the Nature Journal Conference. London, UK.

Bogg, J. (2007). Dr Jekyll & Ms Hide: Where are the women in science? & what would attract them from other sectors? *Nature*, 447.

Bogg, J. (2012). *The ABC model of key steps for change*. Liverpool, UK: University of Liverpool.

Bogost, I. (2008). *Girls prefer 2D games to 3D games*. Retrieved from http://kotaku.com/gaming/research/girls-prefer-2d-games-to-3d-games-335041.php

Bonanno, P., & Kommers, P. A. M. (2008). Exploring the influence of gender & gaming competence on attitudes towards using instructional games. *British Journal of Educational Technology*, *39*(1), 97–109.

Bourgonjon, J., Valcke, M., Soetaert, R., de Wever, B., & Schellens, T. (2011). Parental acceptance of digital game-based learning. *Computers & Education*, *57*, 1434–1444. doi:10.1016/j.compedu.2010.12.012

Bourgonjon, J., Valcke, M., Soetaert, R., & Schellens, T. (2010). Students' perceptions about the use of video games in the classroom. *Computers & Education*, *54*, 1145–1156. doi:10.1016/j.compedu.2009.10.022

Boyle, E., Connolly, T. M., & Hainey, T. (2011). *The role of psychology in understanding the impact of computer games*. Entertainment Computing. doi:10.1016/j.entcom.2010.12.002

Boyle, E., Kennedy, A.-M., Traynor, O., & Hill, A. D. K. (2011). Training surgical skills using nonsurgical tasks- can Nintendo Wii improve surgical performance? *Journal of Surgical Education*. doi:10.1016/j.jsurg.2010.11.005 PMID:21338974

Branden, N. (1969). *The psychology of self-esteem*. New York: Bantam.

Brand, J. E. (2007). *Interactive Australia 2007: Facts about the Australian computer & video game industry*. Queensland, Australia: Bond University.

Brand, J. E., Knight, S., & Majewski, J. (2003). *The diverse worlds of computer games: a content analysis of spaces, population, styles & narratives*. Academic Press.

Brathwaite, B. (2010). *Women in games from famine to Facebook*. Retrieved from http://www.huffingtonpost.com/brenda-brathwaite/women-in-games-from-famin_b_510928.html

Brief, A. P., & Weiss, H. M. (2002). Organizational behavior: Affect in the workplace. *Annual Review of Psychology*, *53*, 279–307. doi:10.1146/annurev.psych.53.100901.135156 PMID:11752487

Brightman, J. (2008, November 25). Guitar Hero, Rock Band players showing increased interest in real instruments. *Game Daily*. Retrieved from http://www.gamedaily.com/games/rock-b&-2/playstation-3/games-news/guitar-hero-rock-b&-players-showing-increased-interest-in-real-instruments/

Brown, J. A., Woodward, C. A., Shannon, H. S., Cunningham, C. E., Lendrum, B., McIntosh, J., & Rosenbloom, D. (1999). Determinants of job stress & job satisfaction among supervisory & non-supervisory employees in a large Canadian teaching hospital. *Healthcare Management Forum*, *12*, 27–33. doi:10.1016/S0840-4704(10)60688-6 PMID:10538924

Brown, J. D., & Dutton, K. A. (1995). Truth and consequences: the costs & benefits of accurate self-knowledge. *Personality and Social Psychology Bulletin*, *21*, 1288–1296. doi:10.1177/01461672952112006

Brown, R., Hal, L., & Holtzer, R. (1997). Gender & video game performance. *Sex Roles*, *36*(11/12), 793–812. doi:10.1023/A:1025631307585

Bryce, J., & Rutter, J. (2001) *In the game – In the flow: Presence in public computer gaming*. Paper presented at Computer Games & Digital Textualities. Copenhagen, Denmark. Retrieved from http://www.digiplay.org.uk

Bryce, J., & Rutter, J. (2002). The gendering of computer gaming: Experience & space. In *Leisure cultures: Investigations in sport, media & technology* (pp. 3–22). Leisure Studies Association.

Bryce, J., & Rutter, J. (2003). Gender dynamics & the social & spatial organization of computer gaming. *Leisure Studies*, *22*, 1–15. doi:10.1080/02614360306571

Bryce, J., & Rutter, J. (2003). The gendering of computer gaming: experience & space. In *Leisure cultures: Investigations in sport, media & technology* (pp. 3–22). Leisure Studies Association.

Bryce, J., Rutter, J., & Sullivan, C. (2005). Gender & digital games. In J. Rutter, & J. Bryce (Eds.), *Understanding digital games*. London: Sage.

Buckley, K. E., & Anderson, C. A. (2006). A theoretical model of the effects & consequences of playing video games. In *Playing video games: Motives, responses, and consequences*. Mahwah, NJ: Lawrence Erlbaum Associates.

Burgess, M. C., Stermer, S. P., & Burgess, S. R. (2007). Sex, lies, & video games: The portrayal of male & female characters on video game covers. *Sex Roles*, *57*, 419–433. doi:10.1007/s11199-007-9250-0

Burke, R. J. (2003). Hospital restructuring, workload, & nursing staff satisfaction & work experiences. *The Health Care Manager*, *22*(2), 99–107. doi:10.1097/00126450-200304000-00003 PMID:12785546

Burke, R. J., Burgess, Z., & Fallon, B. (2005). Organizational practices supporting women & their satisfaction & well-being. *Women in Management Review*, *21*(5), 416–425. doi:10.1108/09649420610676217

Burns, B., Griffiths, M., Moore, K., & Richardson, H. (2007). *Disappearing women: North West ICT final report*. Salford, UK: Salford University.

Burrill, D. A. (2008). *Die tryin': Videogames, masculinity, culture*. New York: Peter Lang Publishing Inc.

Bury, R. (2011). She's geeky: The performance of identity among women working in IT. *International Journal of Gender. Science & Technology*, *3*(1), 33–53.

Bushman, B. J., & Anderson, C. A. (2002). Violent video games & hostile expectations: A test of the general aggression model. *Personality and Social Psychology Bulletin*, *28*, 1679. doi:10.1177/014616702237649

Business, I., & the Skills Committee. (2012). *Women in the workplace*. Retrieved from http://www.parliament.uk/business/committees/committees-a-z/commons-select/business-innovation-&-skills/inquiries/women-in-the-workplace

Bussey-Jones, J., Bernstein, L., Higgins, S., Malebranche, D., Paranjape, A., & Genao, I. et al. (2006). Repaving the road to academic success: The IMeRge (internal medicine research group at emory), approach to peer mentoring. *Academic Medicine*, *81*(7), 674–677. doi:10.1097/01.ACM.0000232425.27041.88 PMID:16799297

Butler, J. (1990). *Gender trouble: Feminism & the subversion of identity*. London: Routledge.

Butler, J. (1993). *Bodies that matter: On the discursive limits of sex*. London: Routledge.

Cable, D. M., & DeRue, D. S. (2002). The convergent & discriminant validity of subjective fit perceptions. *The Journal of Applied Psychology*, *87*, 1–17. doi:10.1037/0021-9010.87.5.875 PMID:12395812

Cable, D. M., & Judge, T. A. (1996). Person-organization fit, job choice decisions, & organizational entry. *Organizational Behavior and Human Decision Processes*, *67*, 294–311. doi:10.1006/obhd.1996.0081

Camicero, L., Cardoso, E., Dempster, A., Liu, K., Mould, O., Pezzana, S. P., & Roodhouse, S. (2008). *Game on! A report on the interactive leisure sorftware subsector in London*. London: University of the Arts London.

Campbell, T., Gillaspy, J. A., & Thompson, B. (1997). The factor structure of the bem sex-role inventory (BSRI), confirmatory analysis of long & short forms. *Educational and Psychological Measurement*, *57*(1), 118–124. doi:10.1177/0013164497057001008

Carless, S. (2006). IGA's Townsend on BF2142 in-game ads. *Gamasutra*. Retrieved from http://www.gamasutra.com/php-bin/news_index.php?story=11300

Carr, D. (1997). The fulfilment of career dreams at midlife: Does it matter for women's mental health? *Journal of Health and Social Behavior*, *38*, 331–344. doi:10.2307/2955429 PMID:9425778

Carr, D. (2005). Contexts, gaming pleasures, & gendered preferences. *Simulation & Gaming*, *36*(4), 464–482. doi:10.1177/1046878105282160

Carr, D., & Pelletier, C. (2008). Games, gender & representation. In E. R. Ferdig (Ed.), *Handbook for research on effective electronic gaming in education* (Vol. 2, pp. 911–921). Hershey, PA: IGI Global. doi:10.4018/978-1-59904-808-6.ch052

Case, S. (2004). *Women in gaming*. Retrieved from http://www.microsoft.com/windowsxp/games/learn-more/womeningames.mspx

Cassell, J., & Jenkins, H. (1998). *From Barbie to Mortal Kombat: Gender & computer games*. Cambridge, MA: MIT Press.

Castel, A., Pratt, J., & Drummond, E. (2005). The effects of action video game experience on the time course of inhibition of return & the efficiency of visual search. *Acta Psychologica*, *119*, 217–230. doi:10.1016/j.actpsy.2005.02.004 PMID:15877981

Casual Games Association. (2007). *Casual games market report 2007: Business & art of games for everyone*. Retrieved from http://www.regonline.com/register/Checkin.aspx?EventId=164417

Cha, J., Kim, Y., & Kim, T.-Y. (2009). Person-career fit & employee outcomes among research & development professionals. *Human Relations*, *20*(10), 1–30.

Chalk, L. M., Meara, N., & Day, J. D. (1994). Possible selves & occupational choices. *Journal of Career Assessment*, *2*(4), 364–383. doi:10.1177/106907279400200404

Chang, T. F. H. (2003). A social psychological model of women's gender-typed occupational mobility. *Career Development International*, *8*(1), 27–39. doi:10.1108/13620430310459496

Chan, V., Stafford, K., Klawe, M., & Chen, G. (2000). Gender differences in Vancouver secondary students: Interests related to information technology careers. In *Women, work & computerization: Charting a course to the future* (pp. 58–69). Boston: Kluwer Academic Publishers.

Chartered Management Institute. (2012). *National management salary survey results*. Retrieved from http://www.managers.org.uk/practical-support/management-community/professional-networks/2012-national-management-salary-survey

Chatard, A., Guimond, S., & Selimbegovic, L. (2007). How good are you in math? The effect of gender stereotypes on students' recollection of their school marks. *Journal of Experimental Social Psychology*, *43*, 1017–1024. doi:10.1016/j.jesp.2006.10.024

Cheong, P. H. (2007). Gender & perceived Internet efficacy: Examining secondary digital divide issues in Singapore. *Women's. Studies in Communications*, *30*(2), 205–228.

Chess, S. (2012). *A 36-24-36 cerebrum: Gendering video game play through advertising*. Retrieved from http://www.shiral&.com/Work/advertising_sample.pdf

Children Now. (2001). *Fair play? Violence, gender, & race in video game's*. Retrieved from www.children-now.org/media/video-games/2001/#race

Choi, N., & Fugua, D. R. (2003). The structure of the bem sex role inventory: A summary report of 23 validation studies. *Educational and Psychological Measurement*, *63*(5), 872–887. doi:10.1177/0013164403258235

Choi, N., Fuqua, D. R., & Newman, J. L. (2007). Hierarchical confirmatory factor analysis of the bem sex role inventory. *Educational and Psychological Measurement*, *67*(5), 818–832. doi:10.1177/0013164406299106

Choi, N., Fuqua, D. R., & Newman, J. L. (2009). Exploratory & confirmatory studies of the structure of the bem sex role inventory short form with two divergent samples. *Educational and Psychological Measurement*, *69*(4), 696–705. doi:10.1177/0013164409332218

Chonin, N. (2006, February 5). MMORPG! WOW! TOS! GLBT! Sexual harassment! *San Francisco Chronicle*.

Chou, C., & Tsai, C.-C. (2002). Developing web-based curricula: Issues & challenges. *Journal of Curriculum Studies*, *34*, 623–636. doi:10.1080/00220270210141909

Clegg, S., & Trayhurn, D. (2000). Gender & computing: Not the same old problem. *British Educational Research Journal*, *26*(1), 75–89. doi:10.1080/014119200109525

Colley, A., Mulhern, G., Maltby, J., & Wood, A. M. (2009). The short form BSRI: Instrumentality, expressiveness & gender associations among a United Kingdom sample. *Personality and Individual Differences*, *46*, 384–387. doi:10.1016/j.paid.2008.11.005

Conley, D., & Stadmark, J. (2012). Gender matters: A call to commission more women writers. *Nature*, *488*(7413), 590. doi:10.1038/488590a PMID:22932370

Connell, J. P., Spencer, M. B., & Aber, J. L. (1994). Educational risk & resilience in African-American youth: Context, self, action, & outcomes in school. *Child Development*, *65*, 493–506. doi:10.2307/1131398 PMID:8013236

Connell, R. (2000). *The men & the boys*. Cambridge, UK: Polity Press.

Consalvo, M. (2003). Hot dates & fairy-tale romances: Studying equality in video games. In *The video game theory reader* (pp. 171–194). London: Routledge.

Consalvo, M. (2003). *It's a queer world after all: Studying the Sims & sexuality*. New York: GLAAD Centre for the Study of Media & Society.

Consalvo, M. (2006). Console video games & global corporations: Creating a hybrid culture. *New Media & Society*, *8*(1), 117–137. doi:10.1177/1461444806059921

Consalvo, M. (2007). *Cheating: Gaining advantage in videogames*. Cambridge, MA: MIT Press.

Consalvo, M. (2008). Crunched by passion: women game developers & workplace challenges. In *Beyond Barbie & Mortal Kombat: New perspectives on gender & gaming* (pp. 177–192). Cambridge, MA: The MIT Press.

Consumer Electronics Association. (2007). *Five tech trends to watch*. Retrieved from http://www.ce.org/PDF/2007–2008_5_Tech_Trends_to_Watch.pdf

Corliss, J. (2011). Introduction: The social science study of video games. *Games and Culture*, *6*(1), 3–16. doi:10.1177/1555412010377323

Corneliussen, H., & Walker Rettberg, J. (Eds.). (2008). *Digital culture, play, & identity a world of warcraft® reader*. Cambridge, MA: MIT Press.

Correll, S. J. (2010). Gender & the career choice process: The role of biased self-assessment. *American Journal of Sociology*, *106*(6), 1691–1730. doi:10.1086/321299

Corrin, L., Lockyer, L., & Bennett, S. (2010). Technological diversity: an investigation of students' technology use in everyday life & academic study. *Learning, Media and Technology*, *35*(4), 387–401. doi:10.1080/17439884.2010.531024

Cotter, D. A., Hermsen, J. A., & Vanneman, R. (2003). The effects of occupational gender segregation across race. *The Sociological Quarterly*, *44*(1), 17–36. doi:10.1111/j.1533-8525.2003.tb02389.x

Crawford, G. (2005). Digital gaming, sport & gender. *Leisure Studies*, *24*(3), 259–270. doi:10.1080/0261436042000290317

Crolla, E., O'Sullivan, H., & Bogg, J. (2011). Gender & medical leadership: Student perceptions & implications for developing future leaders in primary & secondary care - A pilot study. *Journal of Primary Care & Community Health*, *2*(4), 225–228. doi:10.1177/2150131911409413 PMID:23804838

Crompton, R., Dennet, J., & Wigfield, A. (2003). *Organizations, careers & caring*. Retrieved from http://www.jrf.org.uk/sites/files/jrf/n33.pdf

Cross, S., & Bagilhole, B. (2002). Girls' jobs for the boys? Men, masculinity & non-traditional occupations. *Gender, Work and Organization*, *9*(2), 204–226. doi:10.1111/1468-0432.00156

Csikszentmihalyi, M. (1990). *Flow, the psychology of optimal experience*. New York: Harper & Row.

Cunningham, M. (2007). Influences of women's employment on the gendered division of household labor over the life course: Evidence from a 31-year panel study. *Journal of Family Issues, 28*(3), 422–444. doi:10.1177/0192513X06295198 PMID:18458763

Cunningham, S. (2000). Re-inventing the introductory computer graphics course: Providing tools for a wider audience. *Computers & Graphics, 24*(2), 293–296. doi:10.1016/S0097-8493(99)00164-8

D'Amato, A. (2008). Learning orientation, organizational commitment and talent retention across generations: A study of European managers. *Journal of Managerial Psychology, 23*(8), 929–953. doi:10.1108/02683940810904402

Davies, M. (2011). *Women on boards*. Retrieved from http://www.bis.gov.uk/assets/biscore/business-law/docs/w/11-745-women-onboards

Davies, P. G., Spencer, S. J., Quinn, D. M., & Gerhardstein, R. (2002). Consuming images: How television commercials that elicit stereotype threat can restrain women academically & professionally. *Personality and Social Psychology Bulletin, 28*, 1615–1628. doi:10.1177/014616702237644

Davis, F. D. (1989). Perceived usefulness, perceived ease of use, & user acceptance of information technology. *Management Information Systems Quarterly, 13*(3), 319–340. doi:10.2307/249008

Dawson, C. R., Cragg, A., Taylor, C., & Toombs, B. (2007). *Video games*. Retrieved from www.bbfc.co.uk/downloads/pub/Policy%20&%20Research/BBFC%20Video%20Games%20Report.pdf

Day, R., & Allen, T. D. (2004). The relationship between career motivation & self-efficacy with protégé career success. *Journal of Vocational Behavior, 64*, 72–91. doi:10.1016/S0001-8791(03)00036-8

De Castell, S., & Jenson, J. (2006). *You're going to die: Gender, performance & digital gameplay*. Paper presented at the Ninth International Association of Science & Technology for Development Conference on Computers & Advanced Technology in Education. Lima, Peru.

de Freitas, S. I. (2006). Using games & simulations for supporting learning. *Learning, Media and Technology, 31*(4), 343–358. doi:10.1080/17439880601021967

De Lisi, R., & Wolford, J. (2002). Improving children's mental rotation accuracy with computer game playing. *The Journal of Genetic Psychology, 163*, 272–282. doi:10.1080/00221320209598683 PMID:12230149

De Ruijter, E., & Van der Lippe, T. (2007). Effects of job features on domestic outsourcing as a strategy for combining paid & domestic work. *Work and Occupations, 34*(2), 205–230. doi:10.1177/0730888406296510

De Schutter, B. (2010). Never too old to play: The appeal of digital games to an older audience. *Games & Culture: A Journal of Interactive Media*. doi:10.1177/1555412010364978

Deci, E. L., & Ryan, R. M. (1985). *Intrinsic motivation & self determination in human behavior*. New York: Plenum. doi:10.1007/978-1-4899-2271-7

Denner, J., Bean, S., & Martinez, J. (2009). Girl game company: Engaging Latina girls in information technology. *Afterschool Matters, 8*, 26–35.

Denner, J., & Campe, S. (2008). What games made by girls can tell us. In *Beyond Barbie & Mortal Kombat: New perspectives on gender & gaming* (pp. 129–144). Cambridge, MA: The MIT Press.

Deuze, M., Martin, C. B., & Alen, C. (2007). The professional identity of gameworkers. *Convergence: The International Journal of Research into New Media Technologies, 13*(4), 335–353. doi:10.1177/1354856507081947

Devlin, K. (2011). *Mathematical education for a new era: Video games as a medium for learning*. London: AK Peters. doi:10.1201/b10816

DFC. (2004). *DFC intelligence releases new market forecasts for video game industry*. Retrieved from http://www.dfcint.com/news/prsep222004.html

Diamond, C., & Whitehouse, G. (2007). Gender, computing & the organization of working time: Public/private comparisons in the Australian context. *Information Communication and Society, 10*(3), 320–337. doi:10.1080/13691180701409879

Dietz, T. L. (1998). An examination of violence & gender role portrayals in video games: Implications for gender socialization & aggressive behaviour. *Sex Roles*, *38*, 425–442. doi:10.1023/A:1018709905920

Dilchert, S. (2007). Peaks & valleys: Predicting interests in leadership & managerial positions from personality profiles. *International Journal of Selection and Assessment*, *15*(3), 317–334. doi:10.1111/j.1468-2389.2007.00391.x

Dill, K. E., Brown, B. P., & Collins, M. A. (2008). Effects of exposure to sex-stereotyped video game characters on tolerance of sexual harassment. *Journal of Experimental Social Psychology*, *44*, 1402–1408. doi:10.1016/j.jesp.2008.06.002

Dill, K. E., Gentile, D. A., Richter, W. A., & Dill, J. C. (2005). Violence, sex, & age in popular video games: A content analysis. In *Featuring females: Feminist analyses of media* (pp. 115–130). Washington, DC: American Psychological Association. doi:10.1037/11213-008

Dill, K. E., & Thill, K. P. (2007). Video game characters & the socialization of gender roles: Young people's perceptions mirror sexist media depictions. *Sex Roles*, *57*, 851–864. doi:10.1007/s11199-007-9278-1

Divinch, J. (2008). *The Divinich tapes: Females representation in games across genres, consoles.* Academic Press.

Doldor, E., Vinnicombe, S., Gaughan, M., & Sealy, R. (2012). *Gender diversity on boards: The appointment process & the role of executive search firms.* Equality & Human Rights Commission. Retrieved from http://www.equalityhumanrights.com/uploaded_files/research/rr85_final.pdf

Domenico, D. M., & Jones, K. H. (2006). Career aspirations of women in the 20th century. *Journal of Career & Technical Education*, *22*(2), 1–7.

Dovey, J., & Kennedy, H. W. (2006). *Game culture: Computer games as new media.* Berkshire, UK: Open University Press.

Dowley, G. (2011). *Computer games help people with Parkinson's disease, pilot study shows.* Retrieved from http://www.sciencedaily.com/releases/2011/10/111019180024.htm

Downs, E., & Smith, S. (2010). Keeping abreast of hypersexuality: A video game character content analysis. *Sex Roles*, *62*, 721–733. doi:10.1007/s11199-009-9637-1

Drew, E., & Murtagh, E. M. (2005). Work/life balance: Senior management champions or laggards? *Women in Management Review*, *20*(4), 262–278. doi:10.1108/09649420510599089

Ducheneaut, N., Yee, N., Nickel, E., & Moore, R. J. (2006). Building & MMO with mass appeal: A look at gameplay in World of Warcraft. *Games and Culture*, *1*(4), 281–317. doi:10.1177/1555412006292613

Durbin, S. (2011). Creating knowledge through networks: A gender perspective. *Gender, Work and Organization*, *18*, 90–112. doi:10.1111/j.1468-0432.2010.00536.x

Durkin, K., & Barber, B. (2002). Not so doomed: Computer game play & positive adolescent development. *Applied Developmental Psychology*, *23*, 272–392. doi:10.1016/S0193-3973(02)00124-7

Dyer-Whitheford, N., & Sharman, Z. (2005). The political economy of Canada's video & computer game industry. *Canadian Journal of Communication*, *20*, 187–210.

Eachus, P., & Cassidy, S. (2006). Development of the web users self-efficacy scale (WUSE). *Journal of Issues in Informing Science & Information Technology*, *3*, 199–211.

Eagly, A. H. (1987). *Sex differences in social behavior: A social role interpretations.* Hillsdale, NJ: Erlbaum.

Eagly, A. H., & Carli, L. L. (2003). The female leadership advantage: An evaluation of the evidence. *The Leadership Quarterly*, *14*, 807–834. doi:10.1016/j.leaqua.2003.09.004

Eagly, A. H., & Carli, L. L. (2007). Women & the labyrinth of leadership. *Harvard Business Review*, *85*(9), 63–71. PMID:17972496

Eagly, A. H., & Karau, S. J. (2002). Role congruity theory of prejudice toward female leaders. *Psychological Review*, *109*, 573–598. doi:10.1037/0033-295X.109.3.573 PMID:12088246

Eccles, J. (1994). Understanding women's educational & occupational choices. *Psychology of Women Quarterly, 18*, 585–609. doi:10.1111/j.1471-6402.1994.tb01049.x

Eddleston, K. A., Veiga, J. F., & Powell, G. N. (2006). Explaining sex differences in managerial career satisfier preferences: The role of gender self-schema. *The Journal of Applied Psychology, 91*(2), 437–450. doi:10.1037/0021-9010.91.2.437 PMID:16551194

Edge Online. (2009). Retrieved from http://www.edge-online.com/features/gdc-we-need-more-women-games

Egenfeldt-Nielsen, S., Smith, J. H., & Tosca, S. P. (2008). *Understanding video games: The essential introduction*. London: Routledge.

EHRC. (2007). *Gender equality duty: Guidance for public authorities in England March 2007*. London: Equality & Human Rights Commission.

Eklund, L. (2011). Doing gender in cyberspace: the performance of gender by female World of Warcraft players. *Convergence, 17*(3), 323–342.

Ellinger, A. D., Ellinger, A. E., Yang, B., & Howton, S. W. (2002). The relationship between the learning organization concept & firms' financial performance: An empirical assessment. *Human Resource Development Quarterly, 13*, 5–21. doi:10.1002/hrdq.1010

Emes, C. E. (1997). Is Mr Pac Man eating our children? A review of the effects of video games on children. *Canadian Journal of Psychiatry, 42*, 409–414.

England, P., Farkas, G., Kilbourne, B. S., & Dou, T. (1988). Explaining occupational sex segregation & wages: Findings from a model with fixed effects. *American Sociological Review, 53*, 544–558. doi:10.2307/2095848

Entman, R. M., & Rojecki, A. (2011). *The Black image in the White mind: Media & race in America*. Chicago, IL: University of Chicago Press.

Eow, Y. L., Ali, W. Z. B., Mahmud, R. B., & Baki, R. (2009). Form one student's engagement with computer games & its effect on their academic achievement in a Malaysian secondary school. *Computers & Education, 53*(4), 1082–1091. doi:10.1016/j.compedu.2009.05.013

Erfani, M., El-Nasr, M. S., Milam, D., Aghabeigi, B., Lameman, B. A., & Riecke, B. E. et al. (2010). The effect of age, gender, & previous gaming experience on game play performance. *Human-Computer Interaction IFIP Advances in Information & Communication Technology, 332*, 293–296. doi:10.1007/978-3-642-15231-3_33

Ernst, S. B. (1995). Gender issues in books for children & young adults. In *Battling dragons: Issues & controversy in children's literature*. Portsmouth, NH: Heinemann.

ESA. (2001). *State of the industry report 2000-2001*. Entertainment Software Association. Retrieved from http://www.theesa.com/facts/econdata.asp

ESA. (2008). *Essential facts about the computer & videogame industry 2008: Sales, demographics & usage data*. Retrieved from http://www.thesa.com/facts/pdfs/ESA_EF_2008.pdf

ESA. (2010). *Entertainment software association fact sheet*. Retrieved from http://www.theesa.com/facts/gamer_data.php

ESA. (2010). *Sales, demographics & usage: Essential facts about the computer & video games industry*. Retrieved from http://www.theesa.com/facts/pdfs/ESA_Essential_Facts_2010.PDF

ESA. (2011). *Video games & the economy*. Retrieved from http://www.theesa.com/gamesindailylife/economy.pdf

ESA. (2011). *Essential facts about the computer & video game industry*. Retrieved from http://www.theesa.com/facts/pdfs/ESA_EF_About_Games_&_Violence.pdf

ESA. (2011). *Essential facts about games & violence.* Retrieved from http://www.theesa.com/facts/pdfs/ESA_EF_About_Games_&_Violence.pdf

ESA. (2011). *The evolution of mobile games.* Retrieved from http://www.theesa.com/gamesindailylife/mobile_games.pdf

ESA. (2011). *Essential facts about games & violence.* Retrieved from http://www.theesa.com/facts/pdfs/ESA_EF_About_Games_&_Violence.pdf

ESA. (2011). *Video game design influencing art.* Retrieved from http://www.theesa.com/gamedesign-influencingart.pdf

European Commission. (2004). *Widening women's work in information & communication technology.* WWW-ICT. Retrieved from http://www.ftu-namur.org/fichiers/D12-print.pdf

European Commission. (2008). *Women in ICT: Status & the way ahead.* Brussels: European Commission.

Eurostats. (2005). *Comparable time use statistics: National tables from 10 European countries.* European Commission.

Everett, A., & Watkins, S. G. (2008). The power of play: the portrayal & performance of race in video games. In K. Salen (Ed.), *The ecology of games: Connecting youth, games, & learning* (pp. 141–166). Cambridge, MA: The MIT Press.

Fallows, D. (2005). *How women & men use the internet.* Retrieved from http://www.pewInternet.org/pdfs/PIP_Women_&_Men_online.pdf

Faulkner, W. (2001). The technology question in feminism: A view from feminist technology studies. *Women's Studies International Forum, 24*(1), 79–95. doi:10.1016/S0277-5395(00)00166-7

Faulkner, W., & Lie, M. (2007). Gender in the information society: Strategies of inclusion. *Gender, Technology and Development, 11*(2), 157–177. doi:10.1177/097185240701100202

Fawcett Society. (2012). *Fawcett warns of a 'backwards step' on equal pay.* Retrieved from http://fawcettsociety.org.uk/index.asp?PageID=1289

Federation of American Scientists. (2006). *Harnessing the power of video games for learning.* Retrieved from http://www.fas.org/gamesummit/Resources/Summit%20on%20Educational%20Games.pdf

Feiertag, J., & Berge, Z. L. (2008). Training generation N: How educators should approach the net generation. *Education + Training, 50*(6), 457–464. doi:10.1108/00400910810901782

Feldman, D. C., & Ng, T. W. H. (2007). Careers: Mobility, embeddedness, & success. *Journal of Management, 33*(3), 350–377. doi:10.1177/0149206307300815

Felicia, P. (2009). *Digital games in schools: A handbook for teachers.* Retrieved from http://games.eun.org/upload/GIS_HANDBOOK_EN.PDF

Feng, J., Spence, I., & Pratt, J. (2007). Playing an action video game reduces gender differences in spatial cognition. *Psychological Science, 18*(10), 850–855. doi:10.1111/j.1467-9280.2007.01990.x PMID:17894600

Ferguson, C. J. (2007). Evidence for publication bias in video game violence effects literature: A meta-analytic review. *Aggression and Violent Behavior, 12*, 470–482. doi:10.1016/j.avb.2007.01.001

Ferguson, C. J. (2010). Introduction to the special issue on video games. *Review of General Psychology, 14*(2), 66–67. doi:10.1037/a0018940

Ferguson, C. J., Cruz, A. M., & Rueda, S. M. (2008). Gender, video game playing habits and visual memory tasks. *Sex Roles, 58*, 279–286. doi:10.1007/s11199-007-9332-z

Ferguson, C. J., & Kimburn, J. (2009). The public health risks of media violence: A meta-analytic review. *The Journal of Pediatrics, 154*, 759–763. doi:10.1016/j.jpeds.2008.11.033 PMID:19230901

Ferguson, C. J., Rueda, S. M., Cruz, A. M., Ferguson, D. E., Fritz, S., & Smith, S. M. (2008). Violent video games and aggression: Causal relationship or by product of family violence & intrinsic violence motivation? *Criminal Justice and Behavior, 35*, 311. doi:10.1177/0093854807311719

Fertman, C. I., & Chubb, N. H. (1992). The effects of a psychoeducational program on adolescents' activity involvement, self-esteem, & locus of control. *Adolescence, 27*, 517–526. PMID:1414563

Feyerherm, A., & Vick, Y. H. (2005). Generation X women in high technology: Overcoming gender & generational challenges to succeed in the corporate environment. *Career Development International, 10*(3), 216–227. doi:10.1108/13620430510598337

Filiciak, M. (2003). Hyper identities: Postmodern identity patterns in massively multiplayer online role-playing games. In *The video game theory reader*. London: Rouledge.

Flanagan, M. (2000). Navigable narratives: Gender +narrative spatiality in virtual worlds. *Art Journal, 59*(3), 74–85. doi:10.2307/778029

Flanagan, M. (2003). Next level women's digital activism through gaming. In *Digital media revisited: Theoretical & conceptual innovation in digital domains* (pp. 359–388). Cambridge, MA: MIT.

Fletcher, J. (2012). *Sexual harassment in the world of video gaming*. BBC News Magazine.

Forth, J. (2002). The gender pay gap: The research evidence. In *Gender research forum*. London: National Institute of Economic & Social Research.

Fowler, J.L & O'Gorman. (2005). Mentoring functions: A contemporary view of the perceptions of mentees & mentors. *British Journal of Management, 16*, 51–57. doi:10.1111/j.1467-8551.2005.00439.x

Fox, M. (1993). Men who weep, boys who dance: The gender agenda between the lines in children's literature. *Language Arts, 70*(2), 84–88.

Freeman, A. (2007). *London's creative sector working paper 22*. London: GLA. Retrieved from http://www.london.gov.uk/mayor/economic_unit/docs/wp_22_creative.pdf

Fron, J., Fullerton, T., Morie, J. F., & Pearce, C. (2007). *The hegemony of play*. Paper presented at the Situated Play. New York, NY.

Fuegen, K., & Biernat, M. (2002). Re-examining the effects of solo status for women & men. *Personality and Social Psychology Bulletin, 28*, 913–925.

Fullerton, T., Fron, J., Pearce, C., & Morie, J. (2007). Getting girls into the games: Towards a 'virtous cycle. In *Beyond Barbie & Mortal Kombat: New perspectives on gender & computer games*. Cambridge, MA: MIT.

Fullerton, T., Fron, J., Pearce, C., & Morie, J. (2008). Getting girls into the game: Towards a virtous cycle. In *Beyond Barbie & Mortal Kombat: New perspectives on gender & gaming* (pp. 161–176). Cambridge, MA: The MIT Press.

Funk, J. B., & Buchman, D. D. (1996). Playing violent video & computer games & adolescent self-concept. *The Journal of Communication, 46*(2), 19–32. doi:10.1111/j.1460-2466.1996.tb01472.x

Gansmo, H. J., Nordli, H., & Sorensen, K. H. (2003). The gender game: A study of Neregian computer game designers. In *Strategies of inclusion: Gender & the information society: Experiences from private & voluntary sector initiatives* (pp. 139–159). Trondheim, Norway: NTNU.

Gareis, K. C., & Barnett, R. C. (2002). Under what conditions do long hours affect psychological distress: A study of full-time & reduced-hours female doctors. *Work and Occupations, 29*(4), 483–497. doi:10.1177/0730888402029004005

Gaudioso, J. (2003). Magazine names top games suppliers. *Video Store Magazine, 25*(45), 10.

Gee, J. P. (2003). *What video games have to teach us about learning & literacy*. New York: Palgrave Macmillan. doi:10.1145/950566.950595

Gee, J. P. (2005). Learning by design: Good video games as learning machines. *E-Learning & Digital Media, 2*(1), 5–16. doi:10.2304/elea.2005.2.1.5

Gee, J. P. (2007). *Good video games + good learning: Collected essays on video games, learning, & literacy*. New York: Peter Lang.

Gee, J. P., & Hayes, E. (2009). No quitting without saving after bad events: Gaming paradigms & learning in the Sims. *International Journal of Learning and Media*, *1*(3), 1–17. doi:10.1162/ijlm_a_00024

Gelston, S. (2008). *Gen Y, gen X & the baby boomers: Workplace generation wars*. Retrieved from http://www.cio.com

Gentile, D. A., & Anderson, C. A. (2003). Violent video games: The newest media violence hazard. In D. A. Gentile (Ed.), *Media violence & children*. Westport, CT: Praeger Publishing.

Gentile, D. A., Choo, H., Liau, A., Sim, T., Li, D., Fung, D., & Khoo, A. (2011). Pathological video game use among youths: A two-year longitudinal study. *Paediatrics*, *127*(2), e318–e329. doi:10.1542/peds.2010-1353

Gentile, D. A., Yerson, C. A., Yukawa, S., Ihori, N., Saleem, M., & Ming, K. L. et al. (2009). The effects of prosocial video games on prosocial behaviors: International evidence for correlational, longitudinal & experimental studies. *Personality and Social Psychology Bulletin*, *35*, 752–763. doi:10.1177/0146167209333045 PMID:19321812

Gerbner, G., Gross, L., Morgan, M., & Signorielli, N. (1994). *Growing up with television: The cultivation perspective*. Hillsdale, NJ: Lawrence Erlbaum.

Gillespie, R. (2000). When no means no: Disbelief, disregard and deviance as discourses of voluntary childlessness. *Women's Studies International Forum*, *23*(2), 223–234. doi:10.1016/S0277-5395(00)00076-5

Gill, R. (2002). Cool, creative & egalitarian? Exploring gender in project-based new media work in Europe. *Information Communication and Society*, *5*(1), 70–89. doi:10.1080/13691180110117668

Gill, R. (2007). *Technobohemians or the new cybertariat? New media workers in Amsterdam a decade after the web*. Amsterdam: The Institute of Network Cultures.

Gist, M. E., & Mitchell, T. R. (1992). Self-efficacy: A theoretical analysis of its determinants & malleability. *Academy of Management Review*, *17*, 183–211.

Goode, J., Estrella, R., & Margolis, J. (2006). Lost in translation: Gender & high school computer science. In J. M. Cohoon, & W. Aspray (Eds.), *Women in IT: Reasons on the underrepresentation* (pp. 89–114). Cambridge, MA: The MIT Press. doi:10.7551/mitpress/9780262033459.003.0003

Gordon, M., & Denisi, A. (1995). A re-examination of the relationship between union membership & job satisfaction. *Industrial & Labor Relations Review*, *48*, 222–236. doi:10.2307/2524484

Gorriz, C. M., & Medina, C. (2000). Engaging girls with computers through software games. *Communications of the ACM*, *43*, 42–49. doi:10.1145/323830.323843

Gottfredson, G. D., & Duffy, R. D. (2008). Using a theory of vocational personalities & work environments to explore subjective well-being. *Journal of Career Assessment*, *16*(1), 44–59. doi:10.1177/1069072707309609

Gourdin, A. (2005). *Game developers demographics: An exploration of workforce diversity*. International Game Developers Association. Retrieved from http://archives.igda.org/diversity/IGDA_DeveloperDemographics_Oct05.pdf

Graner Ray, S. (2004). *Gender inclusive game design: Expanding the market*. Cambridge, MA: Charles River Media Inc.

Greene, A. L., & Wheatley, S. M. (1992). I've got a lot to do & I don't think I'll have the time: Gender differences in late adolescents' narratives of the future. *Journal of Youth and Adolescence*, *21*, 667–686. doi:10.1007/BF01538738

Greenhaus, J. H., & Powell, G. N. (2003). When work & family collide: Deciding between competing role demands. *Organizational Behavior and Human Decision Processes*, *90*, 291–303. doi:10.1016/S0749-5978(02)00519-8

Green, L., Miles, I., & Rutter, J. (2007). *Hidden innovations in the creative sectors*. Manchester, UK: Manchester Institute for Innovation Research.

Green, S., & Bavelier, D. (2003). Action video game modifies visual selective attention. *Nature*, *423*, 534–537. doi:10.1038/nature01647 PMID:12774121

Green, S., & Bavelier, D. (2006). Enumeration versus multiple object tracking: The case of action video game players. *Cognition*, *101*, 217–245. doi:10.1016/j.cognition.2005.10.004 PMID:16359652

Greitemeyer, T. (2011). Effects of prosocial media on social behavior: When & why does media exposure affect helping & aggression? *Current Directions in Psychological Science*, *20*(4), 251–255. doi:10.1177/0963721411415229

Greitemeyer, T., & Osswald, S. (2009). Prosocial video games reduce aggressive cognitions. *Journal of Experimental Social Psychology*, *45*, 896–900. doi:10.1016/j.jesp.2009.04.005

Greitemeyer, T., & Osswald, S. (2010). Effects of prosocial video games on prosocial behavior. *Journal of Personality and Social Psychology*, *98*(2), 211–221. doi:10.1037/a0016997 PMID:20085396

Greitemeyer, T., Osswald, S., & Brauer, M. (2010). Playing prosocial video games increases empathy & decreases schadenfreude. *Emotion (Washington, D.C.)*, *10*(6), 796–802. doi:10.1037/a0020194 PMID:21171755

Griffiths, M. (2002). The educational benefits of video games. *Education for Health*, *20*(3), 47–51.

Grimley, M., Green, R., Nilsen, T., Thompson, D., & Tomes, R. (2011). Using computer games for instruction: The student experience. *Active Learning in Higher Education*, *12*(1), 45–56. doi:10.1177/1469787410387733

Grusec, J. E., & Lytton, H. (1988). *Social development: History, theory, & research*. New York: Springer-Verlag.

Gupta, V. K., & Bhawe, N. M. (2007). The influence of proactive personality & stereotype threat on women's entrepreneurial intentions. *Journal of Leadership & Organizational Studies*, *13*(4), 73–85. doi:10.1177/1 0717919070130040901

Gursoy, D., Maier, T. A., & Chi, C. G. (2008). Generational differences: An examination of work values and generation gaps in the hospitality workforce. *International Journal of Hospitality Management*, *27*, 448–458. doi:10.1016/j.ijhm.2007.11.002

Gushue, G. V., & Whitson, M. L. (2006). The relationship of ethnic identity & gender role attitudes to the development of career choice goals among Black & Latina girls. *Journal of Counseling Psychology*, *53*(3), 379–385. doi:10.1037/0022-0167.53.3.379

Haines, L. (2004). *Why are there so few women in games?* Research for Media Training North West September. Retrieved from http://archives.igda.org/women/MTNW_Women-in-Games_Sep04.pdf

Haninger, K., & Thompson, K. M. (2004). Content & ratings of teen-rated video games. *Journal of the American Medical Association*, *291*, 856–865. doi:10.1001/jama.291.7.856 PMID:14970065

Hannover, B., & Kessels, U. (2004). Self-to-prototype matching as a strategy for making academic choices: Why high school students do not like maths & science. *Learning and Instruction*, *14*, 51–67. doi:10.1016/j.learninstruc.2003.10.002

Hargittai, E., & Shafer, S. (2006). Differences in actual and perceived online skills: The role of gender. *Social Science Quarterly*, *87*(2), 432–448. doi:10.1111/j.1540-6237.2006.00389.x

Harper, E. P., Baldwin, R. G., Gansneder, B. G., & Chronister, J. L. (2001). Full-time women faculty off the tenure track: Profile & practice. *Review of Higher Education*, *24*, 237–257. doi:10.1353/rhe.2001.0003

Harries, R., & Wilkinson, M. A. (2004). Situating gender: students' perceptions of information work. *Information Technology & People*, *17*(1), 71–86. doi:10.1108/09593840410522189

Harris, J. (2001). *The effect of computer games on young children -A review of the research*. London: Home Office Research, Development & Statistics Directorate. doi:10.1037/e668282007-001

Harrison, B. G., Guy, R. F., & Lupfer, S. L. (1981). Locus of control & self-esteem as correlates of role orientation in traditional & n-traditional women. *Sex Roles*, *7*, 1175–1187. doi:10.1007/BF00287969

Hartmann, T., & Klimmt, C. (2006). Gender & computer games: Exploring females' dislikes. *Journal of Computer-Mediated Communication*, *11*, 910–931. doi:10.1111/j.1083-6101.2006.00301.x

Harvey, A. (2011). Constituting the player: Feminist techno science, gender, & digital play. *International Journal of Gender. Science & Technology*, *3*(1), 170–184.

Hatton, E., & Trautner, M. N. (2011). Equal opportunity objectification? The sexualisation of men & women on the cover of Rolling Stone. *Sexuality & Culture*, *15*, 256–278. doi:10.1007/s12119-011-9093-2

Hayden, J. (2006). Mentoring: Help with climbing the career ladder. *Health Promotion Practice*, *7*(3), 289–292. doi:10.1177/1524839906289269 PMID:16760239

Hayes, E. (2007). Gendered identities at play: Case studies of two women playing Morrowind. *Games and Culture*, *2*(1), 23–48. doi:10.1177/1555412006294768

Hayes, E. (2011). The Sims as a catalyst for girls' IT learning. *International Journal of Gender. Science & Technology*, *3*(1), 121–147.

Heeks, R. (2008). *Current analysis & future research agenda on 'gold framing'*. Retrieved from http://www.sed.manchester.ac.uk/idpm/research/publications/wp/di/di_wp32.htm: University of Manchester.

Heeter, C., Egidio, R., Mishra, P., Winn, B., & Winn, J. (2009). Alien games: Do girls prefer games designed by girls? *Games and Culture*, *4*(1), 74–100. doi:10.1177/1555412008325481

Hegewisch, A., Liepmann, H., Hayes, J., & Hartmann, H. (2010). *Separate & not equal? Gender segregation in the labor market & the gender wage gap*. Washington, DC: Institute for Women's Policy Research. doi:10.1037/e686432011-001

Heilman, M. E. (1983). Sex bias in work settings: The lack of fit model. *Research in Organizational Behavior*, *5*, 269–298.

Heilman, M. E. (2001). Description & prescription: How gender stereotypes prevent women's ascent up the organizational ladder. *The Journal of Social Issues*, *57*, 657–674. doi:10.1111/0022-4537.00234

Heilman, M. E., & Okimoto, T. G. (2007). Why are women penalized for success at male tasks? The implied communality deficit. *The Journal of Applied Psychology*, *92*, 81–92. doi:10.1037/0021-9010.92.1.81 PMID:17227153

Heilman, M. E., Wallen, A. S., Fuchs, D., & Tamkins, M. M. (2004). Penalties for success: Reactions to women who succeed at male gender-typed tasks. *The Journal of Applied Psychology*, *89*, 416–427. doi:10.1037/0021-9010.89.3.416 PMID:15161402

HERA. (2009). *Selection of staff for inclusion in RAE2008*. Retrieved from http://www.hefce.ac.uk/media/hefce1/pubs/hefce/2009/0934/09_34.pdf

Hetty Van Emmerik, I. J., Euwema, M. C., Geschiere, M., & Schouten, M. F. A. G. (2006). Networking your way through the organization: Gender differences in the relationship between network participation & career satisfaction. *Women in Management Review*, *21*(1), 54–66. doi:10.1108/09649420610643411

Hirshfield, L. E. (2010). She won't make me feel dumb: Identity threat in a male-dominated discipline. *International Journal of Gender. Science & Technology*, *2*(1), 6–24.

Hoffmann, L. (2009). Learning through games. *Communications of the ACM*, *52*, 21–22. doi:10.1145/1536616.1536624

Hogg, M. A., & Cooper, J. (2003). *The SAGE handbook of social psychology*. New Delhi: Sage.

Hogue, M., DuBois, L. Z., & Fox-Cardamone, L. (2010). Gender differences in pay expectations: The role of job intention & self-view. *Psychology of Women Quarterly*, *34*, 215–227. doi:10.1111/j.1471-6402.2010.01563.x

Holt, C. L., & Ellis, J. B. (1998). Assessing the current validity of the bem sex-role inventory. *Sex Roles*, *39*(11/12), 929–941. doi:10.1023/A:1018836923919

Hoppes, S., Hally, C., & Sewell, L. (2000). An interest inventory of games for older adults. *Physical & Occupational Therapy in Geriatrics*, *18*(2), 71–83. doi:10.1080/J148v18n02_05

Hosein, A., Ramanau, R., & Jones, C. (2010). Learning & living technologies: A longitudinal study of first-year students' frequency & competence in the use of ICT. *Learning, Media and Technology*, 35(4), 403–418. doi:10.1080/17439884.2010.529913

Huh, S., & Williams, D. (2010). Dude looks like a lady: Gender swapping in an online game. In W. S. Bainbridge (Ed.), *Online worlds: Convergence of the real & virtual, human-computer interaction series* (pp. 161–174). London: Springer-Verlag. doi:10.1007/978-1-84882-825-4_13

Huizinga, J. (1955). *Homo ludens: A study of the play-element in culture*. Boston: BeaconPress.

Hultin, M. (2003). Some take the glass escalator, some hit the glass ceiling? Career consequences of occupational sex segregation. *Work and Occupations*, 30(1), 30–61. doi:10.1177/0730888402239326

Hyman, J., Scholarios, D., & Baldry, C. (2005). Getting on or getting by? Employee flexibility & coping strategies for home & work. *Work, Employment and Society*, 19(4), 705–725. doi:10.1177/0950017005058055

Hyman, J., & Summers, J. (2003). Lacking balance? Work-life employment practices in the modern economy. *Personnel Review*, 33(4), 418–429. doi:10.1108/00483480410539498

Ibarra, H. (1993). Personal networks of women & minorities in management: A conceptual framework. *Academy of Management Review*, 18(1), 56–87.

IBISWord. (2008). Retrieved from http://www.ibisworld.com/pressrelease/pressrelease.aspx?prid=133

IGDA. (2004). *Quality of life white paper*. International Game Developers Association.

Ilies, R., & Judge, T. A. (2004). An experience-sampling measure of job satisfaction & its relationships with affectivity, mood at work, job beliefs, & general job satisfaction. *European Journal of Work and Organizational Psychology*, 13(3), 367–389. doi:10.1080/13594320444000137

ILM. (2011). *Ambition & gender at work*. Institute of Leadership & Management. Retrieved from www.i-l-m.com

Innstrand, S. T., Langballe, E. M., Falkum, E., Espnes, G. A., & Aasland, O. G. (2009). Gender-specific perceptions of four dimensions of the work/family interaction. *Journal of Career Assessment*, 17(4), 402–416. doi:10.1177/1069072709334238

Ivory, J. D. (2006). Still a man's game: Gender representation in online reviews of video games. *Mass Communication & Society*, 9(1), 103–114. doi:10.1207/s15327825mcs0901_6

Ivory, J. D., & Kalanaraman, S. (2007). The effects of technological advancement & violent content in video games on player's feelings of presence, involvement, physiological arousal, & aggression. *The Journal of Communication*, 57, 532–555. doi:10.1111/j.1460-2466.2007.00356.x

Jackson, L. A., Witt, E. A., Games, A. I., Fitzgerald, H. E., von Eye, A., & Zhao, Y. (2011). Information technology use & creativity: Findings from the children & technology project. *Computers in Human Behavior*. doi: doi:10.1016/j.chb.2011.10.006

James, K., & Cardador, J. (2007). Cognitions about technology & science: A measure & its relevance to career decisions. *Journal of Career Assessment*, 15(4), 463–482. doi:10.1177/1069072707305766

Jansz, J., Avis, C., & Vosmeer, M. (2010). Playing the Sims2: An exploration of gender differences in players' motivations & patterns of play. *New Media & Society*, 12(2), 235–251. doi:10.1177/1461444809342267

Jansz, J., & Martis, R. G. (2007). The Laura phenomenon: Powerful female characters in video games. *Sex Roles*, 56, 141–148. doi:10.1007/s11199-006-9158-0

Jenkins, H. (2000, September). *Art form for the digital age*. Retrieved from http://www.geocities.com/lgartclass/h&outs/ArtfortheDigitalAge/ArtFormfortheDigitalAge.html

Jenkins, H. (2001). *From Barbie to Mortal Kombat: Further reflections*. Retrieved from http://culturalpolicy.uchicago.edu/papers/2001-video-games/jenkins.html

Jenkins, H. (2006). *Reality bites: Eight myths about video games debunked*. Retrieved from http://www.pbs.org/kcts/videogamerevolution/impact/myths.html

Jenkins, H. (1999). Voices from the combat zone: Game grrlz talk back. In *From Barbie to Mortal Kombat: Gender & computer games*. Cambridge, MA: MIT Press.

Jenkins, H. (2006). *Fans, bloggers, and gamers: Exploring participatory culture*. New York: NYU Press.

Jenson, J., de Castell, S., & Bryson, M. (2003). Girl talk: Gender, equity & identity discourses in a school-based computer culture. *Women's Studies International Forum, 26*(6), 561–573.

Jenson, J., & deCastell, S. (2010). Gender, simulation, & gaming: Research review & redirections. *Simulation & Gaming, 41*(1), 51–71. doi:10.1177/1046878109353473

Jenson, J., & deCastell, S. (2011). Girls@play. *Feminist Media Studies*. doi:10.1080/14680777.2010.521625

Jin, D. Y., & Chee, F. (2008). Age of new media empires: A critical interpretation of the Korean online game industry. *Games and Culture, 3*(1), 38–58. doi:10.1177/1555412007309528

Johns, J. (2006). Video games production networks: Value capture, power relations & embeddedness. *Journal of Economic Geography, 6*, 151–180. doi:10.1093/jeg/lbi001

Joiner, R., Brosnan, M., Duffield, J., Gavin, J., & Maras, P. (2007). The relationship between internet identification, internet anxiety & Internet use. *Computers in Human Behavior, 23*, 1408–1420. doi:10.1016/j.chb.2005.03.002

Joiner, R., Gavin, J., Duffield, J., Brosnan, M., Crook, C., & Durndell, A. et al. (2005). Gender, internet identification & internet anxiety: Correlates of internet use. *Cyberpsychology & Behavior, 8*(4), 371–378. doi:10.1089/cpb.2005.8.371 PMID:16092894

Jones, J. (2009). Video games help music & math education. *Convergence*. Retried from http://www.convergemag.com/edtech/Video-Games-Music-Math-Education.html

Jones, S. (2003). *Let the games begin: Gaming technology & entertainment amongst college students*. Retrieved from http://www.pewInternet.org/PPF/r/93/report_display.asp

Joy, L., Carter, N., Wagner, H. M., & Narayanan, S. (2012). *The bottom line: Corporate performance & women's representation on boards*. Retrieved from www.catalyst.org/file/139/bottom%20line%202.pdf

Judge, T. A., Locke, E. A., & Durham, C. C. (1997). The dispositional causes of job satisfaction: A core evaluation approach. *Research in Organizational Behavior, 19*, 151–188.

Juul, J. (2010). *A casual revolution: Reinventing video games & their players*. London: MIT Press.

Kafai, Y. (1999). Video game designs by girls & boys: Variability & consistency of gender differences. In M. Kinder (Ed.), *Kids' media culture* (pp. 293–315). Durham, NC: Duke University Press.

Kafai, Y. B. (2006). Playing & making games for learning: Instructionist & constructionist perspectives for games studies. *Games and Culture, 1*(1), 36–40. doi:10.1177/1555412005281767

Kafai, Y. B. (2009). Serious games for girls? Considering gender in learning with digital games. In U. Ritterfield, M. Cody, & P. Vorderer (Eds.), *Serious games mechanisms & effects* (pp. 221–235). London: Routledge.

Kafai, Y. B., Heeter, C., Denner, J., & Sun, J. Y. (2008). *Beyond Barbie and Mortal Kombat: New perspectives on gender and gaming*. Cambridge, MA: MIT Press.

Kambouri, M., Thomas, S., & Mellar, H. (2006). Playing the literacy game: A case study in adult education. *Learning, Media and Technology, 31*(4), 395–410. doi:10.1080/17439880601022015

Kanter, R. (1977). *Men & women of the corporation*. New York: Basic Books.

Karpowitz, C. F., Mendelberg, T., & Shaker, L. (2012). Gender inequality in deliberative participation. *The American Political Science Review, 106*(3), 533. doi:10.1017/S0003055412000329

Kato, P. M. (2010). Video games in health care: Closing the gap. *Review of General Psychology, 14*(2), 113–121. doi:10.1037/a0019441

Kato, P. M., & Beale, I. L. (2006). Factors affecting acceptability to young cancer patients of a psychoeducational video game about cancer. *Journal of Paediatric Oncology, 23*(5), 269–275. doi:10.1177/1043454206289780 PMID:16902082

Kelan, E. K. (2007). Tools & toys: Communicating gendered positions towards technology. *Information Communication and Society, 10*(3), 358–383. doi:10.1080/13691180701409960

Kelleher, C. (2008). Using storytelling to introduce girls to computer programming. In *Beyond Barbie & Mortal Kombat: New perspectives in gender, games & computing*. Boston: MIT Press.

Kellner, D. (2003). *Technological transformation, multiple literacies, & the re-visioning of education.* Retrieved from http://www.gseis.ucla.edu/faculty/kellner/essays.html

Kelly, D. M., Pomerantz, S., & Currie, D. H. (2006). No boundaries? Girls' interactive, online learning about femininities. *Youth & Society, 38*(1), 3–28. doi:10.1177/0044118X05283482

Kennedy, H. W. (2002). Lara Croft: Feminist icon or cyberbimbo? On the limits of textual analysis. *Game Studies. The International Journal of Computer Game Research, 2*(2).

Kennedy, T., Wellman, B., & Clement, K. (2003). Gendering the digital divide. *IT & Society, 1*(5), 72–96.

Kerr, A. (2006). *The business & culture of digital games: Gamework/gameplay.* London: Sage.

Khaleeli, H. (2012). *Will a woman ever run the BBC?* Retrieved from http://www.guardian.co.uk/comment-isfree/2012/sep/28/will-a-woman-ever-run-bbc

Kidd, J. M., & Green, F. (2006). The careers of research scientists: Predicators of three dimensions career commitment & intention to leave science. *Personnel Review, 35*(3), 229–251. doi:10.1108/00483480610656676

Kim, H. (2009). Women's games in Japan: Gendered identity & narrative construction. *Theory, Culture & Society, 26*(2-3), 165–188. doi:10.1177/0263276409103132

Kirkwood, A., & Price, L. (2005). Learners & learning in the twenty-first century: What do we know about students' attitudes towards & experiences of information & communication technologies that will help us design courses? *Studies in Higher Education, 30*(3), 257–274. doi:10.1080/03075070500095689

Kirriernuir, J., & McFarlane, A. (2006). *Literature review in games & learning.* Retrieved from www.futurelab.org.uk

Klawe, M. M. (2005). *Increasing the number of women majoring in CS: What works?* Paper presented at ACM SIGCSE 2005 Symposium. St. Louis, MO. Retrieved from www.princeton.edu/seasWeb/dean/Klawe/SIGCSE 2005.pdf

Kline, S., Dyer-Witheford, N., & de Peuter, G. (2003). *Digital play: The interaction of technology, culture & marketing.* Montreal, Canada: McGill-Queen's University Press.

Knights, D., & Richards, W. (2003). Sex discrimination in UK academia. *Gender, Work and Organization, 10*(2), 213–238. doi:10.1111/1468-0432.t01-1-00012

Kodz, J., Davis, S., Lain, D., Strebler, M., Rick, J., Bates, P., et al. (2002). *Work-life balance: Beyond the rhetoric. institute of employment studies, report 384.* Retrieved from http://www.employment-studies.co.uk/summary/summary.php?id=384

Kodz, J., Harper, H., & Dench, S. (2008). *Work-life balance: Beyond the rhetoric.* Institute of Employment Studies.

Koh, E., Kin, Y. G., Wadhwa, B., & Lim, J. (2012). Teacher perceptions of games in Singapore schools. *Simulation & Gaming, 43*(1), 51–66. doi:10.1177/1046878111401839

Konijn, E. A., & Nije Bijvank, M. (2009). Doors to another me: Identity construction through digital game play. In U. Ritterfield, M. Cody, & P. Vorderer (Eds.), *Serious games mechanisms & effects* (pp. 167–179). London: Routledge.

Konings, K. D., Br-Gruwel, S., & van Merrienboer, J. J. G. (2005). Towards more powerful learning environments through combining the perspectives of designers, teachers, & students. *The British Journal of Educational Psychology*, 75(4), 645–660. doi:10.1348/000709905X43616 PMID:16318683

Korman, A. K. (1966). Self-esteem variable in vocational choice. *The Journal of Applied Psychology*, 50, 479–486. doi:10.1037/h0024039 PMID:5978041

Kotamraju, N. (2002). Keeping up: Web design skill & the reinvented worker. *Information Communication and Society*, 5(1), 1–26. doi:10.1080/13691180110117631

Kovacevic, I., Minovic, M., de Pablos, P. O., & Starcevic, D. (2012). Motivational aspects of different learning contexts: my mom won't let me play this game..... *Computers in Human Behavior*. doi: doi:10.1016/j.chb.2012.01.023 PMID:22393270

Kram, K. E. (1985). *Mentoring at work: Developmental relationships in organizational life*. Glenview, IL: Scott Foresman.

Kron, F. W., Gjerde, G.L., & Sen, A., & Fetters. (2010). Medical students attitudes toward video games & related new media technologies in medical education. *BMC Medical Education*, 10(50), 1–11. PMID:20074350

Krotoski, A. (2004). *Chicks & joysticks: An exploration of women & gaming* (White paper). Entertainment & Leisure Software Publishers Association (ELSPA).

Krotoski, A. (2005). Socialising, subversion & the self: Why women flock to massively multiplayer online role playing games. In N. Garrelts (Ed.), *Digital gameplay: Essays on the nexus of game & gamer*. Jefferson, NC: McFarland Press.

Kupperschmidt, B. R. (2000). Multigeneration employees: Strategies for effective management. *The Health Care Manager*, 19(1), 65–76. doi:10.1097/00126450-200019010-00011 PMID:11183655

Kutnet, L. A., Olson, C. K., Warner, D. E., & Hertozog, S. M. (2008). Parents' & sons' perspectives on video game play: A qualitative study. *Journal of Adolescent Research*, 23(1), 76–96. doi:10.1177/0743558407310721

Lam, S. K., Uduwage, A., Dong, Z., Sen, S., Musicant, D. R., Terveen, L., & Ridel, J. (2011). *WP:Clubhouse? An exploration of Wikipedia's gender imbalance*. Paper presented at WikiSym 2011, Mountain View, CA.

Latham, G. P., & Pinder, C. C. (2005). Work motivation theory & research at the dawn of the twenty-first century. *Annual Review of Psychology*, 56, 485–516. doi:10.1146/annurev.psych.55.090902.142105 PMID:15709944

Lauver, K., & Kristof-Brown, A. (2001). Distinguishing between employees' perceptions of person-job & person-organization fit. *Journal of Vocational Behavior*, 59, 454–470. doi:10.1006/jvbe.2001.1807

Leary, M. R., & Baunmeister, R. (2000). The nature & function of self-esteem: Sociometer theory. In *Advances if experimental social psychology*. San Diego, CA: Academic Press. doi:10.1016/S0065-2601(00)80003-9

Lee, D. (2011). UK 'must act to solve games industry brain drain'. *BBC News Technology*. Retrieved from http://www.bbc.co.uk/newstechnology-15188385?

Lee, Y.-H., & Lin, H. (2011). Gaming is my work: Identity work in Internet-hobbyist game workers. *Work, Employment and Society*, 25(3), 451–467. doi:10.1177/0950017011407975

Lenhart, A., Kahne, J., Middaugh, E., Macgill, A. R., Evans, C., & Vitak, J. (2008). *Teens, video games, & civics*. Pew Internet & American Life Project. Retrieved from http://www.pewInternet.org/Reports/2008/Teens-Video-Games-&-Civics.aspx

Lent, R. W., Brown, S. D., & Hackett, G. (1994). Toward a unifying social cognitive theory of career & academic interest, choice & performance. *Journal of Vocational Behavior*, 45, 79–122. doi:10.1006/jvbe.1994.1027

Leonard, D. J. (2006). Not a hater, just keepin' it real: The importance of race-& gender-based games studies. *Games and Culture*, 1(1), 83–88. doi:10.1177/1555412005281910

Leonard, D. J. (2009). Young, black (& brown) & don't give a fuck: Virtual gangstas in the era of state violence. *Cultural Studies. Critical Methodologies*, 9, 248–272. doi:10.1177/1532708608325938

Lepper, M., & Greene, D. (1978). Over justification research & beyond: Toward a means-ends analysis of intrinsic & extrinsic motivation. In *The hidden costs of reward*. Hillsdale, NJ: Erlbaum.

Lerman, N. E., Oldenziel, R., & Mohun, A. P. (2003). *Gender and technology: A reader*. Baltimore, MD: John Hopkins University Press.

Leupold, T. (2006). Is there room for 'gaymers' in the gaming industry? *Oakland Tribune*. Retrieved from http://findarticles.com/p/aticles/mi_qn4176/is_20060407/ai_n16142589/

Lieberman, D. (2006). What can we learn from playing interactive games? In P. Vorderer, & J. Bryant (Eds.), *Playing video games: Motives, responses, & consequences* (pp. 379–397). Mahwah, NJ: Elbaum.

Lie, M. (2003). *He, she and IT revisited: New perspectives on gender and the information society*. Oslo, Norway: Gyldenhal Akademisk.

Lin, H. (2005). *Gendered gaming experience in social space: From home to Internet cafe*. Paper presented at the Changing Views - Worlds in Play. New York, NY.

Lincoln, A. E., Pincus, S., Koster, J. B., & Leboy, P. S. (2012). The Matilda effect in science: Awards & prizes in the US, 1990s & 2000s. *Social Studies of Science, 42*(2), 307. doi:10.1177/0306312711435830 PMID:22849001

Linehan, M. (2001). Networking for female managers career development. *Journal of Management Development, 20*(10), 823–829. doi:10.1108/EUM0000000006237

Lipinska-Grobelny, A. (2008). Masculinity, femininity, androgyny & work stress. *Medycyna Pracy, 59*(6), 453–460. PMID:19388459

Lipinska-Grobelny, A., & Wasiak, K. (2010). Job satisfaction & gender identity of women managers & non-managers. *International Journal of Occupational Medicine and Environmental Health, 23*(2), 161–166. doi:10.2478/v10001-010-0015-6 PMID:20630833

Lockwood, P. (2006). Someone like me can be successful: Do college students need same-gender role models? *Psychology of Women Quarterly, 30*, 36–46. doi:10.1111/j.1471-6402.2006.00260.x

Long, B. C. (1989). Sex-role orientation, coping strategies, & self-efficacy of women in traditional & non traditional occupations. *Psychology of Women Quarterly, 13*, 307–324. doi:10.1111/j.1471-6402.1989.tb01004.x

Lovejoy, M., & Stone, P. (2011). Opting back In the influence of time at home on professional women's career redirection after opting out. *Gender, Work and Organization*, 1–23.

Lubinski, D., & Benbow, C. P. (2006). Study of mathematically precocious youth after 35 years: Uncovering antecedents for the development of math-science expertise. *Perspectives on Psychological Science, 1*, 316–345. doi:10.1111/j.1745-6916.2006.00019.x

Lucas, K., & Sherry, J. L. (2004). Sex differences in video game play: A communication-based explanation. *Communication Research, 31*, 499–523. doi:10.1177/0093650204267930

Lupton, B. (2000). Maintaining masculinity: men who do 'women's work'. *British Journal of Management, 11*, 33–48. doi:10.1111/1467-8551.11.s1.4

Lynch-Sauer, J., VenBosch, T.M., Kron, F., Livingston Gjerde, G., Arato, N., Sen, A., & Fetters, M.D. (2011). Nursing students' attitudes toward video games & related new media technologies. *The Journal of Nursing Education, 50*, 1–11. doi:10.3928/01484834-20110531-04 PMID:21627050

Lyon, D., & Woodward, A. E. (2004). Gender & time at the top cultural constructions of time in high-level careers & homes. *European Journal of Women's Studies, 11*(2), 205–221. doi:10.1177/1350506804042096

MacCallum-Stewart, E. (2008). Real boys carry girly epics: Normalising gender bending in online games. *Eludamos Journal for Computer Game Culture, 2*(1), 27–40.

Mai, P. (2010). *The highest & lowest grossing video game-based movies.* Retrieved from http://blogs.ocweekly.com/heardmentality/2010/07/hollywoods_lowest_grossing_vid.php

Malone, T. (1981). Toward a theory of intrinsically motivating instruction. *Cognitive Science, 4,* 333–369. doi:10.1207/s15516709cog0504_2

Martins, N., Williams, D. C., Harrison, K., & Ratan, R. A. (2009). A content analysis of female body imagery in video games. *Sex Roles, 61,* 824–836. doi:10.1007/s11199-009-9682-9

Martis, R. G., & Jansz, J. (2004). *The representation of gender & ethnicity in digital interactive games.* Paper presented at the International Communication Association. New Orleans, LA.

Mastro, D. E., Behm-Morawitz, E., & Kopacz, M. A. (2008). Exposure to television portrayals of Latinos: The implications of aversive racism & social identity theory. *Human Communication Research, 34,* 1–27. doi:10.1111/j.1468-2958.2007.00311.x

Matthews, M. (2009). *Exclusive: U.S. year-to-date console top 5s reveal 2009's victors so far.* Retrieved from www.gamasutra.com/phpbin/news_index.php?story=24481

Mayrhofer, W., Steyrer, J., Meyer, M., Strunk, G., Schiffinger, M., & Iellatchitch, A. (2005). Graduates career aspirations & individual characteristics. *Human Resource Management Journal, 15*(1), 38–56. doi:10.1111/j.1748-8583.2005.tb00139.x

Mazman, S. G., & Usluel, Y. K. (2011). Gender differences in using social networks. *The Turkish Online Journal of Educational Technology, 10*(2), 133–139.

McCabe, J., Fairchild, E., Grauerholz, L., Pescosolido, B. A., & Tope, D. (2011). Titles & central characters gender in twentieth-century children's books: Patterns of disparity in titles & central characters. *Gender & Society, 25,* 197. doi:10.1177/0891243211398358

McCarthy, H. (2004). *Girlfriends in high places: How women's networks are changing the workplace.* London: Demos.

McFarlane, A., Sparrowhawk, A., & Heald, Y. (2002). *Report on the educational use of games.* Retrieved from http://www.teem.org.uk/publications/teem_games_ined_full.pdf

McGonigal, J. (2011). *Reality is broken: Why games make us better & how they can change the world.* New York: Penguin Press.

McGuire, G. M. (2000). Gender, race, ethnicity & networks: The factors affecting the status of employees network members. *Work and Occupations, 27*(4), 501–523. doi:10.1177/0730888400027004004

McKinsey. (2012). *Women matter report, 2012.* Retrieved from http://www.mckinsey.com/features/women_matter

McRobbie, A. (1998). *British fashion design: Rag trade or image industry?* London: Routledge. doi:10.4324/9780203168011

MCV. (2008). *Salary survey.* Retrieved from http://www.mcvuk.com/news/29399/Industry-salary-survey

MCV. (2009). *Women earn more than men in the UK games industry.* Retrieved from http://www.mcvuk.com/news/32964/Women-earn-more-than-men-in-the-UK-games-industry

Mead, G. H. (1934). *Mind, self & society.* Chicago: University of Chicago Press.

Meager, N., Anxo, D., Gineste, S., Trinczek, R., & Pamer, S. (2003). *Working long hours: A review of the evidence.* Retrieved from http://www.dti.gov.uk/er/emar/errs16vol1.pdf

Mercier, E. M., Barron, B., & O'Connor, K. M. (2006). Images of self & others as computer users: The role of gender & experience. *Journal of Computer Assisted Learning, 22,* 335–348. doi:10.1111/j.1365-2729.2006.00182.x

Michie, S., & Nelson, D. L. (2006). Barriers women face in information technology careers: Self-efficacy, passion & gender biases. *Women in Management Review, 21*(1), 10–27. doi:10.1108/09649420610643385

Miller, L., Neathey, F., Pollard, E., & Hill, D. (2004). *Occupational segregation, gender gaps & skill gaps.* Equal Opportunities Commission.

Miller, M., & Summers, A. (2007). Gender differences in video game characters' roles, appearances, & attire as portrayed in video game magazines. *Sex Roles, 57,* 733–742. doi:10.1007/s11199-007-9307-0

Millwood Hargrave, A., & Livingstone, S. (2007). *Ofcom's submission to the Byron review.* Retrieved from http://stakeholders.ofcom.org.uk/binaries/research/telecoms-research/annex6.pdf

MMOGchart. (2008). *Total MMOG active subscription.* Retrieved from http://massively.joystiq.com/2008/02/14/mmog-charts-updated-wow-keeps-its-huge-lead/

Moreno-Ger, P., Burgos, D., & Martines-Ortiz, I. (2008). Educational game design for online education. *Computers in Human Behavior, 24,* 2530–2540. doi:10.1016/j.chb.2008.03.012

Morrison, T. G., Kalin, R., & Morrison, M. A. (2004). Body-image evaluation & image investment among adolescents: A test of sociocultural & social comparison theories. *Adolescence, 39,* 571–592. PMID:15673231

Moss-Racusin, C. A., Dovidio, J. F., Brescoll, V. L., Graham, M. J., & Handelsman, J. (2012). Science faculty's subtle gender biases favour male students. In *Proceedings of the National Academy of Sciences of the United States of America.* PNAS. doi:10.1073/pnas.1211286109

Narvaez, D., & Mattan, B. (2006). Practicing goodness: Playing a prosocial video game. *Centre for Ethical Education.* Retrieved from http://cee.nd.edu/news/documents/PracticingGoodnessReportFINAL.pdf

Natale, M. J. (2002). The effect of a male-orientated computer gaming culture on careers in the computer industry. *Computers & Society,* 24–31. doi:10.1145/566522.566526

National Science Foundation. (2011). *Women, minorities & persons with disabilities in science & engineering: 2011 special report NSF.* Arlington, VA: NSF.

National Statistics. (2004). *Focus on gender.* Retrieved from http://www.unece.org/fileadmin/DAM/stats/gender/publications/UK/Focus_on_Gender.pdf

Nelson, D. L., & Burke, R. J. (2000). Women executives: Health, stress & success. *The Academy of Management Executive, 14*(2), 107–121.

Newell, H., & Dopson, S. (1996). Muddle in the middle: Organizational restructuring & middle management careers. *Personnel Review, 25*(4), 4–20. doi:10.1108/00483489610123191

Newman, J. (2002). In search of the video gamplayer: The lives of Mario. *New Media & Society, 4*(3), 404–422.

Newman, J. (2004). *Video games.* London: Routledge.

News, B. B. C. (2012). *UK enforces Pegi video game ratings system.* Retrieved from http://www.bbc.co.uk/news/technology-19042908

Ng, E. S. W., & Burke, R. J. (2005). Person–organization fit & the war for talent: does diversity management make a difference? *International Journal of Human Resource Management, 16*(7), 1195–1210. doi:10.1080/09585190500144038

Ng, T. W. H., Eby, L. T., Sorensen, K. L., & Feldman, D. C. (2005). Predictors of objective & subjective career success: A meta-analysis. *Personnel Psychology, 58,* 367–408. doi:10.1111/j.1744-6570.2005.00515.x

Nielson, T. R., Carlson, D. S., & Lankau, M. J. (2001). The supportive mentor as a means of reducing work-family conflict. *Journal of Vocational Behavior, 59,* 364–381. doi:10.1006/jvbe.2001.1806

Nikken, P., & Jansz, J. (2006). Parental mediation of children's videogame playing: A comparison of reports by parents & children. *Learning, Media and Technology, 31*(2), 181–202. doi:10.1080/17439880600756803

Nikken, P., & Jansz, J. (2007). Parents' interest in videogame ratings & content descriptors in relation to game mediation. *European Journal of Communication, 22*(3), 315–336. doi:10.1177/0267323107079684

Noonan, M. C., Estes, S. B., & Glass, J. L. (2007). Do workplace flexibility policies influence time spent in domestic labor? *Journal of Family Issues*, *28*(2), 263–288. doi:10.1177/0192513X06292703

Nosek, B., Smyth, F., Sriram, N., Lindner, N., Devos, T., & Ayala, A. … Greenwald, A. (2009). National differences in gender-science stereotypes predict national sex differences in science & math achievement. *Proceedings of the National Academy of Sciences, 106* (26), 10593-10597.

O'Neill, R. M., & Blake-Beard, S. D. (2002). Gender barriers to the female mentor – male protégé relationship. *Journal of Business Ethics*, *37*, 51–63. doi:10.1023/A:1014778017993

Oblinger, D., & Oblinger, J. (2005). Is it age or IT: First steps toward understanding the net generation. In *Educating the net generation*. Boulder, CO: EDUCAUSE.

Ochalla, B. (2006). *Boy on boy action: Is gay content on the rise?* Retrieved from http://www.gamasutra.com/features/20061208/ochalla_01.shtml

Ofcom. (2008). *Annex 3 media literacy audit: Report on UK children by platform*. Retrieved from www.ofcom.org.uk/advice/media_literacy/medlitpub/medlitpubrss/ml_childrens08/cannex.pdf

Ofcom. (2011). *UK children's media literacy*. Retreived from http://stakeholders.ofcom.org.uk/binaries/research/media-literacy/media-lit11/childrens.pdf

Ogden, S. M., McTavish, D., & McKean, L. (2006). Clearing the way for gender balance in the management of the UK financial services industry. *Women in Management Review*, *21*(1), 40–53. doi:10.1108/09649420610643402

Ogletree, S. M., & Drake, R. (2007). College students' video game participation & perceptions: Gender differences & implications. *Sex Roles*, *56*, 537–542. doi:10.1007/s11199-007-9193-5

O'Neill, O. A., & O'Reilly, C. A. (2010). Careers as tournaments: the impact of sex & gendered organizational culture preferences on MBAs' income attainment. *Journal of Organizational Behavior*, *31*, 856–876. doi:10.1002/job.641

Ong, J. I. P. L., & Tzuo, P.-W. (2011). Girls' perceptions of characters' gender roles in digital games: A study in Singapore. *International Journal of Gender. Science & Technology*, *3*(3), 620–642.

Ono, H., & Zavodny, M. (2003). Gender & the internet. *Social Science Quarterly*, *84*(1), 111–121. doi:10.1111/1540-6237.t01-1-8401007

ONS. (2008). Statistical bulletin August 2008. In L. F. Statistics (Ed.), *Labour force statistics*. Office for National Statistics.

ONS. (2009). *Statistical bulletin August 2009*. London: Office for National Statistics.

Oosterwegel, A., Littleton, K., & Light, P. (2004). Understanding computer-related attitudes through an idiographic analysis of gender & self-representations. *Learning and Instruction*, *14*, 215–233. doi:10.1016/S0959-4752(03)00093-8

O'Reilly, C. A., Chatman, J., & Caldwell, D. F. (1991). People & organizational culture: A profile comparison approach assessing person-organization fit. *Academy of Management Review*, *34*(3), 487–516. doi:10.2307/256404

Organ, D. W., & Near, J. P. (1985). Cognitive vs. affect measures of job satisfaction. *International Journal of Psychology*, *20*, 241–254.

Orleans, M., & Laney, M. (2000). Children's computer use in the home. *Social Science Computer Review*, *18*, 56–72. doi:10.1177/089443930001800104

Osting, W., Ijsselsteijn, W. A., & de Kort, Y. A. W. (2010). *Parental perceptions & mediation of children's digital, game play at home: A qualitative study*. Retrieved from http://www.carmster.com/families/workshop/uploads/Main/Oosting2.pdf

Ostroff, C. (1992). The relationship between satisfaction, attitudes, & performance: An organizational level analysis. *The Journal of Applied Psychology*, *77*(6), 963–974. doi:10.1037/0021-9010.77.6.963

Oxford Economics. (2008). The economic contribution of the UK games industry: Final report. *Oxford Economics*. Retrieved from http://www.oxfordeconomics.com/publication/open/222646

Palomares, N. A., & Lee, E.-J. (2010). Virtual gender identity: the linguistic assimilation to gendered avatars in computer-mediated communication. *Journal of Language and Social Psychology*, *29*(1), 5–23. doi:10.1177/0261927X09351675

Panteli, N., Stack, J., & Ramsay, H. (2001). Gendered patterns in computing work in the late 1990s'. *New Technology, Work and Employment*, *16*(1), 3–16. doi:10.1111/1468-005X.00073

Papastergiou, M. (2009). Exploring the potential of computer & video games for health & physical education: A literature review. *Computers & Education*, *53*, 603–622. doi:10.1016/j.compedu.2009.04.001

Parker, N., & Dromgoole, S. (2003). *ELSPA game vision report: European consumer intelligence report.* London, UK: Entertainment & Leisure Software Publishers Association.

Pearce, C. (2008). The truth about baby boomer gamers: A study of over-forty computer game players. *Games and Culture*, *3*(2), 142–174. doi:10.1177/1555412008314132

Peixoto, L. M., & Duke, L. (2004). Nothing like a brisk walk & a sort of demon slaughter to make a girl's night: The construction of the female hero in the Buffy video game. *The Journal of Communication Inquiry*, *28*(2), 138–156. doi:10.1177/0196859903261795

Pelletier, C. (2008). Gaming in context: how young people construct their gendered identities in playing & making games. In *Beyond Barbie & Mortal Kombat: New perspectives on gender & gaming* (pp. 145–160). Cambridge, MA: The MIT Press.

Peng, H., Tsai, C.-C., & Wu, Y.-T. (2006). University students' self-efficacy & their attitudes toward the Internet: The role of students' perceptions of Internet. *Educational Studies*, *32*(1), 73–86. doi:10.1080/03055690500416025

Peng, W., Liu, M., & Mou, Y. (2008). Do aggressive people play violent computer games in a more aggressive way? Individual differences & idiosyncratic game-playing experience. *Cyberpsychology & Behavior*, *11*(2), 157–161. doi:10.1089/cpb.2007.0026 PMID:18422407

Perrewe, P. L., & Nelson, D. L. (2004). Gender & career success: The facilitative role of political skill. *Organizational Dynamics*, *33*(4), 366–378. doi:10.1016/j.orgdyn.2004.09.004

Perriton, L. (2006). *Does woman + a network = career progression?* Retrieved from http://eprints.whiterose.ac.uk/2419/1/perritonl2_Leadership._Does_woman_plus_a_network_equal_career_success.pdf

Perrone, K. M., Wright, S. L., & Jackson, Z. V. (2009). Traditional & non-traditional gender roles & work family interface for men & women. *Journal of Career Development*, *36*(1), 8–24. doi:10.1177/0894845308327736

Perryman, R. D. (2004). *Healthy attitudes: Quality of working life in the London NHS, 2000-2002.* Retrieved from http://www.employment-studies.co.uk/pubs/summary.php?id=404

Persky, A. M., Stegall-Zanation, J., & Dupuis, R. E. (2007). Students perceptions of the incorporation of games into classroom instruction for basic & clinical pharmacokinetics. *American Journal of Pharmaceutical Education*, *71*(2), 1–9. doi:10.5688/aj710221 PMID:17429501

Personnel Today. (2010, April 16). Graduates look for work life balance. *Personnel Today*.

Pew Internet & American Life Project. (2008). *Major new study shatters stereotypes about teens & video games.* Retrieved from http://www.pewInternet.org/press-releases/2008/major-new-study-shatters-stereotypes-about-teens-&-video-games.aspx

Pillay, H. (2002). An investigation of cognitive processes engaged in by recreational computer game players: Implications for skills for the future. *Journal of Research on Technology in Education*, *34*(3), 336–350.

Pini, B., Brown, K., & Ryan, C. (2004). Women-only networks as a strategy for change? A case study from local government. *Women in Management Review*, *19*(6), 286–292. doi:10.1108/09649420410555051

PISA. (2006). *Science competencies for tomorrow's world.* The Programme for International Student Assessment. Retrieved from http://www.oecd.org/dataoecd/15/13/39725224.pdf

Plant, S. (1998). *Zeros & ones: Digital women & the new technoculture*. London: Fourth Estate.

Poggio, B. (2000). Between bytes ad bricks: Gender culture in work contexts. *Economic and Industrial Democracy*, *21*(3), 381–402. doi:10.1177/0143831X00213006

Pold, S. (2005). *Interface realisms: The interface as aesthetic form in postmodern culture*. Baltimore, MD: The John Hopkins University Press.

Pollard, E., Connor, H., & Hunt, W. (2008). *Mapping provision & participation in postgraduate creative art & design*. London: National Arts Learning Network.

Poole, S. (2000). *Trigger happy: Videogames & the entertainment revolution*. Arcade Publishing.

Posavac, H. D., Posavac, S. S., & Posavac, E. J. (1998). Exposure to media images of female attractiveness & concern with body weight among young women. *Sex Roles*, *38*, 187–201. doi:10.1023/A:1018729015490

Powell, G. N., & Butterfield, D. A. (2003). Gender, gender identity, & aspirations to top management. *Women in Management Review*, *18*(1/2), 88–96. doi:10.1108/09649420310462361

Powell, G. N., & Greenhaus, J. H. (2010). Sex, gender & the work-to-family interface: Exploring negative & positive interdependencies. *Academy of Management Journal*, *53*(3), 513–534. doi:10.5465/AMJ.2010.51468647

Prensky, M. (2001). Digital natives, digital immigrants. *Horizon*, *9*(5), 1–6. doi:10.1108/10748120110424816

Prensky, M. (2005). Computer games & learning: Digital game-based learning. In J. Raessens, & J. Goldstein (Eds.), *Handbook of computer games studies*. Cambridge, MA: The MIT Press.

Prensky, M. (2006). *Don't bother me, Mom, I'm learning! How computer & video games are preparing your kids for 21st century success & how you can help*. St. Paul, MN: Paragon House.

Prescott, J., & Bogg, J. (2010). The computer games industry: women's experiences of work role in a male dominated environment. In *Women in engineering, science & technology: Education & career challenges*. Hershey, PA: IGI Global. doi:10.4018/978-1-61520-657-5.ch007

Prescott, J., & Bogg, J. (2011). Segregation in a male dominated industry: Women working in the computer games industry. *International Journal of Gender. Science & Technology*, *3*(1), 205–227.

Prescott, J., & Bogg, J. (2012). *Gendered occupational differences in science, engineering, & technology careers*. Hershey, PA: IGI Global. doi:10.4018/978-1-4666-2107-7

Prescott, J., & Bogg, J. (2012). Re-evaluating the BEM sex role inventory (BSRI): A factor analysis of the BSRI. *Assessment and Development Matters*, *3*(2), 28–31.

Provenzo, E. F. (1991). *Video kids: Making sense of Nintendo*. Cambridge, MA: Harvard University Press.

Przybylski, A. K., Weinstein, N., Murayama, K., Lynch, M. F., & Ryan, R. M. (2012). The ideal self at play: The appeal of video games that let you be all you can be. *Psychological Science*, *23*(1), 69–76. doi:10.1177/0956797611418676 PMID:22173739

Quigley, N. R., & Tymon, W. G. (2006). Toward an integrated model of intrinsic motivation & career self-management. *Career Development International*, *11*(6), 522–543. doi:10.1108/13620430610692935

Rapoport, R., Bailyn, L., Fletcher, J. K., & Pruitt, B. H. (2002). *Beyond work-family balance: Advancing gender equity & workplace performance*. San Francisco, CA: Jossey Bass.

Raskin, P. M. (2006). Women, work & family: Three studies of roles & identity among working mothers. *The American Behavioral Scientist*, *49*(10), 1354–1381. doi:10.1177/0002764206286560

Ravaldi, C., Vannacci, A., Bolognesi, E., Mancini, S., Faravelli, C., & Ricca, V. (2006). Gender role, eating disorder symptoms, & body image concern in ballet dancers. *Journal of Psychosomatic Research*, *61*(4), 529–535. doi:10.1016/j.jpsychores.2006.04.016 PMID:17011362

Reiber, L. (1996). Seriously considering play: Designing interactive learning environments based on the blending of microworlds, simulations, & games. *Educational Technology Research and Development*, *44*, 43–58. doi:10.1007/BF02300540

Reinecke, L. (2009). Games at work: The recreational use of computer games during work hours. *Cyberpsychology. Behavior & Social Networking*, *12*(4), 461–465.

Revill, J. (2007, September 9). Pregnancy 'forcing 30,000 out of work' new study reveals British women suffer largest pay gap in Europe. *The Observer*.

Rigotti, T., Schyns, B., & Mohr, G. (2008). A short version of the occupational self-efficacy scale: structural & construct validity across five countries. *Journal of Career Assessment*, *16*(2), 238–255. doi:10.1177/1069072707305763

Robie, C., Ryan, A. M., Schmieder, R. A., Parra, L. F., & Smith, P. C. (1998). The relation between job level & job satisfaction. *Group & Organization Management*, *23*, 470–495. doi:10.1177/1059601198234007

Robinson, J. D., & Cannon, D. L. (2005). Mentoring in the academic medical setting: The gender gap. *Journal of Clinical Psychology*, *12*(3), 265–270.

Robins, R. W., Hendin, H. M., & Trzesniewki, K. H. (2001). Measuring global self-esteem: Construct validation of a single-item measure & the Rosenberg self-esteem scale. *Personality and Social Psychology Bulletin*, *27*(2), 151–161. doi:10.1177/0146167201272002

Rommes, E., Faulkner, W., & Van Slooten, I. (2005). Changing lives: The case for women-only vocational technology training revisited. *Journal of Vocational Education and Training*, *57*(3), 293–318. doi:10.1080/13636820500200288

Rommes, E., Overbeek, G., Scholte, R., Engles, R., & De Kemp, R. (2007). I'm not interested in computers': Gender-based occupational choices of adolescents. *Information Communication and Society*, *10*(3), 299–319. doi:10.1080/13691180701409838

Rosenberg, M. (1965). *Society & adolescent self-image*. Princeton, NJ: Princeton University Press.

Rosser, J., Lynch, P., Cuddihy, L., Gentile, D., Klonsky, J., & Merrell, R. (2007). The impact of video games on training surgeons in the 21st century. *Archives of Surgery*, *142*, 181–186. doi:10.1001/archsurg.142.2.181 PMID:17309970

Royal, C. (200). *Gendered spaces & digital discourse: Framing women's relationship with the internet*. VDM Publishing.

Royse, P., Lee, J., Undrahbuyan, B., Hopson, M., & Consalvo, M. (2007). Woman & games: Technologies of the gendered self. *New Media & Society*, *9*, 555–576. doi:10.1177/1461444807080322

Rusticus, S. A., Hubley, A. M., & Zumbo, B. D. (2004). Cross-national comparability of the rosenberg self-esteem scale. In *Proceedings of 112th Convention of the American Psychological Association*. Honolulu, HI: APA.

Ryan, M. K., Haslam, A., & Kulich, C. (2010). Politics & the glass cliff: Evidence that women are preferentially selected to contest hard-to-win seats. *Psychology of Women Quarterly*, *34*, 56–64. doi:10.1111/j.1471-6402.2009.01541.x

Ryan, M. K., Haslam, S. A., Hersby, M. D., & Bongiorno, R. (2011). Think crisis-think female: The glass cliff & contextual variation in the think manager-think male stereotype. *The Journal of Applied Psychology*, *96*(3), 470–484. doi:10.1037/a0022133 PMID:21171729

Ryan, R. M., Rigby, C. S., & Przybyiski, A. (2006). The motivational pull of video games: A self-determination theory approach. *Motivation and Emotion*, *30*(4), 344–360. doi:10.1007/s11031-006-9051-8

Såks, A. M., & Ashforth, B. E. (1997). A longitudinal investigation of the relationship between job information sources, applicant sources, applicant perceptions of fit, & work outcomes. *Personnel Psychology, 50*(2), 395–426. doi:10.1111/j.1744-6570.1997.tb00913.x

Sayers, R. (2007). The right staff from X to Y: Generational change & professional development in future academic libraries. *Library Management, 28*(8/9), 474–487. doi:10.1108/01435120710837765

Schein, V. (1973). The relationship between sex role stereotypes & requisite management characteristics. *The Journal of Applied Psychology, 57*(1), 95–100. doi:10.1037/h0037128 PMID:4784761

Schoon, I., Hansson, L., & Salmela-Aro, K. (2005). Combining work & family life: Life satisfaction among married & divorced men & women in Estonia, Finland, & the UK. *European Psychologist, 10*(4), 309–319. doi:10.1027/1016-9040.10.4.309

Schott, G., & Horrell, K. (2000). Girl gamers & their relationship with the gaming culture. *Convergence: The International Journal of Research into New Media Technologies, 6*(4), 36–53. doi:10.1177/135485650000600404

Schroder, A. (2008). We don't want it changed, do we? Gender & sexuality in role-playing games. *Eludamos Journal of Computer Game Culture, 2*(2), 241–256.

Schultheiss, D. E. P. (2009). To mother or matter: can women do both? *Journal of Career Development, 36*(1), 25–48. doi:10.1177/0894845309340795

Schyns, B., & von Collani, G. (2002). A new occupational self-efficacy scale & its relations to personality constructs & organisational variables. *European Journal of Work and Organizational Psychology, 11*, 219–241. doi:10.1080/13594320244000148

Seery, M. D., Blasccovich, J., Weisbuch, M., & Vick, S. B. (2004). The relationship between self-esteem level, self-esteem stability, & cardiovascular reactions to performance feedback. *Journal of Personality and Social Psychology, 87*, 133–145. doi:10.1037/0022-3514.87.1.133 PMID:15250798

Sekaquaptewa, D., & Thompson, M. (2003). Solo status, stereotype threat, & performance expectancies: Their effects on women's performance. *Journal of Experimental Social Psychology, 39*, 68–74. doi:10.1016/S0022-1031(02)00508-5

Sellers, M. (2006). Designing the experience of interactive play. In P. Vorderer, & J. Bryant (Eds.), *Playing video games: Motives, responses, & consequences* (pp. 379–397). Mahwah, NJ: Elbaum.

Selwyn, N. (2007). Hi-tech=guy-tech? An exploration of undergraduate students' perceptions of information & communication technologies. *Sex Roles, 56*, 525–536. doi:10.1007/s11199-007-9191-7

Sender, K. (2004). *Business, not politics: The making of the gay market*. New York: Columbia University Press.

Servon, L., & Visser, M. (2011). Progress hindered: The retention & advancement of women in science, engineering & technology careers. *Human Resource Management Journal, 21*(3), 272–284. doi:10.1111/j.1748-8583.2010.00152.x

SET & Royal Society. (2012). *Report: The chemistry PhD: The impact on women's retention*. UK Resource Centre for Women in SET & the Royal Society of Chemistry. Retrieved from http://www.biochemistry.org/Portals/0/SciencePolicy/Docs/Chemistry%20Report%20For%20Web.pdf

Shaffer, D. W. (2006). Epistemic frames for epistemic games. *Computers & Education, 46*(3), 223–234. doi:10.1016/j.compedu.2005.11.003

Shaw, A. (2009). Putting the gay in games: Cultural production & GLBT content in video games. *Games and Culture, 4*(3), 228–253. doi:10.1177/1555412009339729

Shaw, A. (2012). Do you identify as a gamer? Gender, race, sexuality, & gamer identity. *New Media & Society, 14*(1), 28–44. doi:10.1177/1461444811410394

Shaw, I. G. R., & Warf, B. (2009). *Worlds of affect: Virtual geographies of video games*. Environment & Planning. doi:10.1068/a41284

Sheldon, J. P. (2004). Gender stereotypes in educational software for young children. *Sex Roles, 51*(7-8), 433–444. doi:10.1023/B:SERS.0000049232.90715.d9

Sherry, J. L., Lucas, K., Greenberg, B. S., & Lachlan, K. (2004). *Video game uses & gratifications as predictors of use & game preference.* Retrieved from http://icagames.comm.msu.edu/vgu%26g.pdf

Sherry, J. L. (2001). The effects of violent video games on aggression: A meta-analysis. *Human Communication Research, 27*(3), 309–331.

Sherry, J. L., Lucas, K., Greenberg, B. S., & Lachlan, K. (2006). Video game uses & gratifications as predicators of use & game preferences. In *Playing video games: Motives, responses & consequences* (2nd ed., pp. 525–548). Mahwah, NJ: Lawrence Erlbaum Association.

Shields, M. A., & Ward, M. (2001). Improving nurse retention in the national health service in England: The impact of job satisfaction on intentions to quit. *Journal of Health Economics, 20*, 677–701. doi:10.1016/S0167-6296(01)00092-3 PMID:11558644

Shin, W., & Huh, J. (2011). Parental mediation of teenagers' video game playing: antecedents & consequences. *New Media & Society, 13*(6), 945–962. doi:10.1177/1461444810388025

Simpson, B., & Carroll, B. (2008). Re-viewing 'role' in processes of identity construction. *Organization, 15*(1), 29–50. doi:10.1177/1350508407084484

Simpson, R. (1998). Presenteeism, power & organisational change: Long hours as a career barrier & the impact on the working lives of women managers. *British Journal of Management Communication Quarterly, 9*, 37–50.

Simpson, R. (2004). Masculinity at work: The experiences of men in female dominated occupations. *Work, Employment and Society, 18*(2), 349–368. doi:10.1177/09500172004042773

Singh, K., & Allen, K. R. (2007). Women in computer-related majors: A critical synthesis of research & theory from 1994 to 2005. *Review of Educational Research, 77*(4), 500–533. doi:10.3102/0034654307309919

Singh, V., Terjesen, S., & Vinnicombe, S. (2008). Newly appointed directors in the boardroom: How do women & men differ? *European Management Journal, 26*(1), 48–58. doi:10.1016/j.emj.2007.10.002

Singh, V., Vinnicombe, S., & Terjesen, S. (2007). Women advancing onto the corporate board. In *Handbook of women in business & management.* London: Edward Elgar.

Sisler, V. (2008). Digital Arabs: Representation in video games. *European Journal of Cultural Studies, 11*(2), 203–219.

Skiba, D. J. (2008). Games for health. *Nursing Education Perspectives, 29*(4), 230–232. PMID:18770953

Skillset. (2006). *Skillset: Workforce survey 2006.* London: The Sector Skills Council for the Audio Visual Industries.

Skillset. (2008). Retrieved from http://www.skillset.org/skillset/press/releases/article_6286_1.asp

Skillset. (2009). *2009 employment census: The results of the seventh census of the creative media industries december 2009.* The Sector Skills Council for Creative Media.

Skoric, M. M., Ching Teo, L. L., & Neo, R. L. (2009). Children & video games: Addiction, engagement & scholastic achievement. *Cyberpsychology & Behavior, 12*(5), 567–572. doi:10.1089/cpb.2009.0079 PMID:19624263

Smith, J. L., Morgan, C. L., & White, P. H. (2005). Investigating a measure of computer technology domain identification: A tool for understanding gender differences & stereotypes. *Educational and Psychological Measurement, 65*(2), 336–355. doi:10.1177/0013164404272486

Smola, K. W., & Sutton, C. D. (2002). Generational differences: Revisiting generational work values for the new millennium. *Journal of Organizational Behavior, 23*, 363–382. doi:10.1002/job.147

Snider, M. (2009). *Video game sales hit record despite economic downturn.* Retrieved from http://www.gamesindustry.biz/content_page.php?aid=30008

Sorensen, B. H., & Meyer, B. (2007). Serious games in language learning & teaching-a theoretical perspective. In *Proceedings of the 2007 Digital Games Research Association Conference* (pp. 559-560). GRAC.

Spector, P. E. (1985). Measurement of human service staff satisfaction: Development of the job satisfaction survey 1. *American Journal of Community Psychology*, *13*(6), 693–713. doi:10.1007/BF00929796 PMID:4083275

Spencer, S. J., Josephs, R. A., & Steele, C. M. (1993). Low self-esteem: The uphill struggle for self integrity. In *Self-Esteem: The puzzle of low self-regard*. New York: Plenum Press. doi:10.1007/978-1-4684-8956-9_2

Stets, J. E., & Burke, P. J. (2000). Identity theory & social identity theory. *Social Psychology Quarterly*, *63*(3), 224–237. doi:10.2307/2695870

Stickney, L., & Knorad, A. (2007). Gender-role attitudes & earnings: A multinational study of married women & men. *Sex Roles*, *57*(11), 801–811. doi:10.1007/s11199-007-9311-4

Struyven, K., Dochy, F., Gielen, S., & Janssens, S. (2008). Students' experiences with contrasting learning environments: The added value of students' perceptions. *Learning Environments Research*, *11*, 83–109. doi:10.1007/s10984-008-9041-8

Stryker, S., & Burke, P. J. (1968). Identity salience & role performance: The relevance of symbolic interaction theory for family research. *Journal of Marriage and the Family*, *30*, 558–564. doi:10.2307/349494

Stryker, S., & Burke, P. J. (2000). The past, present & future of an identity theory. *Social Psychology Quarterly*, *63*(4), 284–297. doi:10.2307/2695840

Subrahmanyam, K., & Greenfield, P. (2009). Designing serious games for children & adolescents: What developmental psychology can teach us. In U. Ritterfield, M. Cody, & P. Vorderer (Eds.), *Serious games mechanisms & effects* (pp. 167–179). London: Routledge.

Subrahmanyam, K., Smahel, D., & Greenfield, P. M. (2006). Connecting developmental processes to the Internet: Identity presentation & sexual exploration in online teen chatrooms. *Developmental Psychology*, *42*, 1–12. doi:10.1037/0012-1649.42.3.395 PMID:16420114

Symonds, R. (2000). Why IT doesn't appeal to young women. In *Women, work & computerization: Charting a course to the future*. Vancouver, Canada: Kluwer Academic Publishers.

Sypeck, M. F., Gray, J. J., Etu, S. F., Ahrens, A. H., Mosimann, J. E., & Wiseman, C. V. (2006). Cultural representations of thinness in women: Playboy magazine's depiction of beauty from 1979-1999. *Body Image*, *3*, 229–335. doi:10.1016/j.bodyim.2006.07.001 PMID:18089225

Tang, T. L., Singer, M. G., & Roberts, S. (2000). Employees' perceived organizational instrumentality: An examination of the gender differences. *Journal of Managerial Psychology*, *15*(5), 378–406. doi:10.1108/02683940010337112

Tapscott, D. (1998). *Growing up digital: The rise of the net generation*. New York: McGraw-Hill.

Tattersall, A., Keogh, C., & Richardson, H. (2007). *The gender pay gap in the ICT industry*. Salford, UK: University of Salford.

Taub, E. (2006). Nintendo at AAP event to count the grayer gamer. *New York Times*.

Taylor, C. J. (2010). Occupational sex composition & the gendered availability of workplace support. *Gender & Society*, *24*(2), 189–212. doi:10.1177/0891243209359912

Taylor, T. L. (2003). Multiple pleasures: Women & online gaming. *Convergence*, *9*(1), 21–46. doi:10.1177/135485650300900103

Taylor, T. L. (2008). Becoming a player: Networks, structures, & imagined futures. In *Beyond Barbie® & Mortal Kombat: New perspectives on gender & gaming*. Cambridge, MA: MIT Press.

Teague, J. (2002). Women in computing: What brings them to it, what keeps them in it? *SIGCSE Bulletin, 34*(2), 17–158. doi:10.1145/543812.543849

Terlecki, M., Brown, J., Harner-Steeiw, L., Irvin-Hannum, J., Marchetto-Ryan, N., Ruhl, L., & Wiggins, J. (2011). Sex differences & similarities in video game experience, preferences, & self-efficacy: Implications for the gaming industry. *Current Psychology (New Brunswick, N.J.), 30*, 22–33. doi:10.1007/s12144-010-9095-5

Thewlis, M., Miller, L., & Neathey, F. (2004). *Advancing women in the workplace: Statistical analysis.* Manchester, UK: Equal Opportunities Commission.

Thomas, K. W., Jansen, E., & Tymon, W. G. Jr. (1997). Navigating in the realm of theory: An empowering view of construct development. In *Research in organizational change & development.* Greenwich, CT: JAI Press.

Thompson, S. H., & Lougheed, E. (2012). *Frazzled by Facebook? An exploratory study of gender differences In social network communication among undergraduate men & women.* Retrieved from http://www.freepatentsonline.com/article/College-Student-Journal/285532023.html

Thoroughgood, C. N., Sawyer, K. B., & Hunter, S. T. (2012). Real men don't make mistakes: Investigating the effects of leader gender, error type, & the occupational context on leader error perceptions. *Journal of Business and Psychology, 1*(27), 889–227.

Timberlake, S. (2005). Social capital & gender in the workplace. *Journal of Management Development, 24*(1), 34–44. doi:10.1108/02621710510572335

Tinklin, T., Croxford, L., Ducklin, A., & Frame, B. (2005). Gender & attitudes to work & family roles: The views of young people at the millennium. *Gender and Education, 17*(2), 129–142. doi:10.1080/095402 5042000301429

Tinsley, D. J., & Faunce, P. S. (1980). Enabling, facilitating & precipitating factors associated with women's career orientation. *Journal of Vocational Behavior, 17*, 183–194. doi:10.1016/0001-8791(80)90003-2

Tomlinson, J., & Durbin, S. (2010). Female part-time managers work-life balance, aspirations & career mobility. *Equality, Diversity & Inclusion. International Journal (Toronto, Ont.), 29*(3), 255–270.

Ton, M.-T. N., & Hansen, J.-I. C. (2001). Using a person-environment fit framework to predict satisfaction & motivation in work & marital roles. *Journal of Career Assessment, 9*(4), 315–331. doi:10.1177/106907270100900401

Trauth, E. M., Quesenberry, J. L., & Huang, H. (2008). A multicultural analysis of factors influencing career choice for women in the information technology workforce. *Journal of Global Information Management, 16*(4), 1–23. doi:10.4018/jgim.2008100101

Tsai, C.-C. (2001). The interpretation construction design model for teaching science & its applications to Internet-based instruction in Taiwan. *International Journal of Educational Development, 21*, 401–415. doi:10.1016/S0738-0593(00)00038-9

Turhan, D. B., Thomas, W. D., & Lee, F. K. (2001). Gender, race & perceived similarity effects in developmental relationships: The moderating role of relationship duration. *Journal of Vocational Behavior, 61*, 240–262. doi:10.1006/jvbe.2001.1855

Twenge, J. M. (1997). Changes in masculine & feminine traits over time: a meta-analysis. *Sex Roles, 36*(5/6), 305–325. doi:10.1007/BF02766650

Twenge, J. M., & Campbell, S. M. (2008). Generational differences in psychological traits & their impact on the workplace. *Journal of Managerial Psychology, 23*(8), 862–877. doi:10.1108/02683940810904367

UCAS. (2012). *Data search.* Retrieved from http://search1.ucas.co.uk/f&f00/index.html

UKRC. (2008). *Women's underrepresentation in SET in the UK: Key facts.* UK Resource Centre for Women in Science, Engineering & Technology. Retrieved from http://www.theukrc.org/resources/key-facts-&-figures/underrepresentation

Ulicsak, M., Wright, M., & Cranmer, S. (2009). *Gaming in families: A literature review*. Retrieved from http://archive.futurelab.org.uk/resources/documents/lit_reviews/Gaming_Families.pdf

Valenduc, G., et al. (2004). *Widening women's work in information & communication technology*. European Commission. Retrieved from http://www.ftu-namur.org/fichiers/D12-print.pdf

Valkenburg, P. M., Kremar, M., Peeters, A. L., & Marseille, N. M. (1999). Developing a scale to assess three styles of television mediation: Instructive mediation, restrictive mediation, & social co-viewing. *Journal of Broadcasting & Electronic Media*, *43*(1), 523–553. doi:10.1080/08838159909364474

Van der Voort, T., Nikken, P., & van Lil, J. (1992). Determinants of parental guidance of children's television viewing: A Dutch replication study. *Journal of Broadcasting & Electronic Media*, *36*(1), 52–66. doi:10.1080/08838159209364154

Van Dijk, J. G. M. (2005). *The deepening divide: Inequality in the information society*. Thousand Oaks, CA: Sage Publications.

Van Eck, R. (2006). Digital game-based learning: It's not just the digital natives who are restless. *EDUCAUSE Review*, *41*(2), 55–63.

van Vuuren, M., de Jong, M. D. T., & Seydel, E. R. (2008). Contributions of self & organisational efficacy expectations to commitment a fourfold typology. *Employee Relations*, *30*(2), 142–156. doi:10.1108/01425450810843339

Vancouver Film School (VFS). (2009). *The game industry: Now & in the future*. Vancouver, Canada: Vancouver Film School.

Vancouver Film School (VFS). (2010). *The game industry now & in the future 2010: Industry facts, trends & outlook*. Vancouver, Canada: Vancouver Film School.

Vancouver, J. B., Thompson, C. M., & Williams, A. A. (2001). The changing signs in the relationships between self-efficacy, personal goals & performance. *Journal of Applied Psychology of Women Quarterly*, *86*, 605–620. doi:10.1037/0021-9010.86.4.605 PMID:11519645

Vargas, J. A. (2006, March 11). For gay gamers, a virtual reality checks. *The Washington Post*.

Vinnicombe, S., & Singh, V. (2003). Locks & keys to the boardroom. *Women in Management Review*, *18*(6), 325–333. doi:10.1108/09649420310491495

Vinnicombe, S., Singh, V., & Kumra, S. (2004). *Making good connections: Best practice for women's corporate networks*. Cranfield University School of Management.

Vitasari, P., Muhammad, P. V., Wahab, P. N. V., Othman, A., & Awang, A. G. (2010). A research for identifying study anxiety sources among university students. *International Education Studies*, *3*(2), 189–196.

Vorderer, P. (2000). Interactive entertainment & beyond. In D. Zillamann, & P. Vorderer (Eds.), *Media entertainments*. Mahwah, NJ: Erlbaum.

Wajcman, J. (2000). Reflections on gender & technology studies: In what state is the art? *Social Studies of Science*, *30*(3), 447–464. doi:10.1177/030631200030003005

Wajcman, J. (2007). From women & technology to gendered techno science. *Information Communication and Society*, *10*(3), 287–298. doi:10.1080/13691180701409770

Wajcman, J., & Martin, B. (2002). Narratives of identity in modern management: The corrosion of gender difference? *Social Compass*, *36*(4), 985–1002.

Wallop, H. (2009, December 26). Video games bigger than film. *The Daily Telegraph*.

Wang, P., Lawler, J. J., & Shi, K. (2011). Implementing family-friendly employment practices in banking industry: Evidences from some African & Asian countries. *Journal of Occupational and Organizational Psychology*. doi:10.1348/096317910X525363

Wang, Z., & Liu, P. (2000). The influence of motivational factors, learning strategy, & the level of intelligence on the academic achievement of students. *Chinese Journal of Psychology, 32*, 65–69.

Watt, H. M. G. (2008). What motivates females & males to pursue sex-stereotyped careers? In *Gender & occupational outcomes: Longitudinal assessments of individual, social, & cultural influences*. Washington, DC: American Psychological Association. doi:10.1037/11706-003

Weaver, A. J., & Lewis, N. (2012). Mirrored morality: an exploration of moral choice in video games. *Cyberpsychology, Behavior, &. Social Networking, 15*(11), 1–5.

Weeden, K. A., & Grusky, D. B. (2005). The case for a new class map. *American Journal of Sociology, 111*, 141–212. doi:10.1086/428815

Weichselbaumer, D., & Winter-Ebmer, R. (2005). A meta-analysis of the international gender wage gap. *Journal of Economic Surveys, 19*, 483–511. doi:10.1111/j.0950-0804.2005.00256.x

Whitaker, J. L., & Bushman, B. J. (2011). *Remain calm, be kind: Effects of relaxing video games on aggressive & prosocial behavior*. Social Psychological & Personality Science. doi:10.1177/1948550611409760

Whiting, V. R., & de Janasz, S. C. (2004). Mentoring in the 21st century: Using the internet to build skills & networks. *Journal of Management Education, 28*(3), 275–293. doi:10.1177/1052562903252639

Whitley, B. E. (1988). Masculinity, femininity, & self-esteem: A multi trait-multi method analysis. *Sex Roles, 18*(7/8), 419–431. doi:10.1007/BF00288393

Whitlock, L. A., Collins McLaughlin, A., & Allaire, J. C. (2012). Individual differences in response to cognitive training: Using a multi-modal, attentionally demanding game-based intervention for older adults. *Computers in Human Behavior*. doi:10.1016/j.chb.2012.01.012 PMID:22393270

Whitton, N. (2011). Game engagement theory & adult learning. *Simulation & Gaming, 42*(5), 596–609. doi:10.1177/1046878110378587

Wickham, J., Collins, G., Greco, L., & Browne, J. (2008). Individualization & equality: Women's careers & organizational form. *Organization, 15*(2), 211–231. doi:10.1177/1350508407086581

Wilcox, C., & Francis, L. L. (1997). Beyond gender stereotyping: Examining the validity of the bem sex-role inventory among 16 to 19 year old females in England. *Personality and Individual Differences, 23*(1), 9–13. doi:10.1016/S0191-8869(97)00026-3

Wilcox, K., & Laird, J. D. (2000). Impact of media images of super-slender women on women's self-esteem: Identification, social comparison, & self perception. *Journal of Research in Personality, 34*, 278–286. doi:10.1006/jrpe.1999.2281

Willemsen, T. M. (2002). Gender typing of the successful manager - A stereotype reconsidered. *Sex Roles, 46*, 385–391. doi:10.1023/A:1020409429645

Williams, D., Consalvo, M., Caplan, S., & Yee, N. (2009). Looking for gender (LFG), gender roles & behaviors among online gamers. *The Journal of Communication*. doi:10.1111/j.1460-2466.2009.01453.x PMID:20161669

Williams, D., Martins, N., Consalvo, M., & Ivory, J. D. (2009). The virtual census: Representations of gender, race & age in video games. *New Media & Society, 11*, 815–834. doi:10.1177/1461444809105354

Williams, M. J., Levy Paluck, E., & Spence-Rodgers, J. (2010). The masculinity of money: Automatic stereotypes predict gender differences in estimated salaries. *Psychology of Women Quarterly, 34*, 7–20. doi:10.1111/j.1471-6402.2009.01537.x

Williams, S., & Cooper, C. L. (1998). Measuring occupational stress: Development of the pressure management indicator. *Journal of Occupational Health Psychology, 3*(4), 306–321. doi:10.1037/1076-8998.3.4.306 PMID:9805279

Wilson, F. (2003). Can compute, won't compute: Women's participation in the culture of computing. *New Technology, Work and Employment, 18*(2), 127–142. doi:10.1111/1468-005X.00115

Wilson-Kovacs, A. M., Ryan, M., & Haslam, A. (2006). The glass-cliff: women's career paths in the UK private IT sector. *Equal Opportunities International, 25*(8), 674–687. doi:10.1108/02610150610719137

Wimmer, J., & Sitnikova, T. (2011). The professional identity of gameworkers revisited: A qualitative inquiry on the case study of German professionals. In *Proceedings of DiGRA 2011 Conference: Think Design Play*. DiGRA.

Winn, J., & Heeter, C. (2009). Gaming, gender, & time: Who makes time to play? *Sex Roles, 61*, 1–13. doi:10.1007/s11199-009-9595-7

Women & Equality Unit. (2005). *Women & men in the workplace*. Equal Opportunities Commission.

Wood, E., & Eagly, A. (2002). A cross-cultural analysis of the behaviour of women & men: Implications for the origins of sex differences. *Psychological Bulletin, 128*, 699–727. doi:10.1037/0033-2909.128.5.699 PMID:12206191

Wood, J. V., Heimpel, S. A., & Michela, J. L. (2003). Savoring versus dampening: Self-esteem differences in regulating positive effect. *Journal of Personality and Social Psychology, 85*, 566–580. doi:10.1037/0022-3514.85.3.566 PMID:14498791

Work Life Balance Centre. (2007). *The twenty four seven survey 2007*. Work Life Balance Centre.

Yates, S., & Littleton, K. (2001). Understanding computer games culture: A situated approach. In *Virtual gender: Technology, consumption & identity* (pp. 103–123). London: Routledge.

Yee, N. (2006). The demographics, motivations & derived experiences of users of massively-multiuser online graphical environments. *Presence (Cambridge, Mass.), 15*, 309–329. doi:10.1162/pres.15.3.309

Yee, N. (2007). Motivations of play in online games. *Journal of CyberPsychology & Behavior, 9*, 772–775. doi:10.1089/cpb.2006.9.772 PMID:17201605

Yong, S.-T., & Tiong, K.-M. (2008). Video/computer games: Differences in the gender preferences, participation & perception. *Games Journal*. Retrieved from www.gamejournal.org

About the Authors

Julie Prescott (CPsychol, PhD, MA, BSc) is a lecturer of Psychology at the University of Bolton. Julie earned her PhD from the Faculty of Health and Life Sciences at The University of Liverpool, UK, in 2011. Julie has a research career spanning over ten years in academic and public sector environments. Julie's background is in psychology and women's studies; she has a particular interest in women's careers, especially in terms of barriers and drivers, occupational segregation, and the experiences of women working in male dominated occupations/industries, in particular the computer games industry. Julie has published one book entitled *Gendered Occupational Differences in Science, Engineering, and Technology Careers* (again co-authored with Jan)

Jan Bogg (BA, M.Sc, Ph.D, C. Psych, FHEA) is a senior lecturer in the Faculty of Health and Life Sciences, at the University of Liverpool, UK. Her Breaking Barriers research addresses career progression, barriers and drivers for women in science, and equity and diversity issues in the workplace. Jan is an organizational psychologist; her research focuses on workforce issues, leadership, and gender in the workplace; and she is a member of the United Kingdom Athena Swan Steering Committee. The Athena SWAN Charter (http://www.athenaswan.org.uk) recognises commitment to advancing women's careers in science, technology, engineering, mathematics, and medicine (STEMM).

Index